GOD'S BREATH

GOD'S BREATH

SACRED SCRIPTURES OF THE WORLD

Edited by JOHN MILLER & AARON KENEDI

Introduction by THOMAS MOORE

MARLOWE & COMPANY | A BIG FISH BOOK
NEW YORK

Published by
Marlowe & Company
A Division of Avalon Publishing Group Incorporated
841 Broadway, 4th Floor
New York, NY 10003

Copy editor: Pat Thompkins
Illustrations: Stephanie Heald
Cover and interior design: Big Fish
Special thanks to Amy Rennert

Library of Congress Cataloging-in-Publication Data

God's Breath : Sacred Scriptures of the world / edited by
John Miller and Aaron Kenedi.
              p.   cm.
          ISBN 1-56924-623-8
1. Sacred books.   I. Miller, John, 1959–   . II. Kenedi, Aaron.
          BL70.G63   1999
    291.8'2—dc21   99-43283
                                     CIP

Paperback edition ISBN 1-56924-618-1

Distributed by Publishers Group West
Printed in the United States of America

10   9   8   7   6

"It would be worthy of the age to print together the collected Scriptures or Sacred Writings of the several nations, the Chinese, the Hindoos, the Persians, the Hebrews, and others, as the Scripture of mankind."

—Henry David Thoreau

For space reasons, some texts have been edited. From *The Tibetan Book of the Dead*, we have included the beginning and dramatic climax. We have included the first, most popular of the six books of *Rumi*. From *The Qur'an*, we have selected the most beloved and recited sections. From *The Book of Genesis*, we have included the book's tales, omitting repetitious family lineages. *The Gospel of John*, *The Bhagavad Gita*, and *The Tao te Ching* are presented in their entirety.

The editors are indebted to the scholarship of Karen Armstrong, Coleman Barks, Marcus Borg, Joseph Campbell, Thomas Cleary, John Crossan, Carl Jung, Harold Kushner, Thomas Merton, Barbara Stoler Miller, Stephen Mitchell, Reynolds Price, Huston Smith, Jonathan Star, Henry David Thoreau, Robert A.F. Thurman, Alan Watts, and Herman Wouk.

CONTENTS

INTRODUCTION

THOMAS MOORE

IT IS REMARKABLE how the most sophisticated among us need guidance and inspiration. We can't go it alone. For counsel we may turn to a doctor, lawyer, therapist, financial expert, or just a friend. But we also need spiritual instruction. It is easy to get stuck in the busyness of life, to let time pass quickly without a thought to how we want to live. One day we might wake up and say to ourselves that there is more to life than this. But where to turn? How to make sense of it all? We look for someone to offer a word of direction and inspiration.

Perhaps the deepest connection we can have with another person is one of friend and guide. I have been a psychotherapist for twenty years and have taught and lectured to counselors of all stripes for almost that long. I am still overwhelmed by the range of this work—carrying not only the emotional weight of complicated lives but also people's craving for meaning and a spiritual vision. Today therapists are discovering that many people are turning to them for wisdom about the spirit, and often these professionals feel inadequate. They have been trained to manage lives according to ideals of health, but they don't feel confident directing a person's search for meaning and values. In particular, their reading has been technical, and my advice to them is to start reading the spiritual and religious classics.

Where do any of us turn for adequate guidance in that part of our lives that has to do with our mortality, our loves, and the meaning of the whole? Today people in the millions place their trust in writers and leaders who offer one plan or another for health and happiness. But often these sources betray their inadequacy with their easy, outlined answers and their obvious self-interest. There are always those, too, who have been persuaded by a certain tradition or philosophy and who seem too eager to convert others to their vision. They have an unsettling need to help and advise, and their counsel appears to come from deep anxiety. Who knows what we are getting into when we latch onto a plan for salvation that is steeped in neurosis.

As we arrive at the end of a century dedicated to the external world—when technology and science has made an effort to explain everything and promises to solve our problems—the gaps and weaknesses of this wholly secular endeavor are beginning to show. People are turning with new passion to what they call "spirituality." In many cases, they find the institutional churches sexist, authoritarian, and focused too narrowly on morals. The new spirituality inspires them and challenges them to meditate, practice yoga, and bring a positive concern to all beings on the planet. This spirituality is fully engaging. It extends into transcendent realms the psychological movements that developed in the early part of this half-century.

But here, too, we run into problems. Can we trust current popular spiritual leaders? Is there something faddish about the flare-up of new communities and systems? Isn't this spirituality largely narcissistic, as people try to achieve high levels of consciousness and perhaps feel superior in their advancement? Do the many books of inspiration and instruction have sufficient weight to help us deal with matters of our greatest concern? Where are the resources we need that are solid, visionary, profound, free of defensiveness, and unfathomable in their depth?

I grew up in Catholic family and spent my adolescence and early twenties in a Catholic monastery. This foundation in the spiritual life, both warm and intense, gives me the passion I have today for speaking on behalf of the soul and its need for spirit. But for the past thirty years I have been richly educated in the spiritual life by constant reading in the beautiful and intelligent literature of the world's religious traditions. This reading has ripened my Catholicism and given it a depth I never would have imagined, and at the same time it has made me feel like a member of the world's religious community extending beyond the boundaries of tradition and institution.

I can't imagine getting through this maze of modern life without the subtle insights into power found in the Tao te Ching and the profound mystical take on love and devotion in the Sufi poets, especially Rumi. I first read the Tibetan Book of the Dead many years ago when I was a student inspired by Aldous Huxley's devotion to it. It added a dimension, a way of looking at both literal death and the phases of my life, that has stayed with me and helped me keep the eternal and the temporal linked—no small achievement.

Many years ago, too, I discovered the Bhagavad-Gita and felt that it was tailored to fill the gaps in my personal philosophy. I needed all that warrior imagery, no matter how metaphorically interpreted. The Gita helped me see that the spiritual life is not as soft and sentimental as it is often portrayed. Every step of the way it requires courage and challenges us to transcend ourselves. The Qur'an, as well, takes us to a place of absolute dedication to a spiritual vision and a corresponding compassionate way of life. Yes, it is extraordinarily honored by the people of Islam, but that doesn't mean that those of us who are only visiting it can't be profoundly moved by it toward a deeper and more substantive spiritual experience.

This religious literature is not like ordinary writing. Each of the texts in this volume has guided people's lives for many hundreds, in some cases thousands, of years. It is holy, revered, canonical, and the object of ritual attention. Some readers may be so identified with their own tradition that it may seem disloyal to them to read unfamiliar texts seriously. Many imagine religion to be a thing, a set of truths to believe in or an institution in which you become a member. But this literature is also accessible to those who are simply trying to enrich their vision. Religion is sometimes described as a way or a vehicle. We can walk the Taoist or the Tibetan road for a distance and take to heart the teachings we find there.

It might help to remember that in almost all spiritual traditions the arts have been important as a means of conveying ideas and insights that far transcend rational categories. To be on a spiritual journey is to enter the land of mysteries, which can never be fully expressed or understood but which nevertheless plays the most profound role at the very foundation of our lives. We might read these texts, then, as spiritual poetics—a refined, subtle, multilayered exploration of the soul's progress.

People have argued and fought over the cosmological teachings in Genesis, but if we could only decide that its truths are much more deep-seated than fact, that they address the human condition, we could find inspiration there for developing our worldview and for gaining insight into the struggles involved in a meaningful life. The image of the great flood lies deep in the human imagination—we know that we can be flooded with remorse and other consequences of our mistakes and that a whole society can be awash in delusion. The tales of Abraham, Jacob, and Joseph have universal relevance and appeal because they are archetypal stories, narratives about our own faith, loyalty, and weakness. If you have not discovered yet that the spiritual life requires that we wrestle with an angel to get his blessing, then you must read the story of Jacob.

I don't mean to psychologize these sacred stories but rather to dislodge them from the cement of historical thinking. Religion uses history to present eternal truths that are at work in our communities, our families, and our personal lives. The beauty of the Book of John is that it carries us immediately to a mystical place where literalism makes no sense. We are challenged to think of Jesus as a sacred figure, known fully only to a mystical imagination, one that is willing to contemplate how this divine man might be the word of God and how to work out a way of life, based on this tale of God's incarnation, that takes into account both time and eternity.

I confess that sometimes I feel inadequate because so much of my knowledge about religion comes from reading. I have many friends who travel the world, live in spiritual communities, and practice intensely one spiritual method or another. I spend my time reading. But I learned as a monk that reading can be a spiritual practice when it is not done for secular reasons—for information alone or entertainment. The texts in this volume lend themselves to contemplative reading, and so, I believe, they are the stuff of spiritual practice. Reading thoughtfully and actively— with a degree of skepticism and personal interpretation— the spiritual life is fed and deepened.

It's true that in our lifetime we have time to read only a small portion of what has been written. We should be extremely selective, because we are indeed what we read. There is no time for faddish and superficial books about the spiritual life. If we haven't read the basic literature, which is unsurpassed in its wisdom and beauty, then we probably shouldn't waste our time on mediocre sources. If it is inspiration and guidance we want, we could do no better than read the selections in this book slowly and meditatively. We could discuss them with friends, and perhaps read a commentary or two. These passages come from the "great books" of the spiritual life. They can offer a foundation that provides emotional and intellectual security in our search for spirit.

GOD'S BREATH

THE BOOK OF

Prologue by Herman Wouk {

GENESIS

The first chapter of Genesis cut through the murk of ancient mythology with a shaft of light—light that the whole world lives by now, so that we can scarcely picture its effect when it first shone forth. . . . The Genesis account of creation cut the cancer of idolatry out of human discourse. It took a long time to prevail; but at last even the charming Greek and Roman gods withered under the stroke. Genesis is the dividing line between contemporary intelligence and primitive muddle in the realm of first and last things. As such, I do not see how it will ever be superseded. . . . Men still prize Genesis. Modern thinkers now take it for granted—as the rabbis long ago suggested—that Genesis is a mystic vision of the origin of things, put in the purest and strongest words, intelligible to the child, inspiring to adult genius, clear enough to survive in primitive eras, and deep enough to challenge sophisticated cultures.

INTRODUCTION

AS ITS NAME IMPLIES, Genesis traces the early
stages of the human relationship with the divine. It is a
story of beginnings: the beginning of the world, of the
human race, of the people of Israel, and of our experience
of the reality that we call "God." As a story of beginnings, it is full of pain, confusion, and false starts. It
speaks of the difficulty of human generation, of the pangs
of childbirth and the anguish of the family life which
introduces us all into the world. But like any scripture,
Genesis has been treasured not for the light it throws on
the irretrievably distant past but for its timeless relevance to the present. The authors of Genesis do not give
us historical information about life in Palestine during
the second millennium BCE. In fact, as scholars have
shown, they knew nothing about the period. Frequently
they made mistakes, referring to the presence of the
Philistines, for example, who did not arrive in the country until long after this early biblical era. They speak of
towns, such as Beersheva, which did not yet exist. They
make no mention of the strong Egyptian presence in
Palestine at this time. Our authors are not interested in
historical accuracy, however. Instead they bring to the
reader's attention important truths about the human
predicament that still reverberate today. So much is this

4

the case that, while writing this essay and recounting some of these stories, I continually found myself using the present tense and had to make a conscious effort to relegate the events I was describing in the past. It seemed, for example, more natural to say that Jacob fights with his mysterious assailant and *pleads* for a blessing. It is not merely that these stories, learned in childhood, are a familiar part of our imaginative world and are, therefore, in some sense continuously present to us. They have an emblematic, archetypal quality that, for instance, makes Jacob's struggle our own. The author is not simply describing an incident in the life of the patriarch but revealing a mysterious dynamic in the human psyche, and this means that his story speaks as immediately to a reader today as it did in his own time.

The tales of Genesis have a timeless quality because they address those regions of the spirit that remain opaque to us and yet exert an irresistible fascination. A reading of Genesis suggests how it was that psychoanalysis began as a predominantly Jewish discipline. Long before Freud, the authors of ancient Israel had already begun to explore the uncharted realm of the human mind and heart. They saw this struggle with the emotions and with the past as the theater of the religious quest. By seeking reconciliation with the people who have damaged them in the past and by attempting to resolve their inner conflicts, men and women would sense that harmony and peace which characterize the sacred. Yet precisely because the authors of Genesis are dealing with such fundamental and difficult matters, they give us few precise teachings. There are no glib or facile messages in Genesis. It is impossible to find a clear theology in its pages; the authors share no moral consensus, and some have ethics which we would find highly dubious today. There are no paragons in these tales, and even God's behavior occasionally leaves something to be desired. Even though Genesis has played so significant a role in shaping the Judeo-Christian tradition, the book can often challenge our religious preconceptions and show that, like all human reflections on the divine, it cannot adequately express the frequently baffling reality to which it directs our attention.

WRESTLING WITH GOD AND SCRIPTURE

One of the most haunting scenes in Genesis is surely the occasion when Jacob wrestled all night long with a mysterious stranger and discovered that he had in reality been struggling with God (Genesis 32:24–32). It was a moment of crisis. Jacob was returning to his homeland after an absence of twenty years. He feared that his brother, Esau, whom he had gravely wronged, would kill him when they met the next day. He was full of dread and felt inadequate for the task that God had set him. That night Jacob camped alone at the wild gorge of the Jabbok stream on the borders of Canaan. There, the biblical writer tells us laconically, "a man wrestled with him until daybreak." When he found that he could not overpower Jacob, his assailant struck him on the hip, dislocating it, just as the dawn was breaking. Still Jacob refused to let him go and, for once in his confused life, was able to rise superbly to the occasion. He knew that this was no ordinary opponent, yet he did not ask for a revelation or a miracle. Instead, he asked for a blessing and was given a new name: "You shall no longer be called Jacob," said the stranger, "but Israel, for you have striven with God and with humans, and have prevailed."

Then Jacob asked him, "Please tell me your name." But he said, "Why is it that you ask my name?" And there he blessed him. So Jacob called the place Peniel, saying, "For I have seen God face to face, and yet my life is preserved." (32: 29–30)

It is surprising to find this incident in the Hebrew Bible. Later the descendents of Jacob/Israel would insist that no human being could look upon the face of God and live. They would find it blasphemous to imagine their deity appearing to any mortal—however august—in human form. Yet the editors who put together the final text of Genesis in about the fifth century BCE felt able to include the tale because it so eloquently described the religious experience of Israel. There would be no final revelation: God would never fully impart his name and nature to his people. The sacred was too great a reality to be contained within a purely human definition or system of thought. Thus, the people of Israel would have only fleeting and frequently ambiguous glimpses of the divine, though they would know that they had been blessed. Their lives had been touched by a reality that transcended mundane existence, and that elusive contact gave them the strength and insight to face the challenge of an uncertain world. After this strange encounter with

God, Jacob left Peniel, limping from his damaged hip, just as the sun was rising, fully prepared to face his brother and achieve the difficult reconciliation. Above all, the Israelites recognized the image of the wrestling match. They did not imagine their religious heroes achieving enlightenment effortlessly or with the calm serenity of a Buddha. Salvation was a painful, difficult process. Hence the significance of the very name "Israel," which can be translated "One who struggles with God" or even "God-fighter."

Jacob's mysterious combat at the Jabbok is also an emblem of the painful effort that the Bible so often demands of its readers. In almost all cultures, scripture has been one of the tools that men and women have used to apprehend a dimension that transcends their normal lives. People have turned to their holy books not to acquire information but to have an experience. They have encountered a reality there that goes beyond their normal existence but endows it with ultimate significance. They have given this transcendence different names—Brahman, dharma, nirvana, or God—but, however we choose to describe or interpret it, it has been a fact of human life. We are constantly aware of an ideal level that contrasts with the world around us. We may not regard this realm as supernatural; we may prefer to find it in art, music, or poetry rather than in church or synagogue. But human beings have persistently sought a dimension of existence that seems close to our normal lives and yet far from them. Sacred scripture has been one of the principal means of introducing people to a world of ultimate truth, beauty, and goodness. It has helped human beings to cultivate a sense of the eternal and the absolute in the midst of the transient world in which they find themselves.

But we have to know how to read our scriptures. They demand an imaginative effort that can sometimes be as perplexing and painful as Jacob's wresting match. The true meaning of scripture can never be wholly comprised in a literal reading of the text, since that text points beyond itself to a reality which cannot adequately be expressed in words and concepts. Hindus, for example, believe that the sound of the words in the Vedas is just as important as their lexical sense. Thus the syllable om has no conceptual significance, but when people have chanted it, listening to the silence that precedes and follows it, they feel that they have found a mysterious bridge to the divine. Buddhists of the Nichiren school have discovered that chanting the mere title of the Lotus Sutra yields access not only to the truths of the books but to the ineffable reality that lies beyond them. Many Buddhists and Muslims are able to derive inspiration from a scripture written in a language that they do not understand.

This is obviously very different from the way we normally read books in the modern West. Our scientific culture trains us to look for the literal truths of the words on the page. We expect a text to express its ideas as clearly as possible. In a philosophical or historical work, we will often judge writers by the precision and consistency of their arguments; we are likely to condemn a work that is deliberately vague or paradoxical or that presents mutually exclusive arguments. There are many Jews and Christians who have come to apply the same standards to the Bible. Some, for example, have argued that the first chapter of Genesis is a factual account of the beginning of life on earth: they believe that God really did make the world in six days, and that those scientists who maintain that it took billions of years to evolve must be wrong. What we need to understand is that the Bible does not present its truths to us in this way. Reading it demands the same kind of meditative and intuitive attention that we give to a poem. We often have to wrestle with the text, only to learn that we are denied the certainty of a final revelation.

Genesis has been one of the sacred books that have enabled millions of men and women to know at some profound level that human life has an eternal dimension, even though they have not always been able to express this insight in logical, rational form. Like any scripture, Genesis points to a reality that must essentially transcend it. But the writers employ different methods from those of the Hindu Vedas or the Buddhist Sutras. The biblical authors force us to make an imaginative effort. They imply that it is a hard struggle to discern a sacred reality in the flawed and tragic conditions in which we live and that our experience will often be disconcerting or contradictory. Like Jacob, we will have to wrestle in the dark, denied the consolations of final certitude and experiencing at best only transient, elusive blessing. We may even find that we have been wounded in the course of our struggle.

THE BOOK OF GENESIS

IN THE BEGINNING God created the heaven and the earth.

2 And the earth was without form, and void; and darkness *was* upon the face of the deep. And the spirit of God moved upon the face of the waters.

3 And God said, Let there be light: and there was light.

4 And God saw the light, that *it was* good: and God divided the light from the darkness.

5 And God called the light Day, and the darkness he called Night. And the evening and the morning were the first day.

6 And God said, Let there be a firmament in the midst of the waters, and let it divide the waters from the waters.

7 And God made the firmament, and divided the waters which *were* under the firmament from the waters which *were* above the firmament: and it was so.

8 And God called the firmament Heaven. And the evening and the morning were the second day.

9 And God said, Let the waters under the heaven be gathered together unto one place, and let the dry *land* appear: and it was so.

10 And God called the dry *land* Earth; and the gathering together of the waters called he Seas: and God saw that *it was* good.

11 And God said, Let the earth bring forth grass, the herb yielding seed, *and* the fruit tree yielding fruit after his kind, whose seed *is* in itself, upon the earth: and it was so.

12 And the earth brought forth grass, *and* herb yielding seed after his kind, and the tree yielding fruit, whose seed *was* in itself, after his kind: and God saw that *it was* good.

13 And the evening and the morning were the third day.

14 And God said, Let there be lights in the firmament of the heaven to divide the day from the night; and let them be for signs, and for seasons, and for days, and years:

15 And let them be for lights in the firmament of the heaven to give light upon the earth: and it was so.

16 And God made two great lights; the greater light to rule the day, and the lesser light to rule the night: *he made* the stars also.

17 And God set them in the firmament of the heaven to give light upon the earth,

18 And to rule over the day and over the night, and to divide the light from the darkness: and God saw that *it was* good.

19 And the evening and the morning were the fourth day.

20 And God said, Let the waters bring forth abundantly the moving creature that hath life, and fowl *that* may fly above the earth in the open firmament of heaven.

21 And God created great whales, and every living creature that moveth, which the waters brought forth abundantly, after their kind, and every winged fowl after his kind: and God saw that *it was* good.

22 And God blessed them, saying, Be fruitful, and multiply, and fill the waters in the seas, and let fowl multiply in the earth.

23 And the evening and the morning were the fifth day.

24 And God said, Let the earth bring forth the living creature after his kind, cattle, and creeping thing, and beast of the earth after his kind: and it was so.

25 And God made the beast of the earth after his kind, and cattle after their kind, and every thing that creepeth upon the earth after his kind: and God saw that *it was* good.

26 And God said, Let us make man in our image, after our likeness: and let them have dominion over the fish of the sea, and over the fowl of the air, and over the cattle, and over all the earth, and over every creeping thing that creepeth upon the earth.

27 So God created man in his *own* image, in the image of God created he him; male and female created he them.

28 And God blessed them, and God said unto them, Be fruitful, and multiply, and replenish the earth, and subdue it: and have dominion over the fish of the sea, and over the fowl of the air, and over every living thing that moveth upon the earth.

29 And God said, Behold, I have given you every herb bearing seed, which is upon the face of all the earth, and every
tree, in the which is the fruit of a tree yielding seed; to
you it shall be for meat.

30 And to every beast of the earth, and to every fowl of the
air, and to every thing that creepeth upon the earth,
wherein there is life, I have given every green herb for meat:
and it was so.

31 And God saw every thing that he had made, and, behold,
it was very good. And the evening and the morning were
the sixth day.

CHAPTER 2

Thus the heavens and the earth were finished, and all the
host of them.

2 And on the seventh day God ended his work which he had
made; and he rested on the seventh day from all his work
which he had made.

3 And God blessed the seventh day, and sanctified it: because
that in it he had rested from all his work which God created and made.

4 These are the generations of the heavens and of the earth
when they were created, in the day that the LORD God
made the earth and the heavens,

5 And every plant of the field before it was in the earth, and
every herb of the field before it grew: for the LORD God
had not caused it to rain upon the earth, and there was not
a man to till the ground.

6 But there went up a mist from the earth, and watered the
whole face of the ground.

7 And the LORD God formed man *of* the dust of the ground, and breathed into his nostrils the breath of life; and man became a living soul.

8 And the LORD God planted a garden eastward in Eden; and there he put the man whom he had formed.

9 And out of the ground made the LORD God to grow every tree that is pleasant to the sight, and good for food; the tree of life also in the midst of the garden, and the tree of knowledge of good and evil.

10 And a river went out of Eden to water the garden; and from thence it was parted, and became into four heads.

11 The name of the first *is* Pison: that *is* it which compasseth the whole land of Havilah, where *there* is gold;

12 And the gold of that land *is* good: there *is* bdellium and the onyx stone.

13 And the name of the second river *is* Gihon: the same *is* it that compasseth the whole land of Ethiopia.

14 And the name of the third river *is* Hiddekel: that *is* it which goeth toward the east of Assyria. And the fourth river *is* Euphrates.

15 And the LORD God took the man, and put him into the garden of Eden to dress it and to keep it.

16 And the LORD God commanded the man, saying, Of every tree of the garden thou mayest freely eat:

17 But the tree of the knowledge of good and evil, thou shalt not eat of it: for in the day that thou eatest thereof thou shalt surely die.

18 And the LORD God said, It *is* not good that the man should be alone; I will make him an help meet for him.

19 And out of the ground the LORD God formed every beast of

the field, and every fowl of the air; and brought *them* unto Adam to see what he would call them: and whatsoever Adam called every living creature, that *was* the name thereof.

20 And Adam gave names to all cattle, and to the fowl of the air, and to every beast of the field; but for Adam there was not found an help meet for him.

21 And the LORD God caused a deep sleep to fall upon Adam, and he slept: and he took one of his ribs, and closed up the flesh instead thereof;

22 And the rib, which the LORD God had taken from man, made he a woman, and brought her unto the man.

23 And Adam said, This *is* now bone of my bones, and flesh of my flesh: she shall be called Woman, because she is taken out of Man.

24 Therefore shall a man leave his father and his mother, and shall cleave unto his wife: and they shall be one flesh.

25 And they were both naked, the man and his wife, and were not ashamed.

CHAPTER 3

Now the serpent was more subtle than any beast of the field which the LORD God had made. And he said unto the woman, Yea, hath God said, Ye shall not eat of every tree of the garden?

2 And the woman said unto the serpent, We may eat of the fruit of the trees of the garden:

3 But of the fruit of the tree which *is* in the midst of the garden, God hath said, Ye shall not eat of it, neither shall ye touch it, lest ye die.

4 And the serpent said unto the woman, Ye shall not surely die:

5 For God doth know that in the day ye eat thereof, then your eyes shall be opened, and ye shall be as gods, knowing good and evil.

6 And when the woman saw that the tree *was* good for food, and that it *was* pleasant to the eyes, and a tree to be desired to make *one* wise, she took of the fruit thereof, and did eat, and gave also unto her husband with her; and he did eat.

7 And the eyes of them both were opened, and they knew that they *were* naked; and they sewed fig leaves together, and made themselves aprons.

8 And they heard the voice of the LORD God walking in the garden in the cool of the day: and Adam and his wife hid themselves from the presence of the LORD God amongst the trees of the garden.

9 And the LORD God called unto Adam, and said unto him, Where *art* thou?

10 And he said, I heard thy voice in the garden, and I was afraid, because I *was* naked; and I hid myself.

11 And he said, Who told thee that thou *wast* naked? Hast thou eaten of the tree, whereof I commanded thee that thou shouldst not eat?

12 And the man said, The woman whom thou gavest *to be* with me, she gave me of the tree, and I did eat.

13 And the LORD God said unto the woman, What *is* this *that* thou hast done? And the woman said, The serpent beguiled me, and I did eat.

14 And the LORD God said unto the serpent, Because thou hast done this, thou *art* cursed above all cattle, and above every beast of the field; upon thy belly shalt thou go, and dust shalt thou eat all the days of thy life:

15 And I will put enmity between thee and the woman, and between thy seed and her seed; it shall bruise thy head, and thou shalt bruise his heel.

16 Unto the woman he said, I will greatly multiply thy sorrow and thy conception; in sorrow thou shalt bring forth children; and thy desire *shall be* to thy husband, and he shall rule over thee.

17 And unto Adam he said, Because thou hast hearkened unto the voice of thy wife, and hast eaten of the tree, of which I commanded thee, saying, Thou shalt not eat of it: cursed *is* the ground for thy sake; in sorrow shalt thou eat *of* it all the days of thy life;

18 Thorns also and thistles shall it bring forth to thee; and thou shalt eat the herb of the field;

19 In the sweat of thy face shalt thou eat bread, till thou return unto the ground; for out of it wast thou taken: for dust thou *art*, and unto dust shalt thou return.

20 And Adam called his wife's name Eve; because she was the mother of all living.

21 Unto Adam also and to his wife did the LORD God make coats of skins, and clothed them.

22 And the LORD God said, Behold, the man is become as one of us, to know good and evil: and now, lest he put forth his hand, and take also of the tree of life, and eat, and live for ever:

23 Therefore the LORD God sent him forth from the garden of Eden, to till the ground from whence he was taken.

24 So he drove out the man; and he placed at the east of the garden of Eden Cherubims, and a flaming sword which turned every way, to keep the way of the tree of life.

CHAPTER 4

And Adam knew Eve his wife; and she conceived, and bare Cain, and said, I have gotten a man from the LORD.

2 And she again bare his brother Abel. And Abel was a keeper of sheep, but Cain was a tiller of the ground.

3 And in process of time it came to pass, that Cain brought of the fruit of the ground an offering unto the LORD.

4 And Abel, he also brought of the firstlings of his flock and of the fat thereof. And the LORD had respect unto Abel and to his offering:

5 But unto Cain and to his offering he had not respect. And Cain was very wroth, and his countenance fell.

6 And the LORD said unto Cain, Why art thou wroth? and why is thy countenance fallen?

7 If thou doest well, shalt thou not be accepted? and if thou doest not well, sin lieth at the door. And unto thee *shall be* his desire, and thou shalt rule over him.

8 And Cain talked with Abel his brother: and it came to pass, when they were in the field, that Cain rose up against Abel his brother, and slew him.

9 And the LORD said unto Cain, Where *is* Abel thy brother? And he said, I know not: *Am* I my brother's keeper?

10 And he said, What hast thou done? the voice of thy brother's blood crieth unto me from the ground.

11 And now *art* thou cursed from the earth, which hath opened her mouth to receive thy brother's blood from thy hand;

12 When thou tillest the ground, it shall not henceforth yield unto thee her strength; a fugitive and a vagabond shalt thou be in the earth.

13 And Cain said unto the LORD, My punishment *is* greater than I can bear.

14 Behold, thou hast driven me out this day from the face of the earth; and from thy face shall I be hid; and I shall be a fugitive and a vagabond in the earth; and it shall come to pass, *that* every one that findeth me shall slay me.

15 And the LORD said unto him, Therefore whosoever slayeth Cain, vengeance shall be taken on him sevenfold. And the LORD set a mark upon Cain, lest any finding him should kill him.

16 And Cain went out from the presence of the LORD, and dwelt in the land of Nod, on the east of Eden.

17 And Cain knew his wife; and she conceived, and bare Enoch: and he builded a city, and called the name of the city, after the name of his son, Enoch.

18 And unto Enoch was born Irad: and Irad begat Mehujael: and Mehujael begat Methusael: and Methusael begat Lamech.

19 And Lamech took unto him two wives: the name of the one *was* Adah, and the name of the other Zillah.

20 And Adah bare Jabal: he was the father of such as dwell in tents, and *of such as have* cattle.

21 And his brother's name *was* Jubal: he was the father of all such as handle the harp and organ.

22 And Zillah, she also bare Tubal-cain, an instructor of every artificer in brass and iron: and the sister of Tubal-cain *was* Naamah.

23 And Lamech said unto his wives, Adah and Zillah, Hear my voice; ye wives of Lamech, hearken unto my speech: for I have slain a man to my wounding, and a young man to my hurt.

24 If Cain shall be avenged sevenfold, truly Lamech seventy and sevenfold.

25 And Adam knew his wife again; and she bare a son, and called his name Seth: For God, *said she,* hath appointed me another seed instead of Abel, whom Cain slew.

26 And to Seth, to him also there was born a son; and he called his name Enos: then began men to call upon the name of the LORD.

CHAPTER 5

This *is* the book of the generations of Adam. In the day that God created man, in the likeness of God made he him;

2 Male and female created he them; and blessed them, and called their name Adam, in the day when they were created.

3 And Adam lived an hundred and thirty years, and begat *a son* in his own likeness, after his image; and called his name Seth:

4 And the days of Adam after he had begotten Seth were eight hundred years: and he begat sons and daughters:

5 And all the days that Adam lived were nine hundred and thirty years: and he died.

6 And Seth lived an hundred and five years, and begat Enos:

7 And Seth lived after he begat Enos eight hundred and seven years, and begat sons and daughters:

8 And all the days of Seth were nine hundred and twelve years: and he died.

9 And Enos lived ninety years, and begat Cainan:

10 And Enos lived after he begat Cainan eight hundred and fifteen years, and begat sons and daughters:

11 And all the days of Enos were nine hundred and five years: and he died.

12 And Cainan lived seventy years, and begat Mahalaleel:

13 And Cainan lived after he begat Mahalaleel eight hundred and forty years, and begat sons and daughters:

14 And all the days of Cainan were nine hundred and ten years: and died.

15 And Mahalaleel lived sixty and five years, and begat Jared:

16 And Mahalaleel lived after he begat Jared eight hundred and thirty years, and begat sons and daughters:

17 And all the days of Mahalaleel were eight hundred ninety and five years: and he died.

18 And Jared lived an hundred sixty and two years, and he begat Enoch:

19 And Jared lived after he begat Enoch eight hundred years, and begat sons and daughters:

20 And all the days of Jared were nine hundred sixty and two years: and he died.

21 And Enoch lived sixty and five years, and begat Methuselah:

22 And Enoch walked with God after he begat Methuselah three hundred years, and begat sons and daughters:

23 And all the days of Enoch were three hundred sixty and five years:

24 And Enoch walked with God: and he *was* not; for God took him.

25 And Methuselah lived an hundred eighty and seven years, and begat Lamech:

26 And Methuselah lived after he begat Lamech seven hundred

eighty and two years, and begat sons and daughters:

27 And all the days of Methuselah were nine hundred sixty and nine years: and he died.

28 And Lamech lived an hundred eighty and two years, and begat a son:

29 And he called his name Noah, saying, This *same* shall comfort us concerning our work and toil of our hands, because of the ground which the LORD hath cursed.

30 And Lamech lived after he begat Noah five hundred ninety and five years, and begat sons and daughters:

31 And all the days of Lamech were seven hundred seventy and seven years: and he died.

32 And Noah was five hundred years old: and Noah begat Shem, Ham, and Japheth.

CHAPTER 6

And it came to pass, when men began to multiply on the face of the earth, and daughters were born unto them,

2 That the sons of God saw the daughters of men that they *were* fair; and they took them wives of all which they chose.

3 And the LORD said, My spirit shall not always strive with man, for that he also *is* flesh: yet his days shall be an hundred and twenty years.

4 There were giants in the earth in those days; and also after that, when the sons of God came in unto the daughters of men, and they bare *children* to them, the same *became* mighty men which *were* of old, men of renown.

5 And God saw that the wickedness of man *was* great in the earth, and *that* every imagination of the thoughts of his heart *was* only evil continually.

6 And it repented the LORD that he had made man on the earth, and it grieved him at his heart.

7 And the LORD said, I will destroy man whom I have created from the face of the earth; both man, and beast, and the creeping thing, and the fowls of the air; for it repenteth me that I have made them.

8 But Noah found grace in the eyes of the LORD.

9 These *are* the generations of Noah: Noah was a just man *and* perfect in his generations, *and* Noah walked with God.

10 And Noah begat three sons, Shem, Ham, and Japheth.

11 The earth also was corrupt before God, and the earth was filled with violence.

12 And God looked upon the earth, and, behold, it was corrupt; for all flesh had corrupted his way upon the earth.

13 And God said unto Noah, The end of all flesh is come before me; for the earth is filled with violence through them; and, behold, I will destroy them with the earth.

14 Make thee an ark of gopher wood; rooms shalt thou make in the ark, and shalt pitch it within and without with pitch.

15 And this *is the fashion* which thou shalt make it *of*: The length of the ark *shall be* three hundred cubits, the breadth of it fifty cubits, and the height of it thirty cubits.

16 A window shalt thou make to the ark, and in a cubit shalt thou finish it above; and the door of the ark shalt thou set in the side thereof; *with* lower, second, and third *stories* shalt thou make it.

17 And, behold, I, even I, do bring a flood of waters upon the earth, to destroy all flesh, wherein *is* the breath of life, from under heaven; *and* every thing that *is* in the earth shall die.

18 But with thee will I establish my covenant; and thou shalt come into the ark, thou, and thy sons, and thy wife, and thy sons' wives with thee.

19 And of every living thing of all flesh, two of every *sort* shalt come into the ark, to keep *them* alive with thee; they shall be male and female.

20 Of fowls after their kind, and of cattle after their kind, of every creeping thing of the earth after his kind, two of every *sort* shall come unto thee, to keep *them* alive.

21 And take thou unto thee of all food that is eaten, and thou shalt gather *it* to thee; and it shall be for food for thee, and for them.

22 Thus did Noah; according to all that God commanded him, so did he.

CHAPTER 7

And the LORD said unto Noah, Come thou and all thy house into the ark; for thee have I seen righteous before me in this generation.

2 Of every clean beast thou shalt take to thee by sevens, the male and his female: and of beasts that *are* not clean by two, the male and his female.

3 Of fowls also of the air by sevens, the male and the female; to keep seed alive upon the face of all the earth.

4 For yet seven days, and I will cause it to rain upon the earth forty days and forty nights; and every living substance that I have made will I destroy from off the face of the earth.

5 And Noah did according unto all that the LORD commanded him.

6 And Noah *was* six hundred years old when the flood of waters was upon the earth.

7 And Noah went in, and his sons, and his wife, and his sons' wives with him, into the ark, because of the waters of the flood.

8 Of clean beasts, and of beasts that *are* not clean, and of fowls, and of every thing that creepeth upon the earth,

9 There went in two and two unto Noah into the ark, the male and the female, as God had commanded Noah.

10 And it came to pass after seven days, that the waters of the flood were upon the earth.

11 In the six hundredth year of Noah's life, in the second month, the seventeenth day of the month, the same day were all the fountains of the great deep broken up, and the windows of heaven were opened.

12 And the rain was upon the earth forty days and forty nights.

13 In the selfsame day entered Noah, and Shem, and Ham, and Japheth, the sons of Noah, and Noah's wife, and the three wives of his sons with them, into the ark;

14 They, and every beast after his kind, and all the cattle after their kind, and every creeping thing that creepeth upon the earth after his kind, and every fowl after his kind, every bird of every sort.

15 And they went in unto Noah into the ark, two and two of all flesh, wherein *is* the breath of life.

16 And they that went in, went in male and female of all flesh, as God had commanded him: and the LORD shut him in.

17 And the flood was forty days upon the earth; and the

waters increased, and bare up the ark, and it was lift up above the earth.

18 And the waters prevailed, and were increased greatly upon the earth; and the ark went upon the face of the waters.

19 And the waters prevailed exceedingly upon the earth; and all the high hills, that *were* under the whole heaven, were covered.

20 Fifteen cubits upward did the waters prevail; and the mountains were covered.

21 And all flesh died that moved upon the earth, both of fowl, and of cattle, and of beast, and of every creeping thing that creepeth upon the earth, and every man:

22 All in whose nostrils *was* the breath of life, of all that *was* in the dry *land*, died.

23 And every living substance was destroyed which was upon the face of the ground, both man, and cattle, and the creeping things, and the fowl of the heaven; and they were destroyed from the earth: and Noah only remained *alive*, and they that *were* with him in the ark.

24 And the waters prevailed upon the earth an hundred and fifty days.

CHAPTER 8

And God remembered Noah, and every living thing, and all the cattle that *was* with him in the ark: and God made a wind to pass over the earth, and the waters assuaged;

2 The fountains also of the deep and the windows of heaven were stopped, and the rain from heaven was restrained;

3 And the waters returned from off the earth continually:

and after the end of the hundred and fifty days the waters were abated.

4 And the ark rested in the seventh month, on the seventeenth day of the month, upon the mountains of Ararat.

5 And the waters decreased continually until the tenth month: in the tenth *month*, on the first *day* of the month, were the tops of the mountains seen.

6 And it came to pass at the end of forty days, that Noah opened the window of the ark which he had made:

7 And he sent forth a raven, which went forth to and fro, until the waters were dried up from off the earth.

8 Also he sent forth a dove from him, to see if the waters were abated from off the face of the ground;

9 But the dove found no rest for the sole of her foot, and she returned unto him into the ark, for the waters *were* on the face of the whole earth: then he put forth his hand, and took her, and pulled her in unto him into the ark.

10 And he stayed yet other seven days; and again he sent forth the dove out of the ark;

11 And the dove came in to him in the evening; and, lo, in her mouth *was* an olive leaf plucked off: so Noah knew that the waters were abated from off the earth.

12 And he stayed yet other seven days; and sent forth the dove; which returned not again unto him any more.

13 And it came to pass in the six hundredth and first year, in the first *month*, the first *day* of the month, the waters were dried up from off the earth: and Noah removed the covering of the ark, and looked, and, behold, the face of the ground was dry.

14 And in the second month, on the seven and twentieth day

of the month, was the earth dried.

15 And God spake unto Noah, saying,

16 Go forth of the ark, thou, and thy wife, and thy sons, and thy sons' wives with thee.

17 Bring forth with thee every living thing that is with thee, of all flesh, both of fowl, and of cattle, and of every creeping thing that creepeth upon the earth; that they may breed abundantly in the earth, and be fruitful, and multiply upon the earth.

18 And Noah went forth, and his sons, and his wife, and his sons' wives with him:

19 Every beast, every creeping thing, and every fowl, and whatsoever creepeth upon the earth, after their kinds, went forth out of the ark.

20 And Noah builded an altar unto the LORD; and took of every clean beast, and of every clean fowl, and offered burnt offerings on the altar.

21 And the LORD smelled a sweet savour; and the LORD said in his heart, I will not again curse the ground any more for man's sake; for the imagination of man's heart is evil from his youth; neither will I again smite any more every thing living, as I have done.

22 While the earth remaineth, seedtime and harvest, and cold and heat, and summer and winter, and day and night shall not cease.

CHAPTER 9

And God blessed Noah and his sons, and said unto them, Be fruitful, and multiply, and replenish the earth.

2 And the fear of you and the dread of you shall be upon

every beast of the earth, and upon every fowl of the air, upon all that moveth *upon* the earth, and upon all the fishes of the sea; into your hand are they delivered.

3 Every moving thing that liveth shall be meat for you; even as the green herb have I given you all things.

4 But flesh with the life thereof, *which is* the blood thereof, shall ye not eat.

5 And surely your blood of your lives will I require; at the hand of every beast will I require it, and at the hand of man; at the hand of every man's brother will I require the life of man.

6 Whoso sheddeth man's blood, by man shall his blood be shed: for in the image of God made he man.

7 And you, be ye fruitful, and multiply; bring forth abun-dantly in the earth, and multiply therein.

8 And God spake unto Noah, and to his sons with him, saying,

9 And I, behold, I establish my covenant with you, and with your seed after you;

10 And with every living creature that *is* with you, of the fowl, of the cattle, and of every beast of the earth with you; from all that go out of the ark, to every beast of the earth.

11 And I will establish my covenant with you; neither shall all flesh be cut off any more by the waters of a flood; nei-ther shall there any more be a flood to destroy the earth.

12 And God said, This *is* the token of the covenant which I make between me and you and every living creature that *is* with you, for perpetual generations:

13 I do set my bow in the cloud, and it shall be for a token of a covenant between me and the earth.

14 And it shall come to pass, when I bring a cloud over the earth, that the bow shall be seen in the cloud:

15 And I will remember my covenant, which is between me and you and every living creature of all flesh; and the waters shall no more become a flood to destroy all flesh.

16 And the bow shall be in the cloud; and I will look upon it, that I may remember the everlasting covenant between God and every living creature of all flesh that is upon the earth.

17 And God said unto Noah, This is the token of the covenant, which I have established between me and all flesh that is upon the earth.

18 And the sons of Noah, that went forth of the ark, were Shem, and Ham, and Japheth: and Ham is the father of Canaan.

19 These are the three sons of Noah: and of them was the whole earth overspread.

20 And Noah began to be an husbandman, and he planted a vineyard:

21 And he drank of the wine, and was drunken; and he was uncovered within his tent.

22 And Ham, the father of Canaan, saw the nakedness of his father, and told his two brethren without.

23 And Shem and Japheth took a garment, and laid it upon both their shoulders, and went backward, and covered the nakedness of their father; and their faces were backward, and they saw not their father's nakedness.

24 And Noah awoke from his wine, and knew what his younger son had done unto him.

25 And he said, Cursed be Canaan; a servant of servants shall he be unto his brethren.

26 And he said, Blessed *be* the LORD God of Shem; and Canaan shall be his servant.

27 God shall enlarge Japheth, and he shall dwell in the tents of Shem; and Canaan shall be his servant.

28 And Noah lived after the flood three hundred and fifty years.

29 And all the days of Noah were nine hundred and fifty years: and he died.

CHAPTER 12

Now the LORD had said unto Abram, Get thee out of thy country, and from thy kindred, and from thy father's house, unto a land that I will show thee:

2 And I will make of thee a great nation, and I will bless thee, and make thy name great; and thou shalt be a blessing:

3 And I will bless them that bless thee, and curse him that curseth thee: and in thee shall all families of the earth be blessed.

4 So Abram departed, as the LORD had spoken unto him; and Lot went with him: and Abram *was* seventy and five years old when he departed out of Haran.

5 And Abram took Sarai his wife, and Lot his brother's son, and all their substance that they had gathered, and the souls that they had gotten in Haran; and they went forth to go into the land of Canaan; and into the land of Canaan they came.

6 And Abram passed through the land unto the place of Sichem, unto the plain of Moreh. And the Canaanite *was* then in the land.

7 And the LORD appeared unto Abram, and said, Unto thy
seed will I give this land: and there builded he an altar
unto the LORD, who appeared unto him.

8 And he removed from thence unto a mountain on the east
of Beth-el, and pitched his tent, *having* Beth-el on the
west, and Hai on the east: and there he builded an altar
unto the LORD, and called upon the name of the LORD.

9 And Abram journeyed, going on still toward the south.

CHAPTER 15

After these things the word of the LORD came unto Abram
in a vision, saying, Fear not, Abram: I *am* thy shield, *and*
thy exceeding great reward.

2 And Abram said, LORD God, what wilt thou give me,
seeing I go childless, and the steward of my house *is* this
Eliezer of Damascus?

3 And Abram said, Behold, to me thou hast given no seed:
and, lo, one born in my house is mine heir.

4 And, behold, the word of the LORD *came* unto him, saying,
This shall not be thin heir; but he that shall come forth
out of thine own bowels shall be thine heir.

5 And he brought him forth abroad, and said, Look now
toward heaven, and tell the stars, if thou be able to
number them: and he said unto him, So shall thy seed be.

6 And he believed in the LORD; and he counted it to him for
righteousness.

7 And he said unto him, I *am* the LORD that brought thee out
of Ur of the Chaldees, to give thee this land to inherit it.

8 And he said, LORD God, whereby shall I know that I shall
inherit it?

9 And he said unto him, Take me an heifer of three years old, and a she goat of three years old, and a ram of three years old, and a turtledove, and a young pigeon.

10 And he took unto him all these, and divided them in the midst, and laid each piece one against another: but the birds divided he not.

11 And when the fowls came down upon the carcasses, Abram drove them away.

12 And when the sun was going down, a deep sleep fell upon Abram; and, lo, an horror of great darkness fell upon him.

13 And he said unto Abram, Know of a surety that thy seed shall be a stranger in a land *that* is not theirs, and shall serve them; and they shall afflict them four hundred years;

14 And also that nation, whom they shall serve, will I judge: and afterward shall they come out with great substance.

15 And thou shalt go to thy fathers in peace; thou shalt be buried in a good old age.

16 But in the fourth generation they shall come hither again: for the iniquity of the Amorites *is* not yet full.

17 And it came to pass, that, when the sun went down, and it was dark, behold a smoking furnace, and a burning lamp that passed between those pieces.

18 In the same day the LORD made a covenant with Abram, saying, Unto thy seed have I given this land, from the river of Egypt unto the great river, the river Euphrates:

19 The Kenites, and the Kenizzites, and Kadmonites,

20 And the Hittites, and the Perizzites, and the Rephaims,

21 And the Amorites, and the Canaanites, and the Gir-gashites, and the Jebusites.

CHAPTER 16

Now Sarai Abram's wife bare him no children: and she had an handmaid, an Egyptian, whose name *was* Hagar.

2 And Sarai said unto Abram, Behold now, the LORD hath restrained me from bearing: I pray thee, go in unto my maid; it may be that I may obtain children by her. And Abram hearkened to the voice of Sarai.

3 And Sarai Abram's wife took Hagar her maid the Egyptian, after Abram had dwelt ten years in the land of Canaan, and gave her to her husband Abram to be his wife.

4 And he went in unto Hagar, and she conceived: and when she saw that she had conceived, her mistress was despised in her eyes.

5 And Sarai said unto Abram, My wrong *be* upon thee: I have given my maid into thy bosom; and when she saw that she had conceived, I was despised in her eyes: the LORD judge between me and thee.

6 But Abram said unto Sarai, Behold, thy maid *is* in thy hand; do to her as it pleaseth thee. And when Sarai dealt hardly with her, she fled from her face.

7 And the angel of the LORD found her by a fountain of water in the wilderness, by the fountain in the way to Shur.

8 And he said, Hagar, Sarai's maid, whence camest thou? and whither wilt thou go? And she said, I flee from the face of my mistress Sarai.

9 And the angel of the LORD said unto her, Return to thy mistress, and submit thyself under her hands.

10 And the angel of the LORD said unto her, I will multiply thy seed exceedingly, that it shall not be numbered for multitude.

11 And the angel of the LORD said unto her, Behold, thou *art*

with child, and shalt bear a son, and shalt call his name Ishmael; because the LORD hath heard thy affliction.

12 And he will be a wild man; his hand *will be* against every man, and every man's hand against him; and he shall dwell in the presence of all his brethren.

13 And she called the name of the LORD that spake unto her, Thou God seest me: for she said, Have I also here looked after him that seeth me?

14 Wherefore the well was called Beer-lahai-roi; behold, *it is* between Kadesh and Bered.

15 And Hagar bare Abram a son: and Abram called his son's name, which Hagar bare, Ishmael.

16 And Abram *was* fourscore and six years old, when Hagar bare Ishmael to Abram.

CHAPTER 17

And when Abram was ninety years old and nine, the LORD appeared to Abram, and said unto him, I *am* the Almighty God; walk before me, and be thou perfect.

2 And I will make my covenant between me and thee, and will multiply thee exceedingly.

3 And Abram fell on his face: and God talked with him, saying,

4 As for me, behold, my covenant *is* with thee, and thou shalt be a father of many nations.

5 Neither shall thy name any more be called Abram, but thy name shall be Abraham; for a father of many nations have I made thee.

6 And I will make thee exceeding fruitful, and I will make nations of thee, and kings shall come out of thee.

7 And I will establish my covenant between me and thee and thy seed after thee in their generations for an everlasting covenant, to be a God unto thee, and to thy seed after thee.

8 And I will give unto thee, and to thy seed after thee, the land wherein thou art a stranger, all the land of Canaan, for an everlasting possession; and I will be their God.

9 And God said unto Abraham, Thou shalt keep my covenant therefore, thou, and thy seed after thee in their generations.

10 This *is* my covenant, which ye shall keep, between me and you and thy seed after thee; Every man child among you shall be circumcised.

11 And ye shall circumcise the flesh of your foreskin; and it shall be a token of the covenant betwixt me and you.

12 And he that is eight days old shall be circumcised among you, every man child in your generations, he that is born in the house, or bought with money of any stranger, which *is* not of thy seed.

13 He that is born in thy house, and he that is bought with thy money, must needs be circumcised: and my covenant shall be in your flesh for an everlasting covenant.

14 And the uncircumcised man child whose flesh of his foreskin is not circumcised, that soul shall be cut off from his people; he hath broken my covenant.

15 And God said unto Abraham, As for Sarai thy wife, thou shalt not call her name Sarai, but Sarah *shall* her name *be*.

16 And I will bless her, and give thee a son also of her: yea, I will bless her, and she shall be *a mother* of nations; kings of people shall be of her.

17 Then Abraham fell upon his face, and laughed, and said in

his heart, Shall *a child* be born unto him that is an hundred years old? and shall Sarah, that is ninety years old, bear?

18 And Abraham said unto God, O that Ishmael might live before thee!

19 And God said, Sarah thy wife shall bear thee a son indeed; and thou shalt call his name Isaac: and I will establish my covenant with him for an everlasting covenant, *and* with his seed after him.

20 And as for Ishmael, I have heard thee: Behold, I have blessed him, and will make him fruitful, and will multiply him exceedingly; twelve princes shall he beget, and I will make him a great nation.

21 But my covenant will I establish with Isaac, which Sarah shall bear unto thee at this set time in the next year.

22 And he left off talking with him, and God went up from Abraham.

23 And Abraham took Ishmael his son, and all that were born in his house, and all that were bought with his money, every male among the men of Abraham's house; and circumcised the flesh of their foreskin in the selfsame day, as God had said unto him.

24 And Abraham *was* ninety years old and nine, when he was circumcised in the flesh of his foreskin.

25 And Ishmael his son *was* thirteen years old, when he was circumcised in the flesh of his foreskin.

26 In the selfsame day was Abraham circumcised, and Ishmael his son.

27 And all the men of his house, born in the house, and bought with money of the stranger, were circumcised with him.

CHAPTER 21

And the LORD visited Sarah as he had said, and the LORD did unto Sarah as he had spoken.

2 For Sarah conceived, and bare Abraham a son in his old age, at the set time of which God had spoken to him.

3 And Abraham called the name of his son that was born unto him, whom Sarah bare to him, Isaac.

4 And Abraham circumcised his son Isaac being eight days old, as God had commanded him.

5 And Abraham was an hundred years old, when his son Isaac was born unto him.

6 And Sarah said, God hath made me to laugh, *so that* all that hear will laugh with me.

7 And she said, Who would have said unto Abraham, that Sarah should have given children suck? for I have born *him* a son in his old age.

8 And the child grew, and was weaned: and Abraham made a great feast the *same* day that Isaac was weaned.

9 And Sarah saw the son of Hagar the Egyptian, which she had born unto Abraham, mocking.

10 Wherefore she said unto Abraham, Cast out this bond-woman and her son: for the son of this bondwoman shall not be heir with my son, *even* with Isaac.

11 And the thing was very grievous in Abraham's sight because of his son.

12 And God said unto Abraham, Let it not be grievous in thy sight because of the lad, and because of thy bond-woman; in all that Sarah hath said unto thee, hearken unto her voice; for in Isaac shall thy seed by called.

13 And also of the son of the bondwoman will I make a

nation, because his *is* thy seed.

14 And Abraham rose up early in the morning, and took bread, and a bottle of water, and gave *it* unto Hagar, putting it on her shoulder, and the child, and sent her away: and she departed, and wandered in the wilderness of Beer-sheba.

15 And the water was spent in the bottle, and she cast the child under one of the shrubs.

16 And she went, and sat her down over against *him* a good way off, as it were a bowshot: for she said, Let me not see the death of the child. And she sat over against *him*, and lift up her voice, and wept.

17 And God heard the voice of the lad; and the angel of God called to Hagar out of heaven, and said unto her, What aileth thee, Hagar? fear not; for God hath heard the voice of the lad where he *is*.

18 Arise, lift up the lad, and hold him in thine hand; for I will make him a great nation.

19 And God opened her eyes, and she saw a well of water; and she went, and filled the bottle with water, and gave the lad drink.

20 And God was with the lad; and he grew, and dwelt in the wilderness, and became an archer.

21 And he dwelt in the wilderness of Paran: and his mother took him a wife out of the land of Egypt.

22 And it came to pass at that time, that Abimelech and Phichol the chief captain of his host spake unto Abraham, saying, God *is* with thee in all that thou doest:

23 Now therefore swear unto me here by God that thou wilt not deal falsely with me, nor with my son, nor with

my son's son: *but* according to the kindness that I have done unto thee, thou shalt do unto me, and to the land wherein thou hast sojourned.

24 And Abraham said, I will swear.

25 And Abraham reproved Abimelech because of a well of water, which Abimelech's servants had violently taken away.

26 And Abimelech said, I wot not who hath done this thing: neither does thou tell me, neither yet hear I *of it*, but today.

27 And Abraham took sheep and oxen, and gave them unto Abimelech; and both of them made a covenant.

28 And Abraham set seven ewe lambs of the flock by them-selves.

29 And Abimelech said unto Abraham, What *mean* these seven ewe lambs which thou hast set by themselves?

30 And he said, For *these* seven ewe lambs shalt thou take of my hand, that they may be a witness unto me, that I have digged this well.

31 Wherefore he called that place Beer-sheba; because there they sware both of them.

32 Thus they made a covenant at Beer-sheba: then Abimelech rose up, and Phichol the chief captain of his host, and they returned into the land of the Philistines.

33 And *Abraham* planted a grove in Beer-sheba, and called there on the name of the LORD, the everlasting God.

34 And Abraham sojourned in the Philistines' land many days.

CHAPTER 22

And it came to pass after these things, that God did tempt

Abraham, and said unto him, Abraham: and he said, Behold, *here I am*.

2 And he said, Take now thy son, thine only *son* Isaac, whom thou lovest, and get thee into the land of Moriah; and offer him there for a burnt offering upon one of the mountains which I will tell thee of.

3 And Abraham rose up early in the morning, and saddled his ass, and took two of his young men with him, and Isaac his son, and clave the wood for the burnt offering, and rose up, and went unto the place of which God had told him.

4 Then on the third day Abraham lifted up his eyes, and saw the place afar off.

5 And Abraham said unto his young men, Abide ye here with the ass; and I and the lad will go yonder and worship, and come again to you.

6 And Abraham took the wood of the burnt offering, and laid *it* upon Isaac his son; and he took the fire in his hand, and a knife; and they went both of them together.

7 And Isaac spoke unto Abraham his father, and said, My father: and he said, Here *am* I, my son. And he said, Behold the fire and the wood: but where *is* the lamb for a burnt offering?

8 And Abraham said, My son, God will provide himself a lamb for a burnt offering: so they went both of them together.

9 And they came to the place which God had told him of; and Abraham built an altar there, and laid the wood in order, and bound Isaac his son, and laid him on the altar upon the wood.

10 And Abraham stretched forth his hand, and took the knife to slay his son.

11 And the angel of the LORD called unto him out of heaven, and said, Abraham, Abraham: and he said, Here *am* I.

12 And he said, Lay not thine hand upon the lad, neither do thou any thing unto him: for now I know that thou fear-est God, seeing thou hast not withheld thy son, thine only *son* from me.

13 And Abraham lifted up his eyes, and looked, and behold behind *him* a ram caught in a thicket by his horns: and Abraham went and took the ram, and offered him up for a burnt offering in the stead of his son.

14 And Abraham called the name of that place Jehovah-jireh: as it is said *to* this day, In the mount of the LORD it shall be seen.

15 And the angel of the LORD called unto Abraham out of heaven the second time,

16 And said, By myself have I sworn, saith the LORD, for because thou hast done this thing, and hast not withheld thy son, thine only *son*:

17 That in blessing I will bless thee, and in multiplying will multiply thy seed as the stars of the heaven, and as the sand which *is* upon the sea shore; and thy seed shall pos-sess the gate of his enemies;

18 And in thy seed shall all the nations of the earth be blessed; because thou hast obeyed my voice.

19 So Abraham returned unto his young men, and they rose up and went together to Beer-sheba; and Abraham dwelt at Beer-sheba.

CHAPTER 25

7 And these *are* the days of the years of Abraham's life which he lived, an hundred threescore and fifteen years.

8 Then Abraham gave up the ghost, and died in a good old age, an old man, and full *of years*; and was gathered to his people.

9 And his sons Isaac and Ishmael buried him in the cave of Machpelah, in the field of Ephron the son of Zohar the Hittite, which *is* before Mamre;

10 The field which Abraham purchased of the sons of Heth: there was Abraham buried, and Sarah his wife.

11 And it came to pass after the death of Abraham, that God blessed his son Isaac; and Isaac dwelt by the well Lahairoi.

19 And these *are* the generations of Isaac, Abraham's son: Abraham begat Isaac:

20 And Isaac was forty years old when he took Rebekah to wife, the daughter of Bethuel the Syrian of Padan-aram, the sister to Laban the Syrian.

21 And Isaac entreated the LORD for his wife, because she *was* barren: and the LORD was entreated of him, and Rebekah his wife conceived.

22 And the children struggled together within her; and she said, If *it be* so, why *am* I thus? And she went to inquire of the LORD.

23 And the LORD said unto her, Two nations *are* in thy womb, and two manner of people shall be separated from thy bowels; and *the one* people shall be stronger than *the other* people; and the elder shall serve the younger.

24 And when her days to be delivered were fulfilled, behold, *there were* twins in her womb.

25 And the first came out red, all over like an hairy garment; and they called his name Esau.

26 And after that came his brother out, and his hand took hold on Esau's heel; and his name was called Jacob: and Isaac *was* threescore years old when she bare them.

27 And the boys grew: and Esau was a cunning hunter, a man of the field; and Jacob *was* a plain man, dwelling in tents.

28 And Isaac loved Esau, because he did eat of *his* venison: but Rebekah loved Jacob.

29 And Jacob sod pottage: and Esau came from the field, and he *was* faint:

30 And Esau said to Jacob, Feed me, I pray thee, with that same red *pottage*; for I *am* faint: therefore was his name called Edom.

31 And Jacob said, Sell me this day thy birthright.

32 And Esau said, Behold, I *am* at the point to die: and what profit shall this birthright do to me?

33 And Jacob said, Swear to me this day; and he sware unto him: and he sold his birthright unto Jacob.

34 Then Jacob gave Esau bread and pottage of lentiles; and he did eat and drink, and rose up, and went his way: thus Esau despised *his* birthright.

CHAPTER 26

And there was a famine in the land, beside the first famine that was in the days of Abraham. And Isaac went unto Abimeleh king of the Philistines unto Gerar.

2 And the LORD appeared unto him, and said, Go not down into Egypt; dwell in the land which I shall tell thee of:

3 Sojourn in this land, and I will be with thee, and will bless thee; for unto thee, and unto thy seed, I will give all these countries, and I will perform the oath which I sware unto Abraham thy father;

4 And I will make thy seed to multiply as the stars of heaven, and will give unto thy seed all these countries; and in thy seed shall all the nations of the earth be blessed;

5 Because that Abraham obeyed my voice, and kept my charge, my commandments, my statutes, and my laws.

6 And Isaac dwelt in Gerar:

7 And the men of the place asked *him* of his wife; and he said, She *is* my sister: for he feared to say, *She is* my wife; lest, *said he*, the men of the place should kill me for Rebekah; because she *was* fair to look upon.

8 And it came to pass, when he had been there a long time, that Abimelech king of the Philistines looked out at a window, and saw, and, behold, Isaac *was* sporting with Rebekah his wife.

9 And Abimelech called Isaac, and said, Behold, of a surety she *is* thy wife: and how saidst thou, She *is* my sister? And Isaac said unto him, Because I said, Lest I die for her.

10 And Abimelech said, What *is* this thou hast done unto us? one of the people might lightly have lain with thy wife, and thou shouldest have brought guiltiness upon us.

11 And Abimelech charged all *his* people, saying, He that toucheth this man or his wife shall surely be put to death.

12 Then Isaac sowed in that land, and received in the same year an hundredfold: and the LORD blessed him.

13 And the man waxed great, and went forward, and grew until he became very great:

14 For he had possession of flocks, and possession of herds, and great store of servants: and the Philistines envied him.

15 For all the wells which his father's servants had digged in the days of Abraham his father, the Philistines had stopped them, and filled them with earth.

16 And Abimelech said unto Isaac, Go from us; for thou art much mightier than we.

17 And Isaac departed thence, and pitched his tent in the valley of Gerar, and dwelt there.

18 And Isaac digged again the wells of water, which they had digged in the days of Abraham his father; for the Philistines had stopped them after the death of Abraham: and he called their names after the names by which his father had called them.

19 And Isaac's servants digged in the valley, and found there a well of springing water.

20 And the herdmen of Gerar did strive with Isaac's herd-men, saying, The water is ours: and he called the name of the well Esek; because they strove with him.

21 And they digged another well, and strove for that also: and he called the name of it Sitnah.

22 And he removed from thence, and digged another well; and for that they strove not: and he called the name of it Rehoboth; and he said, For now the LORD hath made room for us, and we shall be fruitful in the land.

23 And he went up from thence to Beer-sheba.

24 And the LORD appeared unto him the same night, and said, I am the God of Abraham thy father: fear not, for I am with thee, and will bless thee, and multiply thy seed for my servant Abraham's sake.

25 And he builded an altar there, and called upon the name of the LORD, and pitched his tent there: and there Isaac's servants digged a well.

26 Then Abimelech went to him from Gerar, and Ahuzzath one of his friends, and Phichol the chief captain of his army.

27 And Isaac said unto them, Wherefore come ye to me, seeing ye hate me, and have sent me away from you?

28 And they said, We saw certainly that the LORD was with thee: and we said, Let there be now an oath betwixt us, *even* betwixt us and thee, and let us make a covenant with thee;

29 That thou wilt do us no hurt, as we have not touched thee, and as we have done unto thee nothing but good, and have sent thee away in peace: thou *art* now the blessed of the LORD.

30 And he made them a feast, and they did eat and drink.

31 And they rose up betimes in the morning, and sware one to another: and Isaac sent them away, and they departed from him in peace.

32 And it came to pass the same day, that Isaac's servants came, and told him concerning the well which they had digged, and said unto him, We have found water.

33 And he called it Shebah: therefore the name of the city *is* Beer-sheba unto this day.

34 And Esau was forty years old when he took to wife Judith the daughter of Beeri the Hittite, and Bashemath the daughter of Elon the Hittite:

35 Which were a grief of mind unto Isaac and to Rebekah.

CHAPTER 27

And it came to pass, that when Isaac was old, and his eyes were dim, so that he could not see, he called Esau his eldest son, and said unto him, My son: and he said unto him, Behold, *here am* I.

2 And he said, Behold now, I am old, I know not the day of my death:

3 Now therefore take, I pray thee, thy weapons, thy quiver and thy bow, and go out to the field, and take me *some* venison;

4 And make me savoury meat, such as I love, and bring *it* to me, that I may eat; that my soul may bless thee before I die.

5 And Rebekah heard when Isaac spake to Esau his son. And Esau went to the field to hunt *for* venison, *and* to bring *it*.

6 And Rebekah spake unto Jacob her son, saying, Behold, I heard thy father speak unto Esau thy brother, saying,

7 Bring me venison, and make me savoury meat, that I may eat, and bless thee before the LORD before my death.

8 Now therefore, my son, obey my voice according to that which I command thee.

9 Go now to the flock, and fetch me from thence two good kids of the goats; and I will make them savoury meat for thy father, such as he loveth:

10 And thou shalt bring *it* to thy father, that he may eat, and that he may bless thee before his death.

11 And Jacob said to Rebekah his mother, Behold, Esau my brother *is* a hairy man, and I *am* a smooth man:

12 My father peradventure will feel me, and I shall seem to him as a deceiver; and I shall bring a curse upon me, and not a blessing.

13 And his mother said unto him, Upon me *be* thy curse, my son: only obey my voice, and go fetch me *them*.

14 And he went, and fetched, and brought *them* to his mother: and his mother made savoury meat, such as his father loved.

15 And Rebekah took goodly raiment of her eldest son Esau, which *were* with her in the house, and put them upon Jacob her younger son:

16 And she put the skins of the kids of the goats upon his hands, and upon the smooth of his neck:

17 And she gave the savoury meat and the bread, which she had prepared, into the hand of her son Jacob.

18 And he came unto his father, and said, My father: and he said, Here *am* I; who *art* thou, my son?

19 And Jacob said unto his father, I *am* Esau thy firstborn; I have done according as thou badest me: arise, I pray thee, sit and eat of my venison, that thy soul may bless me.

20 And Isaac said unto his son, How *is it* that thou hast found *it* so quickly, my son? And he said, Because the LORD thy God brought *it* to me.

21 And Isaac said unto Jacob, Come near, I pray thee, that I may feel thee, my son, whether thou *be* my very son Esau or not.

22 And Jacob went near unto Isaac his father; and he felt him, and said, The voice *is* Jacob's voice, but the hands *are* the hands of Esau.

23 And he discerned him not, because his hands were hairy, as his brother Esau's hands: so he blessed him.

24 And he said, *Art* thou my very son Esau? And he said, I *am*.

25 And he said, Bring *it* near to me, and I will eat of my son's

venison, that my soul may bless thee. And he brought *it* near to him, and he did eat: and he brought him wine, and he drank.

26 And his father Isaac said unto him, Come near now, and kiss me, my son.

27 And he came near, and kissed him: and he smelled the smell of his raiment, and blessed him, and said, See, the smell of my son *is* as the smell of a field which the LORD hath blessed:

28 Therefore God give thee of the dew of heaven, and the fatness of the earth, and plenty of corn and wine:

29 Let people serve thee, and nations bow down to thee: be lord over thy brethren, and let thy mother's sons bow down to thee: cursed *be* every one that curseth thee, and blessed *be* he that blesseth thee.

30 And it came to pass, as soon as Isaac had made an end of blessing Jacob, and Jacob was yet scarce gone out from the presence of Isaac his father, that Esau his brother came in from his hunting.

31 And he also had made savoury meat, and brought it unto his father, and said unto his father, Let my father arise, and eat of his son's venison, that thy soul may bless me.

32 And Isaac his father said unto him, Who *art* thou? And he said, I *am* thy son, thy firstborn Esau.

33 And Isaac trembled very exceedingly, and said, Who? where *is* he that hath taken venison, and brought *it* me, and I have eaten of all before thou camest, and have blessed him? yea, *and* he shall be blessed.

34 And when Esau heard the words of his father, he cried with a great and exceeding bitter cry, and said unto his

father, Bless me, *even* me also, O my father.

35 And he said, Thy brother came with subtlety, and hath taken away thy blessing.

36 And he said, Is not he rightly named Jacob? for he hath supplanted me these two times: he took away my birthright; and, behold, now he hath taken away my blessing. And he said, Hast thou not reserved a blessing for me?

37 And Isaac answered and said unto Esau, Behold, I have made him thy lord, and all his brethren have I given to him for servants; and with corn and wine have I sustained him: and what shall I do now unto thee, my son?

38 And Esau said unto his father, Hast thou but one blessing, my father? bless me, *even* me also, O my father. And Esau lifted up his voice, and wept.

39 And Isaac his father answered and said unto him, Behold, thy dwelling shall be the fatness of the earth, and of the dew of heaven from above;

40 And by thy sword shalt thou live, and shalt serve thy brother; and it shall come to pass when thou shalt have the dominion, that thou shalt break his yoke from off thy neck.

41 And Esau hated Jacob because of the blessing wherewith his father blessed him: and Esau said in his heart, The days of mourning for my father are at hand; then will I slay my brother Jacob.

42 And these words of Esau her elder son were told to Rebekah: and she sent and called Jacob her younger son, and said unto him, Behold, thy brother Esau, as touching thee, doth comfort himself, *purposing* to kill thee.

43 Now therefore, my son, obey my voice; and arise, flee thou to Laban my brother to Haran;

44 And tarry with him a few days, until thy brother's fury turn away;

45 Until thy brother's anger turn away from thee, and he forget *that* which thou hast done to him: then I will send, and fetch thee from thence: why should I be deprived also of you both in one day?

46 And Rebekah said to Isaac, I am weary of my life because of the daughters of Heth: if Jacob take a wife of the daughters of Heth, such as these *which are* of the daughters of the land, what good shall my life do me?

CHAPTER 28

And Isaac called Jacob, and blessed him, and charged him, and said unto him, Thou shalt not take a wife of the daughters of Canaan.

2 Arise, go to Padan-aram, to the house of Bethuel thy mother's father; and take thee a wife from thence of the daughters of Laban thy mother's brother.

3 And God Almighty bless then, and make thee fruitful, and multiply thee, that thou mayest be a multitude of people;

4 And give thee the blessing of Abraham, to thee, and to thy seed with thee; that thou mayest inherit the land wherein thou art a stranger, which God gave unto Abraham.

5 And Isaac sent away Jacob: and he went to Padan-aram unto Laban, son of Bethuel the Syrian, the brother of Rebekah, Jacob's and Esau's mother.

6 When Esau saw that Isaac had blessed Jacob, and sent him away to Padan-aram, to take him a wife from thence; and that as he blessed him he gave him a charge, saying, Thou shalt not take a wife of the daughters of Canaan;

7 And that Jacob obeyed his father and his mother, and was gone to Padan-aram;

8 And Esau seeing that the daughters of Canaan pleased not Isaac his father;

9 Then went Esau unto Ishmael, and took unto the wives which he had Mahalath the daughter of Ishmael Abraham's son, the sister of Nebajoth, to be his wife.

10 And Jacob went out from Beer-sheba, and went toward Haran.

11 And he lighted upon a certain place, and tarried there all night, because the sun was set; and he took of the stones of that place, and put *them for* his pillows, and law down in that place to sleep.

12 And he dreamed, and behold a ladder set up on the earth, and the top of it reached to heaven: and behold the angels of God ascending and descending on it.

13 And, behold, the LORD stood above it, and said, I *am* the LORD God of Abraham thy father, and the God of Isaac: the land whereon thou liest, to thee will I give it, and to thy seed;

14 And thy seed shall be as the dust of the earth, and thou shalt spread abroad to the west, and to the east, and to the north, and to the south: and in thee and in thy seed shall all the families of the earth be blessed.

15 And, behold, I *am* with thee, and will keep thee in all *places* whither thou goest, and will bring thee again into this land; for I will not leave thee, until I have done *that* which I have spoken to thee of.

16 And Jacob awaked out of his sleep, and he said, Surely the LORD is in this place; and I knew *it* not.

17 And he was afraid, and said, How dreadful *is* this place! this *is* none other but the house of God, and this *is* the gate of heaven.

18 And Jacob rose up early in the morning, and took the stone that he had put *for* his pillows, and set it up *for* a pillar, and poured oil upon the top of it.

19 And he called the name of that place Beth-el: but the name of that city *was called* Luz at the first.

20 And Jacob vowed a vow, saying, If God will be with me, and will keep me in this way that I go, and will give me bread to eat, and raiment to put on,

21 So that I come again to my father's house in peace; then shall the LORD be my God:

22 And this stone, which I have set *for* a pillar, shall be God's house: and of all that thou shalt give me I will surely give the tenth unto thee.

CHAPTER 29

Then Jacob went on his journey, and came into the land of the people of the east.

2 And he looked, and behold a well in the field, and, lo, there *were* three flocks of sheep lying by it; for out of that well they watered the flocks: and a great stone *was* upon the well's mouth.

3 And thither were all the flocks gathered: and they rolled the stone from the well's mouth, and watered the sheep, and put the stone again upon the well's mouth in his place.

4 And Jacob said unto them, My brethren, whence *be* ye? And they said, Of Haran *are* we.

5 And he said unto them, Know ye Laban the son of Nahor?

And they said, We know *him*.

6 And he said unto them, *Is* he well? And they said, *He is* well: and, behold, Rachel his daughter cometh with the sheep.

7 And he said, Lo, *it is* yet high day, neither *is it* time that the cattle should be gathered together: water ye the sheep, and go *and* feed *them*.

8 And they said, We cannot, until all the flocks be gathered together, and *till* they roll the stone from the well's mouth; then we water the sheep.

9 And while he yet spake with them, Rachel came with her father's sheep: for she kept them.

10 And it came to pass, when Jacob saw Rachel the daughter of Laban his mother's brother, and the sheep of Laban his mother's brother, that Jacob went near, and rolled the stone from the well's mouth, and watered the flock of Laban his mother's brother.

11 And Jacob kissed Rachel, and lifted up his voice, and wept.

12 And Jacob told Rachel that he *was* her father's brother, and that he *was* Rebekah's son: and she ran and told her father.

13 And it came to pass, when Laban heard the tidings of Jacob his sister's son, that he ran to meet him, and embraced him, and kissed him, and brought him to his house. And he told Laban all these things.

14 And Laban said to him, Surely thou *art* my bone and my flesh. And he abode with him the space of a month.

15 And Laban said unto Jacob, Because thou *art* my brother, shouldest thou therefore serve me for nought? tell me, what *shall* thy wages *be?*

16 And Laban had two daughters: the name of the elder *was* Leah, and the name of the younger *was* Rachel.

17 Leah *was* tender eyed; but Rachel was beautiful and well-favoured.

18 And Jacob loved Rachel; and said, I will serve thee seven years for Rachel thy younger daughter.

19 And Laban said, *It is* better that I give her to thee, than that I should give her to another man: abide with me.

20 And Jacob served seven years for Rachel; and they seemed unto him *but* a few days, for the love he had to her.

21 And Jacob said unto Laban, Give *me* my wife, for my days are fulfilled, that I may go in unto her.

22 And Laban gathered together all the men of the place, and made a feast.

23 And it came to pass in the evening, that he took Leah his daughter, and brought her to him; and he went in unto her.

24 And Laban gave unto his daughter Leah Zilpah his maid *for* an handmaid.

25 And it came to pass, that in the morning, behold, it *was* Leah: and he said to Laban, What *is* this thou hast done unto me? did not I serve with thee for Rachel? wherefore then hast thou beguiled me?

26 And Laban said, It must not be so done in our country, to give the younger before the firstborn.

27 Fulfil her week, and we will give thee this also for the service which thou shalt serve with me yet seven other years.

28 And Jacob did so, and fulfilled her week: and he gave him Rachel his daughter to wife also.

29 And Laban gave to Rachel his daughter Bilhah his hand-maid to be her maid.

30 And he went in also unto Rachel, and he loved also Rachel more than Leah, and served with him yet seven other years.

CHAPTER 32

And Jacob went on his way, and the angels of God met him.

2 And when Jacob saw them, he said, This is God's host: and he called the name of that place Mahanaim.

3 And Jacob sent messengers before him to Esau his brother unto the land of Seir, the country of Edom.

4 And he commanded them, saying, Thus shall ye speak unto my lord Esau; Thy servant Jacob saith thus, I have sojourned with Laban, and stayed there until now:

5 And I have oxen, and asses, flocks, and menservants, and womenservants: and I have sent to tell my lord, that I may find grace in thy sight.

6 And the messengers returned to Jacob, saying, We came to thy brother Esau, and also he cometh to meet thee, and four hundred men with him.

7 Then Jacob was greatly afraid and distressed: and he divided the people that was with him, and the flocks, and herds, and the camels, into two bands;

8 And said, If Esau come to the one company, and smite it, then the other company which is left shall escape.

9 And Jacob said, O God of my father Abraham, and God of my father Isaac, the LORD which saidst unto me, Return unto thy country, and to thy kindred, and I will deal well with thee:

10 I am not worthy of the least of all the mercies, and of all the truth, which thou hast shown unto thy servant; for with my staff I passed over this Jordan; and now I am become two bands.

11 Deliver me, I pray thee, from the hand of my brother, from the hand of Esau: for I fear him, lest he will come and smite me, *and* the mother with the children.

12 And thou saidst, I will surely do thee good, and make thy seed as the sand of the sea, which cannot be numbered for multitude.

13 And he lodged there that same night; and took of that which came to his hand a present for Esau his brother;

14 Two hundred she goats, and twenty he goats, two hundred ewes, and twenty rams.

15 Thirty milch camels with their colts, forty kine, and ten bulls, twenty she asses, and ten foals.

16 And he delivered *them* into the hand of his servants, every drove by themselves; and said unto his servants, Pass over before me, and put a space betwixt drove and drove.

17 And he commanded the foremost, saying, When Esau my brother meeteth thee, and asketh thee, saying, Whose *art* thou? and whither goest thou? and whose *are* these before thee?

18 Then thou shalt say, *They be* thy servant Jacob's; it *is* a present sent unto my lord Esau: and, behold, also he *is* behind us.

19 And so commanded he the second, and the third, and all that followed the droves, saying, On this manner shall ye speak unto Esau, when ye find him.

20 And say ye moreover, Behold, thy servant Jacob *is* behind us. For he said, I will appease him with the present that

goeth before me, and afterward I will see his face; peradventure he will accept of me.

21 So went the present over before him: and himself lodged
that night the company.

22 And he rose up that night, and took his two wives, and
his two womenservants, and his eleven sons, and passed
over the ford Jabbok.

23 And he took them, and sent them over the brook, and sent
over that he had.

24 And Jacob was left alone; and there wrestled a man with
him until the breaking of the day.

25 And when he saw that he prevailed not against him, he
touched the hollow of his thigh; and the hollow of Jacob's
thigh was out of joint, as he wrestled with him.

26 And he said, Let me go, for the day breaketh. And he
said, I will not let thee go, except thou bless me.

27 And he said unto him, What *is* thy name? And he said,
Jacob.

28 And he said, Thy name shall be called no more Jacob, but
Israel: for as a prince hast thou power with God and with
men, and hast prevailed.

29 And Jacob asked *him,* and said, Tell *me,* I pray thee, thy
name. And he said, Wherefore *is* it *that* thou dost ask after
my name? And he blessed him there.

30 And Jacob called the name of the place Peniel: for I have
seen God face to face, and my life is preserved.

31 And as he passed over Peniel the sun rose upon him, and
he halted upon his thigh.

32 Therefore the children of Israel eat not *of* the sinew which
shrank, which *is* upon the hollow of the thigh, unto this

day: because he touched the hollow of Jacob's thigh in the sinew that shrank.

CHAPTER 33

And Jacob lifted up his eyes, and look, and, behold, Esau came, and with him four hundred men. And he divided the children unto Leah, and unto Rachel, and unto the two handmaids.

2 And he put the handmaids and their children foremost, and Leah and her children after, and Rachel and Joseph hindermost.

3 And he passed over before them, and bowed himself to the ground seven times, until he came near to his brother.

4 And Esau ran to meet him, and embraced him, and fell on his neck, and kissed him: and they wept.

5 And he lifted up his eyes, and saw the women and the children; and said, Who *are* those with thee? And he said, The children which God hath graciously given thy servant.

6 Then the handmaidens came near, they and their children, and they bowed themselves.

7 And Leah also with her children came near, and bowed themselves: and after came Joseph near and Rachel, and they bowed themselves.

8 And he said, What *meanest* thou by all this drove which I met? And he said, *These are* to find grace in the sight of my lord.

9 And Esau said, I have enough, my brother; keep that thou hast unto thyself.

10 And Jacob said, Nay, I pray thee, if now I have found grace in thy sight, then receive my present at my hand: for

therefore I have seen thy face, as though I had seen the
face of God, and thou wast pleased with me.

11 Take, I pray thee, my blessing that is brought to thee;
because God hath dealt graciously with me, and because
I have enough. And he urged him, and he took it.

12 And he said, Let us take our journey, and let us go, and I
will go before thee.

13 And he said unto him, My lord knoweth that the children
are tender, and the flocks and herds with young are with
me: and if men should overdrive them one day, all the
flock will die.

14 Let my lord, I pray thee, pass over before his servant: and
I will lead on softly, according as the cattle that goeth
before me and the children be able to endure, until I come
unto my lord unto Seir.

15 And Esau said, Let me now leave with thee some of the
folk that are with me: And he said, What needeth it? let
me find grace in the sight of my lord.

16 So Esau returned that day on his way unto Seir.

17 And Jacob journeyed to Succoth, and built him an house,
and made booths for his cattle: therefore the name of the
place is called Succouth.

18 And Jacob came to Shalem, a city of Shechem, which is in
the land of Canaan, when he came from Padan-aram; and
pitched his tent before the city.

19 And he bought a parcel of a field, where he had spread
his tent, at the hand of the children of Hamor, Shechem's
father, for an hundred pieces of money.

20 And he erected there an altar, and called it El-elohe-
Israel.

CHAPTER 37

And Jacob dwelt in the land wherein his father was a stranger, in the land of Canaan.

2 These *are* the generations of Jacob. Joseph, *being* seventeen years old, was feeding the flock with his brethren; and the lad *was* with the sons of Bilhah, and with the sons of Zilpah, his father's wives: and Joseph brought unto his father their evil report.

3 Now Israel loved Joseph more than all his children, because he *was* the son of his old age: and he made him a coat of *many* colours.

4 And when his brethren saw that their father loved him more than all his brethren, they hated him, and could not speak peaceably unto him.

5 And Joseph dreamed a dream, and he told *it* his brethren: and they hated him yet the more.

6 And he said unto them, Hear, I pray you, this dream which I have dreamed:

7 For, behold, we *were* binding sheaves in the field, and, lo, my sheaf arose, and also stood upright; and, behold, your sheaves stood round about, and made obeisance to my sheaf.

8 And his brethren said to him, Shalt thou indeed reign over us? or shalt thou indeed have dominion over us? And they hated him yet the more for his dreams, and for his words.

9 And he dreamed yet another dream, and told it his brethren, and said, Behold, I have dreamed a dream more; and, behold, the sun and the moon and the eleven stars made obeisance to me.

10 And he told *it* to his father, and to his brethren: and his

father rebuked him, and said unto him, What *is* this dream that thou hast dreamed? Shall I and thy mother and thy brethren indeed come to bow down ourselves to thee to the earth?

11 And his brethren envied him; but his father observed the saying.

12 And his brethren went to feed their father's flock in Shechem.

13 And Israel said unto Joseph, Do not thy brethren feed *the flock* in Shechem? come, and I will send thee unto them. And he said to him, Here *am* I.

14 And he said to him, Go, I pray thee, see whether it be well with thy brethren, and well with the flocks; and bring me word again. So he sent him out of the vale of Hebron, and he came to Shechem.

15 And a certain man found him, and, behold, *he was* wandering in the field: and the man asked him, saying, What seekest thou?

16 And he said, I seek my brethren: tell me, I pray thee, where they feed *their flocks.*

17 And the man said, They are departed hence; for I heard them say, Let us go to Dothan. And Joseph went after his brethren, and found them in Dothan.

18 And when they saw him afar off, even before he came near unto them, they conspired against him to slay him.

19 And they said one to another, Behold, this dreamer cometh.

20 Come now therefore, and let us slay him, and cast him into some pit, and we will say, Some evil beast hath devoured him: and we shall see what will become of his dreams.

21 And Reuben heard *it*, and he delivered him out of their hands; and said, Let us not kill him.

22 And Reuben said unto them, Shed no blood, *but* cast him into this pit that *is* in the wilderness, and lay no hand upon him; that he might rid him out of their hands, to deliver him to his father again.

23 And it came to pass, when Joseph was come unto his brethren, that they stripped Joseph out of his coat, *his* coat of *many* colours that *was* on him;

24 And they took him, and cast him into a pit: and the pit *was* empty, *there was* no water in it.

25 And they sat down to eat bread: and they lifted up their eyes and looked, and, behold, a company of Ishmeelites came from Gilead with their camels bearing spicery and balm and myrrh, going to carry *it* down to Egypt.

26 And Judah said unto his brethren, What profit *is it* if we slay our brother, and conceal his blood?

27 Come, and let us sell him to the Ishmeelites, and let not our hand be upon him; for he *is* our brother *and* our flesh. And his brethren were content.

28 Then there passed by Midianites merchantmen; and they drew and lifted up Joseph out of the pit, and sold Joseph to the Ismeelites for twenty *pieces* of silver: and they brought Joseph into Egypt.

29 And Reuben returned unto the pit; and, behold, Joseph *was* not in the pit; and he rent his clothes.

30 And he returned unto his brethren, and said, The child *is* not; and I, whither shall I go?

31 And they took Joseph's coat, and killed a kid of the goats, and dipped the coat in the blood;

32 And they sent the coat of *many* colours, and they brought *it* to their father; and said, This have we found: know now whether it *be* thy son's coat or no.

33 And he knew it, and said, *It is* my son's coat; an evil beast hath devoured him; Joseph is without doubt rent in pieces.

34 And Jacob rent his clothes, and put sackcloth upon his loins, and mourned for his son many days.

35 And all his sons and all his daughters rose up to comfort him; but he refused to be comforted; and he said, For I will go down into the grave unto my son mourning. Thus his father wept for him.

36 And the Midianites sold him into Egypt unto Potiphar, an officer of Pharaoh's, *and* captain of the guard.

CHAPTER 40

And it came to pass after these things, *that* the butler of the king of Egypt and *his* baker had offended their lord the king of Egypt.

2 And Pharaoh was wroth against two *of* his officers, against the chief of the butlers, and against the chief of the bakers.

3 And he put them in ward in the house of the captain of the guard, into the prison, the place where Joseph *was* bound.

4 And the captain of the guard charged Joseph with them, and he served them: and they continued a season in ward.

5 And they dreamed a dream both of them, each man his dream in one night, each man according to the interpreta-tion of his dream, the butler and the baker of the king of Egypt, which *were* bound in the prison.

6 And Joseph came in unto them in the morning, and looked upon them, and, behold, they *were* sad.

7 And he asked Pharaoh's officers that *were* with him in the ward of his lord's house, saying, Wherefore look ye *so* sadly today?

8 And they said unto him, We have dreamed a dream, and *there is* no interpreter of it. And Joseph said unto them, ᴳDo not interpretations *belong* to God? tell me *them,* I pray you.

9 And the chief butler told his dream to Joseph, and said to him, In my dream, behold, a vine *was* before me;

10 And in the vine were three branches: and it *was* as though it budded, *and* her blossoms shot forth; and the clusters thereof brought forth ripe grapes:

11 And Pharaoh's cup *was* in my hand: and I took the grapes, and pressed them into Pharaoh's cup, and I gave the cup into Pharaoh's hand.

12 And Joseph said unto him, This is the interpretation of it: The three branches *are* three days:

13 Yet within three days shall Pharaoh lift up thine head, and restore thee unto thy place: and thou shalt deliver Pharaoh's cup into his hand, after the former manner when thou was his butler.

14 But think on me when it shall be well with thee, and show kindness, I pray thee, unto me, and make mention of me unto Pharaoh, and bring me out of this house:

15 For indeed I was stolen away out of the land of the Hebrews: and here also have I done nothing that they should put me into the dungeon.

16 When the chief baker saw that the interpretation was good, he said unto Joseph, I also *was* in my dream, and, behold, I *had* three white baskets on my head:

17 And in the uppermost basket *there was* of all manner of

bakemeats for Pharaoh; and the birds did eat them out of the basket upon my head.

18 And Joseph answered and said, This *is* the interpretation thereof: The three baskets *are* three days:

19 Yet within three days shall Pharaoh lift up thy head from off thee, and shall hang thee on a tree; and the birds shall eat thy flesh from off thee.

20 And it came to pass the third day, *which was* Pharaoh's birthday, that he made a feast unto all his servants: and he lifted up the head of the chief butler and of the chief baker among his servants.

21 And he restored the chief butler unto his butlership again; and he gave the cup into Pharaoh's hand:

22 But he hanged the chief baker: as Joseph had interpreted to them.

23 Yet did not the chief butler remember Joseph, but forgat him.

CHAPTER 41

And it came to pass at the end of two full years, that Pharaoh dreamed: and, behold, he stood by the river.

2 And, behold, there came up out of the river seven well-favoured kine and fatfleshed; and they fed in a meadow.

3 And, behold, seven other kine came up after them out of the river, ill favoured and leanfleshed; and stood by the *other* kine upon the brink of the river.

4 And the ill favoured and leanfleshed kine did eat up the seven wellfavoured and fat kine. So Pharaoh awoke.

5 And he slept and dreamed the second time: and, behold, seven ears of corn came up upon one stalk, rank and good.

6 And, behold, seven thin ears and blasted with the east wind sprung up after them.

7 And the seven thin ears devoured the seven rank and full ears. And Pharaoh awoke, and, behold, *it was* a dream.

8 And it came to pass in the morning that his spirit was troubled; and he sent and called for all the magicians of Egypt, and all the wise men thereof: and Pharaoh told them his dream; but *there was* none that could interpret them unto Pharaoh.

9 Then spake the chief butler unto Pharaoh, saying, I do remember my faults this day:

10 Pharaoh was wroth with his servants, and put me in ward in the captain of the guard's house, *both* me and the chief baker:

11 And we dreamed a dream in one night, I and he; we dreamed each man according to the interpretation of his dream.

12 And *there was* there with us a young man, an Hebrew, servant to the captain of the guard; and we told him, and he interpreted to us our dreams; to each man according to his dream he did interpret.

13 And it came to pass, as he interpreted to us, so it was; me he restored unto mine office, and him he hanged.

14 Then Pharaoh sent and called Joseph, and they brought him hastily out of the dungeon: and he shaved *himself*, and changed his raiment, and came in unto Pharaoh.

15 And Pharaoh said unto Joseph, I have dreamed a dream, and *there is* none that can interpret it: and I have heard say of thee, *that* thou canst understand a dream and interpret it.

16 And Joseph answered Pharaoh, saying, It *is* not in me:

God shall give Pharaoh an answer of peace.

17 And Pharaoh said unto Joseph, In my dream, behold, I stood upon the bank of the river:

18 And, behold, there came up out of the river seven kine, fatfleshed and wellfavoured; and they fed in a meadow:

19 And, behold, seven other kine came up after them, poor and very ill favoured and leanfleshed, such as I never saw in all the land of Egypt for badness:

20 And the lean and the ill favoured kine did eat up the first seven fat kine:

21 And when they had eaten them up, it could not be known that they had eaten them; but they *were* still ill favoured, as at the beginning. So I awoke.

22 And I saw in my dream, and, behold, seven ears came up in one stalk, full and good:

23 And, behold, seven ears, withered, thin, *and* blasted with the east wind, sprung up after them:

24 And the thin ears devoured the seven good ears: and I told *this* unto the magicians; but *there was* none that could declare *it* to me.

25 And Joseph said unto Pharaoh, The dream of Pharaoh *is* one: God hath shown Pharaoh what he *is* about to do.

26 The seven good kine *are* seven years; and the seven good ears *are* seven years: the dream *is* one.

27 And the seven thin and ill favoured kine that came up after them *are* seven years; and the seven empty ears blasted with the east wind shall be seven years of famine.

28 This *is* the thing which I have spoken unto Pharaoh: What God *is* about to do he showeth unto Pharaoh.

29 Behold, there come seven years of great plenty through-

out all the land of Egypt.

30 And there shall arise after them seven years of famine; and all the plenty shall be forgotten in the land of Egypt; and the famine shall consume the land;

31 And the plenty shall not be known in the land by reason of that famine following; for it *shall be* very grievous.

32 And for that the dream was doubled unto Pharaoh twice; *it is* because the thing *is* established by God, and God will shortly bring it to pass.

33 Now therefore let Pharaoh look out a man discreet and wise, and set him over the land of Egypt.

34 Let Pharaoh do *this,* and let him appoint officers over the land, and take up the fifth part of the land of Egypt in the seven plenteous years.

35 And let them gather all the food of those good years that come, and lay up corn under the hand of Pharaoh, and let them keep food in the cities.

36 And that food shall be for store to the land against the seven years of famine, which shall be in the land of Egypt; that the land perish not through the famine.

37 And the thing was good in the eyes of Pharaoh, and in the eyes of all his servants.

38 And Pharaoh said unto his servants, Can we find *such a one* as this *is,* a man in whom the spirit of God *is?*

39 And Pharaoh said unto Joseph, Forasmuch as God hath shown thee all this, *there is* none so discreet and wise as thou *art:*

40 Thou shalt be over my house, and according unto thy word shall all my people be ruled: only in the throne will I be greater than thou.

41 And Pharaoh said unto Joseph, See, I have set thee over all the land of Egypt.

42 And Pharaoh took off his ring from his hand, and put it upon Joseph's hand, and arrayed him in vestures of fine linen, and put a gold chain about his neck;

43 And he made him to ride in the second chariot which he had; and they cried before him, Bow the knee: and he made him *ruler* over all the land of Egypt.

44 And Pharaoh said unto Joseph, I *am* Pharaoh, and without thee shall no man lift up his hand or foot in all the land of Egypt.

45 And Pharaoh called Joseph's name Zaphnath-paaneah; and he gave him to wife Asenath the daughter of Poti-pherah priest of On. And Joseph went out over *all* the land of Egypt.

46 And Joseph *was* thirty years old when he stood before Pharaoh king of Egypt. And Joseph went out from the presence of Pharaoh, and went throughout all the land of Egypt.

47 And in the seven plenteous years the earth brought forth by handfuls.

48 And he gathered up all the food of the seven years, which were in the land of Egypt, and laid up the food in the cities: the food of the field, which *was* round about every city, laid he up in the same.

49 And Joseph gathered corn as the sand of the sea, very much, until he left numbering; for it *was* without number.

50 And unto Joseph were born two sons before the years of famine came, which Asenath the daughter of Poti-pherah priest of On bare unto him.

51 And Joseph called the name of the firstborn Manasseh:

For God, *said he,* hath made me forget all my toil, and all my father's house.

52 And the name of the second called he Ephraim: For God hath caused me to be fruitful in the land of my affliction.

53 And the seven years of plenteousness, that was in the land of Egypt, were ended.

54 And the seven years of dearth began to come, according as Joseph had said: and the dearth was in all lands; but in all the land of Egypt there was bread.

55 And when all the land of Egypt was famished, the people cried to Pharaoh for bread: and Pharaoh said unto all the Egyptians, Go unto Joseph; what he saith to you, do.

56 And the famine was over all the face of the earth: and Joseph opened all the storehouses, and sold unto the Egyptians; and the famine waxed sore in the land of Egypt.

57 And all countries came into Egypt to Joseph for to buy *corn;* because that the famine was *so* sore in all lands.

CHAPTER 42

Now when Jacob saw that there was corn in Egypt, Jacob said unto his sons, Why do ye look one upon another?

2 And he said, Behold, I have heard that there is corn in Egypt: get you down thither, and buy for us from thence; that we may live, and not die.

3 And Joseph's ten brethren went down to buy corn in Egypt.

4 But Benjamin, Joseph's brother, Jacob sent not with his brethren; for he said, Lest peradventure mischief befall him.

5 And the sons of Israel came to buy *corn* among those that came: for the famine was in the land of Canaan.

6 And Joseph *was* the governor over the land, *and* he *it was* that

sold to all the people of the land: and Joseph's brethren came, and bowed down themselves before him *with* their faces to the earth.

7 And Joseph saw his brethren, and he knew them, but made himself strange unto them, and spake roughly unto them; and he said unto them, Whence came ye? And they said, From the land of Canaan to buy food.

8 And Joseph knew his brethren, but they knew not him.

9 And Joseph remembered the dreams which he dreamed of them, and said unto them, Ye *are* spies; to see the nakedness of the land ye are come.

10 And they said unto him, Nay, my lord, but to buy food are thy servants come.

11 We *are* all one man's sons; we *are* true *men*, thy servants are no spies.

12 And he said unto them, Nay, but to see the nakedness of the land ye are come.

13 And they said, Thy servants *are* twelve brethren, the sons of one man in the land of Canaan; and, behold, the youngest *is* this day with our father, and one *is* not.

14 And Joseph said unto them, That *is it* that I spake unto you, saying, Ye *are* spies:

15 Hereby ye shall be proved: By the life of Pharaoh ye shall not go forth hence, except your youngest brother come hither.

16 Send one of you, and let him fetch your brother, and ye shall be kept in prison, that your words may be proved, whether *there be any* truth in you: or else by the life of Pharaoh surely ye *are* spies.

17 And he put them all together into ward three days.

18 And Joseph said unto them the third day, This do, and live; *for* I fear God:

19 If ye *be* true *men*, let one of your brethren be bound in the house of your prison: go ye, carry corn for the famine of your houses:

20 But bring your youngest brother unto me; so shall your words by verified, and ye shall not die. And they did so.

21 And they said one to another, We *are* verily guilty concerning our brother, in that we saw the anguish of his soul, when he besought us, and we would not hear; therefore is this distress come upon us.

22 And Reuben answered them, saying, Spake I not unto you, saying, Do not sin against the child; and ye would not hear? therefore, behold, also his blood is required.

23 And they knew not that Joseph understood *them*; for he spake unto them by an interpreter.

24 And he turned himself about from them, and wept; and returned to them again, and communed with them, and took from them Simeon, and bound him before their eyes.

25 Then Joseph commanded to fill their sacks with corn, and to restore every man's money into his sack, and to give them provision for the way: and thus did he unto them.

26 And they laded their asses with the corn, and departed thence.

27 And as one of them opened his sack to give his ass provender in the inn, he espied his money; for, behold, it *was* in his sack's mouth.

28 And he said unto his brethren, My money is restored; and, lo, *it is* even in my sack: and their heart failed *them*, and they were afraid, saying one to another, What *is* this

that God hath done unto us?

29 And they came unto Jacob their father unto the land of Canaan, and told him all that befell unto them; saying,

30 The man, *who* is the lord of the land, spake roughly to us, and took us for spies of the country.

31 And we said unto him, We *are* true *men*; we are no spies:

32 We *be* twelve brethren, sons of our father; one *is* not, and the youngest *is* this day with our father in the land of Canaan.

33 And the man, the lord of the country, said unto us, Hereby shall I know that ye *are* true *men*; leave one of your brethren *here* with me, and take *food for* the famine of your households, and be gone:

34 And bring your youngest brother unto me: then shall I know that ye *are* no spies, but *that* ye *are* true *men: so* will I deliver you your brother, and ye shall traffic in the land.

35 And it came to pass as they emptied their sacks, that, behold, every man's bundle of money *was* in his sack: and when *both* they and their father saw the bundles of money, they were afraid.

36 And Jacob their father said unto them, Me have ye bereaved *of my children:* Joseph *is* not, and Simeon *is* not, and ye will take Benjamin *away:* all these things are against me.

37 And Reuben spake unto his father, saying, Slay my two sons, if I bring him not to thee: deliver him into my hand, and I will bring him to thee again.

38 And he said, My son shall not go down with you; for his brother is dead, and he is left alone: if mischief befall him by the way in the which ye go, then shall ye bring down my gray hairs with sorrow to the grave.

CHAPTER 43

And the famine *was* sore in the land.

2 And it came to pass, when they had eaten up the corn which they had brought out of Egypt, their father said unto them, Go again, buy us a little food.

3 And Judah spake unto him, saying, The man did solemnly protest unto us, saying, Ye shall not see my face, except your brother *be* with you.

4 If thou wilt send our brother with us, we will go down and buy thee food:

5 But if thou wilt not send *him*, we will not go down: for the man said unto us, Ye shall not see my face, except your brother *be* with you.

6 And Israel said, Wherefore dealt ye *so* ill with me, *as* to tell the man whether ye had yet a brother?

7 And they said, The man asked us straitly of our state, and of our kindred, saying *Is* your father yet alive? have ye *another* brother? and we told him according to the tenor of these words: could we certainly know that he would say, Bring your brother down?

8 And Judah said unto Israel his father, Send the lad with me, and we will arise and go; that we may live, and not die, both we, and thou, *and* also our little ones.

9 I will be surety for him; of my hand shalt thou require him: if I bring him not unto thee, and set him before thee, then let me bear the blame for ever:

10 For except we had lingered, surely now we had returned this second time.

11 And their father Israel said unto them, If *it must be* so now, do this; take of the best fruits in the land in your vessels,

and carry down the man a present, a little balm, and a little honey, spices, and myrrh, nuts, and almonds:

12 And take double money in your hand; and the money that was brought again in the mouth of your sacks, carry it again in your hand; peradventure it *was* an oversight:

13 Take also your brother, and arise, go again unto the man:

14 And God Almighty give you mercy before the man, that he may send away your other brother, and Benjamin. If I be bereaved *of my children,* I am bereaved.

15 And the men took that present, and they took double money in their hand, and Benjamin; and rose up, and went down to Egypt, and stood before Joseph.

16 And when Joseph saw Benjamin with them, he said to the ruler of his house, Bring *these* men home, and slay, and make ready; for *these* men shall dine with me at noon.

17 And the man did as Joseph bade; and the man brought the men into Joseph's house.

18 And the men were afraid, because they were brought into Joseph's house; and they said, Because of the money that was returned in our sacks at the first time are we brought in; that he may seek occasion against us, and fall upon us, and take us for bondmen, and our asses.

19 And they came near to the steward of Joseph's house, and they communed with him at the door of the house,

20 And said, O sir, we came indeed down at the first time to buy food:

21 And it came to pass, when we came to the inn, that we opened our sacks, and, behold, *every* man's money *was* in the mouth of his sack, our money in full weight: and we have brought it again in our hand.

22 And other money have we brought down in our hands to buy food: we cannot tell who put our money in our sacks.

23 And he said, Peace *be* to you, fear not: your God, and the God of your father, hath given you treasure in your sacks: I had your money. And he brought Simeon out unto them.

24 And the man brought the men into Joseph's house, and gave *them* water, and they washed their feet; and he gave their asses provender.

25 And they made ready the present against Joseph came at noon: for they heard that they should eat bread there.

26 And when Joseph come home, they brought him the present which *was* in their hand into the house, and bowed themselves to him to the earth.

27 And he asked them of *their* welfare, and said, *Is* your father well, the old man of whom ye spake? *Is* he yet alive?

28 And they answered, Thy servant our father *is* in good health, he *is* yet alive. And they bowed down their heads, and made obeisance.

29 And he lifted up his eyes, and saw his brother Benjamin, his mother's son, and said, *Is* this your younger brother, of whom ye spake unto me? And he said, God be gracious unto thee, my son.

30 And Joseph made haste; for his bowels did yearn upon his brother: and he sought *where* to weep; and he entered into *his* chamber, and wept there.

31 And he washed his face, and went out, and refrained himself, and said, Set on bread.

32 And they set on for him by himself, and for them by themselves, and for the Egyptians, which did eat with him, by themselves: because the Egyptians might not eat bread

with the Hebrews; for that *is* an abomination unto the Egyptians.

33 And they sat before him, the firstborn according to his birthright, and the youngest according to his youth: and the men marvelled at one another.

34 And he took *and sent* messes unto them from before him: but Benjamin's mess was five times so much as any of theirs. And they drank, and were merry with him.

CHAPTER 44

And he commanded the steward of his house, saying, Fill the men's sacks *with* food, as much as they can carry, and put every man's money in his sack's mouth.

2 And put my cup, the silver cup, in the sack's mouth of the youngest, and his corn money. And he did according to the word that Joseph had spoken.

3 As soon as the morning was light, the men were sent away, they and their asses.

4 *And* when they were gone out of the city, *and* not *yet* far off, Joseph said unto his steward, Up, follow after the men; and when thou dost overtake them, say unto them, Wherefore have ye rewarded evil for good?

5 Is not this *it* in which my lord drinketh, and whereby indeed he divineth? ye have done evil in so doing.

6 And he overtook them, and he spake unto them these same words.

7 And they said unto him, Wherefore saith my lord these words? God forbid that thy servants should do according to this thing:

8 Behold, the money, which we found in our sacks' mouths, we brought again unto thee out of the land of Canaan: how

then should we steal out of thy lord's house silver or gold?

9 With whomsoever of thy servants it be found, both let him die, and we also will be my lord's bondmen.

10 And he said, Now also *let* it *be* according unto your words: he with whom it is found shall be my servant; and ye shall be blameless.

11 Then they speedily took down every man his sack to the ground, and opened every man his sack.

12 And he searched, *and* began at the eldest, and left at the youngest: and the cup was found in Benjamin's sack.

13 Then they rent their clothes, and laded every man his ass, and returned to the city.

14 And Judah and his brethren came to Joseph's house; for he *was* yet there: and they fell before him on the ground.

15 And Joseph said unto them, What deed *is* this that ye have done? wot ye not that such a man as I can certainly divine?

16 And Judah said, What shall we say unto my lord? what shall we speak? or how shall we clear ourselves? God hath found out the iniquity of thy servants: behold, we *are* my lord's servants, both we, and *he* also with whom the cup is found.

17 And he said, God forbid that I should do so: *but* the man in whose hand the cup is found, he shall be my servant; and as for you, get you up in peace unto your father.

18 Then Judah came near unto him, and said, Oh my lord, let thy servant, I pray thee, speak a word in my lord's ears, and let not thine anger burn against thy servant: for thou *art* even as Pharaoh.

19 My lord asked his servants, saying, Have ye a father, or a brother?

20 And we said unto my lord, We have a father, an old man, and a child of his old age, a little one; and his brother is dead, and he alone is left of his mother, and his father loveth him.

21 And thou saidst unto thy servants, Bring him down unto me, that I may set mine eyes upon him.

22 And we said unto my lord, The lad cannot leave his father: for *if* he should leave his father, *his father* would die.

23 And thou saidst unto thy servants, Except your youngest brother come down with you, ye shall see my face no more.

24 And it came to pass when we came up unto thy servant my father, we told him the words of my lord.

25 And our father said, Go again, *and* buy us a little food.

26 And we said, We cannot go down: if our youngest brother be with us, then will we go down: for we may not see the man's face, except our youngest brother *be* with us.

27 And thy servant my father said unto us, Ye know that my wife bare me two *sons*:

28 And the one went out from me, and I said, Surely he is torn in pieces; and I saw him not since:

29 And if ye take this also from me, and mischief befall him, ye shall bring down my gray hairs with sorrow to the grave.

30 Now therefore when I come to thy servant my father, and the lad *be* not with us; seeing that his life is bound up in the lad's life;

31 It shall come to pass, when he seeth that the lad *is* not *with us,* that he will die: and thy servants shall bring down the gray hairs of thy servant our father with sorrow to the grave.

32 For thy servant became surety for the lad unto my father, saying, If I bring him not unto thee, then I shall bear the blame to my father for ever.

33 Now therefore, I pray thee, let thy servant abide instead of the lad a bondman to my lord; and let the lad go up with his brethren.

34 For how shall I go up to my father, and the lad *be* not with me? lest peradventure I see the evil that shall come on my father.

CHAPTER 45

Then Joseph could not refrain himself before all them that stood by him; and he cried, Cause every man to go out from me. And there stood no man with him, while Joseph made himself known unto his brethren.

2 And he wept aloud: and the Egyptians and the house of Pharaoh heard.

3 And Joseph said unto his brethren, I *am* Joseph; doth my father yet live? And his brethren could not answer him; for they were troubled at his presence.

4 And Joseph said unto his brethren, Come near to me, I pray you. And they came near. And he said, I *am* Joseph your brother, whom ye sold into Egypt.

5 Now therefore be not grieved, nor angry with yourselves, that ye sold me hither: for God did send me before you to preserve life.

6 For these two years *hath the* famine *been* in the land: and yet *there are* five years, in the which *there shall* neither *be* eating nor harvest.

7 And God sent me before you to preserve you a posterity in the earth, and to save your lives by a great deliverance.

8 So now *it was* not you *that* sent me hither, but God: and he hath made me a father to Pharaoh, and lord of all his

house, and a ruler throughout all the land of Egypt.

9 Haste ye, and go up to my father, and say unto him, Thus saith thy son Joseph, God hath made me lord of all Egypt: come down unto me, tarry not:

10 And thou shalt dwell in the land of Goshen, and thou shalt be near unto me, thou, and thy children, and thy children' children, and thy flocks, and thy herds, and all that thou hast:

11 And there will I nourish thee; for yet *there are* five years of famine; lest thou, and thy household, and all that thou hast, come to poverty.

12 And, behold, your eyes see, and the eyes of my brother Benjamin, that *it is* my mouth that speaketh unto you.

13 And ye shall tell my father of all my glory in Egypt, and of all that ye have seen; and ye shall haste and bring down my father hither.

14 And he fell upon his brother Benjamin's neck, and wept; and Benjamin wept upon his neck.

15 Moreover he kissed all his brethren, and wept upon them: and after that his brethren talked with him.

16 And the fame thereof was heard in Pharaoh's house, saying, Joseph's brethren are come: and it pleased Pharaoh well, and his servants.

17 And Pharaoh said unto Joseph, Say unto thy brethren, This do ye; lade your beasts, and go, get you unto the land of Canaan;

18 And take your father and your households, and come unto me: and I will give you the good of the land of Egypt, and ye shall eat the fat of the land.

19 Now thou art commanded, this do ye; take you wagons

out of the land of Egypt for your little ones, and for your wives, and bring your father, and come.

20 Also regard not your stuff; for the good of all the land of Egypt *is* yours.

21 And the children of Israel did so: and Joseph gave them wagons, according to the commandment of Pharaoh, and gave them provision for the way.

22 To all of them he gave each man changes of raiment; but to Benjamin he gave three hundred *pieces* of silver, and five changes of raiment.

23 And to his father he sent after this *manner*; then asses laden with the good things of Egypt, and ten she asses laden with corn and bread and meat for his father by the way.

24 So he sent his brethren away, and they departed: and he said unto them, See that ye fall not out by the way.

25 And they went up out of Egypt, and came into the land of Canaan unto Jacob their father,

26 And told him, saying, Joseph *is* yet alive, and he *is* governor over all the land of Egypt. And Jacob's heart fainted, for he believed them not.

27 And they told him all the words of Joseph, which he had said unto them: and when he saw the wagons which Joseph had sent to carry him, the spirit of Jacob their father revived:

28 And Israel said, It *is* enough; Joseph my son *is* yet alive: I will go and see him before I die.

CHAPTER 48

And it came to pass after these things, that *one* told Joseph, Behold, thy father *is* sick: and he took with him his two sons, Manasseh and Ephraim.

2 And *one* told Jacob, and said, Behold, thy son Joseph cometh unto thee: and Israel strengthened himself, and sat upon the bed.

CHAPTER 49

And Jacob called unto his sons, and said, Gather yourselves together, that I may tell you *that* which shall befall you in the last days.

2 Gather yourselves together, and hear, ye sons of Jacob; and hearken unto Israel your father.

3 Reuben, thou *art* my firstborn, my might, and the beginning of my strength, the excellency of dignity, and the excellency of power:

4 Unstable as water, thou shalt not excel; because thou wentest up to thy father's bed; then defiledst thou *it*: he went up to my couch.

5 Simeon and Levi *are* brethren; instruments of cruelty *are in* their habitations.

6 O my soul, come not thou into their secret; unto their assembly, mine honour, be not thou united: for in their anger they slew a man, and in their selfwill they digged down a wall.

7 Cursed *be* their anger, for *it was* fierce; and their wrath, for it was cruel: I will divide them in Jacob, and scatter them in Israel.

8 Judah, thou *art he* whom thy brethren shall praise: thy hand *shall be* in the neck of thine enemies; thy father's children shall bow down before thee.

9 Judah *is* a lion's whelp: from the prey, my son, thou art

gone up: he stooped down, he couched as a lion, and as an old lion; who shall rouse him up?

10 The sceptre shall not depart from Judah, nor a lawgiver from between his feet, until Shiloh come; and unto him *shall* the gathering of the people *be.*

11 Binding his foal unto the vine, and his ass's colt unto the choice vine; he washed his garments in wine, and his clothes in the blood of grapes:

12 His eyes *shall be* red with wine, and his teeth white with milk.

13 Zebulun shall dwell at the haven of the sea; and he *shall be* for an haven of ships; and his border *shall be* unto Zidon.

14 Issachar *is* a strong ass couching down between two burdens:

15 And he saw that rest *was* good, and the land that *it was* pleasant; and bowed his shoulder to bear, and became a servant unto tribute.

16 Dan shall judge his people, as one of the tribes of Israel.

17 Dan shall be a serpent by the way, an adder in the path, that biteth the horse heels, so that his rider shall fall backward.

18 I have waited for thy salvation, O LORD.

19 Gad, a troop shall overcome him: but he shall overcome at the last.

20 Out of Asher his bread *shall be* fat, and he shall yield royal dainties.

21 Naphtali *is* a hind let loose: he giveth goodly words.

22 Joseph *is* a fruitful bough, *even* a fruitful bough by a well; *whose* branches run over the wall:

23 The archers have sorely grieved him, and shot *at him,* and hated him:

24 But his bow abode in strength, and the arms of his hands were made strong by the hands of the mighty *God* of Jacob; (from thence *is* the shepherd, the stone of Israel:)

25 *Even* by the God of thy father, who shall help thee; and by the Almighty, who shall bless thee with blessings of heaven above, blessings of the deep that lieth under, blessings of the beasts, and of the womb:

26 The blessings of thy father have prevailed above the blessings of my progenitors unto the utmost bound of the everlasting hills: they shall be on the head of Joseph, and on the crown of the head of him that was separate from his brethren.

27 Benjamin shall ravin *as* a wolf: in the morning he shall devour the prey, and at night he shall divide the spoil.

28 All these *are* the twelve tribes of Israel: and this *is it* that their father spake unto them, and blessed them; every one according to his blessing he blessed them.

29 And he charged them, and said unto them, I am to be gathered unto my people: bury me with my fathers in the cave that *is* in the field of Ephron the Hittite,

30 In the cave that *is* in the field of Machpelah, which *is* before Mamre, in the land of Canaan, which Abraham bought with the field of Ephron the Hittite for a possession of a buryingplace.

31 There they buried Abraham and Sarah his wife; there they buried Isaac and Rebekah his wife; and there I buried Leah.

32 The purchase of the field and of the cave that is therein *was* from the children of Heth.

33 And when Jacob had made an end of commanding his

sons, he gathered up his feet into the bed, and yielded up the ghost, and was gathered unto his people.

CHAPTER 50

And Joseph fell upon his father's face, and wept upon him, and kissed him.

2 And Joseph commanded his servants the physicians to embalm his father: and the physicians embalmed Israel.

3 And forty days were fulfilled for him; for so are fulfilled the days of those which are embalmed: and the Egyptians mourned for him threescore and then days.

4 And when the days of his mourning were past, Joseph spake unto the house of Pharaoh, saying, If now I have found grace in you eyes, speak, I pray you, in the ears of Pharaoh, saying,

5 My father made me swear, saying, Lo, I die: in my grave which I have digged for me in the land of Canaan, there shalt thou bury me. Now therefore let me go up, I pray thee, and bury my father, and I will come again.

6 And Pharaoh said, Go up, and bury thy father, according as he made thee swear.

7 And Joseph went up to bury his father: and with him went up all the servants of Pharaoh, the elders of his house, and all the elders of the land of Egypt,

8 And all the house of Joseph, and his brethren, and his father's house: only their little ones, and their flocks, and their herds, they left in the land of Goshen.

9 And there went up with him both chariots and horsemen: and it was a very great company.

10 And they came to the threshingfloor of Atad, which is

beyond Jordan, and there they mourned with a great and very sore lamentation: and he made a mourning for his father seven days.

11 And when the inhabitants of the land, the Canaanites, saw the mourning in the floor of Atad, they said, This is a grievous mourning to the Egyptians: wherefore the name of it was called Abel-mizraim, which is beyond Jordan.

12 And his sons did unto him according as he commanded them:

13 For his sons carried him into the land of Canaan, and buried him in the cave of the field of Machpelah, which Abraham bought with the field for a possession of a burying-place of Ephron the Hittite, before Mamre.

14 And Joseph returned into Egypt, he, and his brethren, and all that went up with him to bury his father, after he had buried his father.

15 And when Joseph's brethren saw that their father was dead, they said, Joseph will peradventure hate us, and will certainly requite us all the evil which we did unto him.

16 And they sent a messenger unto Joseph, saying, Thy father did command before he died, saying,

17 So shall ye say unto Joseph, Forgive, I pray thee now, the trespass of thy brethren, and their sin; for they did unto thee evil: and now, we pray thee, forgive the trespass of the servants of the God of thy father. And Joseph wept when they spake unto him.

18 And his brethren also went and fell down before his face; and they said, Behold, we be thy servants.

19 And Joseph said unto them, Fear not: for am I in the place of God?

20 But as for you, ye thought evil against me; *but* God meant it unto good, to bring to pass, as *it is* this day, to save much people alive.

21 Now therefore fear ye not: I will nourish you, and your little ones. And he comforted them, and spake kindly unto them.

22 And Joseph dwelt in Egypt, he, and his father's house: and Joseph lived an hundred and ten years.

23 And Joseph saw Ephraim's children of the third *generation:* the children also of Machir the son of Manasseh were brought up upon Joseph's knees.

24 And Joseph said unto his brethren, I die: and God will surely visit you, and bring you out of this land unto the land which he sware to Abraham, to Isaac, and to Jacob.

25 And Joseph took an oath of the children of Israel, saying, God will surely visit you, and ye shall carry up my bones from hence.

26 So Joseph died, *being* an hundred and ten years old: and they embalmed him, and he was put in a coffin in Egypt.

THE **TAO TE**

Prologue by Joseph Campbell {

CHING

In the Chinese philosophy of the Tao, of which the classic statement is the Tao te Ching, "the Book (ching) of the Power (tê) of the Way (tao)," it is maintained that a Quietist contemplation of the Tao "gives as the Indians say siddhi, as the Chinese say tê, a power over the outside world undreamt of by those who pit themselves against matter while still in its thralls" [writes Arthur Waley]. . . . The word tao, "the way, the path," is in as much equivalent to dharma as it refers to the law, truth, or order of the universe, which is the law, truth, order, and way of each being and thing within it, according to kind. "It means a road, path, way," [continues Waley] . . . "tao meant 'the way the universe works'; and ultimately, something very like God, in the more abstract and philosophical sense of that term. . . ." There is through all of nature an all-suffusing spiritual harmony: an orderly interaction through all life and lives, through all history and historical institutions, of those two principles or powers, active and passive, light and dark, hot and cold, heavenly and earthly, known as yang and yin. The force of the principle of yang predominates in youth; that of yin, later, and increasingly in old age. Yang is dominant in summer, in the south, and at noon; yin in winter, in the north, and at night. The way of their alterations through all things is the Way of all things, the Tao. And by putting oneself in accord with the Tao—one's time, one's world, oneself—one accomplishes the ends of life and is at peace in the sense of being in harmony with all things.

INTRODUCTION

STEPHEN MITCHELL

TAO TE CHING (pronounced, more or less, Dow Deh Jing) can be translated as *The Book of the Immanence of the Way* or *The Book of the Way and How It Manifests Itself in the World*, or, simply, *The Book of the Way*.

About Lao Tzu, its author, there is practically nothing to be said. He may have been an older contemporary of Confucious (551–479 BCE) and may have held the position of archive keeper in one of the petty kingdoms of the time. But all the information that has come down to us is highly suspect. Even the meaning of his name is uncertain (the most likely interpretations: "the Old Master," or, more picturesquely, "the Old Boy"). Like an Iroquois woodsman, he left no traces. All he left us is his book: the classic manual on the art of living, written in a style of gemlike lucidity, radiant with humor and grace and large heartedness and deep wisdom: one of the wonders of the world.

People usually think of Lao Tzu as a hermit, a dropout from society, dwelling serenely in some mountain hut, unvisited except perhaps by the occasional traveller arriving from a '60s joke to ask, "What's the meaning of life?" But it's clear from his teachings that he deeply cared about society, if society means the welfare of one's fellow human beings; his book is, among other things, a treatise on the art of government, whether of a country or of a child. The misperception may arise from his insistence on *wei wu wei*, literally "doing not doing," which has been seen as passivity. Nothing could be further from the truth. A good athlete can enter a state of body awareness in which the right stroke or right movement happens by itself, effortlessly, without any interference from the conscious will. This is a paradigm for non-action: the purest and most effective form of action. The game plays the game; the poem writes the poem; we can't tell the dancer from the dance.

> Less and less do you need to force things
> until finally you arrive at non action
> When nothing is done
> nothing is left undone

Nothing is done because the doer has wholeheartedly vanished into the deed, the fuel has been completely transformed into flame. This "nothing" is, in fact, everything. It happens when we trust the intelligence of the universe in the same way that an athlete or a dancer trusts the superior intelligence of the body. Hence Lao Tzu's emphasis on softness. Softness means the opposite of rigidity, and is synonymous with suppleness, adaptability, endurance. Anyone who has seen a tai chi or ai-kido master doing not-doing will know how powerful this softness is

Lao Tzu's central figure is a man or woman whose life is in perfect harmony with the way things are. This is not an idea; it is a reality; I have seen it. The Master has mastered Nature: not in the sense of conquering it, but of becoming it. In surrendering to the Tao, in giving up all concepts, judgements and desires, her mind has grown naturally compassionate. She finds deep in her own experience the central truths of the art of living, which are paradoxical only on the surface: that the more truly solitary we are, the more compassionate we can be; the more we let go of what we love, the more present our love becomes; the clearer our insight into what is beyond good and evil, the more we can embody the good. Until finally she is able to say, in all humility, "I am the Tao, the Truth, the Life."

The teaching of the *Tao te Ching* is moral in the deepest sense. Unencumbered by any concept of sin, the Master doesn't see evil as a force to resist, but simply as an opaqueness, a state of self-absorption which is in disharmony with the universal process, so that, as with a dirty window, the light can't shine through. This freedom from moral categories allows him his great compassion for the wicked and the selfish.

Thus the Master is available to all people
and doesn't reject anyone.
He is ready to use all situations
and doesn't waste anything
This is called embodying the light.

What is a good man but a bad man's teacher?
What is a bad man but a good man's job?
If you don't understand this, you will get lost
however intelligent you are.
It is the great secret.

TAO TE CHING

1

THE WAY THAT becomes a way
is not the Immortal Way
the name that becomes a name
is not the Immortal Name
the maiden of Heaven and Earth has no name
the mother of all things has a name
thus in innocence we see the beginning
in passion we see the end
two different names
for one and the same
the one we call dark
the dark beyond dark
the door to all beginnings

2

All the world knows beauty
but if that becomes beautiful
this becomes ugly
all the world knows good
but if that becomes good
this becomes bad
the coexistence of have and have not
the coproduction of hard and easy
the correlation of long and short
the codependence of high and low
the correspondence of note and noise
the coordination of first and last
is endless
thus the sage performs effortless deeds
and teaches wordless lessons
he doesn't start all the things he begins
he doesn't presume on what he does
he doesn't claim what he achieves
and because he makes no claim
he suffers no loss

3

Bestowing no honors
keeps people from fighting
prizing no treasures
keeps people from stealing
displaying no attractions
keeps people from making trouble
thus the rule of the sage

empties the mind
but fills the stomach
weakens the will
but strengthens the bones
by keeping the people from knowing or wanting
and those who know from daring to act
he thus governs them all

4

The Tao is so empty
those who use it
never become full again
and so deep
as if it were the ancestor of us all
dulling our edges
untying our tangles
softening our light
merging our dust
and so clear
as if it were present
I wonder whose child it is
it seems it was here before Ti

5

Heaven and Earth are heartless
treating creatures like straw dogs
heartless is the sage
treating people like straw dogs
between Heaven and Earth
how like a bellows

empty but inexhaustible
each movement produces more
talking only wastes it
better to keep it inside

6

The valley spirit that doesn't die
we call the dark womb
the dark womb's mouth
we call the source of creation
as real as gossamer silk
and yet we can't exhaust it

7

Heaven is eternal and Earth is immortal
the reason they're eternal and immortal
is because they don't live for themselves
hence they can live forever
thus the sage pulls himself back
but ends up in front
he lets himself go
but ends up safe
selflessness must be the reason
whatever he seeks he finds

8

The best are like water
bringing help to all
without competing
choosing what others avoid

hence approaching the Tao
dwelling with earth
thinking with depth
helping with kindness
speaking with truth
governing with peace
working with skill
moving with time
and because they don't compete
they aren't maligned

9

Instead of pouring in more
better stop while you can
making it sharper
won't help it last longer
houses full of treasure
can never be safe
the vanity of success
invites its own failure
when your work is done retire
this is the Way of Heaven

1 0

Can you hold fast your crescent soul and not let it wander
can you make your breath as soft as a baby's
can you wipe your Dark Mirror free of dust
can you serve and govern without effort
can you be the female at Heaven's Gate
can you light up the world without knowledge

beget things and keep them
but beget without possessing
keep without controlling
this is Dark Virtue

1 1

Thirty spokes converge on a hub
but it's the emptiness
that makes a wheel work
pots are fashioned from clay
but it's the hollow that makes a pot work
windows and doors are carved for a house
but it's the spaces that make the house work
existence makes something useful
but nonexistence makes it work

1 2

The five colors make our eyes blind
the five tones make our ears deaf
the five flavors make our mouths numb
riding and hunting make our minds wild
hard-to-get goods make us break laws
thus the rule of the sage
puts the stomach ahead of the eyes
thus he picks this over that

1 3

Favor and disgrace are like warnings
honor and disaster are like the body
and why are favor and disgrace like warnings

favor means descending
to gain it is like a warning
to lose it is like a warning
thus are favor and disgrace like warnings
and why are honor and disaster like the body
the reason we have disaster
is because we have a body
if we didn't have a body
we wouldn't have disaster
who honors his body as much as the world
can be entrusted with the world
who loves his body as much as the world
can be encharged with the world

1 4

We look but don't see it
and call it indistinct
we listen but don't hear it
and call it faint
we reach but don't grasp it
and call it ethereal
three failed means to knowledge
we weave into one
with no light above
with no shade below
too fine to be named
returning to nothing
this is the formless form
the immaterial image
this is the waxing waning

we meet without seeing its face
we follow without seeing its back
holding onto this very Way
we rule this very realm
and discover its ancient past
this is the thread of the Way

1 5

The ancient masters of the Way
aimed at the indiscernible
and penetrated the dark
you would never know them
and because you wouldn't know them
I describe them with reluctance
they were careful as if crossing a river in winter
cautious as if worried about neighbors
reserved like guests
ephemeral like melting ice
simple like uncarved wood
open like valleys
and murky like puddles
but a puddle becomes clear when it's still
and stillness becomes alive when it's roused
those who treasure this Way
don't try to be full
not trying to be full
they can hide and stay hidden

1 6

Let limits be empty
the center be still
ten thousand things rise
we watch them return
creatures without number
all return to their roots
return to their roots to be still
to be still to revive
to revive to endure
knowing how to endure is wisdom
not knowing is to suffer in vain
knowing how to endure is to be all-embracing
all-imbracing means impartial
impartial means the king
the king means Heaven
Heaven means the Way
and the Way means long life
life without trouble

1 7

During the High Ages people knew they were there
then people loved and praised them
then they feared them
finally they despised them
when honesty fails dishonesty prevails
hesitate and guard your words
when their work succeeds
let people think they did it

1 8

When the Great Way disappears
we meet kindess and justice
when reason appears
we meet great deceit
when the six relations fail
we meet obedience and love
when the country is in chaos
we meet honest officials

1 9

Get rid of wisdom and reason
and people will live a hundred times better
get rid of kindness and justice
and people once more will love and obey
get rid of cleverness and profit
and thieves will cease to exist
but these three sayings are not enough
hence let this be added
wear the undyed and hold the uncarved
reduce self-interest and limit desires
get rid of learning and problems will vanish

2 0

Yes and no
aren't so far apart lovely and ugly
aren't so unalike
what others fear
we too must fear before the moon wanes
everyone is gay

as if they were at the Great Sacrifice
or climbing a tower in spring
I sit here and make no sign
like a child that doesn't smile
lost with no one to turn to
while others enjoy more
I alone seem forgotten
my mind is so foolish
so simple
others look bright
I alone seem dim
others are certain
I alone am confused
receding like the ocean
waxing without cease
everyone has a goal
I alone am dumb and backward
for I alone choose to differ
preferring still my mother's breast

2 1
The expression of empty virtue
comes from the Tao alone
the Tao as a thing
waxes and wanes
it waxes and wanes
but inside there is an image
it wanes and waxes
but inside there is a creature
it's distant and dark

but inside there is an essence
an essence fundamentally real
and inside there is a heart
throughout the ages
its name has never changed
so we might follow our fathers
how do we know what our fathers were like
through this

2 2

Partial means whole
crooked means straight
hollow means full
worn-out means new
less means content
more means confused
thus the sage holds onto the one
to use in guiding the world
not watching himself he appears
not displaying himself he flourishes
not flattering himself he succeeds
not parading himself he leads
because he doesn't compete
no one can compete against him
the ancients who said partial means whole
came close indeed
becoming whole depends on this

2 3

Whispered words are natural
a gale doesn't last all morning
a squall doesn't last all day
who else could make these
only Heaven and Earth
if Heaven and Earth can't make things last
what about Man
thus in whatever we do
let those on the Way be one with the Way
let those who succeed be one with success
let those who fail be one with failure
be one with success
for the Way succeeds too
be one with failure
for the Way fails too

2 4

Who tiptoes doesn't stand
who strides doesn't walk
who watches himself doesn't appear
who displays himself doesn't flourish
who flatters himself achieves nothing
who parades himself doesn't lead
on the road they say
too much food and a tiring pace
some things are simply bad
thus the Taoist shuns them

2 5

Imagine a nebulous thing
here before Heaven and Earth
silent and elusive
it stands alone not wavering
it travels everywhere unharmed
it could be the mother of us all
not knowing its name
I call it the Tao
forced to name it
I name it Great
great means ever-flowing
ever-flowing means far-reaching
far-reaching means returning
the Tao is great
Heaven is great
Earth is great
the king is also great
the realm contains four greats
of these the king is one
Man imitates Earth
Earth imitates Heaven
Heaven imitates the Tao
the Tao imitates itself

2 6

Heavy is the root of light
still is the master of busy
thus a lord might travel all day
but never far from his supplies

even in a guarded camp
his manner is calm and aloof
why would the lord of ten thousand chariots
treat himself lighter than his kingdom
too light he loses his base
too busy he loses command

2 7
Good walking leaves no tracks
good talking reveals no flaws
good counting counts no beads
good closing locks no locks
and yet it can't be opened
good tying ties no knots
and yet it can't be undone
thus the sage is good at saving
and yet abandons no one
nor anything of use
this is called cloaking the light
thus the good instruct the bad
the bad learn from the good
not honoring their teachers
not cherishing their students
the wise alone are perfectly blind
this is called peering into the distance

2 8

Recognize the male
but hold onto the female
and be the world's maid
being the world's maid
don't lose your ancient virtue
not losing your ancient virtue
be a newborn child again
recognize the pure
but hold onto the defiled
and be the world's valley
being the world's valley
be filled with ancient virtue
being filled with ancient virtue
be uncarved wood again
recognize the white
but hold onto the black
and be the world's guide
being the world's guide
don't stray from ancient virtue
not straying from ancient virtue
be without limits again
uncarved wood can be split to make tools
the sage makes it his chief official
a master tailor doesn't cut

2 9

Trying to govern the world with force
I see this not succeeding
the world is a spiritual thing
it can't be forced
to force it is to harm it
to control it is to lose it
sometimes things lead
sometimes they follow
sometimes blow hot
sometimes blow cold
sometimes expand
sometimes collapse
therefore the sage avoids extremes
avoids extravagance
avoids excess

3 0

Use the Tao to help your king
don't use weapons to rule the land
such things soon return
where armies camp
brambles grow
best to win then stop
don't make use of force
win but don't be proud
win but don't be vain
win but don't be cruel
win when you have no choice
this is to win without force

virility means old age
this isn't the Tao
what isn't the Tao ends early

3 1

Weapons are not auspicious tools
some things are simply bad
thus the Taoist shuns them
in peace the ruler honors the left
in war he honors the right
weapons are not auspicious
weapons are not a ruler's tools
he wields them when he has no choice
dispassion is the best
thus he does not beautify them
he who beautifies them
enjoys killing others
he who enjoys killing others
achieves no worldly rule
thus we honor the left for joy
we honor the right for sorrow
the left is where the adjutant stands
the commander on the right
which means as at a funeral
when you kill another
honor him with your tears
when the battle is won
treat it as a wake

3 2

The Tao has never had a name
simple and though small
no one can command it
if a lord upheld it
the world would be his guest
when Heaven joins with Earth
they bestow sweet dew
no one gives the order
it comes down to all
the first distinction gives us names
after we have names
we should know restraint
who knows restraint knows no trouble
to picture the Tao in the world
imagine rivers and the sea

3 3

Who knows others is perceptive
who knows himself is wise
who conquers others is forceful
who conquers himself is strong
who knows contentment is wealthy
who strives hard succeeds
who doesn't lose his place endures
who dies but doesn't perish lives on

3 4

The Tao drifts
it can go left or right
everything lives by its grace
but it doesn't speak
when its work succeeds
it makes no claim
it has no desires
shall we call it small
everything turns to it
but it wields no control
shall we call it great
therefore the sage never acts great
thus he can do great things

3 5

Hold up the Great Image
and the world will come
and be beyond harm
safe serene and at one
fine food and song
detain passing guests
when the Tao speaks
it's senseless and plain
we look and don't see it
we listen and don't hear it
but we use it without end

3 6

What you would shorten
you should therefore lengthen
what you would weaken
you should therefore strengthen
what you would topple
you should therefore raise
what you would take
you should therefore give
this is called hiding the light
the weak conquering the strong
fish can't survive out of the deep
a state's greatest tool
is not meant to be shown

3 7

The Tao never does a thing
yet there is nothing it doesn't do
if a ruler could uphold it
people by themselves would change
and changing if their desires stirred
he could make them still
with simplicity that has no name
stilled by nameless simplicity
they would not desire
and not desiring be at peace
the world would fix itself

3 8

Higher Virtue is not virtuous
thus it possesses virtue
Lower Virtue is not without virtue
thus it possesses no virtue
Higher Virtue lacks effort
and the thought of effort
Higher Kindness involves effort
but not the thought of effort
Higher Justice involves effort
and the thought of effort
Higher Ritual involves effort
but no response
until it threatens and compels
when the Way is lost virtue appears
when virtue is lost kindness appears
when kindness is lost justice appears
when justice is lost ritual appears
ritual marks the waning of belief
and onset of confusion
augury is the flower of the Way
and beginning of delusion
thus the great choose thick over thin
the fruit over the flower
therefore they pick this over that

3 9

Of things that became one in the past
Heaven became one and was clear
Earth became one and was still
spirits became one and were active
streams became one and were full
kings became one and ruled the world
but by implication
Heaven would crack if it were always clear
Earth would crumble if it were always still
spirits would fail if they were always active
streams would dry up if they were always full
kings would fall if they were always high and noble
thus the noble is based on the humble
the high is founded on the low
thus do kings refer to themselves
as orphaned widowed and destitute
but is this the basis of humility
counting a carriage as no carriage at all
not wanting to clink like jade
they clunk like rocks

4 0

The Tao moves the other way
the Tao works through weakness
the things of this world come from something
something comes from nothing

4 1

When a great person hears of the Way
he follows it with devotion
when an average person hears of the Way
he doesn't know if it's real or not
when a small person hears of the Way
he laughs out loud
if he didn't laugh
it wouldn't be the Way
hence these sayings arose
the brightest path seems dark
the quickest path seems slow
the smoothest path seems rough
the highest virtue low
the whitest white pitch-black
the greatest virtue wanting
the staunchest virtue timid
the truest truth uncertain
the perfect square lacks corners
the perfect tool does nothing
the perfect sound is hushed
the perfect form is shapeless
the Tao is hidden and has no name
but because it's the Tao
it knows how to start and how to finish

4 2

The Tao gives birth to one
one gives birth to two
two gives birth to three
three gives birth to ten thousand things
ten thousand things with *yin* at their backs
and *yang* in their embrace
and breath between for harmony
what the world hates
to be orphaned widowed or destitute
kings use for their titles
thus some gain by losing
others lose by gaining
thus what people teach
I teach too
tyrants never choose their deaths
this becomes my teacher

4 3

The weakest thing in the world
excels the strongest thing in the world
what doesn't exist finds room where there is none
thus we know doing nothing succeeds
teaching without words
succeeding without effort
few in the world can equal this

4 4

Which is more vital
fame or health
which is more precious
health or riches
which is more harmful
loss or gain
the deeper the love
the higher the cost
the bigger the treasure
the greater the loss
who knows contentment
suffers no shame
who knows restraint
encounters no trouble
and thus lives long

4 5

The greatest thing seems incomplete
yet it never wears out
the fullest thing seems empty
yet it never runs dry
the straightest thing seems crooked
the cleverest thing seems clumsy
the richest thing seems poor
activity overcomes cold
stillness overcomes heat
who can be perfectly still
is able to govern the world

4 6

When the Tao prevails
courier horses manure fields instead of roads
when the Tao fails
war-horses are raised on the border
no crime is worse than yielding to desire
no wrong is greater than discontent
no curse is crueler than getting what you want
the contentment of being content
is true contentment indeed

4 7

Without going out his door
he knows the whole world
without looking out his window
he knows the Way of Heaven
the farther people go
the less people know
therefore the sage knows without moving
names without seeing
succeeds without trying

4 8

Those who seek learning gain every day
those who seek the Way lose every day
they lose and they lose
until they find nothing to do
nothing to do means nothing not done
who rules the world isn't busy
if someone is busy
he can't rule the world

4 9

The sage has no mind of his own
his mind is the mind of the people
to the good he is good
to the bad he is good
until they become good
to the true he is true
to the false he is true
until they become true
in the world the sage withdraws
with others he merges his mind
people open their ears and eyes
the sage covers them up

5 0

Appearing means life
disappearing means death
thirteen are the followers of life
thirteen are the followers of death
but people living to live
join the land of death's thirteen
and why
because they live to live
it's said that those who guard life well
aren't injured by soldiers in battle
or harmed by rhinos or tigers in the world
for rhinos have nowhere to sink their horns
tigers have nowhere to sink their claws
and soldiers have nowhere to sink their blades and why
because for them there is no land of death

5 1

The Way begets them
Virtue keeps them
matter shapes them
usage completes them
thus do all things honor the Way
and glorify Virtue
the honor of the Way
the glory of Virtue
are not confirmed
but always so
the Way begets and keeps them
cultivates and trains them
steadies and adjusts them
nurtures and protects them
but begets without possessing
acts without presuming
and cultivates without controlling
this is called Dark Virtue

5 2

The world has a maiden
she becomes the world's mother
who knows the mother
understands the child
who understands the child
keeps the mother safe
and lives without trouble
who blocks the opening
who closes the gate

lives without toil
who unblocks the opening
who meddles in affairs
lives without hope
who sees the small has vision
who protects the weak has strength
who uses his light
who trusts his vision
lives beyond death
this is the Hidden Immortal

5 3
Were I sufficiently wise
I would follow the Great Way
and only fear going astray
the Great Way is smooth
but people love byways
their palaces are spotless
their fields are overgrown
their granaries are empty
they wear fine clothes
and carry sharp swords
they tire of food and drink
and possess more than they need
this is called robbery
and robbery is not the Way

5 4

What is planted right is not uprooted
what is held right is not ripped away
future generations worship it forever
cultivated in the self virtue becomes real
cultivated in the family virtue multiplies
cultivated in the village virtue increases
cultivated in the state virtue prospers
cultivated in the world virtue abounds
thus view the self through the self
view the family through the family
view the village through the village
view the state through the state
view the world through the world
how do we know what the world is like
through this

5 5

He who contains virtue in abundance
resembles a newborn child
wasps don't sting him
beasts don't claw him
birds of prey don't carry him off
his bones are weak his tendons are soft
and yet his grip is firm
he hasn't known the union of sexes
and yet his penis is stiff
so full of essence is he
he cries all day
yet never gets hoarse

so full of breath is he
who knows how to breathe endures
who knows how to endure is wise
who lengthens his life tempts luck
who breathes with his will is strong
but virility means old age
this isn't the Way
what isn't the Way ends early

5 6
Those who know don't talk
those who talk don't know
seal the opening
close the gate
dull the edge
untie the tangle
soften the light
join the dust
this is called the Dark Union
it can't be embraced
it can't be abandoned
it can't be helped
it can't be harmed
it can't be exalted
it can't be debased
thus does the world exalt it

5 7

Use direction to govern a country
use indirection to fight a war
use inaction to rule the world
how do we know this works
the greater the prohibitions
the poorer the people
the sharper the weapons
the darker the realm
the smarter the scheme
the stranger the outcome
the finer the treasure
the thicker the thieves
thus the sage declares
I change nothing
and the people transform themselves
I stay still
and the people adjust themselves
I do nothing
and the people enrich themselves
I want nothing
and the people simplify themselves

5 8

Where government stands aloof
the people open up
where government steps in
the people slip away
happiness rests in misery
misery hides in happiness

who knows where they end
there is no direction
direction turns into indirection
good turns into evil
the people have been lost
for a long long time
thus the sage is an edge that doesn't cut
a point that doesn't pierce
a line that doesn't extend
a light that doesn't blind

5 9

In governing people and caring for Heaven
nothing surpasses economy
economy means planning ahead
planning ahead means accumulating virtue
accumulating virtue means overcoming all
overcoming all means knowing no limit
knowing no limit means guarding the realm
guarding the realm's mother means living long
this means deep roots and a solid trunk
the Way of long and lasting life

6 0

Ruling a great state
is like cooking a small fish
when you govern the world with the Tao
spirits display no powers
not that they display no powers
their powers do people no harm

not that their powers do people no harm
the sage does people no harm
and neither harms the other
for both rely on Virtue

6 1

The great state is a watershed
the confluence of the world
the female of the world
through stillness the female conquers the male
in order to be still
she needs to be lower
the great state that is lower
governs the small state
the small state that is lower
is governed by the great state
some lower themselves to govern
some lower themselves to be governed
the great state's only desire
is to unite and lead others
the small state's only desire
is to join and serve others
for both to achieve their desire
the greater needs to be lower

6 2

The Tao is creation's sanctuary
treasured by the good
it keeps the bad alive
beautiful words might be the price
noble deeds might be the gift

how can we abandon
people who are bad
thus when emperors are enthroned
or ministers installed
though there be great discs of jade
followed by teams of horses
they don't rival one who sits
and offers up this Way
why the ancients exalted it
did they not proclaim
who searches thereby finds
who errs thereby escapes
thus the world exalts it

6 3

Act without acting
work without working
taste without tasting
great or small many or few
repay each wrong with virtue
plan for the hard while it's easy
work on the great while it's small
the hardest task in the world begins easy
the greatest goal in the world begins small
therefore the sage never acts great
he thus achieves great things
who quickly agrees is seldom trusted
who makes it all easy finds it all hard
therefore the sage makes everything hard
he thus finds nothing hard

6 4

It's easy to rule while it's peaceful
it's easy to plan before it arrives
it's easy to break while it's fragile
it's easy to disperse while it's small
act before it exists
govern before it rebels
a giant tree grows from the tiniest shoot
a great tower rises from a basket of dirt
a thousand-mile journey begins at your feet
but to act is to fail
to control is to lose
therefore the sage doesn't act
he thus doesn't fail
he doesn't control
he thus doesn't lose
when people pursue a task
they always fail near the end
care at the end as well as the start
means an end to failure
the sage thus seeks what no one seeks
he doesn't prize hard-to-get goods
he studies what no one studies
he turns to what others pass by
to help all things be natural
he thus dares not act

6 5

The ancient masters of the Way
tried not to enlighten
but to keep men in the dark
what makes the people hard to rule
is knowledge
who rules the realm with knowledge
spreads evil in the realm
who rules without knowledge
spreads virtue in the realm
who understands these two
understands the universal key
understanding the universal key
this is called Dark Virtue
Dark Virtue goes deep
goes far
goes the other way
until it reaches perfect harmony

6 6

The reason the sea can govern a hundred rivers
is because it has mastered being lower
thus it can govern a hundred rivers
thus if the sage would be above the people
he should speak as if he were below them
if he would be before them
he should act as if he were behind them
thus when the sage is above
the people are not burdened

when he is in front
the people are not hindered
the world never wearies
of pushing him forward
because he doesn't struggle
no one can struggle against him

6 7

The world calls me great
great but useless
because I am great I am useless
if I were of use
I would have stayed small
but I possess three treasures
I treasure and uphold
first is compassion
second is austerity
third is reluctance to excel
because I am compassionate
I can be valiant
because I am austere
I can be extravagant
because I am reluctant to excel
I can be chief of all tools
if I renounced compassion for valor
austerity for extravagance
reluctance for supremacy
I would die
compassion wins every battle

and outlasts every attack
what Heaven creates
let compassion protect

6 8
In ancient times
the perfect officer wasn't armed
the perfect warrior wasn't angry
the perfect victor wasn't hostile
the perfect commander acted humble
this is the virtue of nonaggression
this is using the strength of others
this is uniting with Heaven
which was the ancient end

6 9
In warfare there is a saying
rather than a host
better to be a guest
rather than advance an inch
better to retreat a foot
this means to form no column
to wear no armor
to brandish no weapon
to repulse no enemy
no fate is worse than to have no enemy
without an enemy we would lose our treasure
thus when opponents are evenly matched
the remorseful one prevails

7 0

My words are easy to understand
easy to employ
but no one can understand them
no one can employ them
words have an ancestor
deeds have a master
because they have no understanding
people fail to understand me
rare are they who understand me
thus am I exalted
the sage therefore wears coarse cloth
and keeps his jade inside

7 1

To understand yet not understand
is transcendence
not to understand yet understand
is affliction
the reason the sage is not afflicted
is because he treats affliction as affliction
hence he is not afflicted

7 2

When people no longer fear authority
a greater authority will appear
don't restrict where people dwell
don't repress how people live
if they aren't repressed

they won't protest
thus the sage knows himself
but doesn't reveal himself
he loves himself
but doesn't exalt himself
thus he picks this over that

7 3

Daring to act means death
daring not to act means life
of these two
one benefits
one harms
what Heaven hates
who knows the reason
the Way of Heaven
wins easily without a fight
answers wisely without a word
comes quickly without a summons
plans ingeniously without a thought
the Net of Heaven is all-embracing
its mesh is wide but nothing escapes

7 4

If people no longer fear death
why do we threaten to kill them
and if others fear death
and still act perverse
and we catch and kill them

who else will dare
as long as people fear death
the executioner will exist
to kill in the executioner's place
is to take the carpenter's place
who takes the carpenter's place
is bound to hurt his hands

7 5

The reason the people are hungry
is because those above levy so many taxes
thus the people are hungry
the reason the people are hard to rule
is because those above are so forceful
thus the people are hard to rule
the reason the people think little of death
is because those above think so much of life
thus the people think little of death
meanwhile those who do nothing to live
are more esteemed than those who love life

7 6

When people are born
they are soft and supple
when they perish
they are hard and stiff
when plants shoot forth
they are soft and tender
when they die

they are withered and dry
thus it is said
the hard and strong are followers of death
the soft and weak are followers of life
when an army becomes strong it suffers defeat
when a plant becomes hard it snaps
the hard and strong dwell below
the soft and weak dwell above

7 7

The Way of Heaven
is like stringing a bow
pulling down the high
lifting up the low
shortening the long
lengthening the short
the Way of Heaven
takes from the long
and supplements the short
unlike the Way of Man
taking from the short
and giving to the long
who can find the long
and give it to the world
only those who find the Way
thus the sage does not presume on what he does
or claim what he achieves
thus he chooses to hide his skill

7 8

Nothing in the world is weaker than water
but against the hard and the strong
nothing excels it
for nothing can change it
the soft overcomes the hard
the weak overcomes the strong
this is something everyone knows
but no one is able to practice
thus the sage declares
who accepts a country's disgrace
we call the lord of soil and grain
who accepts a country's misfortune
we call the king of all under Heaven
upright words sound upside down

7 9

In resolving a great dispute
a dispute is sure to remain
how can this be good
thus the sage holds the left marker
he makes no claim on others
thus the virtuous oversee markers
the virtueless oversee taxes
the Way of Heaven favors no one
but always helps the good

8 0

Imagine a small state with a small population
let there be labor-saving tools
that aren't used
let people consider death
and not move far
let there be boats and carts
but no reason to ride them
let there be armor and weapons
but no reason to employ them
let people return to the use of knots
and be satisfied with their food
and pleased with their clothing
and content with their homes
and happy with their customs
let there be a state so near
people hear its dogs and chickens
and live out their lives
without making a visit

8 1

True words aren't beautiful
beautiful words aren't true
the good aren't eloquent
the eloquent aren't good
the wise aren't learned
the learned aren't wise
the sage accumulates nothing
but the more he does for others
the greater his existence

the more he gives to others
the greater his abundance
the Way of Heaven
is to help without harming
the Way of the sage
is to act without struggling

T H E BOOK OF

Prologue by Thomas Merton {

RUMI

The Persian Sufi poet Rumi (thirteenth century) writes about death, showing that our attitude toward death is in reality a reflection of our attitude toward ourselves and toward our life. He who truly loves life and lives it, is able to accept death without sorrow. Rumi's poem is on "The Beauty of Death." It reads in part:

He who deems death to be lovely, as Joseph, gives up his soul in ransom for it; he who deems it to be like the world, turns back from the path of salvation.

Everyone's death is of the same quality as himself, my son: to the enemy of God an enemy, to the friend of God a friend. . . .

Your fear of death is really fear of yourself: see what it is from which you are fleeing!

'Tis your own ugly face, not the visage of death: your spirit is like the tree, death like the leaf.

Yet this "friendship" with death is not the same as a pathological death wish. The death wish is merely a refusal of life, an abdication from the difficulties and sorrows of living, a resentment of its joys. The death wish is an incapacity for life. True acceptance of death in freedom and faith demands a mature and fruitful acceptance of life. He who fears death or he who longs for it—both are in the same condition: they admit they have not lived.

INTRODUCTION

JONATHAN STAR

THERE IS A VOICE in us all that is ever-present, a voice that always sings its melody to the world. This is the voice of truth and certainty, the voice that lays bare the hidden mysteries of the soul. In a burst of inspiration, the German poet Rainer Maria Rilke heard this voice and wrote for three days "in a single breathless obedience . . . without one word being in doubt or having to be changed."

This inspired state that opens up the vistas of the universe—one we glimpse only at peak moments in our life—is the same state that poet-saints live in all the time. That is why their every word is charged with purity and divine refulgence; their poetry is a reflection of their own perfect state. Jalaluddin Rumi was such a poet-saint. For thirty years poetry issued from his lips, infused with such genius and perfection as to belie human origin. He was a pure instrument of the Divine, a flute upon which God played an exquisite song. In one of his quatrains, Rumi writes:

> Do you think I know what I'm doing,
> That for a moment, or even half a moment,
>   I know what verses will come from my mouth?
> I am no more than a pen in a writer's hand,
> No more than a ball smacked around by a polo stick!

Rumi's "breathless obedience" to that inner voice is what

made him a peerless master of ecstatic verse. The Islamic scholar A.J. Arberry writes, "In Rumi we encounter one of the world's greatest poets. In profundity of thought, inventiveness of image, and triumphant mastery of language, he stands out as the supreme genius of Islamic mysticism." And R.A. Nicholson, who dedicated his life to Islamic studies, called Rumi "the greatest mystical poet of any age."

The poetic and mystical achievement of Jalaluddin Rumi is a monument in the annals of spiritual literature. In his vast outpouring he not only captured the whole of Islamic mysticism but polished it, refined it, and transformed it into a thing of exquisite beauty. The most personal experiences are cast in the light of universal truths; the ordinary life of man—crowded, busy, and full of uncertainty—is shown to be a necessary step on one's journey to the ineffable Absolute. Rumi has given every word life; and everyone who reads him beholds the naked words of the soul clothed in living form. In Rumi we hear the pure voice of love—we hear the intimate whispers of lover and beloved, we feel the joyous heart gliding upon the water of its own melting.

SYMBOLS OF GRACE

Sufi poetry is filled with metaphors, the most striking of which revolve around wine, taverns, and drunkenness. In this symbolic language of love, "wine" represents the divine love that intoxicates the soul; "getting drunk" means losing oneself in that love; the "cup" refers to one's body and mind; and the Saaqi (the Cupbearer, the Maiden who pours the wine) is the grace-bestowing aspect of God that fills the soul's empty cup with the wine of love. The Sufis even have a word for "hangover" which suggests the lingering effects of love.

These metaphors of drunkenness are, more than anything else, a call to experience; they reflect the Sufi sentiment that the immediate experience of God is far more crucial than any kind of objective or learned knowledge. In a verse from his famous Rubá'iyát, Omar Khayyám writes:

> The cover on the wine-vat is happier
>> than the empire of King Jamshid,
> The wine more fragrant than a great feast,
> The first sigh of a drunk lover's heart
>> more blessed than the song of the greatest poet.

Although Rumi employed the macabre and bacchanalian symbolism of his tradition, his more endearing themes were based on symbols related to nature. In his poetic verse, the nightingale represents the soul; the rose is the perfect beauty of God; the rosegarden is paradise; and the breeze is God's life-giving breath. When we hear of Winter, it is a soul separated from God; when we hear of Spring, it is union, resurrection, and rebirth. All the elements of nature that come alive in Spring are the outward signs of the soul's inner awakening: the rising Sun is the illumination of divine knowledge, the "festival of color" is the beauty of the soul's awakening, and the warm rain is the pouring down of God's grace.

The Sun had a special significance for Rumi because it alluded to his master, Shams—the one who awakened the truth within Rumi. Rumi's use of the terms "Shams," "Shams-e Tabriz" (Shams of Tabriz), and "Shamsuddin" refers not only to his master but also to the many aspects of the

Beloved, embodied in Shams: "Shams" symbolizes the power of grace, the power that awakens the truth within us; "Shams" symbolizes the inner sunrise, the inner light of consciousness, one's own soul and its awakening. Rumi writes:

O my soul, where can I find rest
　　but in the shimmering love of his heart?
Where can I see the pure light of the Sun
　　but in the eyes of my own Shams-e Tabriz?

THE MEETING OF TWO OCEANS

By all accounts, Rumi lived a grand and illustrious life. He was a respected teacher, a master of Sufi lore, the head of a university in the Anatolian capital city of Konya (in present-day Turkey). At the age of thirty-four he claimed hundreds of disciples, the king being one of them. And what is so remarkable and unforgettable about Rumi's life is that in one moment all this changed—the moment he met a wandering dervish named Shams-e Tabriz.

There are several accounts of this historic meeting. One version says that during a lecture of Rumi's, Shams came in and dumped all of Rumi's books—one handwritten by his own father—into a pool of water. Rumi thought the books were destroyed, but Shams retrieved them, volume by volume, intact. Another version says that at a wave of Shams' hand, Rumi's books were engulfed in flames and burned to ashes. Shams then put his hand in the ashes and pulled out the books. (A story much like the first.) A third account says that Rumi was riding on a mule through a square in the center of Konya. A crowd of eager students walked by his feet. Suddenly a strange figure dressed in black fur approached Rumi, grabbed hold of his mule's bridle, and said: "O scholar of infinite knowledge, who was greater, Muhammad or Bayazid of Bestan?" This seemed like an absurd question since, in all of Islam, Muhammad was held supreme among all the prophets. Rumi replied, "How can you ask such a question?—No one can compare with Muhammad." "O then," Shams asked, "why did Muhammad say, 'We have not known Thee, O God, as thou should be known,' whereas Bayazid said, 'Glory unto me! I know the full glory of God'?"

With this one simple question—and with the piercing gaze of Shams' eyes—Rumi's entire view of reality changed. The question was merely an excuse. Shams' imparting of an inner awakening is what shattered Rumi's world. The truths and assumptions upon which Rumi based his whole life crumbled. This same story is told symbolically in the first two accounts, whereby Rumi's books—representing all his acquired intellectual knowledge, including the knowledge given to him by his father—are destroyed, and then miraculously retrieved or "resurrected" by Shams. The books coming from the ashes, created anew by Shams, represent the replacing of Rumi's book-learned knowledge (and his lofty regard for such knowledge) with divine knowledge and the direct experience of God.

According to an embellished version of this third account, after Sham's question, Rumi entered a mystical state of ego annihilation that the Sufis call *fana*. When he regained consciousness, he looked at Shams with utter amazement, realizing that this was no ordinary dervish, but the Beloved himself in human form. From that moment on, Rumi's life was never again the same. He took Shams to live in his home and the two men were inseparable; they spent hours a day together, sometimes isolating themselves for long periods to pray and fast in divine communion with God.

About this meeting, Rumi's son Sultan Walad wrote: "After meeting Shams, my father danced all day and sang all night. He had been a scholar—he became a poet. He had been an ascetic—he became drunk with love."

Rumi was totally lost in this newfound love that his master revealed, and all his great attainments were blossoming through that love. Every day was a miracle, a new birth for Rumi's soul. He had found the Beloved, he had finally been shown the glory of his own soul.

Then, suddenly, eighteen months after Shams entered Rumi's life, he was gone. He returned some time later, for a brief period, and then he was gone again forever. Some accounts say that Shams left in the middle of the night and that Rumi wandered in search of him for two years. (Perhaps a symbolic and romantic portrayal of the lover in search of his missing Beloved.) Other accounts report that Shams was murdered by Rumi's jealous disciples (symbolizing how one's desires and lower tendencies can destroy the thing held most dear).

Without Shams, Rumi found himself in a state of utter and incurable despair; and his whole life thereafter became one of longing and divine remembrance. Rumi's emptiness was that of a person who has just lost a husband or a wife, or a dear friend. Rumi's story shows us that the longing and emptiness we feel for a lost loved one is only a reflection, a hologram, of the longing we feel for God; it is the longing we feel to become whole again, the longing to return to the root from which we are cut. (Rumi uses the metaphor of a reed cut from a reed bed and then made into a flute—which becomes a symbol of a human separated from its source, the Beloved. And as the reed flute wails all day, telling about its separation from the reed bed, so Rumi wails all day telling about being separated from his Beloved.)

It was Sham's disappearance, however, that ignited the fire of longing within Rumi; and it was this very longing that brought him the glorious union with the Beloved. Years later Rumi wrote: "It is the burn of the heart that I want. It is this burning which is everything—more precious than a worldly empire—because it calls God secretly in the night."

THE PATH OF LOVE

In Rumi's poetry, love is the soul of the universe, and this soul knows no bounds—it embraces all people, all countries, and all religions. The goal of Sufism is to know love in all of its glorious forms; and every prophet, every practice, and every form of worship that leads toward love is, in essence, Sufism. The great Sufi philosopher Ibn Arabi writes:

My heart holds within it every form,
    it contains a pasture for gazelles,
    a monastery for Christian monks.
There is a temple for idol-worshippers,
    a holy shrine for pilgrims;
There is the table of the Torah,
    and the Book of the Koran.

I follow the religion of Love
  and go whichever way His camel leads me.
This is the true faith;
This is the true religion.

Just as the Sufis honored all traditions, seeing each as a path leading to the highest truth, they also honored the prophets of these traditions. They looked upon each for guidance and inspiration. Many Sufis, including the great Mansur al-Hallaj, idealized Jesus as the embodiment of perfect love; they built their philosophy around him, rather than the Prophet. The renowned Sufi saint Junayd gives this prescription for Sufi practice based on the lives of the prophets

Sufism is founded on the eight qualities exemplified by the eight prophets: The generosity of Abraham, who was willing to sacrifice his son. The surrender of Ishmael, who submitted to the command of God and gave up his dear life. The patience of Job, who endured the affliction of worms and the jealousy of the Merciful. The mystery of Zacharias, to whom God said, "Thou shalt not speak unto men for three days save by sign." The solitude of John, who was a stranger in his own country and an alien to his own kind. The detachment of Jesus, who was so removed from worldly things that he kept only a cup and a comb—the cup he threw away when he saw a man drinking in the palms of his hand, and the comb likewise when he saw another man using his fingers instead of a comb. The wearing of wool by Moses, whose garment was woolen. And the poverty of Muhammad, to whom God sent the key of all treasures that are upon the face of the earth.

The supreme vision of Sufism is to see God everywhere, to view every portion of creation as a reflection of God's glory. The poet Jami writes: "Every branch and leaf and fruit reveals some aspect of God's perfection: the cypress gives hint of His majesty; the rose gives tidings of His beauty." Every atom was created by God so that men know the highest truth and learn the secrets of love.

Rumi's poetry has the magical ability to show us this truth and to unlock love's precious secrets. Within the folds of his words we gain entrance to a hidden chamber; we hear whispers that are ancient, yet intimate; we behold the endless love story between the individual soul and God. Like looking into a polished mirror, or like being in the presence of a holy being, reading Rumi's poetry shows us ourselves and our state, but more than that, it shows us the boundless glory of what we can become.

THE BOOK OF RUMI

HEARKEN TO THE reed-flute, how it discourses
When complaining of the pains of separation—
"Ever since they tore me from my osier bed,
My plaintive notes have moved men and women to tears.
I burst my breast, striving to give vent to sighs,
And to express the pangs of my yearning for my home.
He who abides far away from his home
Is ever longing for the day he shall return.
My wailing is heard in every throng,
In concert with them that rejoice and them that weep.
Each interprets my notes in harmony with his own
feelings,

But not one fathoms the secrets of my heart.
My secrets are not alien from my plaintive notes,
Yet they are not manifest to the sensual ear.
Body is not veiled from soul, neither soul from body,
Yet no man hath ever seen a soul."

 This plaint of the flute is fire, not mere air.
Let him who lacks this fire be accounted dead!
'Tis the fire of love that inspires the flute,
'Tis the ferment of love that possesses the wine.
The flute is the confidant of all unhappy lovers;
Yea, its strains lay bare my inmost secrets.
Who hath seen a poison and an antidote like the flute?
Who hath seen a sympathetic consoler like the flute?
The flute tells the tale of love's bloodstained path,
It recounts the story of Majnun's love toils.
None is privy to these feelings save one distracted,
As ear inclines to the whispers of the tongue.
Through grief my days are as labour and sorrow,
My days move on, hand in hand with anguish.
Yet, though my days vanish thus, 'tis no matter,
Do thou abide, O Incomparable Pure One!

 But all who are not fishes are soon tired of water;
And they who lack daily bread find the day very long;
So the "Raw" comprehend not the state of the "Ripe;"
Therefore it behoves me to shorten my discourse.

 Arise, O son! burst they bonds and be free!
How long wilt thou be captive to silver and gold?
Though thou pour the ocean into thy pitcher,
It can hold no more than one day's store.
The pitcher of the desire of the covetous never fills,

The oyster-shell fills not with pearls till it is content;
Only he whose garment is rent by the violence of love
Is wholly pure from covetousness and sin.

    Hail to thee, then, O LOVE, sweet madness!
Thou who healest all our infirmities!
Who art the physician of our pride and self-conceit!
Who art our Plato and our Galen!
Love exalts our earthly bodies to heaven,
And makes the very hills to dance with joy!
O lover, 'twas love that gave life to Mount Sinai,
When "it quaked, and Moses fell down in a swoon."
Did my Beloved only touch me with his lips,
I too, like the flute, would burst out in melody.
But he who is parted from them that speak his tongue,
Though he possess a hundred voices, is perforce dumb.
When the rose has faded and the garden is withered,
The song of the nightingale is no longer to be heard.
The BELOVED is all in all, the lover only veils Him;
The BELOVED is all that lives, the lover a dead thing.
When the lover feels no longer LOVE'S quickening,
He becomes like a bird who has lost its wings. Alas!
How can I retain my senses about me,
When the BELOVED shows not the light of His
countenance?

    LOVE desires that this secret should be revealed,
For if a mirror reflects not, of what use is it?
Knowest thou why thy mirror reflects not?
Because the rust has not been scoured from its face.
If it were purified from all rust and defilement,
It would reflect the shining of the SUN of GOD.

O friends, ye have now heard this tale,
Which sets forth the very essence of my case.

THE PRINCE AND THE HANDMAID

A prince, while engaged on a hunting excursion, espied a fair maiden, and by promises of gold induced her to accompany him. After a time she fell sick, and the prince had her tended by divers physicians. As, however, they all omitted to say, "*God willing*, we will cure her," their treatment was of no avail. So the prince offered prayer, and in answer thereto a physician was sent from heaven. He at once condemned his predecessors' view of the case, and by a very skilful diagno-sis, discovered that the real cause of the maiden's illness was her love for a certain goldsmith of Samarcand. In accordance with the physician's advice, the prince sent to Samarcand and fetched the goldsmith, and married him to the lovesick maiden, and for six months the pair lived together in the utmost harmony and happiness. At the end of that period the physician, by divine command, gave the goldsmith a poisonous draught, which caused his strength and beauty to decay, and he then lost favour with the maiden, and she was reunited to the king. This divine command was precisely similar to God's command to Abraham to slay his son Ishmael, and to the act of the angel in slaying the servant of Moses, and is therefore beyond human criticism.

DESCRIPTION OF LOVE

A true lover is proved such by his pain of heart;
No sickness is there like sickness of heart.

The lover's ailment is different from all ailments;
Love is the astrolabe of God's mysteries.
A lover may hanker after this love or that love,
But at the last he is drawn to the KING of love.
However much we describe and explain love,
When we fall in love we are ashamed of our words.
Explanation by the tongue makes most things clear,
But love unexplained is clearer.
When pen hasted to write,
On reaching the subject of love it split in twain.
When the discourse touched on the matter of love,
Pen was broken and paper torn.
In explaining it Reason sticks fast, as an ass in mire;
Naught but Love itself can explain love and lovers!
None but the sun can display the sun,
If you would see it displayed, turn not away from it.
Shadows, indeed, may indicate the sun's presence,
But only the sun displays the light of life.
Shadows induce slumber, like evening talks,
But when the sun arises the "moon is split asunder."
In the world there is naught so wondrous as the sun,
But the Sun of the soul sets not and has no yesterday.
Though the material sun is unique and single,
We can conceive similar suns like to it.
But the Sun of the soul, beyond this firmament,—
No like thereof is seen in concrete or abstract.
Where is there room in conception for HIS essence,
So that similitudes of HIM should be conceivable?

SHAMSU-D-DIN IMPORTUNES JALALU-'D-DIN
TO COMPOSE THE MASNAVI

The sun (*Shams*) of Tabriz is a perfect light,
A sun, yea, one of the beams of God!
When the praise was heard of the "Sun of Tabriz,"
The sun of the fourth heaven bowed its head.
Now that I have mentioned his name, it is but right
To set forth some indications of his beneficence.

 That precious Soul caught my skirt,
Smelling the perfume of the garment of Yusuf;
And said, "For the sake of our ancient friendship,
Tell forth a hint of those sweet states of ecstasy,
That earth and heaven may be rejoiced,
And also Reason and Spirit, a hundredfold."

 I said, "O thou who art far from 'The Friend,'
Like a sick man who has strayed from his physician,
Importune me not, for I am beside myself;
My understanding is gone, I cannot sing praises.
Whatsoever one says, whose reason is thus astray,
Let him not boast; his efforts are useless.
Whatever he says is not to the point,
And is clearly inapt and wide of the mark.
What can I say when not a nerve of mine is sensible?
Can I explain 'The Friend' to one to whom He is no Friend?
Verily my singing His praise were dispraise,
For 'twould prove me existent, and existence is error.
Can I describe my separation and my bleeding heart?
Nay, put off this matter till another season."

 He said, "Feed me, for I am an hungred,
And at once, for 'the time is a sharp sword.'

O comrade, the Sufi is 'the son of time present.'
It is not the rule of his canon to say, 'To-morrow.'
Can it be that thou art not a true Sufi?
Ready money is lost by giving credit."

    I said, "'Tis best to veil the secrets of 'The Friend.'
So give good heed to the morals of these stories.
That is better than that the secrets of 'The Friend'
Should be noised abroad in the talk of strangers."

    He said, "Without veil or covering or deception,
Speak out, and vex me not, O man of many words!
Strip off the veil and speak out, for do not I
Enter under the same coverlet as the Beloved?"

    I said, "If the Beloved were exposed to outward view,
Neither wouldst thou endure, nor embrace, nor form.
Press thy suit, yet with moderation;
A blade of grass cannot pierce a mountain.
If the sun that illumines the world
Were to draw nigher, the world would be consumed.
Close thy mouth and shut the eyes of this matter,
That the world's life be not made a bleeding heart.
No longer seek this peril, this bloodshed;
Hereafter impose silence on the 'Sun of Tabriz.'"
He said, "Thy words are endless. Now tell forth
All thy story from its beginning."

THE OILMAN AND HIS PARROT

An oilman possessed a parrot which used to amuse him
with its agreeable prattle, and to watch his shop when he
went out. One day, when the parrot was alone in the shop,
a cat upset one of the oil-jars. When the oilman returned

home he thought that the parrot had done this mischief, and in his anger he smote the parrot such a blow on the head as made all its feathers drop off, and so stunned it that it lost the power of speech for several days. But one day the parrot saw a bald-headed man passing the shop, and recovering its speech, it cried out, "Pray, whose oil-jar did you upset?" The passers-by smiled at the parrot's mistake in confounding baldness caused by age with the loss of its own feathers due to a blow.

CONFUSION OF SAINTS WITH HYPOCRITES

Worldly senses are the ladder of earth,
Spiritual senses are the ladder of heaven.
The health of the former is sought of the leech,
The health of the latter from "The Friend."
The health of the former arises from tending the body,
That of the latter from mortifying the flesh.
    The kingly soul lays waste the body,
And after its destruction he builds it anew.
Happy the soul who for love of God
Has lavished family, wealth, and goods!—
Has destroyed its house to find the hidden treasure,
And with that treasure has rebuilt it in fairer sort;
Has dammed up the stream and cleansed the channel,
And then turned a fresh stream into the channel;—
Has cut its flesh to extract a spear-head,
Causing a fresh skin to grow again over the wound;—
Has razed the fort to oust the infidel in possession,
And then rebuilt it with a hundred towers and bulwarks.
    Who can describe the unique work of Grace?

I have been forced to illustrate it by these similes.

Sometimes it presents one appearance, sometimes another.

Yea, the affair of religion is only bewilderment.

Not such as occurs when one turns one's back on God,

But such as when one is drowned and absorbed in Him.

That latter has his face ever turned to God,

The former's face shows his undisciplined self-will.

 Watch the face of each one, regard it well,

It may be by serving thou wilt recognise Truth's face.

As there are many demons with men's faces,

It is wrong to join hand with every one.

When the fowler sounds his decoy whistle,

That the birds may be beguiled by that snare,

The birds hear that call simulating a bird's call,

And, descending from the air, find net and knife.

So vile hypocrites steal the language of Darveshes,

In order to beguile the simple with their trickery.

The works of the righteous are light and heat,

The works of the evil treachery and shamelessness.

They make stuffed lions to scare the simple,

They give the title of Muhammad to false Musailima.

But Musailima retained the name of "Liar,"

And Muhammad that of "Sublimest of beings."

That wine of God (the righteous) yields a perfume of musk;

Other wine (the evil) is reserved for penalties and pains.

THE JEWISH KING, HIS VAZIR, AND THE CHRISTIANS

A certain Jewish king used to persecute the Christians, desiring to exterminate their faith. His Vazir persuaded him to try a stratagem, namely, to mutilate the Vazir himself, and expel him from his court, with the intent that he might take refuge with the Christians, and stir up mutual dissensions amongst them. The Vazir's suggestion was adopted. He fled to the Christians, and found no difficulty in persuading them that he had been treated in that barbarous way on account of his attachment to the Christian faith. He soon gained complete influence over them, and was accepted as a saintly martyr and a divine teacher. Only a few discerning men divined his treachery; the majority were all deluded by him. The Christians were divided into twelve legions, and at the head of each was a captain. To each of these captains the Vazir gave secretly a volume of religious directions, taking care to make the directions in each volume different from and contradictory to those in the others. One volume enjoined fasting, another charity, another faith, another works, and so on. Afterwards the Vazir withdrew into a cave, and refused to come out to instruct his disciples, in spite of all their entreaties. Calling the captains to him, he gave secret instructions to each to set himself up as his successor, and to be guided by the instructions in the volume secretly confided to him, and to slay all other claimants of the apostolic office. Having given these directions, he slew himself. In the event each captain set himself up as the Vazir's successor, and the Christians were split up into many sects at enmity with one another, even as the Vazir had intended. But the malicious scheme did not altogether succeed, as one faithful band cleaved to the name of "Ahmad," mentioned in the Gospel, and were thus saved from sharing the ruin of the rest.

THE VAZIR'S TEACHING

Myriads of Christians flocked round him,
One after another they assembled in his street.
Then he would preach to them of mysteries,—
Mysteries of the Gospel, of stoles, of prayers.
He would preach to them with eloquent words
Concerning the words and acts of the Messiah.
Outwardly he was a preacher of religious duties,
But within a decoy call and a fowler's snare.
Therefore the followers of the Prophet ('Isa)
Were beguiled by the fraud of that demon soul.
He mingled in his discourses many secret doctrines
Concerning devotion and sincerity of soul.
He taught them to make a fair show of devotion,
But to say of secret sins, "What do they matter?"
Hair by hair and jot by jot they learned of him
Fraud of soul, as roses might learn of garlic.
Hair-splitters and all their disciples
Are darkened by similar preaching and discourse.
The Christians gave their hearts to him entirely,
For the blind faith of the vulgar has no discernment.
In their inmost breasts they planted love of him,
And fancied him to be the Vicar of Christ;—
Yea, him, that one-eyed and cursed Dajjál!
Save us, O God! who art our only defender!
O God, there are hundreds of snares and baits,
And we are even as greedy and foolish birds;
Every moment our feet are caught in a fresh snare;
Yea, each one of us, though he be a falcon or Simurgh!

Thou dost release us every moment, and straightway
We again fly into the snare, O Almighty One!

SLEEP OF THE BODY THE SOUL'S AWAKING

Every night Thou freest our spirits from the body
And its snare, making them pure as rased tablets.
Every night spirits are released from this cage,
And set free, neither lording it nor lorded over.
At night prisoners are unaware of their prison,
At night kings are unaware of their majesty.
Then there is no thought or care for loss or gain,
No regard to such an one or such an one.
The state of the "knower" is such as this, even when
awake.
God says, "Thou wouldst deem him awake though asleep,
Sleeping to the affairs of the world, day and night,
Like a pen in the directing hand of the writer.
He who sees not the hand which effects the writing
Fancies the effects proceeds from the motion of the pen.
If the "knower" revealed the particulars of this state,
'Twould rob the vulgar of their sensual sleep.
His soul wanders in the desert that has no similitude;
Like his body, his spirit is enjoying perfect rest;—
Freed from desire of eating and drinking,
Like a bird escaped from cage and snare.
But when he is again beguiled into the snare,
He cries for help to the Almighty.

LAILA AND THE KHALIFA

The Khalifa said to Laila, "Art thou really she
For whom Majnun lost his head and went distracted?
Thou art not fairer than many other fair ones."
She replied, "Be silent; thou art not Majnun!"

    If thou hadst Majnun's eyes,
The two worlds would be within thy view.
Thou art in thy senses, but Majnun is beside himself.
In love to be wide awake is treason.
The more a man is awake, the more he sleeps (to love);
His (critical) wakefulness is worse than slumbering.

    Our wakefulness fetters our spirits,
Then our souls are a prey to divers whims,
Thoughts of loss and gain and fears of misery.
They retain not purity, nor dignity, nor lustre,
Nor aspiration to soar heavenwards.
That one is really sleeping who hankers after each whim
And holds parley with each fancy.

THE TWELVE VOLUMES OF THEOLOGY

He drew up a separate scroll to the address of each,
The contents of each scroll of a different tenor;
The rules of each of a different purport,
This contradictory of that, from beginning to end.
In one the road of fasting and asceticism
Was made the pillar and condition of right devotion.
In one 'twas said, "Abstinence profits not;
Sincerity in this path is naught but charity."
In one 'twas said, "Thy fasting and thy charity

Are both a making thyself equal with God;
Save faith and utter resignation to God's will
In weal and woe, all virtues are fraud and snares."
In one 'twas said, "Works are the one thing needful;
The doctrine of faith without works is delusion."
In one 'twas said, "Commands and prohibitions are
Not for observance, but to demonstrate our weakness,
That we may see our own weakness (to carry them out),
And thereby recognise and confess God's power."
In one 'twas said, "Reference to thine own weakness
Is ingratitude for God's mercies towards us.
Rather regard thy power, for thou hast power from God,
Know thy power to be God's grace, for 'tis of Him."
In one 'twas said, "Leave power and weakness alone;
Whatever withdraws thine eyes from God is an idol."
In one 'twas said, "Quench not thy earthy torch,
That it may be a light to lighten mankind.
If thou neglectest regard and care for it,
Thou wilt quench at midnight the lamp of union."
In one 'twas said, "Quench that torch without fear,
That in lieu of one thou may'st see a thousand joys,
For by quenching the light the soul is rejoiced,
And thy Laila is then as bold as her Majnun.
Whoso to display his devotion renounces the world,
The world is ever with him, before and behind."
In one 'twas said, "Whatsoever God has given thee
In His creation, that He has made sweet to thee;
Yea, pleasant to thee and allowable. Take it, then,
And cast not thyself into the pangs of abstinence."
In one 'twas said, "Give up all thou possessest,

For to be ruled by covetousness is grievous sin."
    (Ah! how many diverse roads are pointed out,
And each followed by some sect for dear life!
If the right road were easily attainable,
Every Jew and Gueber would have hit on it!)
    In one 'twas said, "The right road is attainable,
For the heart's life is the food of the soul.
Whatever is enjoyed by the carnal man
Yields no fruit, even as salt and waste land.
Its result is naught by remorse,
Its traffic yields only loss.
It is not profitable in the long run;
Its name is called 'bankrupt' in the upshot.
Discern, then, the bankrupt from the profitable,
Consider the eventual value of this and that."
In one 'twas said, "Choose ye a wise Director,
But foresight of results is not found in dignities."
    (Each sect looked to results in a different way,
And so, perforce, became captive to errors.
Real foresight of results is not simple jugglery,
Otherwise all these differences would not have arisen.)
    In one 'twas said, "Thyself art thy master,
Inasmuch as thou art acquainted with the Master of all;
Be a man, and not another man's beast of burden!
Follow thine own way and lose not thy head!"
In one 'twas said, "All we see is One.
Whoever says, 'tis two is suffering from double vision."
In one 'twas said, "A hundred are even as one."
But whoso thinks this is a madman.
Each scroll had its contrary piece of rhetoric,

In form and substance utterly opposed to it;
This contrary to that, from first to last,
As if each was compounded of poison and antidotes.

ANOTHER TYRANNICAL JEWISH KING

A certain Jewish king, the same who is referred to in the Sura "Signs of the Zodiac," made up his mind to utterly exterminate the Christian faith, and with that view he set up a huge idol, and issued commands that all who refused to worship it should be cast into the fire. Thereupon his officers seized a Christian woman with her babe, and as she refused to worship it, they cast the babe into the fire. But the babe cried out to its mother, "Be not afraid, the fire has no power to burn me; it is as cool as water!" Hearing this, the rest of the Christians leapt into the fire, and found that it did not burn them. The king reproached the fire for failing to do its office, but the fire replied that it was God's servant, and that its consuming properties were not to be used for evil purposes. It then blazed up and consumed the king, and all his Jews with him.

SECOND CAUSES ONLY OPERATE IN SUBORDINATION TO, AND FROM THE IMPULSION OF, THE FIRST CAUSE

Air, earth, water, and fire are God's servants.
To us they seem lifeless, but to God living.
In God's presence fire ever waits to do its service,
Like a submissive lover with no will of its own.
When you strike steel on flint fire leaps forth;
But 'tis by God's command it thus steps forth.

Strike not together the flint and steel of wrong,

For the pair will generate more, like man and woman.

The flint and the steel are themselves causes, yet

Look higher for the First Cause, O righteous man!

For that Cause precedes this second cause.

How can a cause exist of itself without precedent cause?

That Cause makes this cause operative,

And again helpless and inoperative.

That Cause, which is a guiding light to the prophets,

That, I say, is higher than these second causes.

Men's minds recognise these second causes,

But only prophets perceive the action of the First Cause.

PRAISE COMPARED TO VAPOUR DRAWN UPWARDS, AND THEN DESCENDING IN RAIN

Though water by enclosed in a reservoir,

Yet air will absorb it, for 'tis its supporter;

It sets it free and bears it to its source,

Little by little, so that you see not the process.

    In like manner this breath of ours by degrees

Steals away our souls from the prison-house of earth.

"The good word riseth up to Him,"

Rising from us wither He knoweth.

Our breathings are lifted up in fear of God,

Offerings from us to the throne of Eternity.

Then come down to us rewards for our praises,

The double thereof, yea, mercies from the King of Glory.

Therefore are we constrained to utter these praises,

That slaves may attain the height of God's gifts.

And so this rising and descent go on evermore,

And cease not for ever and aye.

To speak in plain Persian, this attraction

Comes from the same quarter whence comes this sweet savour.

THE LION AND THE BEASTS

In the book of Kalila and Damna a story is told of a lion who held all the beasts of the neighbourhood in subjection, and was in the habit of making constant raids upon them, to take and kill such of them as he required for his daily food. At last the beasts took counsel together, and agreed to deliver up one of their company every day, to satisfy the lion's hunger, if he, on his part, would cease to annoy them by his continual forays. The lion was at first unwilling to trust to their promise, remarking that he always preferred to rely on his own exertions; but the beasts succeeded in persuading him that he would do well to trust Providence and their word. To illustrate the thesis that human exertions are vain, they related a story of a man who got Solomon to transport him to Hindustan to escape the angel of death, but was smitten by the angel the moment he got there. Having carried their point, the beasts continued for some time to perform their engagement. One day it came to the turn of the hare to be delivered up as a victim to the lion; but he requested the others to let him practise a stratagem. They scoffed at him, asking how such a silly beast as he could pretend to outwit the lion. The hare assured them that wisdom was of God, and God might choose weak things to confound the strong. At last they consented to let him try his luck. He took his way slowly to the lion, and found him sorely enraged. In excuse for his tardy arrival he represented that he and another hare had set out together to appear before the lion, but a strange lion had seized the second hare, and carried it off in spite of his remonstrances. On hearing this the lion was exceeding wroth, and commanded the hare to show him the foe who had trespassed on his preserves. Pretending to be afraid, the hare got the lion to take him upon his back, and directed him to a well. On looking down the well, the lion saw in the water the reflection of himself and of the hare on his back; and thinking that he saw his foe with the stolen hare, he plunged in to attack him, and was drowned, while the hare sprang off his back and escaped. This folly on the part of the lion was predestined to punish him for denying God's ruling providence. So Adam, though he knew the names of all things, in accordance with God's predestination, neglected to obey a single prohibition, and his disobedience cost him dearly.

TRUST IN GOD, AS OPPOSED TO HUMAN EXERTIONS

The beasts said, "O enlightened sage,
Lay aside caution; it cannot help thee against destiny;
To worry with precaution is toil and moil;
Go, trust in Providence, trust is the better part.
War not with the divine decree, O hot-headed one,
Lest that decree enter into conflict with thee.
Man should be as dead before the commands of God,
Lest a blow befall him from the Lord of all creatures."

He said, "True; but though trust be our mainstay,
Yet the prophet teaches us to have regard to means.
The Prophet cried with a loud voice,

'Trust in God, yet tie the camel's leg.'
Hear the adage, 'The worker is the friend of God;'
Through trust in Providence neglect not to use means.
Go, O Fatalists, practise trust with self-exertion,
Exert yourself to attain your objects, bit by bit.
In order to succeed, strive and exert yourselves;
If you strive not for your objects, ye are fools."

    They said, "What is gained from the poor by exertions
Is a fraudulent morsel that will bring ill luck.
Again, know that self-exertion springs from weakness;
Relying on other means is a blot upon perfect trust.
Self-exertion is not more noble than trust in God.
What is more lovely than committing oneself to God?
Many there are who flee from one danger to a worse;
Many flee from a snake and meet a dragon.
Man plans a stratagem, and thereby snares himself;
What he takes for life turns out to be destruction.
He shuts the door after his foe is in the house.
After this sort were the schemes of Pharaoh.
That jealous kings slew a myriad babes,
While Moses, whom he sought, was in his house.
Our eyes are subject to many infirmities;
Go! annihilate your sight in God's sight.
For our foresight His foresight is a fair exchange;
In His sight is all that ye can desire.
So long as a babe cannot grasp or run,
It takes its father's back for its carriage.
But when it becomes independent and uses its hands,
It falls into grievous troubles and disgrace.
The souls of our first parents, even before their hands,

Flew away from fidelity after vain pleasure.

Being made captives by the command, 'Get down hence,'

They became bond-slaves of enmity, lust, and vanity.

We are the family of the Lord and His sucking babes.

The Prophet said, 'The people are God's family;'

He who sends forth the rain from heaven,

Can He not also provide us our daily bread?"

    The lion said, "True; yet the Lord of creatures

Sets a ladder before our feet.

Step by step must we mount up to the roof!

The notion of fatalism is groundless in this place.

Ye have feet—why then pretend ye are lame?

Ye have hands—why then conceal your claws?

When a master places a spade in the hand of a slave,

The slave knows his meaning without being told.

Like this spade, our hands are our Master's hints to us;

Yea, if ye consider, they are His directions to us.

When ye have taken to heart His hints,

Ye will shape your life in reliance on their direction;

Wherefore these hints disclose His intent,

Take the burden from you, and appoint your work.

He that bears it makes it bearable by you,

He that is able makes it within your ability.

Accept His command, and you will be able to execute it;

Seek union with Him, and you will find yourselves united.

Exertion is giving thanks for God's blessings;

Think ye that your fatalism gives such thanks?

Giving thanks for blessings increases blessings,

But fatalism snatches those blessings from your hands.

Your fatalism is to sleep on the road; sleep not

Till ye behold the gates of the King's palace.
Ah! sleep not, O unreflecting fatalists,
Till ye have reached that fruit-laden Tree of Life
Whose branches are ever shaken by the wind,
And whose fruit is showered on the sleepers' heads.
Fatalism means sleeping amidst highwaymen.
Can a cock who crows too soon expect peace?
If ye cavil at and accept not God's hints,
Though ye count yourselves men, see, ye are women.
The quantum of reason ye possessed is lost,
And the head whose reason has fled is a tail.
Inasmuch as the unthankful are despicable,
They are at last cast into the fiery pit.
If ye really have trust in God, exert yourselves,
And strive, in constant reliance on the Almighty."

WISDOM IS GRANTED OFTENTIMES TO THE WEAK

He said, "O friends, God has given me inspiration.
Oftentimes strong counsel is suggested to the weak.
The wit taught by God to the bee
Is withheld from the lion and the wild ass.
It fills its cells with liquid sweets,
For God opens the door of this knowledge to it.
The skill taught by God to the silkworm
Is a learning beyond the reach of the elephant.
The earthly Adam was taught of God names,
So that his glory reached the seventh heaven.
He laid low the name and fame of the angels,
Yet blind indeed are they whom God dooms to doubt!

The devotee of seven hundred thousand years (Satan)
Was made a muzzle for that yearling calf (Adam),
Lest he should suck milk of the knowledge of faith,
And soar on high even to the towers of heaven.
The knowledge of men of external sense is a muzzle
To stop them sucking the milk of that sublime knowledge.
But God drops into the heart a single pearl-drop
Which is not bestowed on oceans or skies!"

"How long regard ye mere form, O form-worshippers?
Your souls, void of substance, rest still in forms.
If the form of man were all that made man,
Ahmad and Abu Jahl would be upon a par.
A painting on a wall resembles a man,
But see what is lacking in that empty form.
'Tis life that is lacking to that mere semblance of man.
Go! seek for that pearl it never will find.
The heads of earth's lions were bowed down
When God gave might to the Seven Sleepers' dog.
What mattered its despised form
When its soul was drowned in the sea of light?"

HUMAN WISDOM THE MANIFESTATION OF DIVINE

On his way to the lion the hare lingered,
Devising a stratagem with himself.
He proceeded on his way after delaying long,
In order to have a secret or two for the lion

What worlds the principle of Reason embraces!
How broad is this ocean of Reason!
Yea, the Reason of man is a boundless ocean.

O son, that ocean requires, as it were, a diver.
On this fair ocean our human forms
Float about, like bowls on the surface of water;
Yea, like cups on the surface, till they are filled;
And when filled, these cups sink into the water.

   The ocean of Reason is not seen; reasoning men are seen;
But our forms (minds) are only as waves or spray thereof.
Whatever form that ocean uses as its instrument,
Therewith it casts its spray far and wide.
Till the heart sees the Giver of the secret,
Till it espies that Bowman shooting from afar,
It fancies its own steed lost, while in bewilderment
It is urging that steed hither and thither;
It fancies its own steed lost, when all the while
That swift steed is bearing it on like the wind.
In deep distress that blunderhead
Runs from door to door, searching and inquiring,
"Who and where is he that hath stolen my steed?"
They say, "What is this thou ridest on, O master?"
He says, "True, 'tis a steed; but where is mine?"
They say, "Look to thyself, O rider; thy steed is there."

   The real Soul is lost to view, and seems far off;
Thou art like a pitcher with full belly but dry lip;
How canst thou ever see red, green, and scarlet
Unless thou see'st the light first of all?
When thy sight is dazzled by colours,
These colours veil the light from thee.
But when night veils those colours from thee,
Thou seest that colours are seen only through light.
As there is no seeing outward colours without light,

So it is with the mental colours within.

Outward colours arise from the light of sun and stars,

And inward colours from the Light on high.

The light that lights the eye is also the heart's Light.

The eye's light proceeds from the Light of the heart.

But the light that lights the heart is the Light of God,

Which is distinct from the light of reason and sense.

    At night there is no light, and colours are not seen;

Hence we know what light is by its opposite, darkness.

At night no colours are visible, for light is lacking.

How can colour be the attribute of dark blackness?

Looking on light is the same as looking on colours;

Opposite shows up opposite, as a Frank a Negro.

The opposite of light shows what is light,

Hence colours too are known by their opposite.

God created pain and grief for this purpose,

To wit, to manifest happiness by its opposites.

Hidden things are manifested by their opposites;

But, as God has no opposite, He remains hidden.

God's light has no opposite in the range of creation

Whereby it may be manifested to view.

Perforce "Our eyes see not Him, though He sees us."

Behold this in the case of Moses and Mount Sinai.

Discern form from substance, as lion from desert,

Or as sound and speech from the thought they convey.

The sound and speech arise from the thought;

Thou knowest not where is the Ocean of thought;

Yet when thou seest fair waves of speech,

Thou knowest there is a glorious Ocean beneath them.

When waves of thought arise from the Ocean of Wisdom,

They assume the forms of sound and speech.
These forms of speech are born and die again,
These waves cast themselves back into the Ocean.
Form is born of That which is without form,
And goes again, for, "Verily to Him do we return."
Wherefore to thee every moment come death and "return."
Mustafa saith, "The world endureth only a moment."
So, thought is an arrow shot by God into the air.
How can it stay in the air? It returns to God.

Every moment the world and we are renewed,
Yet we are ignorant of this renewing for ever and aye.
Life, like a stream of water, is renewed and renewed,
Though it wears the appearance of continuity in form.
That seeming continuity arises from its swift renewal,
As when a single spark of fire is whirled round swiftly.
If a single spark by whirled round swiftly,
It seems to the eye a continuous line of fire.
This apparent extension, owing to the quick motion,
Demonstrates the rapidity with which it is moved.
If ye seek the deepest student of this mystery,
Lo! 'tis Husamu-'d-Din, the most exalted of creatures!

'OMAR AND THE AMBASSADOR

The hare, having delivered his companions from the tyranny of the lion, in the manner just described, proceeds to improve the occasion by exhorting them to engage in a greater and more arduous warfare, viz., the struggle against their inward enemy, the lusts of the flesh. He illustrates his meaning by the story of an ambassador who was sent by the Emperor of Rum to the Khalifa 'Omar. On approaching

Medina this ambassador inquired for 'Omar's palace, and learned that 'Omar dwelt in no material palace, but in a spiritual tabernacle, only visible to purified hearts. At last he discerned 'Omar lying under a palm-tree, and drew near to him in fear and awe. 'Omar received him kindly, and instructed him in the doctrine of the mystical union with God. The ambassador heard him gladly, and asked him two questions, first, How can souls descend from heaven to earth? and secondly, With what object are souls imprisoned in the bonds of flesh and blood? 'Omar responded, and the ambassador accepted his teaching, and became a pure-hearted Sufi. The hare urged his companions to abjure lust and pride, and to go and do likewise.

GOD'S AGENCY RECONCILED WITH MAN'S FREEWILL

The ambassador said, "O Commander of the faithful,
How comes the soul down from above the earth?
How can so noble a bird be confined in a cage?"
    He said, "God speaks words of power to souls,—
To things of naught, without eyes or ears,
And at these words they all spring into motion;
At His words of power these nothings arise quickly,
And strong impulse urges them into existence.
Again, He speaks other spells to these creatures,
And swiftly drives them back again into not-being.
He speaks to the rose's ear, and causes it to bloom;
He speaks to the tulip, and makes it blossom.
He speaks a spell to body, and it becomes soul;
He speaks to the sun, and it becomes a fount of light.

Again, in its ear He whispers a word of power,

And its face is darkened as by a hundred eclipses.

What is it that God says to the ear of earth,

That it attends thereto and rests steadfast?

What is it that Speaker says to the cloud,

That it pours forth rain-water like a water-skin?

Whosoever is bewildered by wavering will,

In his ear hath God whispered His riddle,

That He may bind him on the horns of a dilemma;

For he says, 'Shall I do this or its reverse?'

Also from God comes the preference of one alternative;

'Tis from God's impulsion that man chooses one of the two.

If you desire sanity in this embarrassment,

Stuff not the ear of your mind with cotton.

Take the cotton of evil suggestions from the mind's ear,

That the heavenly voice from above may enter it,

That you may understand that riddle of His,

That you may be cognisant of that open secret.

Then the mind's ear becomes the sensorium of inspiration;

For what is this Divine voice but the inward voice?

The spirit's eye and ear possess this sense,

The eye and ear of reason and sense lack it.

The word 'compulsion' makes me impatient for love's sake;

'Tis he who loves not who is fettered by compulsion.

This is close communion with God, not compulsion,

The shining of the sun, and not a dark cloud.

Or, if it be compulsion, 'tis not common compulsion,

It is not the domination of wanton wilfulness.

O son, they understand this compulsion

For whom God opens the eyes of the inner man.

Things hidden and things future are plain to them;

To speak of the past seems to them despicable.

They posses freewill and compulsion besides,

As in oyster-shells raindrops become pearls.

Outside the shell they are raindrops, great and small;

Inside they are precious pearls, big and little.

These men also resemble the musk deer's bag;

Outside it is blood, but inside pure musk;

Yet, say not that outside 'twas mere blood,

Which on entering the bag becomes musk.

Nor say that outside the alembic 'twas mere copper,

And becomes gold inside, when mixed with elixir.

In you freewill and compulsion are vain fancies,

But in them they are the light of Almighty power.

On the table bread is a mere lifeless thing,

When taken into the body it is a life-giving spirit.

This transmutation occurs not in the table's heart,

'Tis soul effects this transmutation with water of life.

Such is the power of the soul, O man of right views!

Then what is the power of the Soul of souls? (God).

Bread is the food of the body, yet consider,

How can it be the food of the soul, O son?

Flesh-born man by force of soul

Cleaves mountains with tunnels and mines.

The might of Ferhad's soul cleft a hill;

The might of the Soul's soul cleaves the moon.

If the heart opens the mouth of mystery's store,

The soul springs up swiftly to highest heaven.

If tongue discourses of hidden mysteries,

It kindles a fire that consumes the world.

Behold, then, God's action and man's action;
Know, action does belong to us; this is evident.
If no actions proceeded from men,
How could you say, 'Why act ye thus?'
The agency of God is the cause of our action,
Our actions are the signs of God's agency;
Nevertheless our actions are freely willed by us,
Whence our recompense is either hell or 'The Friend.'

THE MERCHANT AND HIS CLEVER PARROT

There was a certain merchant who kept a parrot in a cage. Being about to travel to Hindustan on business, he asked the parrot if he had any message to send to his kinsmen in that country, and the parrot desired him to tell them that he was kept confined in a cage. The merchant promised to deliver this message, and on reaching Hindustan, duly delivered it to the first flock of parrots he saw. On hearing it one of them at once fell down dead. The merchant was annoyed with his own parrot for having sent such a fatal message, and on his return home sharply rebuked his parrot for doing so. But the parrot no sooner heard the merchant's tale than he too fell down dead in his cage. The merchant, after lamenting his death, took his corpse out of the cage and threw it away; but, to his surprise, the corpse immediately recovered life, and flew away, explaining that the Hindustani parrot had only feigned death to suggest this way of escaping from confinement in a cage.

SAINTS ARE PRESERVED FROM ALL HARM

As to a "man of heart," he takes no hurt,

Even though he should eat deadly poison.

He who gains health from practising abstinence is safe;

The poor disciple is safe in the midst of fever.

The prophet said, "O disciple, though you be bold,

Yet enter not into conflict with every foe."

Within you is a Nimrod; enter not his fire;

But if you must do so, first become an Abraham.

If you are neither swimmer nor seaman,

Cast not yourself into the sea out of self-conceit.

A swimmer brings pearls from the deep sea;

Yea, he plucks gain from the midst of perils.

If the saint handles earth, it becomes gold;

If a sinner handles gold, it turns to dust.

Whereas the saint is well-pleasing to God,

In his actions his hand is the hand of God.

But the sinner's hand is the hand of Satan and demons,

Because he is ensnared in falsity and fraud.

If folly meets him, he takes it for wisdom;

Yea, the learning gained by the wicked is folly.

Whatever a sick man eats is a source of sickness,

But if a saint imbibe infidelity it becomes faith.

Ah! footman who contendest with horsemen,

Thou wilt not succeed in carrying the day!

THE JEALOUSY OF GOD

The whole world is jealous for this cause,

That God surpasseth the world in jealousy.

God is as a soul and the world as a body,
And bodies derive their good and evil from souls.
He to whom the sanctuary of true prayer is revealed
Deems it shameful to turn back to mere formal religion.
He who is master of the robes of a king
Brings shame on his lord by petty huckstering.
He who is admitted to the king's presence-chamber
Would show disrespect by tarrying at the doorway.
If the king grants him license to kiss his hand,
He would err were he to kiss merely the king's foot.
Though to lay head at the king's feet is due obeisance,
In the case supposed it would be wrong to kiss the feet.
The king's jealousy would be kindled against him
Who, after he had seen his face, preferred his mere perfume.
God's jealousy may be likened to a grain of wheat,
But man's jealousy is but empty chaff.
For know ye that the source of jealousy is in God,
And man's jealousy is only an offshoot from God's.
But let me now quit this subject, and make complaint
Of the severity of That Fickle Fair One.

COMPLAINTS OF GOD'S HARSH DEALINGS WITH HIS ADORING SLAVES

"Wherefore dost thou abandon thy creed and faith?
What matters it if it be heathen or true?
Why hast thou forsaken thy Beloved?
What matters it if she be fair or ugly?"

Let me then, I say, make complaint
Of the severity of That Fickle Fair One.

I cry, and my cries sound sweet in His ear;
He requires from the two worlds cries and groans.
How shall I not wail under His chastening hand?
How shall I not be in the number of those bewitched by Him?
How shall I be other than night without His day?
Without the vision of His face that illumes the day?
His bitters are very sweets to my soul,
My sad heart is a lively sacrifice to my Beloved.
I am enamoured of my own grief and pain,
For it makes me well-pleasing to my peerless King.
I use the dust of my grief as salve for my eyes,
That my eyes, like seas, may teem with pearls.
The tears which are shed because of His chastening
Are very pearls, though men deem them mere tears.
'Tis "The Soul of souls," of whom I am making complaint;
Yet I do not complain;—I merely state my case.
My heart says, "He has injured me,"
But I laugh at these pretended injuries.
Do me justice, O Thou who art the glory of the just,
Who art the throne, and I the lintel of Thy door!
But, in sober truth, where are throne and doorway?
Where are "We" and "I?" There where our Beloved is!
O Thou, who art exempt from "Us" and "Me,"—
Who pervadest the spirits of all men and women;
When man and woman become one, Thou art that One!
When their union is dissolved, lo! Thou abidest!
Thou hast made these "Us" and "Me" for this purpose,
To wit, to play chess with them by Thyself.
When Thou shalt become one entity with "Us" and "You,"
Then wilt Thou show true affection for these lovers.

When these "We" and "Ye" shall all become one Soul,
Then they will be lost and absorbed in the "Beloved."
These are plain truths. Come then, O Lord!
Who art exalted above description and explanation!
Is it possible for the bodily eye to behold Thee?
Can mind of man conceive Thy frowns and Thy smiles?
Are hearts, when bewitched by Thy smiles and frowns,
In a fit state to see the vision of Thyself?
When our hearts are bewitched by Thy smiles and frowns,
Can we gain life from these two alternating states?
The fertile garden of love, as it is boundless,
Contains other fruits besides joy and sorrow.
The true lover is exalted above these two states,
He is fresh and green independently of autumn or spring!
Pay tithe on Thy beauty, O Beauteous One!
Tell forth the tale of the Beloved, every whit!
For through coquetry His glances
Are still inflicting fresh wounds on my heart.
I gave him leave to shed my blood, if He willed it;
I only said, "Is it right?" and He forsook me.
Why dost Thou flee from the cries of us on earth?
Why pourest Thou sorrow on the heart of the sorrowful?
O Thou who, as each new morn dawns from the east,
Art seen uprising anew, like a bright fountain!
What excuse makest Thou for Thy witcheries?
O Thou whose lips are sweeter than sugar,
Thou that ever renewest the life of this old world,
Hear the cry of this lifeless body and heart!
But, for God's sake, leave off telling of the Rose;
Tell of the Bulbul who is severed from his Rose.

My ardour arises not from joy or grief,
My sense mates not with illusion and fancy.
My condition is different, for it is strange.
Deny it not! God is all-powerful.
Argue not from the condition of common men,
Stumble not at severity and at mercy.
For mercy and severity, joy and sorrow, are transient,
And transient things die; "God is heir of all."

 'Tis dawn! O Protector and Asylum of the dawn!
Make excuse for me to my lord Husamu-'d-Din!
Thou makest excuses for "Universal Reason and Soul;"
Soul of souls and Gem of life art Thou!
The light of my dawn is a beam from Thy light,
Shining in the morning draught of Thy protection!
Since Thy gift keeps me, as it were, intoxicated,
What is this spiritual wine that causes me this joy?
Natural wine lacks the ferment in my breast,
The spheres lag behind me in revolutions!
Wine is intoxicated with me, not I with it!
The world takes its being from me, not I from it!
I am like bees, and earthly bodies like wax,
I build up these bodies as with my own wax!

THE HARPER

In the time of the Khalifa 'Omar there lived a harper, whose
voice was as sweet as that of the angel Isráfil, and who was
in great request at all feasts. But he grew old, and his voice
broke, and no one would employ him any longer. In despair
he went to the burial-ground of Yathrub, and there played
his harp to God, looking to Him for recompense. Having

finished his melody he fell asleep, and dreamed he was in heaven. The same night a divine voice came to 'Omar, directing him to go to the burial-ground, and relieve an old man whom he should find there. 'Omar proceeded to the place, found the harper, and gave him money, promising him more when he should need it. The harper cast away his harp, saying that it had diverted him from God, and expressed great contrition for his past sins. 'Omar then instructed him that his worldly journey was now over, and that he must not give way to contrition for the past, as he was now entered into the state of ecstasy and intoxication of union with God, and in this exalted state regard to past and future should be swept away. The harper acted on his instructions, and sang no more.

APOLOGY FOR APPLYING THE TERM "BRIDE" TO GOD

Mustafa became beside himself at that sweet call,
His prayer failed on "the night of the early morning halt."
He lifted not head from that blissful sleep,
So that his morning prayer was put off till noon.
On that, his wedding night, in presence of his bride,
His pure soul attained to kiss her hands.
Love and mistress are both veiled and hidden,
Impute it not as a fault if I call Him "Bride."
I would have kept silence from fear of my Beloved,
If He had granted me but a moment's respite.
But He said, "Speak on, 'tis no fault,
'Tis naught but the necessary result of the hidden decree,
'Tis a fault only to him who only sees faults.

How can the Pure Hidden Spirit notice faults?"
Faults seems so to ignorant creatures,
Not in the sight of the Lord of Benignity.
Blasphemy even may be wisdom in the Creator's sight,
Whereas from our point of view it is grievous sin.
If one fault occur among a hundred beauties,
'Tis as one dry stick in a garden of green herbs.
Both weigh equally in the scales,
For the two resemble body and soul.
Wherefore the sages have said not idly,
"The bodies of the righteous are as pure souls."
Their words, their actions, their praises,
Are all as a pure soul without spot or blemish.

'OMAR REBUKES THE HARPER FOR BROODING OVER AND BEWAILING THE PAST

Then 'Omar said to him, "This wailing of thine
Shows thou art still in a state of 'sobriety.'"
Afterwards he thus urged him to quit that state,
And called him out of his beggary to absorption in God:
    "Sobriety savours of memory of the past;
Past and future are what veil God from our sight.
Burn up both of them with fire! How long
Wilt thou be partitioned by these segments as a reed?
So long as a reed has partitions 'tis not privy to secrets,
Nor is it vocal in response to lip and breathing.
While circumambulating the house thou art a stranger;
When thou enterest in thou art at home.
Thou whose knowledge is ignorance of the Giver of
knowledge,

Thy wailing contrition is worse than thy sin.
The road of the 'annihilated' is another road;
Sobriety is wrong, and a straying from that other road.
O thou who seekest to be contrite for the past,
How wilt thou be contrite for this contrition?
At one time thou adorest the music of the lute,
At another embracest wailing and weeping."

　　While the "Discerner" reflected these mysteries,
The heart of the harper was emancipated.
Like a soul he was freed from weeping and rejoicing,
His old life died, and he was regenerated.
Amazement fell upon him at that moment,
For he was exalted above earth and heaven,
An uplifting of the heart surpassing all uplifting;—
I cannot describe it; if you can, say on!
Ecstasy and words beyond all ecstatic words;—
Immersion in the glory of the Lord of glory!
Immersion wherefrom was no extrication,—
As it were identification with the Very Ocean!
Partial Reason is as naught to Universal Reason,
If one impulse dependent on another impulse be naught;
But when *that* impulse moves *this* impulse,
The waves of *that* sea rise to *this* point.

THE ARAB AND HIS WIFE

An Arab lived with his wife in the desert in extreme
poverty, so that they became a reproach to their neighbours.
The wife at last lost patience, and began to abuse her husband, and to urge him to improve their condition. The Arab
rebuked her for her covetousness, reminding her that the

Prophet had said, "Poverty is my glory," and showing her how poverty was a better preparation for death than riches, and finally threatening to divorce her if she persisted in her querulous ways. The wife, however, by blandishments reduced her husband to obedience, as wives always do, and made him promise to carry out her wishes. She directed him to go and represent their case to the Khalifa at Bagdad, and to make him an offering of a pot of water, that being the only present they could afford to make. Accordingly the Arab traveled to Bagdad, and laid his offering at the feet of the Khalifa, who received it graciously, and in return filled the pot with pieces of gold, and then sent him back to his home in a boat up the river Tigris. The Arab was lost in wonder at the benignity of the Khalifa, who had recompensed him so bountifully for his petty offering of a drop of water. The story contains several digressions, on Pharaoh, on the prophet Salih, and on Adam and the angels, and the poet, *apropos* of its disconnectedness, compares it to eternity, as it has no beginning and no end.

MEN SUBDUED BY WOMEN'S WILES

In this manner she pleaded with gentle coaxing,
The while her tears fell upon her cheeks.
How could his firmness and endurance abide
When even without tears she could charm his heart?
That rain brought forth a flash of lightning
Which kindled a spark in the heart of that poor man.
Since the man was the slave of her fair face,
How was it when she stooped to slavish entreaties?
When she whose airs set thy heart a-quaking,—

When she weeps, how feelest thou then?
When she whose coquetry makes thy heart bleed
Condescends to entreaties, how is it then?
She who subdues us with her pride and severity,
What plea is left us when she begins to plead?
When she who traded in naught but bloodshed
Submits at last, ah! what a profit she makes!
God has adorned them "fair in the sight of men;"
From her whom God has adorned how can man escape?
Since He created him "to dwell together with her,"
How can Adam sever himself from his Eve?
Though he be Rustum, son of Zal, and braver than Hamza,
Yet he is submissive to the behests of his dame.
He by whose preaching the world was entranced
Was he who spake the two words, "O Humaira!"
Though water prevails over fire in might,
Yet it boils by fire when in a cauldron.
When the cauldron intervenes between these two,
Air (desire) makes as naught the action of the water.
Apparently thou art the ruler of thy wife, like water;
In reality thou art ruled by and suppliant to her.
Such is the peculiarity of man,
He cannot withstand animal desire; that is his failing.
The Prophet said that women hold dominion
Over sages and over men of heart,
But that fools, again, hold the upper hand over women,
Because fools are violent and exceedingly froward.
They have no tenderness or gentleness or amity,
Because the animal nature sways their temperament.
Love and tenderness are qualities of humanity,

Passion and lust are qualities of animality.
Woman is a ray of God, not a mere mistress,
The Creator's self, as it were, not a mere creature!

MOSES AND PHARAOH, ALIKE DOERS OF GOD'S WILL
AS LIGHT AND DARKNESS, POISON AND ANTIDOTE

Verily, both Moses and Pharaoh walked in the right way,
Though seemingly the one did so, and the other not.
By day Moses wept before God,
At midnight Pharaoh lifted up his cry,
Saying, "What a yoke is this upon my neck, O God!
Were it not for this yoke who would boast, 'I am?'
Because Thou hast made Moses' face bright as the moon,
And hast made the moon of my face black in the face.
Can my star ever shine brighter than the moon?
If it be eclipsed, what remedy have I?
Though princes and kings beat drums,
And men beat cymbals because of my eclipse,
They beat their brass dishes and raise a clamour
And make my moon ashamed thereby,
I who am Pharoah, woe is me! The people's clamour
Confounds my boast, 'I am Lord Supreme!'
Moses and I are Thy nurslings both alike,
Yet Thy axe cuts down the branches in Thy woods.
Some of these branches Thou plantest in the ground,
Others Thou castest away as useless.
Can branch strive against axe? Not so.
Can branch elude the power of the axe? Nay,
O Lord of the power that dwells in Thy axe,
In mercy make these crooked things straight!"

MAN AND WIFE TYPES OF THE SPIRIT AND THE FLESH

The dissension of this husband and wife is a parable;
They are types of thy animal and rational souls.
This husband and wife are the reason and the flesh,
A couple joined together for good and for evil.
And in this earthly house this linked pair
Day and night are ever at variance and strife.
The wife is ever seeking dainties for domestic needs,
Namely, bread and meat and her own dignity and position.
Like the wife, the animal soul seeks comfort,
Sometimes carnal, sometimes ambitious;
Reason has no care for these matters,
In its mind is naught but regard to Allah.
Though the secret moral hereof is a bait and snare,
Hear its outward form to the end.
If spiritual manifestations had been sufficient,
The creation of the world had been needless and vain.
If spiritual thought were equivalent to love of God,
Outward forms of temples and prayers would not exist.
Presents which friends make one to another
Are naught but signs and indications,
To give outward testimony and witness
Of the love concealed within the heart.
Because outward attentions are evidence
Of secret love, O beloved!
The witness may be true or false,—
Now drunk with real wine, now with sour whey;
He who drinks fermented whey displays drunkenness,
Makes a noise, and reels to and fro.

That hypocrite in prayers and fasts
Displays exceeding diligence,
That men may think him drunk with love of God;
But if you look into the truth, he is drowned in hypocrisy.
In fine, outward actions are guides
To show the way to what is concealed within.
Sometimes the guide is true, sometimes false,
Sometimes a help, and at other times a hindrance.
O Lord, grant, in answer to my prayers, discernment,
That I may know such false signs from the true!
Know you how discernment accrues to the sense?
'Tis when sense "sees by the light of Allah."
If effects are obscure, still causes testify;
Kindred, for instance, shows that there is love.
But he to whom God's light is the guide
Is no longer a slave to effects and causes.
When the light of Allah illumes his senses,
A man is no longer a slave to effects.
When love of God kindles a flame in the inward man,
He burns, and is freed from effects.
He has no need of signs to assure him of love,
For love casts its own light up to heaven.
Other details are wanting to complete this subject,
But take this much, and all hail to you!
Though reality is exposed to view in this form,
Form is at once nigh to and far from reality.
For instance, these two resemble water and a tree;
When you look to their essence they are far apart;
Yet see how quickly a seed becomes a high tree
Out of water, along with earth and sunshine!

If you turn your eyes to their real essence,

These two are far, far apart from each other!

But let us quit this talk of essences and properties,

And return to the story of those two wealth-seekers.

HOW GOD MADE ADAM SUPERIOR TO THE ANGELS IN WISDOM AND HONOUR

He said, "By Allah, who knoweth hidden secrets,

Who created pure Adam out of dust;—

In the form, three cubits high, which he gave him,

He displayed the contents of all spirits, all decrees!—

Communicated to him the indelible tablet of existence,

That he might know all that is written on those tablets,

All that should be first and last to endless eternity

He taught him, with the knowledge of his own 'names,'

So that the angels were beside themselves at his instruction,

And gained more sanctity from his sanctification.

The expansion of their minds, which Adam brought about,

Was a thing unequaled by the expansion of the heavens.

For the wide expanse of that pure mind

The wide space of the seven heavens was not enough."

The Prophet said that God has declared,

"I am not contained in aught above or below,

I am not contained in earth or sky, or even

In highest heaven. Know this for a surety, O beloved!

Yet am I contained in the believer's heart!

If ye seek me, search in such hearts!"

He said also, "Enter the hearts of my servants

To gain the paradise of beholding Me, O fearer of God."

Highest heaven, with all its light and wide expanse,
When it beheld Adam, was shaken from its place!
Highest heaven is greatness itself revealed;
But what is form when reality draws nigh?
Every angel declared, "In times of yore
We bore friendship to the plains of earth;
We were wont to sow the seed of service on the earth,
Wherefore we bore a wondrous attachment to it.
What was this attachment to that house of earth
When our own natures are heavenly?
What was the friendship of lights like us to darkness?
How can light dwell together with darkness?
O Adam! that friendship arose from the scent of thee,
Because the earth is the warp and weft of thy body.
Thy earthly body was taken from *there*,
Thy pure spirit of light was shed down from *here*!
But our souls were enlightened by thy spirit
Long, long before earth had diverted it to itself.
We used to be on earth, ignorant of the earth,—
Ignorant of the treasure buried within it.
When we were commanded to depart from that place,
We felt sorrow at turning our steps away from it.
So that we raised many questions, saying,
'O Lord! who will come to take our place?
Wilt Thou barter the glory of our praises and homage
For the vain babble (of men)?'
The commands of God then diffused joy upon us; He said,
'What are ye saying at such length?
What ye give tongue to so foolishly
Is as the words of spoiled children to their father.

I knew of myself what ye thought,
But I desired that ye should speak it;
As this boasting of yours is very improper,
So shall my mercy be shown to prevail over my wrath:
O angels, in order to show forth that prevailing,
I inspired that pretension to cavil and doubt;
If you say your say, and I forbear to punish you,
The gainsayers of my mercy must hold their peace.
My mercy equals that of a hundred fathers and mothers;
Every soul that is born is amazed thereat.
Their mercy is as the foam of the sea of my mercy;
It is mere foam of waves, but the sea abides ever!
What more shall I say? In that earthly shell
There is naught but foam of foam of foam of foam!'"
God is that foam; God is also that pure sea,
For His words are neither a temptation nor a vain boast.

PLURALITY AND PARTIAL EVIL, THOUGH SEEMINGLY OPPOSED TO UNITY, SUBSERVE GOOD

The story is now concluded, with its ups and downs,
Like lovers' musings, without beginning or ending.
It has no beginning, even as eternity,
Nor ending, for 'tis akin to world without end.
Or like water, each drop whereof is at once
Beginning and end, and also has no beginning or end.
But God forbid! This story is not a vain fable,
'Tis the ready money of your state and mine, be sure!
Before every Sufi who is enlightened
Whatever is past is never mentioned.
When his whole thoughts are absorbed in present ecstasy,

No thought of consequences enters his mind.
Arab, water-pot, and angels are all ourselves!
"Whatsoever turneth from God is turned from Him."
Know the husband is reason, the wife lust and greed;
She is vested with darkness and a gainsayer of reason.
Learn now whence springs the root of this circumstance,
From this, that the Whole has parts of divers kinds.
These parts of the Whole are not parts in relation to it,—
Not in the way that rose's scent is a part of the rose.
The beauty of the green shoot is part of the rose's beauty,
But the turtle-dove's cooing is a part of *that* Bulbul's music.
But if I engage in doubts and answers,
How can I give water to thirsty souls?
Yet, if you are perplexed by Whole and finite parts,
Have patience, for "patience is the key of joy."
Be abstinent,—abstinent from vague thoughts,
Since there are lions in that desert (of thoughts).
Abstinence is the prince of medicines,
As scratching only aggravates a scab.
Abstinence is certainly the root of medicine;
Practise abstinence, see how it invigorates thy soul!
Accept this counsel and give ear thereto,
That it may be to thee as an earring of gold!
Nay, not a mere earring, but that thou mayest be a mine
of gold,
Or that thou mayest surpass moon and Pleiades.

    First, know creation is in various forms;
Souls are as various as the letters from *Alif* to *Yá*.
In this variety of letters there seems disorder,
Though in fact they agree in an integral unity.

In one aspect they are opposed, in another united;

In one aspect capricious, in another serious.

The day of judgment is the day of the great review;

Whoso is fair and enlightened longs for that review;

Whoso, like a Hindoo, is black (with sin),

The day of review will sound the knell of his disgrace.

Since he has not a face like a sun,

He desires only night like to a veil!

If his thorn puts not forth a single rosebud,

The spring in disclosing him is his foe.

But he who is from head to foot a perfect rose or lily,

To him spring brings rejoicing.

The useless thorn desires the autumn,

That autumn may associate itself with the garden;

And hide the rose's beauty and the thorn's shame,

That men may not see the bloom of the one and the
other's shame,

That common stone and pure ruby may appear all as one.

True, the Gardener knows the difference even in autumn,

But the sight of *One* is better than the world's sight.

That *One* Person is Himself the world, as He is the sun,

And every star in heaven is a part of the sun;

That *One* Person is Himself the world, and the rest

Are all His dependents and parasites, O man!

He is the perfect world, yet He is single;

He holds in hand the writing of the whole existence.

Wherefore all forms and colours of beauty cry out,

"Good news! good news! Lo! the spring is at hand!"

If the blossoms did not shine as bright helmets,

How could the fruits display their globes?

When the blossoms are shed the fruits come to a head,
When the body is destroyed the soul lifts up its head.
The fruit is in the substance, the blossom only its form,
Blossom the good news, and fruit the promised boon.
When the blossoms fall the fruit appears,
When the former vanish the fruit is tasted.
Till bread is broken, how can it serve as food?
Till the grapes are crushed, how can they yield wine?
Till citrons be pounded up with drugs,
How can they afford healing to the sick?

THE MAN WHO WAS TATTOOED

It was the custom of the men of Qazwin to have various devices tattooed upon their bodies. A certain coward went to the artist to have such a device tattooed on his back, and desired that it might be the figure of a lion. But when he felt the pricks of the needles he roared with pain, and said to the artist, "What part of the lion are you now painting?" The artist replied, "I am doing the tail." The patient cried, "Never mind the tail; go on with another part." The artist accordingly began in another part, but the patient again cried out and told him to try somewhere else. Wherever the artist applied his needles, the patient raised similar objections, till at last the artist dashed all his needles and pigments on the ground, and refused to proceed any further.

THE PROPHET'S COUNSELS TO 'ALI TO FOLLOW THE DIRECTION OF THE PIR OR SPIRITUAL GUIDE, AND TO ENDURE HIS CHASTISEMENTS PATIENTLY

The Prophet said to 'Ali, "O 'Ali,
Thou art the Lion of God, a hero most valiant;

Yet confide not in thy lion-like valour,

But seek refuge under the palm-trees of the 'Truth.'

Whoso takes obedience as his exemplar

Shares its proximity to the ineffable Presence.

Do thou seek to draw near to Reason; let not thy heart

Rely, like others, on thy own virtue and piety.

Come under the shadow of the Man of Reason,

Thou canst not find it in the road of the traditionists.

That man enjoys close proximity to Allah;

Turn not away from obedience to him in any wise;

For he makes the thorn a bed of roses,

And gives sight to the eyes of the blind.

His shadow on earth is as that of Mount Qáf,

His spirit is as a Simurgh soaring on high.

He lends aid to the slaves of the friends of God,

And advances to high place them who seek him.

Were I to tell his praises till the last day,

My words would not be too many nor admit of

curtailment,

He is the sun of the spirit, not that of the sky,

For from his light men and angels draw life.

That sun is hidden in the form of a man,

Understand me! Allah knows the truth.

O 'Ali, out of all forms of religious service

Choose thou the shadow of that dear friend of God!

Every man takes refuge in some form of service,

And chooses for himself some asylum;

Do thou seek refuge in the shadow of the wise man,

That thou mayest escape thy fierce secret foes,

Of all forms of service this is the fittest for thee;

Thou shalt surpass all who were before thee.

Having chosen thy Director, be submissive to him,

Even as Mosses submitted to the commands of Khizr.

Have patience with Khizr's actions, O sincere one!

Lest he say, 'There is a partition between us.'

Though he stave in thy boat, heave not a sigh.

God declares his hand to be even as God's hand,

For He saith, 'The hand of God is over their hands.'

The hand of God impels him and gives him life;

Nay, not life only, but an eternal soul.

A friend is needed; travel not the road alone,

Take not thy own way through this desert!

Whoso travels this road alone

Only does so by aid of the might of holy men.

The hand of the Director is not weaker than theirs;

His hand is none other than the grasp of Allah!

If absent saints can confer such protection,

Doubtless present saints are more powerful than absent.

If such food be bestowed on the absent,

What dainties may not the guest who is present expect?

The courtier who attends in the presence of the king

Is served better than the stranger outside the gate.

The difference between them is beyond calculation;

One sees the light, the other only the veil.

Strive to obtain entrance within,

If thou wouldst not remain as a ring outside the door.

Having chosen thy Director, be not weak of heart,

Nor yet sluggish and lax as water and mud;

But if thou takest umbrage at every rub,

How wilt thou become a polished mirror?"

THE LION WHO HUNTED WITH THE WOLF AND THE FOX

A lion took a wolf and a fox with him on a hunting excursion, and succeeded in catching a wild ox, an ibex, and a hare. He then directed the wolf to divide the prey. The wolf proposed to award the ox to the lion, the ibex to himself, and the hare to the fox. The lion was enraged with the wolf because he had presumed to talk of "I" and "Thou," and "My share" and "Thy share," when it all belonged of right to the lion, and he slew the wolf with one blow of his paw. Then, turning to the fox, he ordered him to make the division. The fox, rendered wary by the fate of the wolf, replied that the whole should be the portion of the lion. The lion, please with his self-abnegation, gave it all up to him, saying, "Thou art no longer a fox, but myself."

TILL MAN DESTROYS "SELF" HE IS NO TRUE FRIEND OF GOD

Once a man cam and knocked at the door of his friend.
His friend said, "Who art thou, O faithful one?"
He said, "'Tis I." He answered, "There is no admittance.
There is no room for the 'raw' at my well-cooked feast.
Naught but fire of separation and absence
Can cook the raw one and free him from hypocrisy!
Since thy 'self' has not yet left thee,
Thou must be burned in fiery flames."
The poor man went away, and for one whole year
Journeyed burning with grief for his friend's absence.
His heart burned till it was cooked; then he went again
And drew near to the house of his friend.

He knocked at the door in fear and trepidation
Lest some careless word might fall from his lips.
His friend shouted, "Who is that at the door?"
He answered, "'Tis Thou who art at the door, O Beloved!"
The friend said, "Since 'tis I, let me come in,
There is not room for two 'I's' in one house."

JOSEPH AND THE MIRROR

An old friend came to pay his respects to Joseph, and after some remarks upon the bad behaviour of his brethren, Joseph asked him what present he had brought to show his respect. The friend replied that he had long considered what gift would be most suitable to offer, and at last had fixed upon a mirror, which he accordingly produced from his pocket and presented to Joseph, at the same time begging him to admire his own beauteous face in it.

DEFECT AND NOT-BEING THE MIRROR WHEREIN ABSOLUTE PERFECT BEING IS REFLECTED

He drew forth a mirror from his side
A mirror is what Beauty busies itself with.
Since Not-being is the mirror of Being,
If you are wise, choose Not-being (self-abnegation).
Being may be displayed in that Not-being,
Wealthy men show their liberality on the poor.
He who is an hungered is the clear mirror of bread,
The tinder is the mirror of the flint and steel.
Not-being and Defect, wherever they occur,
Are the mirrors of the Beauty of all beings.
Because Not-being is a clear filtered essence,

Wherein all these beings are infused.
When a garment is made by a good tailor,
'Tis an evidence of the tailor's art.
Logs of wood would not be duly shaped
Did not the carpenter plan outline and detail.
The leech skilled in setting bones goes
Where lies the patient with a broken leg.
If there were no sick and infirm,
How could the excellence of the leech's art be seen?
If vile base copper were not mingled,
How could the alchemist show his skill?
Defects are the mirrors of the attributes of Beauty,
The base is the mirror of the High and Glorious One,
Because one contrary shows forth its contrary,
As honey's sweetness is shown by vinegar's sourness.
Whoso recognises and confesses his own defects
Is hastening in the way that leads to perfection!
But he advances not towards the Almighty
Who fancies himself to be perfect.
No sickness worse than fancying thyself perfect
Can infect thy soul, O arrogant misguided one!
Shed many tears of blood from eyes and heart,
That this self-satisfaction may be driven out.
The fault of Iblis lay in saying, "I am better than he,"
And this same weakness lurks in the soul of all creatures.

THE PROPHET'S SCRIBE

The Prophet had a scribe who used to write down the texts
that fell from his lips. At last this scribe became so conceited
that he imagined all this heavenly wisdom proceeded from his

own wit, and not from the Prophet. Puffed up with self-importance, he fancied himself inspired, and his heart was hardened against his master, and he became a renegade, like the fallen angels Harut and Marut. He took his own foolish surmises to be the truth, whereas they were all wide of the mark, as those of the deaf man who went to condole with a sick neighbour, and answered all his remarks at cross purposes.

HOW PHILOSPHERS DECEIVE THEMSELVES

On the last day, "when Earth shall quake with quaking,"
This earth shall give witness of her condition.
For she "shall tell out her tidings openly,"
Yea, earth and her rocks shall tell them forth!
The philosopher reasons from base analogies
(True reason comes not out of a dark corner);
The philosopher (I say) denies this in his pride of intellect.
Say to him, "Go, dash thy head against a wall!"
The speech of water, of earth, of mire,
Is audible by the ears of men of heart!
The philosopher, who denies Divine Providence,
Is a stranger to the perceptions of saints.
He says that the flashes of men's morbid imaginations
Instill many vain fancies into men's minds.
But, on the contrary, 'tis his perverseness and want of faith
Which implant in himself this vain fancy of negation.
The philosopher denies the existence of the Devil;
At the same time he is the Devil's laughing-stock.
If thou hast not seen the Devil, look at thyself,
Without demon's aid how came that blue turban on
thy brow?

Whosoever has a doubt or disquietude in his heart
Is a secret denier and philosopher.
Now and then he displays firm belief,
But that slight dash of philosophy blackens his face.
Beware, O believers! That lurks in you too;
You may develop innumerable states of mind.
All the seventy and two heresies lurk in you;
Have a care lest one day they prevail over you!
He in whose breast the leaf of true faith is grown
Must tremble as a leaf from fear of such catastrophe.
Thou makest a mock of Iblis and the Devil,
Because thou art a fine man in thy own sight;
But when thy soul shall tell thy wretched faults,
What lamentation thou wilt cause to the faithful!
The sellers of base gold sit smiling in their shops,
Because the touchstone is not as yet in their sight.
O Veiler of sins! strip not the veil from us;
Lend us aid on the day of trial!

THE CHINESE AND THE GREEK ARTISTS

The Chinese and the Greeks disputed before the Sultan
which of them were the better painters; and, in order to
settle the dispute, the Sultan allotted to each a house to be
painted by them. The Chinese procured all kinds of paints,
and coloured their house in the most elaborate way. The
Greeks, on the other hand, used no colours at all, but con-
tented themselves with cleansing the walls of their house
from all filth, and burnishing them till they were as clear
and bright as the heavens. When the two houses were
offered to the Sultan's inspection, that painted by the

Chinese was much admired; but the Greek house carried off
the palm, as all the colours of the other house were reflected
on its walls with an endless variety of shades and hues.

KNOWLEDGE OF THE HEART PREFERABLE TO THE KNOWLEDGE OF THE SCHOOLS

The knowledge of men of heart bears them up,
The knowledge of men of the body weighs them down.
When 'tis knowledge of the heart, it is a friend;
When knowledge of the body, it is a burden.
God saith, "As an ass bearing a load of books,"
The knowledge which is not of Him is a burden.
Knowledge which comes not immediately from Him
Endures no longer than the rouge of the tirewoman.
Nevertheless, if you bear this burden in a right spirit
'Twill be removed, and you will obtain joy.
See you bear not that burden out of vainglory,
Then you will behold a store of true knowledge within.
When you mount the steed of this true knowledge,
Straightway the burden will fall from your back.
If you drink not His cup, how will you escape lusts?
You, who seek no more of Him than to name His name?
What do His name and fame suggest? The idea of Him.
And the idea of Him guides you to union with Him.
Know you a guide without something to which it guides?
Were there no roads there would be no *ghouls*.
Know you a name without a thing answering to it?
Have you ever plucked a rose (Gul) from Gáf and Lám?
You name His name; go, seek the reality named by it!
Look for the moon in heaven, not in the water!

If you desire to rise above mere names and letters,
Make yourself free from self at one stroke!
Like a sword be without trace of soft iron;
Like a steel mirror, scour off all rust with contrition;
Make yourself pure from all attributes of self,
That you may see your own pure bright essence!
Yea, see in your heart the knowledge of the Prophet,
Without book, without tutor, without preceptor.
The Prophet saith, "He is one of my people,
Whoso is of like temper and spirit with me.
His soul beholds me by the selfsame light
Whereby I myself behold him,—
Without traditions and scriptures of histories,
In the fount of the water of life."
Learn the mystery, "I was last night a Kurd,
And this morning am become an Arab."
This mystery of "last night" and "this morning"
Leads you into the road that brings you to God.
But if you want an insurance of this secret knowledge,
Hear the story of the Greeks and the Chinese.

COUNSELS OF RESERVE GIVEN BY THE PROPHET TO HIS FREEDMAN ZAID

At dawn the Prophet said to Zaid,
"How is it with thee this morning, O pure disciple?"
He replied, "They faithful slave am I." Again he said,
"If the garden of faith has bloomed, show a token of it."
He answered, "I was athirst many days,
By night I slept not for the burning pangs of love;

So that I passed by days and nights,
As the point of a spear glances off a shield.
For in that state all faith is one,
A hundred thousand years and a moment are all one;
World without beginning and world without end are one;
Reason finds no entrance when mind is thus lost."

The Prophet again urged Zaid to deliver to him a present from that celestial region, as a token that he had really been there in the spirit. Zaid answered that he had seen the eight heavens and the seven hells, and the destinies of all men, whether bound to heaven or hell. The body, he said, is as a mother, and the soul as her infant, and death is the time of parturition, when it becomes manifest to what class the infant soul belongs. As on the day of judgment it will be manifest to all men whether a soul belongs to the saved or to the lost, so now it was plain and manifest to him. He went on to ask the Prophet if he should publish this secret knowledge of his to all men, or hold his peace. The Prophet told him to hold his peace. Zaid, however, proceeded to detail the vision of the last judgment, which he had seen when in the spirit; and the Prophet again commanded him to pause, adding that "God is never ashamed to say the truth," and allows His Prophet to speak forth the truth, but that for Zaid to blab forth the secrets seen in ecstatic vision would be wrong. Zaid replied that it was impossible for one who had once beheld the Sun of "The Truth" to keep his vision a secret. But the Prophet in reply instructed him that all men are masters of their own wills, and that he must not reveal what God has determined to keep secret till the last day, in order to leave men till then under the stimulus of hope and fear, and to give them the credit of "believing what is not seen." More honour is given to the warder of a castle who faithfully executes his trust at a distance from the court than to those courtiers who serve constantly under the king's own eye. Zaid submitted to the Prophet's injunctions, and remained self-contained in his ecstatic visions. Anecdotes of the sage Luqman, of King Solomon, and of a conflagration in the days of the Khalifa 'Omar complete the section.

THE PROPHET'S FINAL COUNSELS OF "RESERVE"

The Prophet said, "My companions are as the stars,
Lights to them that walk aright, missiles against Satan.
If every man had strength of eyesight
To look straight at the light of the sun in heaven,
What need were there of stars, O humble one,
To one who was guided by the light of the sun?
Neither moon nor planets would be needed
By one who saw directly the Sun of 'The Truth.'
The Moon declares, as also the clouds and shadows,
'I am a man, yet it hath been revealed to me.'
Like you, I was naturally dark,
'Twas the Sun's revelation that gave me such light.
I still am dark compared to the Sun,
Though I am light compared to the dark souls of men.
Therefore is my light weak, that you may bear it,
For you are not strong enough to bear the dazzling Sun.
I have, as it were, mixed honey with vinegar,

To succour the sickness of your hearts.

When you are cured of your sickness, O invalid,

Then leave out the vinegar and eat pure honey.

When the heart is garnished and swept clear of lust,

Therein 'The God of Mercy sitteth on His throne.'

Then God rules the heart immediately,

When it has gained this immediate connection with Him.

This subject is endless; but where is Zaid,

That I may tell him again not to seek notoriety?

'Tis not wise to publish these mysteries,

Since the last day is approaching to reveal all things."

Now you will not find Zaid, for he is fled,

He sprang from the place where the shoes were left,

Scattering the shoes in his hurry.

If you had been Zaid, you too would have been lost,

As a star is lost when the sun shines on it;

For then you see no trace or sign of it,

No place or track of it in the milky way.

Our senses and our endless discourses

Are annihilated in the light of the knowledge of our King.

Our senses and our reason with us

Are as waves on waves "assembled before us."

When night returns and 'tis the time of the sky's levée,

The stars that were hidden come forth to their work.

The people of the world lie unconscious,

With veils drawn over their faces, and asleep;

But when the morn shall burst forth and the sun arise

Every creature will raise its head from its couch;

To the unconscious God will restore consciousness;

They will stand in rings as slaves with rings in their ears;

Dancing and clapping hands with songs of praise,
Singing with joy, "Our Lord hath restored us to life!"
Shedding their old skins and bones,
As horsemen stirring up a cloud of dust.
All pressing on from Not-being to Being,
On the last day, as well the thankful as the unthankful.

'ALI'S FORBEARANCE

'Ali, the "Lion of God," was once engaged in conflict with a Magian chief, and in the midst of the struggle the Magian spat in his face. 'Ali, instead of taking vengeance on him, at once dropped his sword, to the Magian's great astonishment. On his inquiring the reason of such forbearance, 'Ali informed him that the "Lion of God" did not destroy life for the satisfaction of his own vengeance, but simply to carry out God's will, and that whenever he saw just cause, he held his hand even in the midst of the strife, and spared the foe. The Prophet, 'Ali continued, had long since informed him that he would die by the hand of his own stirrup-bearer (Ibn Maljun), and the stirrup-bearer had frequently implored 'Ali to kill him, and thus save him from the commission of that great crime; but 'Ali said he always refused to do so, as to him death was as sweet as life, and he felt no anger against his destined assassin, who was only the instrument of God's eternal purpose. The Magian chief, on hearing 'Ali's discourse, was so much affected that he embraced Islam, together with all his family, to the number of fifty souls.

HOW THE PROPHET WHISPERED TO 'ALI'S STIRRUP-BEARER THAT HE WOULD ONE DAY ASSASSINATE HIS MASTER

The Prophet whispered in the ear of my servant
That one day he would sever my head from my neck.
The Prophet also warned by inspiration me, his friend,
That the hand of my servant would destroy me.
My servant cried, "O kill me first,
That I may not become guilty of so grievous a sin!"
I replied, "Since my death is to come from thee,
How can I balk the fateful decree?"
He fell at my feet and cried, "O gracious lord,
For God's sake cleave now my body in twain,
That such an evil deed may not be wrought by me,
And my soul burn with anguish for its beloved."
I replied, "What God's pen has written, it has written;
In presence of its writings knowledge is confounded;
There is no anger in my soul against thee,
Because I attribute not this deed to thee;
Thou art God's instrument, God's hand is the agent.
How can I chide or fret at God's instrument?"
He said, "If this be so, why is there retaliation?"
I answered, "'Tis from God, and 'tis God's secret;
If He shows displeasure at His own acts,
From His displeasure He evolves a Paradise;
He feels displeasure at His own acts,
Because He is a God of vengeance as of mercy.
In this city of events He is the Lord,

In this realm He is the King who plans all events.
If He crushes His own instruments,
He makes those crushed ones fair in His sight.
Know the great mystery of 'Whatever verses we cancel,
Or cause you to forget, we substitute better for them.'
Whatever law God cancels, He makes as a weed,
And in its stead He brings forth a rose.
So night cancels the business of the daytime,
When the reason that lights our minds becomes inanimate.
Again, night is cancelled by the light of day,
And inanimate reason is rekindled to life by its rays.
Though darkness produces this sleep and quiet,
Is not the 'water of life' in the darkness?
Are not spirits refreshed in that very darkness?
Is not that silence the season of heavenly voices?
For from contraries contraries are brought forth,
Out of darkness was created light.
The Prophet's wars brought about the present peace,
The peace of these latter days resulted from those wars.
That conqueror of hearts cut off a thousand heads,
That the heads of his people might rest in peace."

GOD'S REBUKE TO ADAM FOR SCORNING IBLIS

To whomsoever God's order comes,
He must smite with his sword even his own child.
Fear then, and revile not the wicked,
For the wicked are impotent under God's commands.
In presence of God's commands bow down the neck
of pride.
Scoff not nor chide even them that go astray!

One day Adam cast a look of contempt and scorn
Upon Iblis, thinking what a wretch he was.
He felt self-important and proud of himself,
And he smiled at the actions of cursed Iblis.
God Almighty cried out to him, "O pure one,
Thou art wholly ignorant of hidden mysteries.
If I were to blab the faults of the unfortunate,
I should root up the mountains from their bases,
And lay bare the secrets of a hundred Adams,
And convert a hundred fresh Iblises into Musulmans."
Adam answered, "I repent me of my scornful looks;
Such arrogant thoughts shall not be mine again.
O Lord, pardon this rashness in Thy slave;
I repent; chastise me not for these words!"

    O Aider of aid-seekers, guide us,
For there is no security in knowledge or wealth;
"Lead not our hearts astray after Thou hast guided us,"
And avert the evil that the "Pen" has written.
Turn aside from our souls the evil written on our fates.
Repel us not from the tables of purity!
O God, Thy grace is the proper object of our desire;
To couple others with Thee is not proper.
Nothing is bitterer than severance from Thee,
Without Thy shelter there is naught but perplexity.
Our worldly good rob us of our heavenly goods,
Our body rends the garment of our soul.
Our hands, as it were, prey on our feet;
Without reliance on Thee how can we live?
And if the soul escapes these great perils,
It is made captive as a victim of misfortunes and fears,

Inasmuch as when the soul lacks union with the Beloved,
It abides for ever blind and darkened by itself.
If Thou showest not the way, our life is lost;
A life living without Thee esteem as dead!
If Thou findest fault with Thy slaves,
Verily it is right in Thee, O Blessed One!
If Thou shouldst call sun and moon obscure,
If Thou shouldst call the straight cypress crooked,
If Thou shouldst declare the highest heaven base,
Or rich mines and oceans paupers,—
All this is the truth in relation to Thy perfection!
Thin is the dominion and the glory and the wealth!
For Thou art exempt from defect and not-being,
Thou givest existence to things non-existent, and again
Thou makest them non-existent.

EPILOGUE

Alas! the forbidden fruits were eaten,
And thereby the warm life of reason was congealed.
A grain of wheat eclipsed the sun of Adam,
Like as the Dragon's tail dulls the brightness of the moon.
Behold how delicate is the heart, that a morsel of dust
Clouded its moon with foul obscurity!
When bread is "substance," to eat it nourishes us;
When 'tis empty "form," it profits nothing.
Like as the green thorn which is cropped by the camel,
And then yields him pleasure and nutriment;
When its greenness has gone and it becomes dry,—
If the camel crops that same thorn in the desert,
It wounds his palate and mouth without pity,

As if conserve of roses should turn to sharp swords.
When bread is "substance," it is as a green thorn;
When 'tis "form," 'tis as the dry and coarse thorn.
And thou eatest it in the same way as of yore
Thou wert wont to eat it, O helpless being,—
Eatest this dry thing in the same manner,
After the real "substance" is mingled with dust;
It has become mingled with dust, dry in pith and rind.
O camel, now beware of that herb!
The Word is become foul with mingled earth;
The water is become muddy; close the mouth of the well,
Till God makes it again pure and sweet;
Yea, till He purifies what He has made foul.
Patience will accomplish thy desire, not haste.
Be patient, God knows what is best.

THE GOSPEL

Prologue by Marcus Borg {

OF JOHN

The Gospel of John is familiar and much loved. The opening words of its magnificent prologue take us back to creation: "In the beginning was the Word." It contains the best-known verse in the New Testament: "For God so loved the world that he gave his only begotten Son; whoever believes in him shall not perish, but have everlasting life." Its story of Jesus is strikingly different from the first three gospels, Matthew, Mark, and Luke. Only in John does Jesus speak of himself with the great "I am" statement: as "the light of the world," "the bread of life," "the way," "the truth," "the resurrection and the life," "the true vine," and more. Only John has the wedding at Cana, the conversations with Nicodemus and the Samaritan woman, the resurrection of Lazarus, and the "farewell discourses" of chapters 13-17. These differences were recognized by Christians in antiquity. Around the year 200, Clement of Alexandria called John "the spiritual gospel" to distinguish it from the first three gospels. This designation is the key to understanding it. In John, we do not directly encounter the historical Jesus, we encounter what the risen living Christ had become in the experience of the early Christian community in the decades after the first Easter. In short, John's portrait of Jesus is not history remembered, but history metaphorized. Its powerful images and stories are best read as metaphorical narratives whose truth does not depend upon their historical factuality. About John's story of Jesus, one may say "Although it may not have happened this way, this story is true."

INTRODUCTION

REYNOLDS PRICE

THE GOSPEL ACCORDING TO JOHN is the most mysterious document that survives from the early years of the Jesus sect. . . . Not long after the end of the first century, the document we know as The Good News According to John was widely (if not universally) acknowledged throughout the scattered and threatened world of the Jesus sect as one of four unparalleled stories of the acts and the meaning of Jesus. With the possible exception of the apocryphal *Gospel of Thomas*, which confines itself strictly to the sayings of Jesus, none of the other first-century gospels alluded to by Luke in the preface to his own gospel has yet come to light in its entirety. So John with all its bafflements—and above all with its unique claim of firsthand authority—has, from near the first, been seen as the unmatched pearl of the four. And it stands unchallenged as the crown of firsthand witness to a life as shocking, and as crucial to the history of the world, as any life known.

Yet again, the heart of that shock is seldom noticed. And a poll of modern readers would likely show that John stands with Luke as the most beloved of gospels, primarily because of its many consolations. A further poll might show that, among possible readers, Christian readers prize John for two reasons—his steady picture of a Jesus who boldly announces his godhead yet knows our human weakness so well that he promises the love and hope which most hearts crave. Few readers versed in Anglo-Saxon culture fail to know some of the words by heart, and in the King James Version—

> For God so loved the world, that he gave his only begotten Son: that whosoever believeth in him, should not perish, but have everlasting life. . . . Let not your heart be troubled: ye believe in God, believe also in me. In my Father's house are many mansions; if it were not so, I would have told you: I go to prepare a place for you . . . that where I am, there ye may be also.

But centuries of familiarity with such assurance—and with John's near omission of that awful Judge who spreads his terror through the other gospels—has muffled the rank outrage of John. Seen head-on, John demands that his readers choose—is he a truthful reporter, as he vows, or a fantast? Is he fraudulent or raving? And if we feel that John's report rings true, then all the questions must be judged once more in the matter of his hero. Is this man Jesus a whole-cloth fictional creation, a village lunatic, a deluded visionary, a skillful charlatan, the "only begotten Son of God"; or as John's Jesus announces, is he somehow the power of God himself? If veteran readers of John can make the effort to approach his gospel freshly, in a new and relatively literal translation, they may begin to see what atheists and agnostics will sight at once— the hair-raising newness of one slender tract. Anyone coming to the book afresh will spot that newness at once.

Forget that you ever read a gospel; forget you ever heard

of Jesus. Read John watchfully and what do you see? For me, first and last, he offers two things. The things are a few human acts, some of which John calls "signs," and a number of speeches. The story concerns the final years of one man's life. The important speeches come from that man. Alone among gospel writers, John claims that he himself witnessed the signs and heard the speeches (the second such claim, at the end of the gospel, appears to be made by John's surviving disciples). He claims to report a few of those significant moments—and to report them truly—and he adds in clarification at the very end, "There were many other things Jesus did which if each were written I think the world couldn't hold the books written." Also near the end, and again in his own voice (or that of his stenographer or editor), John says that he makes his record for an urgent reason—to convince each reader "that Jesus is Messiah, the Son of God and that trusting you may have life in his name." Compared with the world's other urgent stories, however—the early books of Hebrew scripture, the Koran, and the founding texts of most Eastern religions for instance—John delivers his strike in a few thousand words and ends. He can be read through in little more than an hour; and he stands, after Mark, as the second-shortest of the gospels.

What is the story John can tell so quickly? Does he mean us to read it as "realistic," even by his time's different standards of veracity? If he writes symbolically, allegorically, anagogically, does he give us sufficient signals when he goes into a nonrepresentational gear, into rigged descriptions of acts that never happened or improvisations on the gestures and voices of a distantly remembered Jesus? (Ancient writers and readers of John's time make it amply clear that they were capable of differentiating between a visible historical event and the transmutation of that event into metaphor.) Again, is John's evident passion to change at least the lives of his ini-tial readers a folly, a delusion, or a sanely built plan?

With unprecedented daring, he packs the whole story—veiled but intact—into his first three paragraphs. A further surprise in traversing the length of John's pamphlet comes in our eventual discovery that we knew his whole story from the first page but were unaware of our knowledge. "At the start was the Word. The Word was with God and God was the Word—he was at the start with God." The Word, then, or the Idea, is one of God's presumably infinite natures—a nature that was present before the creation of things and that caused all things. After a glance at another John, who will forerun Messiah, John the gospel writer races with a speed and aim as sure as the start of Genesis toward his first shock. Though he would be refused by the world, "the Word became flesh and tented among us. We watched his glory, glory like that of a father's one son full of grace and truth." In the early years of our era, then, God's active power embodied itself in a visible man called Jesus.

Having calmly hung the assertion before us, John begins his human story. The Word has now been among us through the concealed years of Jesus' childhood and has grown to manhood in ways likewise undescribed. Now at a moment of historical time that ends in the known Palestinian gover-norship of Pontius Pilate, the Word in its tent of flesh—Jesus from the village of Nazareth in Galilee—comes south to the teacher called John (the writer never calls him *the*

Baptizer or *the Baptist*). This John is performing a ritual wash-
ing of sinners near Jerusalem. Though the writer omits the
scene itself, Jesus apparently accepts this rite that he (as a
sinless God-man) cannot need. At once John both recognizes
Jesus as Messiah and predicts his unsuspected nature, the
shock and scandal he will bring to his people.

Jesus Messiah will not be the longed-for chieftain to lead
his people in victory over Rome. He will be more nearly the
Suffering Servant whom Isaiah foresaw—"He was despised
and rejected by men . . . by his wounds we are healed." In
another flare of insight, this Baptizer finds yet another name
for the man Jesus who walks before him—"Look, the Lamb
of God who cancels the wrongs of the world." Lambs are
common objects of affection. They are also slaughtered by
the thousands in sacrifice to God's just wrath, in his Temple
a few miles west of the baptism site. But while the Baptizer
sees so far at the start, even he fails to glimpse the horror to
come in the life of this lamb and the glory to follow.

Among those around the Baptizer are five particular men.
At least three of them are from Galilee—Andrew, his
brother Simon (whom Jesus soon calls *Peter* or *Rock*), and
Nathanael (a man not mentioned in the other gospels). The
fourth is Philip. Is the unnamed fifth that man whom John
later calls "the disciple [or pupil] whom Jesus loved"? Since
John bar Zebedee is named in each of the other gospels as one
of the first four disciples called by Jesus, the guess is likely.
In any case, all five men seem young, impressionable, and
game to roam; and they are so impressed by the Baptizer's
witness, by the undescribed magnetism and wit of Jesus,
by Jesus' assent to Nathanael's belief that here indeed is

Messiah, that they promptly leave the Baptizer and follow Jesus north.

Back in Galilee, Jesus soon impresses the new disciples, his mother, and numerous others with a first display of power, the first unearthly sign. In a forthright kitchen wonder—the response to nothing more urgent than a friend's social embarrassment—Jesus changes water to delicious wine at a wedding in Cana, a town near Nazareth. Despite the symbolic meanings deduced by two millennia of commentators, it seems unlikely that John would describe such a homely feat unless he had been present and convinced of its actual and inexplicable occurrence. If not, why invent—for the inaugural sign of Jesus' great career—a miraculous solution to a mere social oversight?

Then with his disciples, his mother, and now his brothers, Jesus visits the fishing town of Capernaum of the Lake of Galilee. The other gospels tell us that, hereabouts, Jesus found and enlisted more disciples, to a final number of twelve. John will later mention others—Judas, Thomas Didymus, and "the disciple whom Jesus loved"—but he passes over their calling in silence. And he omits the numerous early Galilean signs and wonders described by Mark and repeated in Matthew and Luke.

Next Jesus and the disciples go to Jerusalem for Passover, the solemn spring feast in memory of the night when God's angel of death spared those Hebrew sons with lamb's blood on their doors. It is the first of three such visits to the capital described by John; the other gospels describe only one. And here at Jesus' first appearance on the main stage of his country, he at once scores his fame on the public air by committing a serious breach of the civil and religious peace. In the other gospels such a breach comes only a few days before Jesus' death and is clearly a weighty matter in his condemnation; with John's own unapologetic authority, he sets it as the headpiece of Jesus' dealings with the interlopers who defile his Father's house. With an impromptu whip, Jesus drives the licensed livestock dealers and money changers from the Temple (though John does not specify, it seems implicit that his Jesus actually strikes some of the dealers; in Mark he merely overturns their tables). Unaccountably, such an alarming outburst goes unpunished—in fact, it is never again alluded to by Jesus' enemies—and on the same visit Jesus is free to perform other signs, unspecified.

Then he moves in bold contrast to the Jesus of Mark, who demands that his disciples keep silent about his nature. John's Jesus moves from his violent breach to a meeting with a member of the same hierarchy he has challenged. Poised on the edge of national fame, Jesus tells Nicodemus (who is a member of the Jewish ruling council and visits Jesus by night) that he Jesus is the only Son of God. He has been sent, here and now, from the depths of God's love to save whoever believes in him. Here and constantly hereafter, Jesus affirms that eternal life is available to those who believe in him, and to them alone. In the teeth of such a blasphemous claim, strangely Nicodemus makes no reply; but when Jesus is dead, it is John alone who tells us that Nicodemus shares the burial costs with Joseph of Arimathea.

In the remaining three-fourths of the gospel, Jesus will give more signs; he will suffer death and rise from the dead. By the end of Jesus' first visit to Jerusalem, however, John's story has set its pattern and made its sole demand—*Trust in this man or die forever.* But who is the man and what do we mean if we say we "trust or believe in him"? How would that belief change our daily lives, our thoughts and acts? What would be the long-range outcome of such a vague faith? The balance of the story, and the speeches, work at telling us, with no trace of doubt (though not always clearly) in the voice of the teller. . . .

That seems a fair outline of John's story. Yet the outline can be pressed further down, to a sentence—*The force that conceived and bore all things came here among us, proved his identity in visible human acts, was killed by men no worse than we, rose from death, and walked again with his early believers, vowing eternal life beside him to those who also come to believe that he is God and loves us as much as his story shows.* None of the other active world religions says anything remotely similar or comparable. John's story, which—more than the story of the other gospels—became the orthodox Christian faith . . . [has] no parallel in the theologies of John's contemporaries—the dead myths of Greece or Rome, with their demigods and deified bureaucrats. Again, John hands us a brand-new thing.

Bizarre as it is in so many parts, his gospel speaks—in the clearest voice we have—that sentence all humankind craves from stories: *The Maker of all things loves and wants me.* In no other book our culture possesses can we see a clearer graph

of that need, that tall enormous radiant arc—fragile creatures made by the Father's hand, hurled into space, then
caught at last by a man in some ways like ourselves, though
the ark of God.

THE GOSPEL OF JOHN

IN THE BEGINNING was the Word, and the Word
was with God, and the Word was God.

2 The same was in the beginning with God.

3 All things were made by him; and without him was not
any thing made that was made.

4 In him was life; and the life was the light of men.

5 And the light shineth in darkness; and the darkness com-
prehended it not.

6 There was a man sent from God, whose name *was* John.

7 The same came for a witness, to bear witness of the Light,
that all *men* through him might believe.

8 He was not that Light, but *was sent* to bear witness of that
Light.

9 *That* was the true Light, which lighteth every man that cometh into the world.

10 He was in the world, and the world was made by him, and the world knew him not.

11 He came unto his own, and his own received him not.

12 But as many as received him, to them gave he power to become the sons of God, *even* to them that believe on his name:

13 Which were born, not of blood, nor of the will of the flesh, nor of the will of man, but of God.

14 And the Word was made flesh, and dwelt among us, (and we beheld his glory, the glory as of the only begotten of the Father,) full of grace and truth.

15 John bare witness of him, and cried, saying, This was he of whom I spake, He that cometh after me is preferred before me: for he was before me.

16 And of his fulness have all we received, and grace for grace.

17 For the law was given by Moses, *but* grace and truth came by Jesus Christ.

18 No man hath seen God at any time; the only begotten Son, which is in the bosom of the Father, he hath declared *him*.

19 And this is the record of John, when the Jews sent priests and Levites from Jerusalem to ask him, Who art thou?

20 And he confessed, and denied not; but confessed, I am not the Christ.

21 And they asked him, What then? Art thou Elias? And he saith, I am not. Art thou that prophet? And he answered, No.

22 Then said they unto him, Who art thou? that we may

give an answer to them that sent us. What sayest thou of thyself?

23 He said, I *am* the voice of one crying in the wilderness, Make straight the way of the Lord, as said the prophet Esaias.

24 And they which were sent were of the Pharisees.

25 And they asked him, and said unto him, Why baptizest thou then, if thou be not that Christ, nor Elias, neither that prophet?

26 John answered them, saying, I baptize with water: but there standeth one among you, whom ye know not;

27 He it is, who coming after me is preferred before me, whose shoe's latchet I am not worthy to unloose.

28 These things were done in Bethabara beyond Jordan, where John was baptizing.

29 The next day John seeth Jesus coming unto him, and saith, Behold the Lamb of God, which taketh away the sin of the world.

30 This is he of whom I said, After me cometh a man which is preferred before me: for he was before me.

31 And I knew him not: but that he should be made manifest to Israel, therefore am I come baptizing with water.

32 And John bare record, saying, I saw the Spirit descending from heaven like a dove, and it abode upon him.

33 And I knew him not: but he that sent me to baptize with water, the same said unto me, Upon whom thou shalt see the Spirit descending, and remaining on him, the same is he which baptizeth with the Holy Ghost.

34 And I saw, and bare record that this is the Son of God.

35 Again the next day after John stood, and two of his disciples;

36 And looking upon Jesus as he walked, he saith, Behold the Lamb of God!

37 And the two disciples heard him speak, and they followed Jesus.

38 Then Jesus turned, and saw them following, and saith unto them, What seek ye? They said unto him, Rabbi, (which is to say, being interpreted, Master,) where dwellest thou?

39 He saith unto them, Come and see. They came and saw where he dwelt, and abode with him that day: for it was about the tenth hour.

40 One of the two which heard John *speak*, and followed him, was Andrew, Simon Peter's brother.

41 He first findeth his own brother Simon, and saith unto him, We have found the Messias, which is, being interpreted, the Christ.

42 And he brought him to Jesus. And when Jesus beheld him, he said, Thou art Simon the son of Jona: thou shalt be called Cephas, which is by interpretation, A stone.

43 The day following Jesus would go forth into Galilee, and findeth Philip, and saith unto him, Follow me.

44 Now Philip was of Bethsaida, the city of Andrew and Peter.

45 Philip findeth Nathanael, and saith unto him, We have found him, of whom Moses in the law, and the prophets, did write, Jesus of Nazareth, the son of Joseph.

46 And Nathanael said unto him, Can there any good thing come out of Nazareth? Philip saith unto him, Come and see.

47 Jesus saw Nathanael coming to him, and saith of him, Behold an Israelite indeed, in whom is no guile!

48 Nathanael saith unto him, Whence knowest thou me? Jesus answered and said unto him, Before that Philip called thee, when thou wast under the fig tree, I saw thee.

49 Nathanael answered and saith unto him, Rabbi, thou art the Son of God; thou art the King of Israel.

50 Jesus answered and said unto him, Because I said unto thee, I saw thee under the fig tree, believest thou? thou shalt see greater things than these.

51 And he saith unto him, Verily, verily, I say unto you, Hereafter ye shall see heaven open, and the angels of God ascending and descending upon the Son of man.

CHAPTER 2

And the third day there was a marriage in Cana of Galilee; and the mother of Jesus was there:

2 And both Jesus was called, and his disciples, to the marriage.

3 And when they wanted wine, the mother of Jesus saith unto him, They have no wine.

4 Jesus saith unto her, Woman, what have I to do with thee? mine hour is not yet come.

5 His mother saith unto the servants, Whatsoever he saith unto you, do it.

6 And there were set there six waterpots of stone, after the manner of the purifying of the Jews, containing two or three firkins apiece.

7 Jesus saith unto them, Fill the waterpots with water. And they filled them up to the brim.

8 And he saith unto them, Draw out now, and bear unto the governor of the feast. And they bare it.

9 When the ruler of the feast had tasted the water that was made wine, and knew not whence it was: (but the servants which drew the water knew;) the governor of the feast called the bridegroom,

10 And saith unto him, Every man at the beginning doth set forth good wine; and when men have well drunk, then that which is worse: *but* thou hast kept the good wine until now.

11 This beginning of miracles did Jesus in Cana of Galilee, and manifested forth his glory; and his disciples believed on him.

12 After this he went down to Capernaum, he, and his mother, and his brethren, and his disciples: and they continued there not many days.

13 And the Jews' passover was at hand, and Jesus went up to Jerusalem.

14 And found in the temple those that sold oxen and sheep and doves, and the changers of money sitting:

15 And when he had made a scourge of small cords, he drove them all out of the temple, and the sheep, and the oxen; and poured out the changers' money, and overthrew the tables;

16 And said unto them that sold doves, Take these things hence; make not my Father's house an house of merchandise.

17 And his disciples remembered that it was written, The zeal of thine house hath eaten me up.

18 Then answered the Jews and said unto him, What sign showest thou unto us, seeing that thou doest these things?

19 Jesus answered and said unto them, Destroy this temple, and in three days I will raise it up.

20 Then said the Jews, Forty and six years was this temple in building, and wilt thou rear it up in three days?

21 But he spake of the temple of his body.

22 When therefore he was risen from the dead, his disciples remembered that he had said this unto them; and they believed the scripture, and the word which Jesus had said.

23 Now when he was in Jerusalem at the passover, in the feast *day*, many believed in his name, when they saw the miracles which he did.

24 But Jesus did not commit himself unto them, because he knew all *men*,

25 And needed not that any should testify of man: for he knew what was in man.

CHAPTER 3

There was a man of the Pharisees, named Nicodemus, a ruler of the Jews:

2 The same came to Jesus by night, and said unto him, Rabbi, we know that thou art a teacher come from God: for no man can do these miracles that thou doest, except God be with him.

3 Jesus answered and said unto him, Verily, verily, I say unto thee, Except a man be born again, he cannot see the kingdom of God.

4 Nicodemus saith unto him, How can a man be born when he is old? can he enter the second time into his mother's womb, and be born?

5 Jesus answered, Verily, verily, I say unto thee, Except a man be born of water and *of* the Spirit, he cannot enter into the kingdom of God.

6 That which is born of the flesh is flesh; and that which is born of the Spirit is spirit.

7 Marvel not that I said unto thee, Ye must be born again.

8 The wind bloweth where it listeth, and thou hearest the sound thereof, but canst not tell whence it cometh, and whither it goeth: so is every one that is born of the Spirit.

9 Nicodemus answered and said unto him, How can these things be?

10 Jesus answered and said unto him, Art thou a master of Israel, and knowest not these things?

11 Verily, verily, I say unto thee, We speak that we do know, and testify that we have seen; and ye receive not our witness.

12 If I have told you earthly things, and ye believe not, how shall ye believe, if I tell you *of* heavenly things?

13 And no man hath ascended up to heaven, but he that came down from heaven, *even* the Son of man which is in heaven.

14 And as Moses lifted up the serpent in the wilderness, even so must the Son of man be lifted up:

15 That whosoever believeth in him should not perish, but have eternal life.

16 For God so loved the world, that he gave his only begotten Son, that whosoever believeth in him should not perish, but have everlasting life.

17 For God sent not his Son into the world to condemn the world; but that the world through him might be saved.

18 He that believeth on him is not condemned: but he that believeth not is condemned already, because he hath not believed in the name of the only begotten Son of God.

19 And this is the condemnation, that light is come into the world, and men loved darkness rather than light, because their deeds were evil.

20 For every one that doeth evil hateth the light, neither cometh to the light, lest his deeds should be reproved.

21 But he that doeth truth cometh to the light, that his deeds may be made manifest, that they are wrought in God.

22 After these things came Jesus and his disciples into the land of Judaea; and there he tarried with them, and baptized.

23 And John also was baptizing in Aenon near to Salim, because there was much water there: and they came, and were baptized.

24 For John was not yet cast into prison.

25 Then there arose a question between *some* of John's disciples and the Jews about purifying.

26 And they came unto John, and said unto him, Rabbi, he that was with thee beyond Jordan, to whom thou barest witness, behold, the same baptizeth, and all *men* come to him.

27 John answered and said, A man can receive nothing, except it be given him from heaven.

28 Ye yourselves bear me witness, that I said, I am not the Christ, but that I am sent before him.

29 He that hath the bride is the bridegroom: but the friend of the bridegroom, which standeth and heareth him, rejoiceth greatly because of the bridegroom's voice: this my joy therefore is fulfilled.

30 He must increase, but I *must* decrease.

31 He that cometh from above is above all: he that is of the

earth is earthly, and speaketh of the earth: he that cometh from heaven is above all.

32 And what he hath seen and heard, that he testifieth; and no man receiveth his testimony.

33 He that hath received his testimony hath set to his seal that God is true.

34 For he whom God hath sent speaketh the words of God: for God giveth not the Spirit by measure *unto him*.

35 The Father loveth the Son, and hath given all things into his hand.

36 He that believeth on the Son hath everlasting life: and he that believeth not the Son shall not see life; but the wrath of God abideth on him.

CHAPTER 4

When therefore the LORD knew how the Pharisees had heard that Jesus made and baptized more disciples than John,

2 (Though Jesus himself baptized not, but his disciples,)

3 He left Judaea, and departed again into Galilee.

4 And he must needs go through Samaria.

5 Then cometh he to a city of Samaria, which is called Sychar, near to the parcel of ground that Jacob gave to his son Joseph.

6 Now Jacob's well was there. Jesus therefore, being wearied with *his* journey, sat thus on the well: *and* it was about the sixth hour.

7 There cometh a woman of Samaria to draw water: Jesus saith unto her, Give me to drink.

8 (For his disciples were gone away unto the city to buy meat.)

9 Then saith the woman of Samaria unto him, How is it that

thou, being a Jew, askest drink of me, which am a woman of Samaria? for the Jews have no dealings with the Samaritans.

10 Jesus answered and said unto her, If thou knewest the gift of God, and who it is that saith to thee, Give me to drink; thou wouldest have asked of him, and he would have given thee living water.

11 The woman saith unto him, Sir, thou hast nothing to draw with, and the well is deep: from whence then hast thou that living water?

12 Art thou greater than our father Jacob, which gave us the well, and drank thereof himself, and his children, and his cattle?

13 Jesus answered and said unto her, Whosoever drinketh of this water shall thirst again:

14 But whosoever drinketh of the water that I shall give him shall never thirst; but the water that I shall give him shall be in him a well of water springing up into everlasting life.

15 The woman saith unto him, Sir, give me this water, that I thirst not, neither come hither to draw.

16 Jesus saith unto her, Go, call thy husband, and come hither.

17 The woman answered and said, I have no husband. Jesus said unto her, Thou hast well said, I have no husband:

18 For thou hast had five husbands; and he whom thou now hast is not thy husband: in that saidst thou truly.

19 The woman saith unto him, Sir, I perceive that thou art a prophet.

20 Our fathers worshipped in this mountain; and ye say, that in Jerusalem is the place where men ought to worship.

21 Jesus saith unto her, Woman, believe me, the hour cometh, when ye shall neither in this mountain, nor yet at Jerusalem, worship the Father.

22 Ye worship ye know not what: we know what we worship: for salvation is of the Jews.

23 But the hour cometh, and now is, when the true worshippers shall worship the Father in spirit and in truth: for the Father seeketh such to worship him.

24 God *is* a Spirit: and they that worship him must worship *him* in spirit and in truth.

25 The woman saith unto him, I know that Messias cometh, which is called Christ: when he is come, he will tell us all things.

26 Jesus saith unto her, I that speak unto thee am *he*.

27 And upon this came his disciples, and marvelled that he talked with the woman: yet no man said, What seekest thou? or, Why talkest thou with her?

28 The woman then left her waterpot, and went her way into the city, and saith to the men,

29 Come, see a man, which told me all things that ever I did: is not this the Christ?

30 Then they went out of the city, and came unto him.

31 In the mean while his disciples prayed him, saying, Master, eat.

32 But he said unto them, I have meat to eat that ye know not of.

33 Therefore said the disciples one to another, Hath any man brought him *aught* to eat?

34 Jesus saith unto them, My meat is to do the will of him that sent me, and to finish his work.

35 Say not ye, There are yet four months, and *then* cometh harvest? behold, I say unto you, Lift up your eyes, and look on the fields; for they are white already to harvest.

36 And he that reapeth receiveth wages, and gathereth fruit unto life eternal: that both he that soweth and he that reapeth may rejoice together.

37 And herein is that saying true, One soweth, and another reapeth.

38 I sent you to reap that whereon ye bestowed no labour: other men laboured, and ye are entered into their labours.

39 And many of the Samaritans of that city believed on him for the saying of the woman, which testified, He told me all that ever I did.

40 So when the Samaritans were come unto him, they besought him that he would tarry with them: and he abode there two days.

41 And many more believed because of his own word;

42 And said unto the woman, Now we believe, not because of thy saying: for we have heard *him* ourselves, and know that this is indeed the Christ, the Saviour of the world.

43 Now after two days he departed thence, and went into Galilee.

44 For Jesus himself testified, that a prophet hath no honour in his own country.

45 Then when he was come into Galilee, the Galilaeans received him, having seen all the things that he did at Jerusalem at the feast: for they also went unto the feast.

46 So Jesus came again into Cana of Galilee, where he made the water wine. And there was a certain nobleman, whose son was sick at Capernaum.

47 When he heard that Jesus was come out of Judaea into Galilee, he went unto him, and besought him that he would come down, and heal his son: for he was at the point of death.

48 Then said Jesus unto him, Except ye see signs and wonders, ye will not believe.

49 The nobleman saith unto him, Sir, come down ere my child die.

50 Jesus saith unto him, Go thy way; thy son liveth. And the man believed the word that Jesus had spoken unto him, and he went his way.

51 And as he was now going down, his servants met him, and told *him*, saying, Thy son liveth.

52 Then enquired he of them the hour when he began to amend. And they said unto him, Yesterday at the seventh hour the fever left him.

53 So the father knew that *it was* at the same hour, in which Jesus said unto him, Thy son liveth: and himself believed, and his whole house.

54 This *is* again the second miracle *that* Jesus did, when he was come out of Judaea into Galilee.

CHAPTER 5

After this there was a feast of the Jews; and Jesus went up to Jerusalem.

2 Now there is at Jerusalem by the sheep *market* a pool, which is called in the Hebrew tongue Bethesda, having five porches.

3 In these lay a great multitude of impotent folk, of blind, halt, withered, waiting for the moving of the water.

4 For an angel went down at a certain season into the pool, and troubled the water: whosoever then first after the troubling of the water stepped in was made whole of whatsoever disease he had.

5 And a certain man was there, which had an infirmity thirty and eight years.

6 When Jesus saw him lie, and knew that he had been now a long time *in that case*, he saith unto him, Wilt thou be made whole?

7 The impotent man answered him, Sir, I have no man, when the water is troubled, to put me into the pool: but while I am coming, another steppeth down before me.

8 Jesus saith unto him, Rise, take up thy bed, and walk.

9 And immediately the man was made whole, and took up his bed, and walked: and on the same day was the sabbath.

10 The Jews therefore said unto him that was cured, It is the sabbath day: it is not lawful for thee to carry *thy* bed.

11 He answered them, He that made me whole, the same said unto me, Take up thy bed, and walk.

12 Then asked they him, What man is that which said unto thee, Take up thy bed, and walk?

13 And he that was healed wist not who it was: for Jesus had conveyed himself away, a multitude being in *that* place.

14 Afterward Jesus findeth him in the temple, and said unto him, Behold, thou art made whole: sin no more, lest a worse thing come unto thee.

15 The man departed, and told the Jews that it was Jesus, which had made him whole.

16 And therefore did the Jews persecute Jesus, and sought to

slay him, because he had done these things on the sabbath day.

17 But Jesus answered them, My Father worketh hitherto, and I work.

18 Therefore the Jews sought the more to kill him, because he not only had broken the sabbath, but said also that God was his Father, making himself equal with God.

19 Then answered Jesus and said unto them, Verily, verily, I say unto you, The Son can do nothing of himself, but what he seeth the Father do: for what things soever he doeth, these also doeth the Son likewise.

20 For the Father loveth the Son, and showeth him all things that himself doeth: and he will show him greater works than these, that ye may marvel.

21 For as the Father raiseth up the dead, and quickeneth *them*; even so the Son quickeneth whom he will.

22 For the Father judgeth no man, but hath committed all judgment unto the Son:

23 That all *men* should honour the Son, even as they honour the Father. He that honoureth not the Son honoureth not the Father which hath sent him.

24 Verily, verily, I say unto you, He that heareth my word, and believeth on him that sent me, hath everlasting life, and shall not come into condemnation; but is passed from death unto life.

25 Verily, verily, I say unto you, The hour is coming, and now is, when the dead shall hear the voice of the Son of God: and they that hear shall live.

26 For as the Father hath life in himself; so hath he given to the Son to have life in himself;

27 And hath given him authority to execute judgment also, because he is the Son of man.

28 Marvel not at this: for the hour is coming, in the which all that are in the graves shall hear his voice,

29 And shall come forth; they that have done good, unto the resurrection of life; and they that have done evil, unto the resurrection of damnation.

30 I can of mine own self do nothing: as I hear, I judge: and my judgment is just; because I seek not mine own will, but the will of the Father which hath sent me.

31 If I bear witness of myself, my witness is not true.

32 There is another that beareth witness of me; and I know that the witness which he witnesseth of me is true.

33 Ye sent unto John, and he bare witness unto the truth.

34 But I receive not testimony from man: but these things I say, that ye might be saved.

35 He was a burning and a shining light: and ye were willing for a season to rejoice in his light.

36 But I have greater witness than *that* of John: for the works which the Father hath given me to finish, the same works that I do, bear witness of me, that the Father hath sent me.

37 And the Father himself, which hath sent me, hath borne witness of me. Ye have neither heard his voice at any time, nor seen his shape.

38 And ye have not his word abiding in you: for whom he hath sent, him ye believe not.

39 Search the scriptures; for in them ye think ye have eternal life: and they are they which testify of me.

40 And ye will not come to me, that ye might have life.

41 I receive not honour from men.

42 But I know you, that ye have not the love of God in you.

43 I am come in my Father's name, and ye receive me not: if another shall come in his own name, him ye will receive.

44 How can ye believe, which receive honour one of another, and seek not the honour that *cometh* from God only?

45 Do not think that I will accuse you to the Father: there is *one* that accuseth you, *even* Moses, in whom ye trust.

46 For had ye believed Moses, ye would have believed me; for he wrote of me.

47 But if ye believe not his writings, how shall ye believe my words?

CHAPTER 6

After these things Jesus went over the sea of Galilee, which is *the sea* of Tiberias.

2 And a great multitude followed him, because they saw his miracles which he did on them that were diseased.

3 And Jesus went up into a mountain, and there he sat with his disciples.

4 And the passover, a feast of the Jews, was nigh.

5 When Jesus then lifted up *his* eyes, and saw a great company come unto him, he saith unto Philip, Whence shall we buy bread, that these may eat?

6 And this he said to prove him: for he himself knew what he would do.

7 Philip answered him, Two hundred pennyworth of bread is not sufficient for them, that every one of them may take a little.

8 One of his disciples, Andrew, Simon Peter's brother, saith unto him,

9 There is a lad here, which hath five barley loaves, and two small fishes: but what are they among so many?

10 And Jesus said, Make the men sit down. Now there was much grass in the place. So the men sat down, in number about five thousand.

11 And Jesus took the loaves; and when he had given thanks, he distributed to the disciples, and the disciples to them that were set down; and likewise of the fishes as much as they would.

12 When they were filled, he said unto his disciples, Gather up the fragments that remain, that nothing be lost.

13 Therefore they gathered *them* together, and filled twelve baskets with the fragments of the five barley loaves, which remained over and above unto them that had eaten.

14 Then those men, when they had seen the miracle that Jesus did, said, This is of a truth that prophet that should come into the world.

15 When Jesus therefore perceived that they would come and take him by force, to make him a king, he departed again into a mountain himself alone.

16 And when even was *now* come, his disciples went down unto the sea,

17 And entered into a ship, and went over the sea toward Capernaum. And it was now dark, and Jesus was not come to them.

18 And the sea arose by reason of a great wind that blew.

19 So when they had rowed about five and twenty or thirty furlongs, they see Jesus walking on the sea, and drawing

nigh unto the ship: and they were afraid.

20 But he saith unto them, It is I; be not afraid.

21 Then they willingly received him into the ship: and immediately the ship was at the land whither they went.

22 The day following, when the people which stood on the other side of the sea saw that there was none other boat there, save that one whereinto his disciples were entered, and that Jesus went not with his disciples into the boat, but *that* his disciples were gone away alone;

23 (Howbeit there came other boats from Tiberias nigh unto the place where they did eat bread, after that the LORD had given thanks:)

24 When the people therefore saw that Jesus was not there, neither his disciples, they also took shipping, and came to Capernaum, seeking for Jesus.

25 And when they had found him on the other side of the sea, they said unto him, Rabbi, when camest thou hither?

26 Jesus answered them and said, Verily, verily, I say unto you, Ye seek me, not because ye saw the miracles, but because ye did eat of the loaves, and were filled.

27 Labour not for the meat which perisheth, but for that meat which endureth unto everlasting life, which the Son of man shall give unto you: for him hath God the Father sealed.

28 Then said they unto him, What shall we do, that we might work the works of God?

29 Jesus answered and said unto them, This is the work of God, that ye believe on him whom he hath sent.

30 They said therefore unto him, What sign showest thou then, that we may see, and believe thee? what dost thou work?

31 Our fathers did eat manna in the desert; as it is written, He gave them bread from heaven to eat.

32 Then Jesus said unto them, Verily, verily, I say unto you, Moses gave you not that bread from heaven; but my Father giveth you the true bread from heaven.

33 For the bread of God is he which cometh down from heaven, and giveth life unto the world.

34 Then said they unto him, Lord, evermore give us this bread.

35 And Jesus said unto them, I am the bread of life: he that cometh to me shall never hunger; and he that believeth on me shall never thirst.

36 But I said unto you, That ye also have seen me, and believe not.

37 All that the Father giveth me shall come to me; and him that cometh to me I will in no wise cast out.

38 For I came down from heaven, not to do mine own will, but the will of him that sent me.

39 And this is the Father's will which hath sent me, that of all which he hath given me I should lose nothing, but should raise it up again at the last day.

40 And this is the will of him that sent me, that every one which seeth the Son, and believeth on him, may have everlasting life: and I will raise him up at the last day.

41 The Jews then murmured at him, because he said, I am the bread which came down from heaven.

42 And they said, Is not this Jesus, the son of Joseph, whose father and mother we know? how is it then that he saith, I came down from heaven?

43 Jesus therefore answered and said unto them, Murmur not among yourselves.

44 No man can come to me, except the Father which hath sent me draw him: and I will raise him up at the last day.

45 It is written in the prophets, And they shall be all taught of God. Every man therefore that hath heard, and hath learned of the Father, cometh unto me.

46 Not that any man hath seen the Father, save he which is of God, he hath seen the Father.

47 Verily, verily, I say unto you, He that believeth on me hath everlasting life.

48 I am that bread of life.

49 Your fathers did eat manna in the wilderness, and are dead.

50 This is the bread which cometh down from heaven, that a man may eat thereof, and not die.

51 I am the living bread which came down from heaven: if any man eat of this bread, he shall live for ever: and the bread that I will give is my flesh, which I will give for the life of the world.

52 The Jews therefore strove among themselves, saying, How can this man give us *his* flesh to eat?

53 Then Jesus said unto them, Verily, verily, I say unto you, Except ye eat the flesh of the Son of man, and drink his blood, ye have no life in you.

54 Whoso eateth my flesh, and drinketh my blood, hath eternal life; and I will raise him up at the last day.

55 For my flesh is meat indeed, and my blood is drink indeed.

56 He that eateth my flesh, and drinketh my blood, dwelleth in me, and I in him.

57 As the living Father hath sent me, and I live by the

Father: so he that eateth me, even he shall live by me.

58 This is that bread which came down from heaven: not as your fathers did eat manna, and are dead: he that eateth of this bread shall live for ever.

59 These things said he in the synagogue, as he taught in Capernaum.

60 Many therefore of his disciples, when they had heard *this*, said, This is an hard saying; who can hear it?

61 When Jesus knew in himself that his disciples murmured at it, he said unto them, Doth this offend you?

62 *What* and if ye shall see the Son of man ascend up where he was before?

63 It is the spirit that quickeneth; the flesh profiteth nothing: the words that I speak unto you, *they* are spirit, and *they* are life.

64 But there are some of you that believe not. For Jesus knew from the beginning who they were that believed not, and who should betray him.

65 And he said, Therefore said I unto you, that no man can come unto me, except it were given unto him of my Father.

66 From that *time* many of his disciples went back, and walked no more with him.

67 Then said Jesus unto the twelve, Will ye also go away?

68 Then Simon Peter answered him, Lord, to whom shall we go? thou hast the words of eternal life.

69 And we believe and are sure that thou art that Christ, the Son of the living God.

70 Jesus answered them, Have not I chosen you twelve, and one of you is a devil?

71 He spake of Judas Iscariot *the son* of Simon: for he it was that should betray him, being one of the twelve.

CHAPTER 7

After these things Jesus walked in Galilee: for he would not walk in Jewry, because the Jews sought to kill him.

2 Now the Jew's feast of tabernacles was at hand.

3 His brethren therefore said unto him, Depart hence, and go into Judaea, that thy disciples also may see the works that thou doest.

4 For *there is* no man *that* doeth any thing in secret, and he himself seeketh to be known openly. If thou do these things, show thyself to the world.

5 For neither did his brethren believe in him.

6 Then Jesus said unto them, My time is not yet come: but your time is always ready.

7 The world cannot hate you; but me it hateth, because I testify of it, that the works thereof are evil.

8 Go ye up unto this feast: I go not up yet unto this feast: for my time is not yet full come.

9 When he had said these words unto them, he abode *still* in Galilee.

10 But when his brethren were gone up, then went he also up unto the feast, not openly, but as it were in secret.

11 Then the Jews sought him at the feast, and said, Where is he?

12 And there was much murmuring among the people concerning him: for some said, He is a good man: others said, Nay; but he deceiveth the people.

13 Howbeit no man spake openly of him for fear of the Jews.

14 Now about the midst of the feast Jesus went up into the temple, and taught.

15 And the Jews marvelled, saying, How knoweth this man letters, having never learned?

16 Jesus answered them, and said, My doctrine is not mine, but his that sent me.

17 If any man will do his will, he shall know of the doctrine, whether it be of God, or *whether* I speak of myself.

18 He that speaketh of himself seeketh his own glory: but he that seeketh his glory that sent him, the same is true, and no unrighteousness is in him.

19 Did not Moses give you the law, and *yet* none of you keepeth the law? Why go ye about to kill me?

20 The people answered and said, Thou hast a devil: who goeth about to kill thee?

21 Jesus answered and said unto them, I have done one work, and ye all marvel.

22 Moses therefore gave unto you circumcision; (not because it is of Moses, but of the fathers;) and ye on the sabbath day circumcise a man.

23 If a man on the sabbath day receive circumcision, that the law of Moses should not be broken; are ye angry at me, because I have made a man every whit whole on the sabbath day?

24 Judge not according to the appearance, but judge righteous judgment.

25 Then said some of them of Jerusalem, Is not this he, whom they seek to kill?

26 But, lo, he speaketh boldly, and they say nothing unto him. Do the rulers know indeed that this is the very Christ?

27 Howbeit we know this man whence he is: but when Christ cometh, no man knoweth whence he is.

28 Then cried Jesus in the temple as he taught, saying, Ye both know me, and ye know whence I am: and I am not come of myself, but he that sent me is true, whom ye know not.

29 But I know him: for I am from him, and he hath sent me.

30 Then they sought to take him: but no man laid hands on him, because his hour was not yet come.

31 And many of the people believed on him, and said, When Christ cometh, will he do more miracles than these which this *man* hath done?

32 The Pharisees heard that the people murmured such things concerning him; and the Pharisees and the chief priests sent officers to take him.

33 Then said Jesus unto them, Yet a little while am I with you, and *then* I go unto him that sent me.

34 Ye shall seek me, and shall not find me: and where I am, *thither* ye cannot come.

35 Then said the Jews among themselves, Whither will he go, that we shall not find him? will he go unto the dispersed among the Gentiles, and teach the Gentiles?

36 What *manner of* saying is this that he said, Ye shall seek me, and shall not find *me*: and where I am, *thither* ye cannot come?

37 In the last day, that great *day* of the feast, Jesus stood and cried, saying, If any man thirst, let him come unto me, and drink.

38 He that believeth on me, as the scripture hath said, out of his belly shall flow rivers of living water.

39 (But this spake he of the Spirit, which they that believe on him should receive: for the Holy Ghost was not yet *given*; because that Jesus was not yet glorified.)

40 Many of the people therefore, when they heard this saying, said, Of a truth this is the Prophet.

41 Others said, This is the Christ. But some said, Shall Christ come out of Galilee?

42 Hath not the scripture said, That Christ cometh of the seed of David, and out of the town of Bethlehem, where David was?

43 So there was a division among the people because of him.

44 And some of them would have taken him; but no man laid hands on him.

45 Then came the officers to the chief priests and Pharisees; and they said unto them, Why have ye not brought him?

46 The officers answered, Never man spake like this man.

47 Then answered them the Pharisees, Are ye also deceived?

48 Have any of the rulers or of the Pharisees believed on him?

49 But this people who knoweth not the law are cursed.

50 Nicodemus saith unto them, (he that came to Jesus by night, being one of them,)

51 Doth our law judge *any* man, before it hear him, and know what he doeth?

52 They answered and said unto him, Art thou also of Galilee? Search, and look: for out of Galilee ariseth no prophet.

53 And every man went unto his own house.

CHAPTER 8

Jesus went unto the mount of Olives.

2 And early in the morning he came again into the temple,

and all the people came unto him; and he sat down, and taught them.

3 And the scribes and Pharisees brought unto him a woman taken in adultery; and when they had set her in the midst,

4 They say unto him, Master, this woman was taken in adultery, in the very act.

5 Now Moses in the law commanded us, that such should be stoned: but what sayest thou?

6 This they said, tempting him, that they might have to accuse him. But Jesus stooped down, and with *his* finger wrote on the ground, *as though he heard them not.*

7 So when they continued asking him, he lifted up himself, and said unto them, He that is without sin among you, let him first cast a stone at her.

8 And again he stooped down, and wrote on the ground.

9 And they which heard *it*, being convicted by *their own* conscience, went out one by one, beginning at the eldest, *even* unto the last: and Jesus was left alone, and the woman standing in the midst.

10 When Jesus had lifted up himself, and saw none but the woman, he said unto her, Woman, where are those thine accusers? hath no man condemned thee?

11 She said, No man, Lord. And Jesus said unto her, Neither do I condemn thee: go, and sin no more.

12 Then spake Jesus again unto them, saying, I am the light of the world: he that followeth me shall not walk in darkness, but shall have the light of life.

13 The Pharisees therefore said unto him, Thou bearest record of thyself; thy record is not true.

14 Jesus answered and said unto them, Though I bear record

of myself, *yet* my record is true: for I know whence I came, and whither I go; but ye cannot tell whence I come, and whither I go.

15 Ye judge after the flesh; I judge no man.

16 And yet if I judge, my judgment is true: for I am not alone, but I and the Father that sent me.

17 It is also written in your law, that the testimony of two men is true.

18 I am one that bear witness of myself, and the Father that sent me beareth witness of me.

19 Then said they unto him, Where is thy Father? Jesus answered, Ye neither know me, nor my Father: if ye had known me, ye should have known my Father also.

20 These words spake Jesus in the treasury, as he taught in the temple: and no man laid hands on him; for his hour was not yet come.

21 Then said Jesus again unto them, I go my way, and ye shall seek me, and shall die in your sins: whither I go, ye cannot come.

22 Then said the Jews, Will he kill himself? because he saith, Whither I go, ye cannot come.

23 And he said unto them, Ye are from beneath; I am from above: ye are of this world; I am not of this world.

24 I said therefore unto you, that ye shall die in your sins: for if ye believe not that I am *he*, ye shall die in your sins.

25 Then said they unto him, Who art thou? And Jesus saith unto them, Even *the same* that I said unto you from the beginning.

26 I have many things to say and to judge of you: but he that sent me is true; and I speak to the world those things

which I have heard of him.

27 They understood not that he spake to them of the Father.

28 Then said Jesus unto them, When ye have lifted up the Son of man, then shall ye know that I am *he*, and *that* I do nothing of myself; but as my Father hath taught me, I speak these things.

29 And he that sent me is with me: the Father hath not left me alone; for I do always those things that please him.

30 As he spake these words, many believed on him.

31 Then said Jesus to those Jews which believed on him, If ye continue in my word, *then* are ye my disciples indeed;

32 And ye shall know the truth, and the truth shall make you free.

33 They answered him, We be Abraham's seed, and were never in bondage to any man: how sayest thou, Ye shall be made free?

34 Jesus answered them, Verily, verily, I say unto you, Whosoever committeth sin is the servant of sin.

35 And the servant abideth not in the house for ever: *but* the Son abideth ever.

36 If the Son therefore shall make you free, ye shall be free indeed.

37 I know that ye are Abraham's seed; but ye seek to kill me, because my word hath no place in you.

38 I speak that which I have seen with my Father: and ye do that which ye have seen with your father.

39 They answered and said unto him, Abraham is our father. Jesus saith unto them, If ye were Abraham's children, ye would do the works of Abraham.

40 But now ye seek to kill me, a man that hath told you the

truth, which I have heard of God: this did not Abraham.

41 Ye do the deeds of your father. Then said they to him, We be not born of fornication; we have one Father, *even* God.

42 Jesus said unto them, If God were your Father, ye would love me: for I proceeded forth and came from God; neither came I of myself, but he sent me.

43 Why do ye not understand my speech? *even* because ye cannot hear my word.

44 Ye are of *your* father the devil, and the lusts of your father ye will do. He was a murderer from the beginning, and abode not in the truth, because there is no truth in him. When he speaketh a lie, he speaketh of his own: for he is a liar, and the father of it.

45 And because I tell *you* the truth, ye believe me not.

46 Which of you convinceth me of sin? And if I say the truth, why do ye not believe me?

47 He that is of God heareth God's words: ye therefore hear *them* not, because ye are not of God.

48 Then answered the Jews, and said unto him, Say we not well that thou art a Samaritan, and hast a devil?

49 Jesus answered, I have not a devil; but I honour my Father, and ye do dishonour me.

50 And I seek not mine own glory: there is one that seeketh and judgeth.

51 Verily, verily, I say unto you, If a man keep my saying, he shall never see death.

52 Then said the Jews unto him, Now we know that thou hast a devil. Abraham is dead, and the prophets; and thou sayest, If a man keep my saying, he shall never taste of death.

53 Art thou greater than our father Abraham, which is dead?

and the prophets are dead: whom makest thou thyself?

54 Jesus answered, If I honour myself, my honour is nothing: it is my Father that honoureth me; of whom ye say, that he is your God:

55 Yet ye have not known him; but I know him: and if I should say, I know him not, I shall be a liar like unto you: but I know him, and keep his saying.

56 Your father Abraham rejoiced to see my day: and he saw it, and was glad.

57 Then said the Jews unto him, Thou art not yet fifty years old, and hast thou seen Abraham?

58 Jesus said unto them, Verily, verily, I say unto you, Before Abraham was, I am.

59 Then took they up stones to cast at him: but Jesus hid himself, and went out of the temple, going through the midst of them, and so passed by.

CHAPTER 9

And as *Jesus* passed by, he saw a man which was blind from his birth.

2 And his disciples asked him, saying, Master, who did sin, this man, or his parents, that he was born blind?

3 Jesus answered, Neither hath this man sinned, nor his parents: but that the works of God should be made manifest in him.

4 I must work the works of him that sent me, while it is day: the night cometh, when no man can work.

5 As long as I am in the world, I am the light of the world.

6 When he had thus spoken, he spat on the ground, and made clay of the spittle, and he anointed the eyes of the blind man with the clay,

7 And said unto him, Go, wash in the pool of Siloam, (which is by interpretation, Sent.) He went his way therefore, and washed, and came seeing.

8 The neighbours therefore, and they which before had seen him that he was blind, said, Is not this he that sat and begged?

9 Some said, This is he: others *said*, He is like him: *but* he said, I am *he*.

10 Therefore said they unto him, How were thine eyes opened?

11 He answered and said, A man that is called Jesus made clay, and anointed mine eyes, and said unto me, Go to the pool of Siloam, and wash: and I went and washed, and I received sight.

12 Then said they unto him, Where is he? He said, I know not.

13 They brought to the Pharisees him that aforetime was blind.

14 And it was the sabbath day when Jesus made the clay, and opened his eyes.

15 Then again the Pharisees also asked him how he had received his sight. He said unto them, He put clay upon mine eyes, and I washed, and do see.

16 Therefore said some of the Pharisees, This man is not of God, because he keepeth not the sabbath day. Others said, How can a man that is a sinner do such miracles? And there was a division among them.

17 They say unto the blind man again, What sayest thou of him, that he hath opened thine eyes? He said, He is a prophet.

18 But the Jews did not believe concerning him, that he had been blind, and received his sight, until they called the parents of him that had received his sight.

19 And they asked them, saying, Is this your son, who ye say was born blind? how then doth he now see?

20 His parents answered them and said, We know that this is our son, and that he was born blind:

21 But by what means he now seeth, we know not; or who hath opened his eyes, we know not: he is of age; ask him: he shall speak for himself.

22 These *words* spake his parents, because they feared the Jews: for the Jews had agreed already, that if any man did confess that he was Christ, he should be put out of the synagogue.

23 Therefore said his parents, He is of age; ask him.

24 Then again called they the man that was blind, and said unto him, Give God the praise: we know that this man is a sinner.

25 He answered and said, Whether he be a sinner *or no*, I know not: one thing I know, that, whereas I was blind, now I see.

26 Then said they to him again, What did he to thee? how opened he thine eyes?

27 He answered them, I have told you already, and ye did not hear: wherefore would ye hear *it* again? will ye also be his disciples?

28 Then they reviled him, and said, Thou art his disciple; but we are Moses' disciples.

29 We know that God spake unto Moses: *as for* this *fellow*, we know not from whence he is.

30 The man answered and said unto them, Why herein is a marvellous thing, that ye know not from whence he is, and *yet* he hath opened mine eyes.

31 Now we know that God heareth not sinners: but if any man be a worshipper of God, and doeth his will, him he heareth.

32 Since the world began was it not heard that any man opened the eyes of one that was born blind.

33 If this man were not of God, he could do nothing.

34 They answered and said unto him, Thou wast altogether born in sins, and dost thou teach us? And they cast him out.

35 Jesus heard that they had cast him out; and when he had found him, he said unto him, Dost thou believe on the Son of God?

36 He answered and said, Who is he, Lord, that I might believe on him?

37 And Jesus said unto him, Thou hast both seen him, and it is he that talketh with thee.

38 And he said, Lord, I believe. And he worshipped him.

39 And Jesus said, For judgment I am come into this world, that they which see not might see; and that they which see might be made blind.

40 And *some* of the Pharisees which were with him heard these words, and said unto him, Are we blind also?

41 Jesus said unto them, If ye were blind, ye should have no sin: but now ye say, We see; therefore your sin remaineth.

CHAPTER 10

Verily, verily, I say unto you, He that entereth not by the door into the sheepfold, but climbeth up some other way, the same is a thief and a robber.

2 But he that entereth in by the door is the shepherd of the sheep.

3 To him the porter openeth; and the sheep hear his voice: and he calleth his own sheep by name, and leadeth them out.

4 And when he putteth forth his own sheep, he goeth before them, and the sheep follow him: for they know his voice.

5 And a stranger will they not follow, but will flee from him: for they know not the voice of strangers.

6 This parable spake Jesus unto them: but they understood not what things they were which he spake unto them.

7 Then said Jesus unto them again, Verily, verily, I say unto you, I am the door of the sheep.

8 All that ever came before me are thieves and robbers: but the sheep did not hear them.

9 I am the door: by me if any man enter in, he shall be saved, and shall go in and out, and find pasture.

10 The thief cometh not, but for to steal, and to kill, and to destroy: I am come that they might have life, and that they might have it more abundantly.

11 I am the good shepherd: the good shepherd giveth his life for the sheep.

12 But he that is an hireling, and not the shepherd, whose own the sheep are not, seeth the wolf coming, and leaveth the sheep, and fleeth: and the wolf catcheth them, and scattereth the sheep.

13 The hireling fleeth, because he is an hireling, and careth not for the sheep.

14 I am the good shepherd, and know my *sheep*, and am known of mine.

15 As the Father knoweth me, even so know I the Father: and I lay down my life for the sheep.

16 And other sheep I have, which are not of this fold: them

also I must bring, and they shall hear my voice; and there shall be one fold, *and* one shepherd.

17 Therefore doth my Father love me, because I lay down my life, that I might take it again.

18 No man taketh it from me, but I lay it down of myself. I have power to lay it down, and I have power to take it again. This commandment have I received of my Father.

19 There was a division therefore again among the Jews for these sayings.

20 And many of them said, He hath a devil, and is mad; why hear ye him?

21 Others said, These are not the words of him that hath a devil. Can a devil open the eyes of the blind?

22 And it was at Jerusalem the feast of the dedication, and it was winter.

23 And Jesus walked in the temple in Solomon's porch.

24 Then came the Jews round about him, and said unto him, How long dost thou make us to doubt? If thou be the Christ, tell us plainly.

25 Jesus answered them, I told you, and ye believed not: the works that I do in my Father's name, they bear witness of me.

26 But ye believe not, because ye are not of my sheep, as I said unto you.

27 My sheep hear my voice, and I know them, and they follow me:

28 And I give unto them eternal life; and they shall never perish, neither shall any *man* pluck them out of my hand.

29 My Father, which gave *them* me, is greater than all; and no *man* is able to pluck *them* out of my Father's hand.

30 I and *my* Father are one.

31 Then the Jews took up stones again to stone him.

32 Jesus answered them, Many good works have I shown you from my Father; for which of those works do ye stone me?

33 The Jews answered him, saying, For a good work we stone thee not; but for blasphemy; and because that thou, being a man, makest thyself God.

34 Jesus answered them, Is it not written in your law, I said, Ye are gods?

35 If he called them gods, unto whom the word of God came, and the scripture cannot be broken;

36 Say ye of him, whom the Father hath sanctified, and sent into the world, Thou blasphemest; because I said, I am the Son of God?

37 If I do not the works of my Father, believe me not.

38 But if I do, though ye believe not me, believe the works: that ye may know, and believe, that the Father is in me, and I in him.

39 Therefore they sought again to take him: but he escaped out of their hand,

40 And went away again beyond Jordan into the place where John at first baptized; and there he abode.

41 And many resorted unto him, and said, John did no miracle: but all things that John spake of this man were true.

42 And many believed on him there.

CHAPTER 11

Now a certain *man* was sick, *named* Lazarus, of Bethany, the town of Mary and her sister Martha.

2 (It was *that* Mary which anointed the LORD with ointment,

and wiped his feet with her hair, whose brother Lazarus was sick.)

3 Therefore his sisters sent unto him, saying, Lord, behold, he whom thou lovest is sick.

4 When Jesus heard *that*, he said, This sickness is not unto death, but for the glory of God, that the Son of God might be glorified thereby.

5 Now Jesus loved Martha, and her sister, and Lazarus.

6 When he had heard therefore that he was sick, he abode two days still in the same place where he was.

7 Then after that saith he to *his* disciples, Let us go into Judaea again.

8 *His* disciples say unto him, Master, the Jews of late sought to stone thee; and goest thou thither again?

9 Jesus answered, Are there not twelve hours in the day? If any man walk in the day, he stumbleth not, because he seeth the light of this world.

10 But if a man walk in the night, he stumbleth, because there is no light in him.

11 These things said he: and after that he saith unto them, Our friend Lazarus sleepeth; but I go, that I may awake him out of sleep.

12 Then said his disciples, Lord, if he sleep, he shall do well.

13 Howbeit Jesus spake of his death: but they thought that he had spoken of taking of rest in sleep.

14 Then said Jesus unto them plainly, Lazarus is dead.

15 And I am glad for your sakes that I was not there, to the intent ye may believe; nevertheless let us go unto him.

16 Then said Thomas, which is called Didymus, unto his

fellow disciples, Let us also go, that we may die with him.

17 Then when Jesus came, he found that he had *lain* in the grave four days already.

18 Now Bethany was nigh unto Jerusalem, about fifteen fur-longs off:

19 And many of the Jews came to Martha and Mary, to com-fort them concerning their brother.

20 Then Martha, as soon as she heard that Jesus was coming, went and met him: but Mary sat *still* in the house.

21 Then said Martha unto Jesus, Lord, if thou hadst been here, my brother had not died.

22 But I know, that even now, whatsoever thou wilt ask of God, God will give *it* thee.

23 Jesus saith unto her, Thy brother shall rise again.

24 Martha saith unto him, I know that he shall rise again in the resurrection at the last day.

25 Jesus said unto her, I am the resurrection, and the life: he that believeth in me, though he were dead, yet shall he live:

26 And whosoever liveth and believeth in me shall never die. Believest thou this?

27 She saith unto him, Yea, Lord: I believe that thou art the Christ, the Son of God, which should come into the world.

28 And when she had so said, she went her way, and called Mary her sister secretly, saying, The Master is come, and calleth for thee.

29 As soon as she heard *that*, she arose quickly, and came unto him.

30 Now Jesus was not yet come into the town, but was in that place where Martha met him.

31 The Jews then which were with her in the house, and comforted her, when they saw Mary, that she rose up hastily and went out, followed her, saying, She goeth unto the grave to weep there.

32 Then when Mary was come where Jesus was, and saw him, she fell down at his feet, saying unto him, Lord, if thou hadst been here, my brother had not died.

33 When Jesus therefore saw her weeping, and the Jews also weeping which came with her, he groaned in the spirit, and was troubled.

34 And said, Where have ye laid him? They said unto him, Lord, come and see.

35 Jesus wept.

36 Then said the Jews, Behold how he loved him!

37 And some of them said, Could not this man, which opened the eyes of the blind, have caused that even this man should not have died?

38 Jesus therefore again groaning in himself cometh to the grave. It was a cave, and a stone lay upon it.

39 Jesus said, Take ye away the stone. Martha, the sister of him that was dead, saith unto him, Lord, by this time he stinketh: for he hath been *dead* four days.

40 Jesus saith unto her, Said I not unto thee, that, if thou wouldest believe, thou shouldest see the glory of God?

41 Then they took away the stone *from the place* where the dead was laid. And Jesus lifted up *his* eyes, and said, Father, I thank thee that thou hast heard me.

42 And I knew that thou hearest me always: but because of

the people which stand by I said *it*, that they may believe that thou hast sent me.

43 And when he thus had spoken, he cried with a loud voice, Lazarus, come forth.

44 And he that was dead came forth, bound hand and foot with graveclothes: and his face was bound about with a napkin. Jesus saith unto them, Loose him, and let him go.

45 Then many of the Jews which came to Mary, and had seen the things which Jesus did, believed on him.

46 But some of them went their ways to the Pharisees, and told them what things Jesus had done.

47 Then gathered the chief priests and the Pharisees a council, and said, What do we? for this man doeth many miracles.

48 If we let him thus alone, all *men* will believe on him: and the Romans shall come and take away both our place and nation.

49 And one of them, *named* Caiaphas, being the high priest that same year, said unto them, Ye know nothing at all,

50 Nor consider that it is expedient for us, that one man should die for the people, and that the whole nation perish not.

51 And this spake he not of himself: but being high priest that year, he prophesied that Jesus should die for that nation;

52 And not for that nation only, but that also he should gather together in one the children of God that were scattered abroad.

53 Then from that day forth they took counsel together for to put him to death.

54 Jesus therefore walked no more openly among the Jews; but went thence unto a country near to the wilderness, into a city called Ephraim, and there continued with his disciples.

55 And the Jews' passover was nigh at hand: and many went out of the country up to Jerusalem before the passover, to purify themselves.

56 Then sought they for Jesus, and spake among themselves, as they stood in the temple, What think ye, that he will not come to the feast?

57 Now both the chief priests and the Pharisees had given a commandment, that, if any man knew where he were, he should show it, that they might take him.

CHAPTER 12

Then Jesus six days before the passover came to Bethany, where Lazarus was, which had been dead, whom he raised from the dead.

2 There they made him a supper; and Martha served: but Lazarus was one of them that sat at the table with him.

3 Then took Mary a pound of ointment of spikenard, very costly, and anointed the feet of Jesus, and wiped his feet with her hair: and the house was filled with the odour of the ointment.

4 Then saith one of his disciples, Judas Iscariot, Simon's *son*, which should betray him,

5 Why was not this ointment sold for three hundred pence, and given to the poor?

6 This he said, not that he cared for the poor; but because he was a thief, and had the bag, and bare what was put therein.

7 Then said Jesus, Let her alone: against the day of my bury-
ing hath she kept this.

8 For the poor always ye have with you; but me ye have not
always.

9 Much people of the Jews therefore knew that he was
there: and they came not for Jesus' sake only, but that they
might see Lazarus also, whom he had raised from the
dead.

10 But the chief priests consulted that they might put
Lazarus also to death;

11 Because that by reason of him many of the Jews went
away, and believed on Jesus.

12 On the next day much people that were come to the feast,
when they heard that Jesus was coming to Jerusalem,

13 Took branches of palm trees, and went forth to meet him,
and cried, Hosanna: Blessed is the King of Israel that
cometh in the name of the Lord.

14 And Jesus, when he had found a young ass, sat thereon; as
it is written,

15 Fear not, daughter of Zion: behold, thy King cometh,
sitting on an ass's colt.

16 These things understood not his disciples at the first: but
when Jesus was glorified, then remembered they that
these things were written of him, and that they had done
these things unto him.

17 The people therefore that was with him when he called
Lazarus out of his grave, and raised him from the dead,
bare record.

18 For this cause the people also met him, for that they
heard that he had done this miracle.

19 The Pharisees therefore said among themselves, Perceive ye how ye prevail nothing? behold, the world is gone after him.

20 And there were certain Greeks among them that came up to worship at the feast:

21 The same came therefore to Philip, which was of Bethsaida of Galilee, and desired him, saying, Sir, we would see Jesus.

22 Philip cometh and telleth Andrew: and again Andrew and Philip tell Jesus.

23 And Jesus answered them, saying, The hour is come, that the Son of man should be glorified.

24 Verily, verily, I say unto you, Except a corn of wheat fall into the ground and die, it abideth alone: but if it die, it bringeth forth much fruit.

25 He that loveth his life shall lose it; and he that hateth his life in this world shall keep it unto life eternal.

26 If any man serve me, let him follow me; and where I am, there shall also my servant be: if any man serve me, him will my Father honour.

27 Now is my soul troubled; and what shall I say? Father, save me from this hour: but for this cause came I unto this hour.

28 Father, glorify thy name. Then came there a voice from heaven, *saying*, I have both glorified *it*, and will glorify *it* again.

29 The people therefore, that stood by, and heard *it*, said that it thundered: others said, An angel spake to him.

30 Jesus answered and said, This voice came not because of me, but for your sakes.

31 Now is the judgment of this world: now shall the prince of this world be cast out.

32 And I, if I be lifted up from the earth, will draw all *men* unto me.

33 This he said, signifying what death he should die.

34 The people answered him, We have heard out of the law that Christ abideth for ever: and how sayest thou, The Son of man must be lifted up? who is this Son of man?

35 Then Jesus said unto them, Yet a little while is the light with you. Walk while ye have the light, lest darkness come upon you: for he that walketh in darkness knoweth not whither he goeth.

36 While ye have light, believe in the light, that ye may be the children of light. These things spake Jesus, and departed, and did hide himself from them.

37 But though he had done so many miracles before them, yet they believed not on him:

38 That the saying of Esaias the prophet might be fulfilled, which he spake, Lord, who hath believed our report? and to whom hath the arm of the LORD been revealed?

39 Therefore they could not believe, because that Esaias said again,

40 He hath blinded their eyes, and hardened their heart; that they should not see with *their* eyes, nor understand with *their* heart, and be converted, and I should heal them.

41 These things said Esaias, when he saw his glory, and spake of him.

42 Nevertheless among the chief rulers also many believed on him; but because of the Pharisees they did not confess *him*, lest they should be put out of the synagogue:

43 For they loved the praise of men more than the praise of God.

44 Jesus cried and said, He that believeth on me, believeth not on me, but on him that sent me.

45 And he that seeth me seeth him that sent me.

46 I am come a light into the world, that whosoever believeth on me should not abide in darkness.

47 And if any man hear my words, and believe not, I judge him not: for I came not to judge the world, but to save the world.

48 He that rejecteth me, and receiveth not my words, hath one that judgeth him: the word that I have spoken, the same shall judge him in the last day.

49 For I have not spoken of myself; but the Father which sent me, he gave me a commandment, what I should say, and what I should speak.

50 And I know that his commandment is life everlasting: whatsoever I speak therefore, even as the Father said unto me, so I speak.

CHAPTER 13

Now before the feast of the passover, when Jesus knew that his hour was come that he should depart out of this world unto the Father, having loved his own which were in the world, he loved them unto the end.

2 And supper being ended, the devil having now put into the heart of Judas Iscariot, Simon's *son*, to betray him;

3 Jesus knowing that the Father had given all things into his hands, and that he was come from God, and went to God;

4 He riseth from supper, and laid aside his garments; and

took a towel, and girded himself.

5 After that he poureth water into a basin, and began to wash the disciples' feet, and to wipe *them* with the towel wherewith he was girded.

6 Then cometh he to Simon Peter: and Peter saith unto him, Lord, dost thou wash my feet?

7 Jesus answered and said unto him, What I do thou knowest not now; but thou shalt know hereafter.

8 Peter saith unto him, Thou shalt never wash my feet. Jesus answered him, If I wash thee not, thou hast no part with me.

9 Simon Peter saith unto him, Lord, not my feet only, but also *my* hands and *my* head.

10 Jesus saith to him, He that is washed needeth not save to wash *his* feet, but is clean every whit: and ye are clean, but not all.

11 For he knew who should betray him; therefore said he, Ye are not all clean.

12 So after he had washed their feet, and had taken his garments, and was set down again, he said unto them, Know ye what I have done to you?

13 Ye call me Master and Lord: and ye say well; for *so* I am.

14 If I then, *your* LORD and Master, have washed your feet; ye also ought to wash one another's feet.

15 For I have given you an example, that ye should do as I have done to you.

16 Verily, verily, I say unto you, The servant is not greater than his lord; neither he that is sent greater than he that sent him.

17 If ye know these things, happy are ye if ye do them.

18 I speak not of you all: I know whom I have chosen: but

that the scripture may be fulfilled, He that eateth bread with me hath lifted up his heel against me.

19 Now I tell you before it come, that, when it is come to pass, ye may believe that I am *he*.

20 Verily, verily, I say unto you, He that receiveth whomsoever I send receiveth me; and he that receiveth me receiveth him that sent me.

21 When Jesus had thus said, he was troubled in spirit, and testified, and said, Verily, verily, I say unto you, that one of you shall betray me.

22 Then the disciples looked one on another, doubting of whom he spake.

23 Now there was leaning on Jesus' bosom one of his disciples, whom Jesus loved.

24 Simon Peter therefore beckoned to him, that he should ask who it should be of whom he spake.

25 He then lying on Jesus' breast saith unto him, Lord, who is it?

26 Jesus answered, He it is, to whom I shall give a sop, when I have dipped *it*. And when he had dipped the sop, he gave *it* to Judas Iscariot, *the son* of Simon.

27 And after the sop Satan entered into him. Then said Jesus unto him, That thou doest, do quickly.

28 Now no man at the table knew for what intent he spake this unto him.

29 For some *of them* thought, because Judas had the bag, that Jesus had said unto him, Buy *those things* that we have need of against the feast; or, that he should give something to the poor.

30 He then having received the sop went immediately out: and it was night.

31 Therefore, when he was gone out, Jesus said, Now is the Son of man glorified, and God is glorified in him.

32 If God be glorified in him, God shall also glorify him in himself, and shall straightway glorify him.

33 Little children, yet a little while I am with you. Ye shall seek me: and as I said unto the Jews, Whither I go, ye cannot come; so now I say to you.

34 A new commandment I give unto you, That ye love one another; as I have loved you, that ye also love one another.

35 By this shall all *men* know that ye are my disciples, if ye have love one to another.

36 Simon Peter said unto him, Lord, whither goest thou? Jesus answered him, Whither I go, thou canst not follow me now; but thou shalt follow me afterwards.

37 Peter said unto him, Lord, why cannot I follow thee now? I will lay down my life for thy sake.

38 Jesus answered him, Wilt thou lay down thy life for my sake? Verily, verily, I say unto thee, The cock shall not crow, till thou hast denied me thrice.

CHAPTER 14

Let not your heart be troubled: ye believe in God, believe also in me.

2 In my Father's house are many mansions: if *it were* not *so*, I would have told you. I go to prepare a place for you.

3 And if I go and prepare a place for you, I will come again, and receive you unto myself; that where I am, *there* ye may be also.

4 And whither I go ye know, and the way ye know.

5 Thomas saith unto him, Lord, we know not whither thou goest; and how can we know the way?

6 Jesus saith unto him, I am the way, the truth, and the life: no man cometh unto the Father, but by me.

7 If ye had known me, ye should have known my Father also: and from henceforth ye know him, and have seen him.

8 Philip saith unto him, Lord, show us the Father, and it sufficeth us.

9 Jesus saith unto him, Have I been so long time with you, and yet hast thou not known me, Philip? he that hath seen me hath seen the Father; and how sayest thou *then*, Show us the Father?

10 Believest thou not that I am in the Father, and the Father in me? the words that I speak unto you I speak not of myself: but the Father that dwelleth in me, he doeth the works.

11 Believe me that I *am* in the Father, and the Father in me: or else believe me for the very works' sake.

12 Verily, verily, I say unto you, He that believeth on me, the works that I do shall he do also; and greater *works* than these shall he do; because I go unto my Father.

13 And whatsoever ye shall ask in my name, that will I do, that the Father may be glorified in the Son.

14 If ye shall ask any thing in my name, I will do *it*.

15 If ye love me, keep my commandments.

16 And I will pray the Father, and he shall give you another Comforter, that he may abide with you for ever;

17 *Even* the Spirit of truth; whom the world cannot receive, because it seeth him not, neither knoweth him: but ye know him; for he dwelleth with you, and shall be in you.

18 I will not leave you comfortless: I will come to you.

19 Yet a little while, and the world seeth me no more; but

ye see me: because I live, ye shall live also.

20 At that day ye shall know that I *am* in my Father, and ye in me, and I in you.

21 He that hath my commandments, and keepeth them, he it is that loveth me: and he that loveth me shall be loved of my Father, and I will love him, and will manifest myself to him.

22 Judas saith unto him, not Iscariot, Lord, how is it that thou wilt manifest thyself unto us, and not unto the world?

23 Jesus answered and said unto him, If a man love me, he will keep my words: and my Father will love him, and we will come unto him, and make our abode with him.

24 He that loveth me not keepeth not my sayings: and the word which ye hear is not mine, but the Father's which sent me.

25 These things have I spoken unto you, being yet present with you.

26 But the Comforter, *which is* the Holy Ghost, whom the Father will send in my name, he shall teach you all things, and bring all things to your remembrance, whatsoever I have said unto you.

27 Peace I leave with you, my peace I give unto you: not as the world giveth, give I unto you. Let not your heart be troubled, neither let it be afraid.

28 Ye have heard how I said unto you, I go away, and come *again* unto you. If ye loved me, ye would rejoice, because I said, I go unto the Father: for my Father is greater than I.

29 And now I have told you before it come to pass, that, when it is come to pass, ye might believe.

30 Hereafter I will not talk much with you: for the prince of

this world cometh, and hath nothing in me.

31 But that the world may know that I love the Father; and as the Father gave me commandment, even so I do. Arise, let us go hence.

CHAPTER 15

I am the true vine, and my Father is the husbandman.

2 Every branch in me that beareth not fruit he taketh away: and every *branch* that beareth fruit, he purgeth it, that it may bring forth more fruit.

3 Now ye are clean through the word which I have spoken unto you.

4 Abide in me, and I in you. As the branch cannot bear fruit of itself, except it abide in the vine; no more can ye, except ye abide in me.

5 I am the vine, ye *are* the branches: He that abideth in me, and I in him, the same bringeth forth much fruit: for without me ye can do nothing.

6 If a man abide not in me, he is cast forth as a branch, and is withered; and men gather them, and cast *them* into the fire, and they are burned.

7 If ye abide in me, and my words abide in you, ye shall ask what ye will, and it shall be done unto you.

8 Herein is my Father glorified, that ye bear much fruit; so shall ye be my disciples.

9 As the Father hath loved me, so have I loved you: continue ye in my love.

10 If ye keep my commandments, ye shall abide in my love; even as I have kept my Father's commandments, and abide in his love.

11 These things have I spoken unto you, that my joy might remain in you, and *that* your joy might be full.

12 This is my commandment, That ye love one another, as I have loved you.

13 Greater love hath no man than this, that a man lay down his life for his friends.

14 Ye are my friends, if ye do whatsoever I command you.

15 Henceforth I call you not servants; for the servant knoweth not what his LORD doeth: but I have called you friends; for all things that I have heard of my Father I have made known unto you.

16 Ye have not chosen me, but I have chosen you, and ordained you, that ye should go and bring forth fruit, and *that* your fruit should remain: that whatsoever ye shall ask of the Father in my name, he may give it you.

17 These things I command you, that ye love one another.

18 If the world hate you, ye know that it hated me before it *hated* you.

19 If ye were of the world, the world would love his own: but because ye are not of the world, but I have chosen you out of the world, therefore the world hateth you.

20 Remember the word that I said unto you, The servant is not greater than his lord. If they have persecuted me, they will also persecute you; if they have kept my saying, they will keep yours also.

21 But all these things will they do unto you for my name's sake, because they know not him that sent me.

22 If I had not come and spoken unto them, they had not had sin: but now they have no cloak for their sin.

23 He that hateth me hateth my Father also.

24 If I had not done among them the works which none other man did, they had not had sin: but now have they both seen and hated both me and my Father.

25 But *this cometh to pass*, that the word might be fulfilled that is written in their law, They hated me without a cause.

26 But when the Comforter is come, whom I will send unto you from the Father, *even* the Spirit of truth, which pro-ceedeth from the Father, he shall testify of me:

27 And ye also shall bear witness, because ye have been with me from the beginning.

CHAPTER 16

These things have I spoken unto you, that ye should not be offended.

2 They shall put you out of the synagogues: yea, the time cometh, that whosoever killeth you will think that he doeth God service.

3 And these things will they do unto you, because they have not known the Father, nor me.

4 But these things have I told you, that when the time shall come, ye may remember that I told you of them. And these things I said not unto you at the beginning, because I was with you.

5 But now I go my way to him that sent me; and none of you asketh me, Whither goest thou?

6 But because I have said these things unto you, sorrow hath filled your heart.

7 Nevertheless I tell you the truth; It is expedient for you that I go away: for if I go not away, the Comforter will not come unto you; but if I depart, I will send him unto you.

8 And when he is come, he will reprove the world of sin, and of righteousness, and of judgment:

9 Of sin, because they believe not on me;

10 Of righteousness, because I go to my Father, and ye see me no more;

11 Of judgment, because the prince of this world is judged.

12 I have yet many things to say unto you, but ye cannot bear them now.

13 Howbeit when he, the Spirit of truth, is come, he will guide you into all truth: for he shall not speak of himself; but whatsoever he shall hear, *that* shall he speak: and he will show you things to come.

14 He shall glorify me: for he shall receive of mine, and shall show *it* unto you.

15 All things that the Father hath are mine: therefore said I, that he shall take of mine, and shall show it unto you.

16 A little while, and ye shall not see me: and again, a little while, and ye shall see me, because I go to the Father.

17 Then said *some* of his disciples among themselves, What is this that he saith unto us, A little while, and ye shall not see me: and again, a little while, and ye shall see me: and, Because I go to the Father?

18 They said therefore, What is this that he saith, A little while? we cannot tell what he saith.

19 Now Jesus knew that they were desirous to ask him, and said unto them, Do ye inquire among yourselves of that I said, A little while, and ye shall not see me: and again, a little while, and ye shall see me?

20 Verily, verily, I say unto you, That ye shall weep and lament, but the world shall rejoice: and ye shall be sor-

rowful, but your sorrow shall be turned into joy.

21 A woman when she is in travail hath sorrow, because her hour is come: but as soon as she is delivered of the child, she remembereth no more the anguish, for joy that a man is born into the world.

22 And ye now therefore have sorrow: but I will see you again, and your heart shall rejoice, and your joy no man taketh from you.

23 And in that day ye shall ask me nothing. Verily, verily, I say unto you, Whatsoever ye shall ask the Father in my name, he will give it you.

24 Hitherto have ye asked nothing in my name: ask, and ye shall receive, that your joy may be full.

25 These things have I spoken unto you in proverbs: but the time cometh, when I shall no more speak unto you in proverbs, but I shall show you plainly of the Father.

26 At that day ye shall ask in my name: and I say not unto you, that I will pray the Father for you:

27 For the Father himself loveth you, because ye have loved me, and have believed that I came out from God.

28 I came forth from the Father, and am come into the world: again, I leave the world, and go to the Father.

29 His disciples said unto him, Lo, now speakest thou plainly, and speakest no proverb.

30 Now are we sure that thou knowest all things, and needest not that any man should ask thee: by this we believe that thou camest forth from God.

31 Jesus answered them, Do ye now believe?

32 Behold, the hour cometh, yea, is now come, that ye shall be scattered, every man to his own, and shall leave

me alone: and yet I am not alone, because the Father is with me.

33 These things I have spoken unto you, that in me ye might have peace. In the world ye shall have tribulation: but be of good cheer; I have overcome the world.

CHAPTER 17

These words spake Jesus, and lifted up his eyes to heaven, and said, Father, the hour is come; glorify thy Son, that thy Son also may glorify thee:

2 As thou hast given him power over all flesh, that he should give eternal life to as many as thou hast given him.

3 And this is life eternal, that they might know thee the only true God, and Jesus Christ, whom thou hast sent.

4 I have glorified thee on the earth: I have finished the work which thou gavest me to do.

5 And now, O Father, glorify thou me with thine own self with the glory which I had with thee before the world was.

6 I have manifested thy name unto the men which thou gavest me out of the world: thine they were, and thou gavest them me; and they have kept thy word.

7 Now they have known that all things whatsoever thou hast given me are of thee.

8 For I have given unto them the words which thou gavest me; and they have received *them*, and have known surely that I came out from thee, and they have believed that thou didst send me.

9 I pray for them: I pray not for the world, but for them which thou hast given me; for they are thine.

10 And all mine are thine, and thine are mine; and I am glorified in them.

11 And now I am no more in the world, but these are in the world, and I come to thee. Holy Father, keep through thine own name those whom thou hast given me, that they may be one, as we *are*.

12 While I was with them in the world, I kept them in thy name: those that thou gavest me I have kept, and none of them is lost, but the son of perdition; that the scripture might be fulfilled.

13 And now come I to thee; and these things I speak in the world, that they might have my joy fulfilled in themselves.

14 I have given them thy word; and the world hath hated them, because they are not of the world, even as I am not of the world.

15 I pray not that thou shouldest take them out of the world, but that thou shouldest keep them from the evil.

16 They are not of the world, even as I am not of the world.

17 Sanctify them through thy truth: thy word is truth.

18 As thou hast sent me into the world, even so have I also sent them into the world.

19 And for their sakes I sanctify myself, that they also might be sanctified through the truth.

20 Neither pray I for these alone, but for them also which shall believe on me through their word;

21 That they all may be one; as thou, Father, *art* in me, and I in thee, that they also may be one in us: that the world may believe that thou hast sent me.

22 And the glory which thou gavest me I have given them; that they may be one, even as we are one:

23 I in them, and thou in me, that they may be made perfect in one; and that the world may know that thou hast sent me, and hast loved them, as thou hast loved me.

24 Father, I will that they also, whom thou hast given me, be with me where I am; that they may behold my glory, which thou hast given me: for thou lovedst me before the foundation of the world.

25 O righteous Father, the world hath not known thee: but I have known thee, and these have known that thou hast sent me.

26 And I have declared unto them thy name, and will declare *it:* that the love wherewith thou hast loved me may be in them, and I in them.

CHAPTER 18

When Jesus had spoken these words, he went forth with his disciples over the brook Cedron, where was a garden, into the which he entered, and his disciples.

2 And Judas also, which betrayed him, knew the place: for Jesus ofttimes resorted thither with his disciples.

3 Judas then, having received a band *of men* and officers from the chief priests and Pharisees, cometh thither with lanterns and torches and weapons.

4 Jesus therefore, knowing all things that should come upon him, went forth, and said unto them, Whom seek ye?

5 They answered him, Jesus of Nazareth. Jesus saith unto them, I am *he.* And Judas also, which betrayed him, stood with them.

6 As soon then as he had said unto them, I am *he,* they went backward, and fell to the ground.

7 Then asked he them again, Whom seek ye? And they said, Jesus of Nazareth.

8 Jesus answered, I have told you that I am *he*: if therefore ye seek me, let these go their way:

9 That the saying might be fulfilled, which he spake, Of them which thou gavest me have I lost none.

10 Then Simon Peter having a sword drew it, and smote the high priest's servant, and cut off his right ear. The servant's name was Malchus.

11 Then said Jesus unto Peter, Put up thy sword into the sheath: the cup which my Father hath given me, shall I not drink it?

12 Then the band and the captain and officers of the Jews took Jesus, and bound him,

13 And led him away to Annas first; for he was father-in-law to Caiaphas, which was the high priest that same year.

14 Now Caiaphas was he, which gave counsel to the Jews, that it was expedient that one man should die for the people.

15 And Simon Peter followed Jesus, and *so did* another disciple: that disciple was known unto the high priest, and went in with Jesus into the palace of the high priest.

16 But Peter stood at the door without. Then went out that other disciple, which was known unto the high priest, and spake unto her that kept the door, and brought in Peter.

17 Then saith the damsel that kept the door unto Peter, Art not thou also *one* of this man's disciples? He saith, I am not.

18 And the servants and officers stood there, who had made a fire of coals; for it was cold: and they warmed themselves: and Peter stood with them, and warmed himself.

19 The high priest then asked Jesus of his disciples, and of his doctrine.

20 Jesus answered him, I spake openly to the world; I ever taught in the synagogue, and in the temple, whither the Jews always resort; and in secret have I said nothing.

21 Why askest thou me? ask them which heard me, what I have said unto them: behold, they know what I said.

22 And when he had thus spoken, one of the officers which stood by struck Jesus with the palm of his hand, saying, Answerest thou the high priest so?

23 Jesus answered him, If I have spoken evil, bear witness of the evil: but if well, why smitest thou me?

24 Now Annas had sent him bound unto Caiaphas the high priest.

25 And Simon Peter stood and warmed himself. They said therefore unto him, Art not thou also *one* of his disciples? He denied *it*, and said, I am not.

26 One of the servants of the high priest, being *his* kinsman whose ear Peter cut off, saith, Did not I see thee in the garden with him?

27 Peter then denied again: and immediately the cock crew.

28 Then led they Jesus from Caiaphas unto the hall of judgment: and it was early; and they themselves went not into the judgment hall, lest they should be defiled; but that they might eat the passover.

29 Pilate then went out unto them, and said, What accusation bring ye against this man?

30 They answered and said unto him, If he were not a malefactor, we would not have delivered him up unto thee.

31 Then said Pilate unto them, Take ye him, and judge him

according to your law. The Jews therefore said unto him, It is not lawful for us to put any man to death:

32 That the saying of Jesus might be fulfilled, which he spake, signifying what death he should die.

33 Then Pilate entered into the judgment hall again, and called Jesus, and said unto him, Art thou the King of the Jews?

34 Jesus answered him, Sayest thou this thing of thyself, or did others tell it thee of me?

35 Pilate answered, Am I a Jew? Thine own nation and the chief priests have delivered thee unto me: what hast thou done?

36 Jesus answered, My kingdom is not of this world: if my kingdom were of this world, then would my servants fight, that I should not be delivered to the Jews: but now is my kingdom not from hence.

37 Pilate therefore said unto him, Art thou a king then? Jesus answered, Thou sayest that I am a king. To this end was I born, and for this cause came I into the world, that I should bear witness unto the truth. Every one that is of the truth heareth my voice.

38 Pilate saith unto him, What is truth? And when he had said this, he went out again unto the Jews, and saith unto them, I find in him no fault *at all*.

39 But ye have a custom, that I should release unto you one at the passover: will ye therefore that I release unto you the King of the Jews?

40 Then cried they all again, saying, Not this man, but Barabbas. Now Barabbas was a robber.

CHAPTER 19

Then Pilate therefore took Jesus, and scourged *him*.

2 And the soldiers platted a crown of thorns, and put *it* on his head, and they put on him a purple robe,

3 And said, Hail, King of the Jews! and they smote him with their hands.

4 Pilate therefore went forth again, and saith unto them, Behold, I bring him forth to you, that ye may know that I find no fault in him.

5 Then came Jesus forth, wearing the crown of thorns, and the purple robe. And *Pilate* saith unto them, Behold the man!

6 When the chief priests therefore and officers saw him, they cried out, saying, Crucify *him*, crucify *him*. Pilate saith unto them, Take ye him, and crucify *him*: for I find no fault in him.

7 The Jews answered him, We have a law, and by our law he ought to die, because he made himself the Son of God.

8 When Pilate therefore heard that saying, he was the more afraid;

9 And went again into the judgment hall, and saith unto Jesus, Whence art thou? But Jesus gave him no answer.

10 Then saith Pilate unto him, Speakest thou not unto me? knowest thou not that I have power to crucify thee, and have power to release thee?

11 Jesus answered, Thou couldest have no power *at all* against me, except it were given thee from above: therefore he that delivered me unto thee hath the greater sin.

12 And from thenceforth Pilate sought to release him: but the Jews cried out, saying, If thou let this man go, thou

art not Caesar's friend: whosoever maketh himself a king speaketh against Caesar.

13 When Pilate therefore heard that saying, he brought Jesus forth, and sat down in the judgment seat in a place that is called the Pavement, but in the Hebrew, Gabbatha.

14 And it was the preparation of the passover, and about the sixth hour: and he saith unto the Jews, Behold your King!

15 But they cried out, Away with *him*, away with *him*, crucify him. Pilate saith unto them, Shall I crucify your King? The chief priests answered, We have no king but Caesar.

16 Then delivered he him therefore unto them to be crucified. And they took Jesus, and led *him* away.

17 And he bearing his cross went forth into a place called *the place* of a skull, which is called in the Hebrew Golgotha:

18 Where they crucified him, and two other with him, on either side one, and Jesus in the midst.

19 And Pilate wrote a title, and put it on the cross. And the writing was JESUS OF NAZARETH THE KING OF THE JEWS.

20 This title then read many of the Jews: for the place where Jesus was crucified was nigh to the city: and it was written in Hebrew, *and* Greek, *and* Latin.

21 Then said the chief priests of the Jews to Pilate, Write not, The King of the Jews; but that he said, I am King of the Jews.

22 Pilate answered, What I have written I have written.

23 Then the soldiers, when they had crucified Jesus, took his garments, and made four parts, to every soldier a part; and also *his* coat: now the coat was without seam, woven from the top throughout.

24 They said therefore among themselves, Let us not rend it, but cast lots for it, whose it shall be: that the scripture might be fulfilled, which saith, They parted my raiment among them, and for my vesture they did cast lots. These things therefore the soldiers did.

25 Now there stood by the cross of Jesus his mother, and his mother's sister, Mary the *wife* of Cleophas, and Mary Magdalene.

26 When Jesus therefore saw his mother, and the disciple standing by, whom he loved, he saith unto his mother, Woman, behold thy son!

27 Then saith he to the disciple, Behold thy mother! And from that hour that disciple took her unto his own *home*.

28 After this, Jesus knowing that all things were now accomplished, that the scripture might be fulfilled, saith, I thirst.

29 Now there was set a vessel full of vinegar: and they filled a sponge with vinegar, and put *it* upon hyssop, and put *it* to his mouth.

30 When Jesus therefore had received the vinegar, he said, It is finished: and he bowed his head, and gave up the ghost.

31 The Jews therefore, because it was the preparation, that the bodies should not remain upon the cross on the sabbath day, (for that sabbath day was an high day,) besought Pilate that their legs might be broken, and *that* they might be taken away.

32 Then came the soldiers, and brake the legs of the first, and of the other which was crucified with him.

33 But when they came to Jesus, and saw that he was dead already, they brake not his legs:

34 But one of the soldiers with a spear pierced his side, and forthwith came there out blood and water.

35 And he that saw *it* bare record, and his record is true: and he knoweth that he saith true, that ye might believe.

36 For these things were done, that the scripture should be fulfilled, A bone of him shall not be broken.

37 And again another scripture saith, They shall look on him whom they pierced.

38 And after this Joseph of Arimathaea, being a disciple of Jesus, but secretly for fear of the Jews, besought Pilate that he might take away the body of Jesus: and Pilate gave *him* leave. He came therefore, and took the body of Jesus.

39 And there came also Nicodemus, which at the first came to Jesus by night, and brought a mixture of myrrh and aloes, about an hundred pound *weight*.

40 Then took they the body of Jesus, and wound it in linen clothes with the spices, as the manner of the Jews is to bury.

41 Now in the place where he was crucified there was a garden; and in the garden a new sepulchre, wherein was never man yet laid.

42 There laid they Jesus therefore because of the Jews' preparation *day*; for the sepulchre was nigh at hand.

CHAPTER 20

The first *day* of the week cometh Mary Magdalene early, when it was yet dark, unto the sepulchre, and seeth the stone taken away from the sepulchre.

2 Then she runneth, and cometh to Simon Peter, and to the

other disciple, whom Jesus loved, and saith unto them, They have taken away the LORD out of the sepulchre, and we know not where they have laid him.

3 Peter therefore went forth, and that other disciple, and came to the sepulchre.

4 So they ran both together: and the other disciple did outrun Peter, and came first to the sepulchre.

5 And he stooping down, *and looking in*, saw the linen clothes lying; yet went he not in.

6 Then cometh Simon Peter following him, and went into the sepulchre, and seeth the linen clothes lie,

7 And the napkin, that was about his head, not lying with the linen clothes, but wrapped together in a place by itself.

8 Then went in also that other disciple, which came first to the sepulchre, and he saw, and believed.

9 For as yet they knew not the scripture, that he must rise again from the dead.

10 Then the disciples went away again unto their own home.

11 But Mary stood without at the sepulchre weeping: and as she wept, she stooped down, *and looked* into the sepulchre,

12 And seeth two angels in white sitting, the one at the head, and the other at the feet, where the body of Jesus had lain.

13 And they say unto her, Woman, why weepest thou? She saith unto them, Because they have taken away my LORD , and I know not where they have laid him.

14 And when she had thus said, she turned herself back, and saw Jesus standing, and knew not that it was Jesus.

15 Jesus saith unto her, Woman, why weepest thou? whom

seekest thou? She, supposing him to be the gardener, saith unto him, Sir, if thou have borne him hence, tell me where thou hast laid him, and I will take him away.

16 Jesus saith unto her, Mary. She turned herself, and saith unto him, Rabboni; which is to say, Master.

17 Jesus saith unto her, Touch me not; for I am not yet ascended to my Father: but go to my brethren, and say unto them, I ascend unto my Father, and your Father; and *to* my God, and your God.

18 Mary Magdalene came and told the disciples that she had seen the LORD , and *that* he had spoken these things unto her.

19 Then the same day at evening, being the first *day* of the week, when the doors were shut where the disciples were assembled for fear of the Jews, came Jesus and stood in the midst, and saith unto them, Peace *be* unto you.

20 And when he had so said, he showed unto them *his* hands and his side. Then were the disciples glad, when they saw the LORD .

21 Then said Jesus to them again, Peace *be* unto you: as *my* Father hath sent me, even so send I you.

22 And when he had said this, he breathed on *them*, and saith unto them, Receive ye the Holy Ghost:

23 Whosesoever sins ye remit, they are remitted unto them; *and* whosesoever *sins* ye retain, they are retained.

24 But Thomas, one of the twelve, called Didymus, was not with them when Jesus came.

25 The other disciples therefore said unto him, We have seen the LORD. But he said unto them, Except I shall see in his hands the print of the nails, and put my finger into the

print of the nails, and thrust my hand into his side, I will not believe.

26 And after eight days again his disciples were within, and Thomas with them: *then* came Jesus, the doors being shut, and stood in the midst, and said, Peace *be* unto you.

27 Then saith he to Thomas, Reach hither thy finger, and behold my hands; and reach hither thy hand, and thrust *it* into my side: and be not faithless, but believing.

28 And Thomas answered and said unto him, My LORD and my God.

29 Jesus saith unto him, Thomas, because thou hast seen me, thou hast believed: blessed *are* they that have not seen, and *yet* have believed.

30 And many other signs truly did Jesus in the presence of his disciples, which are not written in this book:

31 But these are written, that ye might believe that Jesus is the Christ, the Son of God; and that believing ye might have life through his name.

CHAPTER 21

After these things Jesus showed himself again to the disciples at the sea of Tiberias; and on this wise showed he *himself.*

2 There were together Simon Peter, and Thomas called Didymus, and Nathanael of Cana in Galilee, and the *sons* of Zebedee, and two other of his disciples.

3 Simon Peter saith unto them, I go a-fishing. They say unto him, We also go with thee. They went forth, and entered into a ship immediately; and that night they caught nothing.

4 But when the morning was now come, Jesus stood on the

shore: but the disciples knew not that it was Jesus.

5 Then Jesus saith unto them, Children, have ye any meat? They answered him, No.

6 And he said unto them, Cast the net on the right side of the ship, and ye shall find. They cast therefore, and now they were not able to draw it for the multitude of fishes.

7 Therefore that disciple whom Jesus loved saith unto Peter, It is the LORD . Now when Simon Peter heard that it was the Lord, he girt *his* fisher's coat *unto him,* (for he was naked,) and did cast himself into the sea.

8 And the other disciples came in a little ship; (for they were not far from land, but as it were two hundred cubits,) dragging the net with fishes.

9 As soon then as they were come to land, they saw a fire of coals there, and fish laid thereon, and bread.

10 Jesus saith unto them, Bring of the fish which ye have now caught.

11 Simon Peter went up, and drew the net to land full of great fishes, an hundred and fifty and three: and for all there were so many, yet was not the net broken.

12 Jesus saith unto them, Come *and* dine. And none of the disciples durst ask him, Who art thou? knowing that it was the Lord.

13 Jesus then cometh, and taketh bread, and giveth them, and fish likewise.

14 This is now the third time that Jesus showed himself to his disciples, after that he was risen from the dead.

15 So when they had dined, Jesus saith to Simon Peter, Simon, *son* of Jonas, lovest thou me more than these? He saith unto him, Yea, Lord; thou knowest that I love thee.

He saith unto him, Feed my lambs.

16 He saith to him again the second time, Simon, *son* of Jonas, lovest thou me? He saith unto him, Yea, Lord; thou knowest that I love thee. He saith unto him, Feed my sheep.

17 He saith unto him the third time, Simon, *son* of Jonas, lovest thou me? Peter was grieved because he said unto him the third time, Lovest thou me? And he said unto him, Lord, thou knowest all things; thou knowest that I love thee. Jesus saith unto him, Feed my sheep.

18 Verily, verily, I say unto thee, When thou wast young, thou girdest thyself, and walkedst whither thou wouldest: but when thou shalt be old, thou shalt stretch forth thy hands, and another shall gird thee, and carry *thee* whither thou wouldest not.

19 This spake he, signifying by what death he should glorify God. And when he had spoken this, he saith unto him, Follow me.

20 Then Peter, turning about, seeth the disciple whom Jesus loved following; which also leaned on his breast at supper, and said, Lord, which is he that betrayeth thee?

21 Peter seeing him saith to Jesus, Lord, and what *shall* this man *do?*

22 Jesus saith unto him, If I will that he tarry till I come, what *is that* to thee? follow thou me.

23 Then went this saying abroad among the brethren, that that disciple should not die: yet Jesus said not unto him, He shall not die; but, If I will that he tarry till I come, what *is that* to thee?

24 This is the disciple which testifieth of these things, and wrote these things: and we know that his testimony is true.

25 And there are also many other things which Jesus did, the which, if they should be written every one, I suppose that even the world itself could not contain the books that should be written. Amen.

THE BHAGAVAD-

Prologue by Henry David Thoreau {

GITA

I would say to the readers of Scriptures, if they wish for a good book, read the Bhagvat-Geeta, an episode to the Mahabharat, said to have been written by Kreeshna Dwypayen Veias,—known to have been written by —--- more than four thousand years ago,—it matters not whether three or four, or when. It deserves to be read with reverence even by Yankees, as part of the sacred writings of a devout people . . . a Hebrew will rejoice to find in it a moral grandeur and sublimity akin to those of his own Scriptures. . . . In every one's youthful dreams philosophy is still vaguely but inseparably, and with singular truth, associated with the East, nor do after years discover its local habitation in the Western world. In comparison with the philosophers of the East, we may say that modern Europe has yet given birth to none. Beside the vast and cosmogonal philosophy of the Bhagvat-Geeta, even our Shakespeare seems sometimes youthfully green and practical merely. Some of these sublime sentences, as the Chaldaean oracles of Zoroaster, still surviving after a thousand revolutions and translations, alone make us doubt if the poetic form and dress are not transitory, and not essential to the most effective and enduring expression of thought. Ex oriente lux may still be the motto of scholars, for the Western world has not yet derived from the East all the light which it is destined to receive thence.

INTRODUCTION

BARBARA STOLER MILLER

THE BHAGAVAD-GITA has been the exemplary text of Hindu culture for centuries, both in India and in the West. The Sanskrit title *Bhagavad-Gita* has usually been interpreted to mean "Song of the Lord," but this is misleading. It is not a lyric but a philosophical poem composed in the form of a dialogue between the warrior Arjuna and his charioteer, the god Krishna.

As we read the *Bhagavad-Gita* today we can understand the paralyzing conflict Arjuna suffers knowing that the enemies it is his warrior duty to destroy are his own kinsmen and teachers. We can sympathize with his impulse to shrink from the violence he sees in the human condition, and we can learn from the ways Krishna teaches him to understand his own and others' mortality. Krishna's exposition of the relationship between death, sacrifice, and devotion dramatizes the Hindu idea that one must heroically confront death in order to transcend the limits of worldly existence. We may not share Arjuna's developing faith in Krishna's authority or be convinced by Krishna's insistence that one must perform one's sacred duty, even when it requires violence. But if we listen carefully to the compelling arguments and imagery of the discourse, we cannot but hear the voice of a larger reality.

The dramatic moral crisis that is central to the *Bhagavad-Gita* has inspired centuries of Indian philosophers and practical men of wisdom, as well as Western thinkers such as Thoreau, Emerson, and Eliot. Interpretations of the *Gita*, as it is commonly referred to in India, are as varied as the figures who have commented on it. From Shankara, the great Hindu philosopher of the eighth century, to Mahatma Gandhi, the leader of India's independence struggle in the twentieth century, each thinker has emphasized the path to spiritual liberation that was suited to his view of reality. These various interpretations reflect the intentionally multifaceted message of Krishna's teaching. The *Gita's* significance for Hindu life continues to be debated in India today.

Hinduism is not based on the teachings of a founder, such as Buddha, Christ, or Muhammad. It has evolved over centuries through the continual interplay of diverse religious beliefs and practices: popular local cults; orthodox traditions, including the ancient Vedic hymns, the ritual texts of the Brahmanas, and the mystical Upanishads; as well as heterodox challenges from Buddhist and Jain ideas and institutions. Even the word *Hindu* is a foreign idea, used by Arab invaders in the eighth century A.D. to refer to the customs and beliefs of people who worshiped sectarian gods such as Vishnu and Shiva.

Although the *Gita* exists as an independent sacred text, its placement within the sixth book of the great Indian war epic, the *Mahabharata*, gives it a concrete context. The religious and cultural life of the Indian subcontinent, and much of the rest of Asia, has been deeply influenced by the *Mahabharata*, as well as by the *Ramayana*, the other ancient Indian epic. Both poems have their roots in legendary events that took place in the period following the entry of nomadic

Indo-Aryan-speaking tribes into northwestern India around 1200 B.C. The composition of the epics began as these tribes settled in the river valleys of the Indus and the Ganges during the first millennium B.C., when their nomadic sacrificial cults began to develop into what are now the religious traditions of Hinduism.

The Hindu concept of religion is expressed by the Sanskrit term *dharma* ("sacred duty"), which refers to the moral order that sustains the cosmos, society, and the individual. The continual reinterpretation of *dharma* attests to its significance in Indian civilization. Derived from a Sanskrit form meaning "that which sustains," within Hindu culture it generally means religiously ordained duty, that is, the code of conduct appropriate to each group in the hierarchically ordered Hindu society. Theoretically, right and wrong are not absolute in this system; practically, right and wrong are decided according to the categories of social rank, kinship, and stage of life. For modern Westerners who have been raised on ideals of universality and egalitarianism, this relativity of values and obligations is the aspect of Hinduism most difficult to understand. However, without an attempt to understand it, the Hindu view of life remains opaque.

The epics are repositories of myths, ideals, and concepts that Hindu culture has always drawn upon to represent aspects of *dharma*. As befits their social position as warrior-kings, the figures of the epic heroes embody order and sacred duty (*dharma*); while their foes, whether human or demonic, embody chaos (*adharma*). The rituals of warrior life and the demands of sacred duty define the religious and moral meaning of heroism throughout the *Mahabharata*. Acts of heroism are characterized less by physical prowess than by the fulfillment of *dharma*, which often involves extraordinary forms of sacrifice, penance, devotion to a divine authority, and spiritual victory over evil. The distinctive martial religion of this epic emerges from a synthesis of values derived from the ritual traditions of the Vedic sacrificial cult combined with loyalty to a personal diety.

Most scholars agree that the *Mahabharata* was composed over the centuries between 400 B.C. and A.D. 400. Beyond its kernel story of internecine war, it is difficult to summarize. The work has its stylistic and mythological roots in the *Rig Veda*; its narrative sources are the oral tales of a tribal war fought in the Punjab early in the first millennium B.C. As the tradition was taken over by professional storytellers and intellectuals, many sorts of legend, myth, and speculative thought were absorbed, including the *Bhagavad-Gita*, which belongs to that layer of the epic which took form around the first century A.D. In its present form the *Mahabharata* is a rich encyclopedia of ancient Indian culture consisting of over one hundred thousand verses divided into eighteen books. The multiple layers of the text reflect its long history as well as attempts to reconcile conflicting religious and social values.

The epic's main narrative revolves around a feud over succession to the ancient kingdom of Kurukshetra in northern India. The rivals are two sets of cousins descended from the legendary king Bharata—the five sons of Pandu and the one hundred sons of Dhritarashtra. The feud itself is based on genealogical complications that are a result of a series of divine interventions. Pandu had become king because his elder brother, Dhritarashtra, was congenitally blind and thus ineligible for direct succession to the throne. But Pandu was unable to beget offspring because of a curse that forbade him intercourse with his two wives on penalty of death. After a long reign he renounces the throne and retires to the forest, where he fathers five sons (the Pandava brothers) with the help of five gods, and then dies.

The Pandava brothers are taken to be educated with their cousins at the court of Dhritarashtra, who has assumed the throne as regent in the absence of another adult heir. The princes' two teachers are their great-uncle Bhishma, who is revered for the spiritual power symbolized by his vow of celibacy, and the priest Drona, who is a master of archery and the teacher chosen by Bhishma to educate the princes in the martial arts. Arjuna becomes Drona's favored pupil when he vows to avenge his teacher's honor at the end of his training. The Pandavas excel their cousins in every warrior skill and virtue, which arouses the jealousy of Dhritarashtra's eldest son, Duryodhana.

Although Yudhishthira, Pandu's eldest son, has the legitimate right to be king, Duryodhana covets the throne, and in various episodes he attempts to assassinate his cousins or otherwise frustrate their rights. After thirteen years of exile imposed on them as the penalty for Yudhishthira's defeat in a crooked dice game played as part of a ritual, the Pandavas return to reclaim their kingdom. Duryodhana's refusal to step aside makes war inevitable. The description of the eighteen-day-long battle and concomitant philosophizing by various teachers takes up the bulk of the epic. The battle ends with the triumph of the Pandavas over their cousins—the triumph of order over chaos.

The setting of the *Gita* is the battlefield of Kurukshetra as the war is about to begin. It is not only a physical place but is representative of a state of mind. When the assembled troops are arrayed on the field awaiting battle, the sage Vyasa, the traditional author of the *Mahabharata*, appears to the blind Dhritarashtra and grants him a boon. He will be able to hear an account of the battle from Sanjaya, who is endowed with immediate vision of all things past, present, and future, thus enabling him to see every detail of the battle. Vyasa says to Dhritarashtra: "Sanjaya shall see all the events of the battle directly. He shall have a divine inner eye. . . . O King, Sanjaya has an inner eye. He will tell you everything about the battle. He will be all-knowing. Whenever he thinks with his mind, Sanjaya will see everything taking place during day or night, in public or in secret."

Sanjaya, the visionary narrator who serves as the personal bard and charioteer of Dhritarashtra, is thus the mediating voice through whom the audience of the *Gita* learns Krishna's secret teaching. Through Sanjaya's retelling, the mystery of life and death revealed to Arjuna enters into the bardic tradition that preserves it for all to hear. . . .

For Arjuna, and for the audience of the *Gita*, Krishna is a companion and teacher, as well as the god who commands devotion. Krishna's mythology suggests that he is a tribal hero transformed into cult divinity. In the *Gita*, Krishna is the incarnation of cosmic power, who periodically descends to earth to accomplish the restoration of order in times of chaos. The mundane and cosmic levels of his activity are interwoven to provide the background for his role as divine charioteer to Arjuna. The mightiest warrior in the epic, Arjuna is characterized not only by his physical prowess but by his spiritual prowess, which involves a mystical friendship with Krishna. From the start Arjuna knows that his charioteer is no ordinary mortal; he begs Krishna to dispel his uncertainty, and Krishna speaks with the authority of omniscience. As Arjuna's confidence and faith increase, the power of Krishna's divinity gradually unfolds before him in all its terrible glory, and Arjuna comes to see himself mirrored in the divine. Krishna's revelation of the cosmic spectacle forces Arjuna to accept the necessity of his own part in it. . . .

Each of the eighteen teachings that comprise the *Gita* highlights some aspect of Krishna's doctrine, but there is much repetition throughout them as the central themes are developed and subtly interpreted within the text. The text also has a broader triadic structure. In the first six teachings the dramatic narrative modulates into a series of theoretical and practical teachings on self-knowledge and the nature of action. The third and fourth teachings develop the crucial relation between sacrifice and action. The fifth and sixth teachings explore the tension between renunciation and action; Arjuna's query is resolved in the ideal of disciplined action. It is Arjuna's probing questions and his dissatisfaction with the apparent inconsistencies in Krishna's answers that expose Arjuna's state of mind and open him now to more advanced teachings. In the seventh teaching, focus shifts toward knowledge of Krishna. The language of paradox intensifies and hyperbole heightens, culminating in the dazzling theophany of the eleventh teaching. The theophany ends in a cadence on devotion, and the twelfth teaching develops this idea. Arjuna is transformed, not by a systematic argument, but by a mystical teaching in which Krishna becomes the object of Arjuna's intense devotion (*bhakti*). The representation of Arjuna's mystical experience of Krishna is poetically structured within the dialogue form to engage the participation of the audience in its drama.

In the final six teachings, the dialogue recedes as Krishna emphatically recapitulates the basic ideas he has already taught and integrates them into the doctrine of devotion. Devotion allows for a resolution of the conflict between the worldly life of allotted duties and the life of renunciation. By purging his mind of attachments and dedicating the fruits of his actions to Krishna, Arjuna can continue to act in a world of pain without suffering despair. The core of this devotion to Krishna is discipline (*yoga*) which enables the warrior to control his passions and become a man of discipline (*yogi*). . . .

At every stage of Arjuna's dramatic journey of self-discovery, the charioteer Krishna is aware of his pupil's spiritual conflict and guides him to the appropriate path for resolving it. Krishna urges him not to resign himself to killing but instead to renounce his selfish attachment to the fruits of his actions. By learning how to discipline his emotion and his action, Arjuna journeys far without ever leaving the battlefield. Krishna draws him into a universe beyond the world of everyday experience but keeps forcing him back to wage the battle of life. He advocates, on the one hand, the life of action and moral duty, and on the other, the transcendence of empirical experience in search of knowledge and liberation. Though much of Krishna's teaching seems remote from the moral chaos that Arjuna envisions will be a consequence of his killing his kinsmen, Krishna's doctrine of disciplined action is a way of bringing order to life's destructive aspect. When the puzzled Arjuna asks, "Why do you urge me to do this act of violence?" Krishna does not condone physical violence. Instead, he identifies the real enemy as desire, due to attachment, an enemy that can only be overcome by arming oneself with discipline and acting to transcend the narrow limits of individual desire.

The text of the *Gita* ends by commenting on itself through the witness of Sanjaya, who re-creates the dialogue in all its compelling power as he keeps remembering it. He recalls for the blind king Dhritarashtra, and for every other member of his audience, the correspondence between Krishna's wondrous form and the language of poetry that represents that form. Anyone who listens to his words gains consciousness of Krishna's presence.

THE
BHAGAVAD-GITA

HERE THE BLESSED LORD'S Song is begun.

Dhritarâshtra said:

On the holy plain, on the field of Kuru, gathered together, eager for battle, what did they, O Sanjaya, my people and the Pândavas?

Sanjaya said:

Having seen arrayed the army of the Pândavas, the Râjâ Duryodhana approached his teacher, and spake these words:

Behold this mighty host of the sons of Pându, O teacher, arrayed by the son of Drupada, thy wise disciple.

Heroes are these, mighty bowmen, to Bhîma and Arjuna equal in battle; Yuyudhâna, Virâta, and Drupada of the great car.

Dhrishtaketu, Chekitâna, and the valiant Râjâ of Kâshî;

Purujit and Kuntibhoja, and Shaibya, bull among men;

Yudhâmanyu the strong, and Uttamaujâ the brave; Saubhadra and the Draupadeyas, all of great cars.

Know further all those who are our chiefs, O best of the twice-born, the leaders of my army; these I name to thee for thy information:

Thou, lord and Bhîshma, and Karna, and Kripa, conquering in battle; Ashvatthâma, Vikarna, and Saumadatti also;

And many others, heroes, for my sake renouncing their lives, with divers weapons and missiles, and all well-skilled in war.

Yet insufficient seems this army of ours, though marshalled by Bhîshma, while that army of theirs seems sufficient, though marshalled by Bhîma;

Therefore in the rank and file let all, standing firmly in their respective divisions, guard Bhîshma, even all ye Generals.

To enhearten him, the Ancient of the Kurus, the Grandsire, the glorious, blew his conch, sounding on high a lion's roar.

Then conches and kettledrums, tabors and drums and cowhorns suddenly blared forth, and the sound was tumultuous.

Then, stationed in their great war-chariot, yoked to white horses, Mâdhava and the son of Pându blew their divine conches,

Pânchajanya by Hrishîkesha, and Devadatta by Dhananjaya. Vrikodara, of terrible deeds, blew his mighty conch, Paundra;

The Râjâ Yudhishthira, the son of Kuntî, blew

Anatavijaya; Nakula and Sahadeva, Sughosha and Manipushpaka.

And Kâshya, of the great bow, and Shikhandî, the mighty car-warrior, Dhrishtadyumna and Virâta and Sâtyaki, the unconquered.

Drupada and the Draupadeyas, O Lord of earth, and Saubhadra, the mighty-armed, on all sides their several conches blew.

That tumultuous uproar rent the hearts of the sons of Dhritarâshtra, filling the earth and sky with sound.

Then, beholding the sons of Dhritarâshtra standing arrayed, and the flight of missiles about to begin, he whose crest is an ape, the son of Pându, took up his bow,

And spake this word to Hrishîkesha, O Lord of earth:

Arjuna said:

"In the midst, between the two armies, stay my chariot, O Achyuta,

That I may behold these standing, longing for battle, with whom I must strive in this out-breaking war;

And gaze on those here gathered together, ready to fight, desirous of pleasing in battle the evil-minded son of Dhritarâshtra."

Sanjaya said:

Thus addressed by Gudâkesha, Hrishîkesha, O Bhârata, having stayed that best of chariots in the midst, between the two armies,

Over against Bhîshma, Drona and all the rulers of the world, said: "O Pârtha, behold these Kurus gathered together."

Then saw Pârtha standing there uncles and grandfathers,

teachers, mother's brothers, cousins, sons and grandsons, comrades,

Fathers-in-law and friends also in both armies. Seeing all these kinsmen, thus standing arrayed, Kaunteya,

Deeply moved to pity, this uttered in sadness:

Arjuna said:

Seeing these, my kinsmen, O Krishna, arrayed eager to fight,

My limbs fail and my mouth is parched, my body quivers, and my hair stands on end,

Gândîva slips from my hand, and my skin burns all over; I am not able to stand, and my mind is whirling,

And I see adverse omens, O Keshava. Nor do I foresee any advantage from slaying kinsmen in battle,

For I desire not victory, O Krishna, nor kingdom, nor pleasures; what is kingdom to us, O Govinda, what enjoyment, or even life?

Those for whose sake we desire kingdom, enjoyments and pleasures, they stand here in battle, abandoning life and riches—

Teachers, fathers, sons, as well as grandfathers, mother's brothers, fathers-in-law, grandsons, brothers-in-law, and other relatives.

These I do not wish to kill, though myself slain, O Madhusûdana, even for the sake of the kingship of the three worlds; how then for earth?

Slaying these sons of Dhritarâshtra, what pleasure can be ours, O Janârdana? killing these desperadoes sin will but take hold of us.

Therefore we should not kill the sons of Dhritarâshtra,

our relatives; for how, killing our kinsmen, may we be happy, O Mâdhava?

Although these, with intelligence overpowered by greed, see no guilt in the destruction of a family, no crime in hostility to friends,

Why should not we learn to turn away from such a sin, O Janârdana, who see the evils in the destruction of a family?

In the destruction of a family the immemorial family traditions perish; in the perishing of traditions lawlessness overcomes the whole family;

Owing to predominance of lawlessness, O Krishna, the women of the family become corrupt; women, corrupted, O Vârshneya, there ariseth caste-confusion;

This confusion draggeth to hell the slayers of the family and the family; for their ancestors fall, deprived of rice-balls and libations.

By these caste-confusing misdeeds of the slayers of the family, the everlasting caste customs and family customs are abolished.

The abode of the men whose family customs are extinguished, O Janârdana, is everlastingly in hell. Thus have we heard.

Alas! in committing a great sin are we engaged, we who are endeavoring to kill our kindred from greed of the pleasures of kingship.

If the sons of Dhritarâshtra, weapon-in-hand, should slay me, unresisting, unarmed, in the battle, that would for me be the better.

Sanjaya said:

Having thus spoken on the battle-field, Arjuna sank

down on the seat of the chariot, casting away his bow and arrow, his mind overborne by grief.

SECOND DISCOURSE

Sanjaya said:

To him thus with pity overcome, with smarting brimming eyes, despondent, Madhusûdana spake these words:

The Blessed Lord said:

Whence hath this dejection befallen thee in this perilous strait, ignoble, heaven-closing, infamous, O Arjuna?

Yield not to impotence, O Pârtha! it doth not befit thee. Shake off this paltry faint-heartedness! Stand up, Parantapa!

Arjuna said:

How, O Madhusûdana, shall I attack Bhîshma and Drona with arrows in battle? they who are worthy of reverence, O slayer of foes.

Better in this world to eat even the beggars' crust, than to slay these most noble Gurus. Slaying these Gurus, our well-wishers, I should taste of blood-besprinkled feasts.

Nor know I which for us be the better, that we conquer them or they conquer us—these, whom having slain we should not care to live, even these arrayed against us, the sons of Dhritarâshtra.

My heart is weighed down with the vice of faintness; my mind is confused as to duty. I ask thee which may be the better—that tell me decisively. I am thy disciple, suppliant to Thee; teach me.

For I see not that it would drive away this anguish that withers up my senses, if I should attain unrivalled monarchy on earth, or even the sovereignty of the Shining Ones.

Sanjaya said:

Gudâkesha, conqueror of his foes, having thus addressed Hrishîkesha, and said to Govinda, "I will not fight!" became silent.

Then Hrishîkesha, smiling, as it were O Bhârata, spake these words, in the midst of the two armies, to him, despondent.

The Blessed Lord said:

Thou grievest for those that should not be grieved for, yet speakest words of wisdom. The wise grieve neither for the living nor for the dead.

Nor at any time verily was I not, nor thou, nor these princes of men, nor verily shall we ever cease to be, hereafter.

As the dweller in the body experienceth, in the body, childhood, youth and old age, so passeth he on to another body; the steadfast one grieveth not thereat.

The contacts of matter, O son of Kuntî, giving cold and heat, pleasure and pain, they come and go, impermanent; endure them bravely, O Bhârata.

The man whom these torment not, O chief of men, balanced in pain and pleasure, steadfast, he is fitted for immortality.

The unreal hath no being; the real never ceaseth to be; the truth about both hath been perceived by the seers of the Essence of things.

Know that to be indestructible by whom all this is pervaded. Nor can any work the destruction of that imperishable One.

These bodies of the embodied One, who is eternal, indestructible and boundless, are known as finite. Therefore fight, O Bhârata.

He who regardeth this as a slayer, and he who thinketh he is slain, both of them are ignorant. He slayeth not, nor is he slain.

He is not born, nor doth he die: nor having been, ceaseth he any more to be; unborn, perpetual, eternal and ancient, he is not slain when the body is slaughtered.

Who knoweth him indestructible, perpetual, unborn, undiminishing, how can that man slay, O Pârtha, or cause to be slain?

As a man, casting off worn-out garments, taketh new ones, so the dweller in the body, casting off worn-out bodies, entereth into others that are new.

Weapons cleave him not, nor fire burneth him, nor waters wet him, nor wind drieth him away.

Uncleavable he, incombustible he, and indeed neither to be wetted nor dried away; perpetual, all-pervasive, stable, immovable, ancient,

Unmanifest, unthinkable, immutable, he is called; therefore knowing him as such, thou shouldst not grieve.

Or if thou thinkest of him as being constantly born and constantly dying, even then, O mighty-armed, thou shouldst not grieve.

For certain is death for the born, and certain is birth for the dead; therefore over the inevitable thou shouldst not grieve.

Beings are unmanifest in their origin, manifest in their midmost state, O Bhârata, unmanifest likewise are they in dissolution. What room then for lamentation?

As marvellous one regardeth him; as marvellous another

speaketh thereof; as marvellous another heareth thereof; yet heaving heard, none indeed understandeth.

This dweller in the body of everyone is ever invulnerable, O Bhârata; therefore thou shouldst not grieve for any creature.

Further, looking to thine own duty, thou shouldst not tremble; for there is nothing more welcome to a Kshattriya than righteous war.

Happy the Kshattriyas, O Pârtha, who obtain such a fight, offered unsought as an open door to heaven.

But if thou wilt not carry on this righteous warfare, then, casting away thine own duty and thine honour, thou wilt incur sin.

Men will recount thy perpetual dishonor, and, to one highly esteemed, dishonor exceedeth death.

The great car-warriors will think thee fled from the battle from fear, and thou that wast highly thought of by them, wilt be lightly held.

Many unseemly words will be spoken by thine enemies, slandering thy strength; what more painful than that?

Slain, thou wilt obtain heaven; victorious, thou wilt enjoy the earth; therefore stand up, O son of Kuntî, resolute to fight.

Taking as equal pleasure and pain, gain and loss, victory and defeat, gird thee for the battle; thus thou shalt not incur sin.

This teaching set forth to thee is in accordance with the Sânkya; hear it now according to the Yoga, imbued with which teaching, O Pârtha, thou shalt cast away the bonds of action.

In this there is no loss of effort, nor is there transgression. Even a little of this knowledge protects from great fear.

The determinate reason is but one-pointed, O joy of the Kurus; many-branched and endless are the thoughts of the irresolute.

Flowery speech is uttered by the foolish, rejoicing in the letter of the Vedas, O Pârtha, saying: "There is naught but this."

With desire for self, with heaven for goal, they offer birth as the fruit of action, and prescribe many and various ceremonies for the attainment of pleasure and lordship.

For them who cling to pleasure and lordship, whose minds are captivated by such teaching, is not designed this determinate Reason, on contemplation steadily bent.

The Vedas deal with the three attributes; be thou above these three attributes, O Arjuna; beyond the pairs of opposites, ever steadfast in purity, careless of possessions, full of the Self.

All the Vedas are as useful to an enlightened Brâhmana as is a tank in a place covered all over with water.

Thy business is with the action only, never with its fruits; so let not the fruit of action be thy motive, nor be thou to inaction attached.

Perform action, O Dhanañjaya, dwelling in union with the divine, renouncing attachments, and balanced evenly in success and failure: equilibrium is called yoga.

Far lower than the Yoga of Discrimination is action, O Dhanañjaya. Take thou refuge in the Pure Reason; pitiable are they who work for fruit.

United to the Pure Reason, one abandoneth here both good and evil deeds, therefore cleave thou to yoga; yoga is skill in action.

The Sages, united to the Pure Reason, renounce the fruit which action yieldeth, and, liberated from the bonds of birth, they go to the blissful seat.

When thy mind shall escape from this tangle of delusion, then thou shalt rise to indifference as to what has been heard and shall be heard.

When thy mind, bewildered by the Shruti, shall stand immovable, fixed in contemplation, then shalt thou attain unto yoga.

Arjuna said:

What is the mark of him who is stable of mind, steadfast in contemplation, O Keshava? how doth the stable-minded talk, how doth he sit, how walk?

The Blessed Lord said:

When a man abandoneth, O Pârtha, all the desires of the heart, and is satisfied in the Self by the Self, then is he called stable in mind.

He whose mind is free from anxiety amid pains, indifferent amid pleasures, loosed from passion, fear and anger, he is called a sage of stable mind.

He who on every side is without attachments, whatever hap of fair and foul, who neither likes nor dislikes, of such a one the understanding is well-poised.

When, again, as a tortoise draws in on all sides its limbs, he withdraws his senses from the objects of sense, then in his understanding well-poised.

The objects of sense, but not the relish for them, turn away from an abstemious dweller in the body; and even relish turneth away from him after the Supreme is seen.

O son of Kuntî, the excited senses of even a wise man,

though he be striving, impetuously carry away his mind.

Having restrained them all, he should sit harmonised, I his supreme goal; for whose senses are mastered, of him the understanding is well-poised.

Man, musing on the objects of sense, conceiveth an attachment to these; from attachment ariseth desire; from desire anger cometh forth;

From anger proceedeth delusion; from delusion confused memory; from confused memory the destruction of Reason; from destruction of Reason he perishes.

But the disciplined self, moving among sense-objects with senses free from attraction and repulsion mastered by the Self, goeth to Peace.

In that Peace the extinction of all pains ariseth for him; for of him whose heart is peaceful the Reason soon attaineth equilibrium.

There is no pure Reason for the non-harmonised, nor for the non-harmonised is there concentration; for him without concentration there is no peace, and for the unpeaceful how can there be happiness?

Such of the roving sense as the mind yieldeth to, that hurries away the understanding, just as the gale hurries away a ship upon the waters.

Therefore, O mighty-armed, whose senses are all completely restrained from the objects of sense, of him the understanding is well-poised.

That which is the night of all beings, for the disciplined man is the time of waking; when other beings are waking, then is night for the Muni who seeth.

He attaineth Peace, into whom all desires flow as rivers

flow into the ocean, which is filled with water but remaineth unmoved—not he who desireth desires.

Who so forsaketh all desires and goeth onwards free from yearnings, selfless and without egoism—he goeth to Peace.

This is the Eternal state, O son of Prithâ. Having attained thereto none is bewildered. Who, even at the death-hour, is established therein, he goeth to the Nirvâna of the Eternal.

THIRD DISCOURSE

Arjuna said:

If it be thought by thee that knowledge is superior to action, O Janârdana, why dost thou, O Keshava, enjoin on me this terrible action?

With these perplexing words Thou only confusest my understanding; therefore tell me with certainty the one way by which I may reach bliss?

The Blessed Lord said:

In this world there is a twofold path, as I before said, O sinless one: that of yoga by knowledge, of the Sânkhyas; and that of yoga by action, of the Yogis.

Man winneth not freedom from action by abstaining from activity, nor by mere renunciation doth he rise to perfection.

Nor can anyone, even for an instant, remain really actionless; for helplessly is everyone driven to action by the qualities born of nature.

Who sitteth, controlling the organs of action, but dwelling in his mind on the objects of the senses, that bewildered man is called a hypocrite.

But who, controlling the senses by the mind, O Arjuna, with the organs of action, without attachment performeth yoga by action, he is worthy.

Perform thou right action, for action is superior to inaction, and, inactive, even the maintenance of thy body would not be possible.

The world is bound by action, unless performed for the sake of sacrifice; for that sake, free from attachment, O son of Kuntî, perform thou action.

Having in ancient times emanated mankind together with sacrifice, the Lord of emanation said: "By this shall ye propagate; be this to you the giver of desires;

"With this nourish ye the shining ones and may the shining ones nourish you; thus nourishing one another, ye shall reap the supremest good.

"For, nourished by sacrifice, the Shining Ones shall bestow on you the enjoyments you desire." A thief verily is he who enjoyeth what is given by Them without returning Them aught.

The righteous, who eat the remains of the sacrifice, are freed from all sins; but the impious, who dress food for their own sakes, they verily eat sin.

From food creatures become; from rain is the production of food; rain proceedeth from sacrifice; sacrifice ariseth out of action;

Know thou that from Brahma action groweth, and Brahman from the Imperishable cometh. Therefore the Eternal, the all-permeating, is ever present in sacrifice.

He who on earth doth not follow the wheel thus revolving, sinful of life and rejoicing in the senses, he, O son of Prithâ, liveth in vain.

But the man who rejoiceth in the Self, with the Self is satisfied, and is content in the Self, for him verily there is nothing to do.

For him there is no interest in things done in this world, nor any in things not done, nor doth any object of his depend on any being.

Therefore, without attachment, constantly perform action which is duty, for by performing action without attachment, man verily reacheth the Supreme.

Janaka and others indeed attained to perfection by action; then having an eye to the welfare of the world also, thou shouldst perform action.

Whatsoever a great man doeth, that other men also do; the standard he setteth up, by that the people go.

There is nothing in the three worlds, O Pârtha, that should be done by Me, nor anything unattained that might be attained; yet I mingle in action.

For if I mingled not ever in action, unwearied, men all around would follow My path, O son of Prithâ.

These worlds would fall into ruin, if I did not perform action; I should be the author of confusion of castes, and should destroy these creatures.

As the ignorant act from attachment to action, O Bhârata, so should the wise act without attachment, desiring the welfare of the world.

Let no wise man unsettle the mind of ignorant people attached to action; but acting in harmony with Me let him render all action attractive.

All actions are wrought by the qualities of nature only. The self, deluded by egoism, thinketh: "I am the doer."

But he, O mighty-armed, who knoweth the essence of the divisions of the qualities and functions, holding that "the qualities move amid the qualities," is not attached.

Those deluded by the qualities of nature are attached to the functions of the qualities. The man of perfect knowledge should not unsettle the foolish whose knowledge is imperfect.

Surrendering all actions to Me, with thy thoughts resting on the supreme Self, from hope and egoism freed, and of mental fever cured, engage in battle.

Who abide ever in this teaching of Mine, full of faith and free from cavilling, they too are released from actions.

Who carp at My teaching and act not thereon, senseless, deluded in all knowledge, know thou these mindless ones as fated to be destroyed.

Even the man of knowledge behaves in conformity with his own nature; beings follow nature; what shall restraint avail?

Affection and aversion for the objects of sense abide in the senses; let none come under the dominion of these two; they are obstructors of the path.

Better one's own duty, though destitute of merit, than the duty of another well-discharged. Better death in the discharge of one's own duty; the duty of another is full of danger.

Arjuna said:

But dragged on by what does a man commit sin, reluctantly indeed, O Vârshneya, as it were by force constrained?

The Blessed Lord said:

It is desire, it is wrath, begotten by the quality of mobility; all-consuming, all-polluting, know thou this as our foe here on earth.

As a flame is enveloped by smoke, as a mirror by dust, as an embryo is wrapped by the amnion, so This is enveloped by it.

Enveloped is wisdom by this constant enemy of the wise in the form of desire, which is insatiable as a flame.

The senses, the mind and the Reason are said to be its seat; by these, enveloping wisdom, it bewilders the dweller in the body.

Therefore, O best of the Bharatas, mastering first the senses, do thou slay this thing of sin, destructive of wisdom and knowledge.

It is said that the senses are great; greater than the senses is the mind; greater than the mind is the Reason; but what is greater than the Reason, is He.

Thus understanding Him as greater than the Reason, restraining the self by the Self, slay thou, O mighty-armed, the enemy in the form of desire, difficult to overcome.

FOURTH DISCOURSE

The Blessed Lord said:

This imperishable yoga I declared to Vivasvân; Vivasvân taught it to Manu; Manu to Ikshvâku told it.

This, handed on down the line, the King-Sages knew. This yoga by great efflux of time decayed in the world, O Parantapa.

This same ancient yoga hath been to-day declared to thee by Me, for thou art My devotee and My friend; it is the supreme Secret.

Arjuna said:

Later was thy birth, earlier the birth of Vivasvân; how then am I to understand that Thou declaredst it in the beginning?

The Blessed Lord said:

Many births have been left behind by Me and by thee, O Arjuna. I know them all, but thou knowest not thine, O Parantapa.

Though unborn, the imperishable Self, and also the Lord of all beings, brooding over nature, which is Mine own, yet I am born through My own Power.

Whenever there is decay of righteousness, O Bhârata, and there is exaltation of unrighteousness, then I Myself come forth;

For the protection of the good, for the destruction of evil-doers, for the sake of firmly establishing righteousness, I am born from age to age.

He who thus knoweth My divine birth and action, in its essence, having abandoned the body, cometh not to birth again, but cometh unto Me, O Arjuna.

Freed from passion, fear and anger, filled with Me, taking refuge in Me, purified in the fire of wisdom, many have entered into My being.

However men approach Me, even so do I welcome them, for the path men take from every side is Mine, O Pârtha.

They who long after success in action on earth sacrifice to the Shining Ones; for in brief space verily, in this world of men, success is born of action.

The four castes were emanated by Me, by the different distribution of qualities and actions; know Me to be the author of them, though the actionless and inexhaustible.

Nor do actions affect Me, nor is the fruit of action desired by Me. He who thus knoweth Me is not bound by actions.

Having thus known, our forefathers, ever seeking liberation, performed action; therefore do thou also perform action, as did our forefathers in the olden time.

"What is action, what inaction?" Even the wise are herein perplexed. Therefore I will declare to thee the action by knowing which thou shalt be loosed from evil.

It is needful to discriminate action, to discriminate unlawful action, and to discriminate inaction; mysterious is the path of action.

He who seeth inaction in action, and action in inaction, he is wise among men, he is harmonious, even while performing all action.

Whose works are all free from the moulding of desire, whose actions are burned up by the fire of wisdom, him the wise have called a Sage.

Having abandoned attachment to the fruit of action, always content, nowhere seeking refuge, he is not doing anything, although doing actions.

Hoping for naught, his mind and self controlled, having abandoned all greed, performing action by the body alone he doth not commit sin.

Content with whatsoever he obtaineth without effort, free from the pairs of opposites, without envy, balanced in success and failure, though acting he is not bound.

Of one with attachment dead, harmonious, with his thoughts established in wisdom, his works sacrifices, all action melts away.

The Eternal the oblation, the Eternal the clarified butter, are offered in the Eternal the fire by the Eternal; unto the Eternal verily shall he go who in his action meditateth wholly upon the Eternal.

Some Yogîs offer up sacrifice to the Shining Ones; others sacrifice only by pouring sacrifice into the fire of the Eternal;

Some pour as sacrifice hearing and the other senses into the fires of restraint; some pour sound and the other objects of sense into the fires of the senses as sacrifice;

Others again into the wisdom-kindled fire of union attained by self-control, pour as sacrifice all the functions of the senses and the functions of life;

Yet others the sacrifice of wealth, the sacrifice of austerity, the sacrifice of yoga, the sacrifice of silent reading and wisdom, men concentrated and of effectual vows;

Yet others pour as sacrifice the outgoing breath in the incoming, and the incoming in the outgoing, restraining the flow of the outgoing and incoming breaths, solely absorbed in the control of breathing;

Others, regular in food, pour as sacrifice their life-breaths in life-breaths. All these are knowers of sacrifice, and by sacrifice have destroyed their sins.

The eaters of the life-giving remains of sacrifice go to the changeless Eternal. This world is not for the non-sacrificer, much less the other, O best of the Kurus.

Many and various sacrifices are thus spread out before the Eternal. Know thou that all these are born of action, and thus knowing thou shalt be free.

Better than the sacrifice of any objects is the sacrifice of wisdom, O Parantapa. All actions in their entirety, O

Pârtha, culminate in wisdom.

Learn thou this by discipleship, by investigation, and by service. The wise, the seers of the Essence of things, will instruct thee in wisdom.

And having known this, thou shalt not again fall into this confusion, O Pândava; for by this thou wilt see all beings without exception in the Self, and thus in Me.

Even if thou art the most sinful of all sinners, yet shalt thou cross over all sin by the raft of wisdom.

As the burning fire reduces fuel to ashes, O Arjuna, so doth the fire of wisdom reduce all actions to ashes.

Verily there is no purifier in this world like wisdom; he that is perfected in yoga finds it in the Self in due season.

The man who is full of faith obtaineth wisdom, and he also who hath mastery over his senses; and having obtained wisdom he goeth swiftly to the Supreme Peace.

But the ignorant, faithless, doubting self goeth to destruction; nor this world, nor that beyond, nor happiness, is there for the doubting self.

He who hath renounced action by yoga, who hath cloven asunder doubt by wisdom, who is ruled by the Self, actions do not bind him, O Dhanañjaya.

Therefore with the sword of the wisdom of the Self cleaving asunder this ignorance-born doubt, dwelling in thy heart, be established in yoga. Stand up, O Bhârata.

FIFTH DISCOURSE

Arjuna said:

Renunciation of actions, thou praisest, O Krishna, and then also yoga. Of the two which one is the better? That tell me conclusively.

The Blessed Lord said:

Renunciation and yoga by action both lead to the highest bliss; of the two, yoga by action is verily better than renunciation of action.

He should be known as a perpetual ascetic, who neither hateth nor desireth; free from the pairs of opposites, O mighty-armed, he is easily set free from bondage.

Children, not Sages, speak of the Sânkhya and Yoga as different; he who is duly established in one obtaineth the fruits of both.

That place which is gained by the Sânkhyas is reached by the Yogas also. He seeth who seeth that the Sânkhya and the Yoga are one.

But without yoga, O mighty-armed, renunciation is hard to attain to; the yoga-harmonised Muni swiftly goeth to the Eternal.

He who is harmonised by yoga, the self purified, Self-ruled, the senses subdued, whose Self is the Self of all beings, although acting he is not affected.

"I do not anything," should think the harmonised one, who knoweth the Essence of things; seeing, hearing, touching, smelling, eating, moving, sleeping, breathing,

Speaking, giving, grasping, opening and closing the eyes, he holdeth: "The senses move among the objects of the senses."

He who acteth, placing all actions in the Eternal, abandoning attachment, is unaffected by sin as a lotus leaf by the waters.

Yogîs, having abandoned attachment, perform action

only by the body, by the mind, by the Reason, and even by the senses, for the purification of the self.

The harmonised man, having abandoned the fruit of action, attaineth to the eternal Peace; the non-harmonised, impelled by desire, attached to fruit, are bound.

Mentally renouncing all actions, the sovereign dweller in the body resteth serenely in the nine-gated city, neither acting nor causing to act.

The Lord of the world produceth not the idea of agency, nor actions, nor the union together of action and its fruit; nature, however, manifesteth.

The Lord accepteth neither the evil-doing nor yet the well-doing of any. Wisdom is enveloped by unwisdom; therewith mortals are deluded.

Verily, in whom unwisdom is destroyed by the wisdom of the Self, in them wisdom, shining as the sun, reveals the Supreme.

Thinking on That, merged in That, established in That, solely devoted to That, they go whence there is no return, their sins dispelled by wisdom.

Sages look equally on a Brâhmana adorned with earning and humility, a cow, an elephant, and even a dog, and an outcast.

Even here on earth everything is overcome by those whose mind remains balanced; the Eternal is incorruptible and balanced; therefore they are established in the Eternal.

With Reason firm, unperplexed, the knower of the Eternal, established in the Eternal, neither rejoiceth on obtaining what is pleasant, nor sorroweth on obtaining what is unpleasant.

He whose self is unattached to external contacts, and

findeth joy in the Self, having the self harmonised with the Eternal by yoga, enjoys happiness exempt from decay.

The delights that are contact-born, they are verily wombs of pain, for they have beginning and ending, O Kaunteya; not in them may rejoice the wise.

He who is able to endure here on earth, ere he be liberated from the body, the force born from desire and passion, he is harmonised, he is a happy man.

He who is happy within, who rejoiceth within, who is illuminated within, that Yogî, becoming the Eternal, goeth to the Peace of the Eternal.

Rishis, their sins destroyed, their duality removed, their selves controlled, intent upon the welfare of all beings, obtain the Peace of the Eternal.

The Peace of the Eternal lies near to those who know themselves, who are disjoined from desire and passion, subdued in nature, of subdued thoughts.

Having external contacts excluded, and with gaze fixed between the eye-brows; having made equal the outgoing and incoming breaths moving within the nostrils,

With senses, mind and Reason ever controlled, solely pursuing liberation, the Sage, having for ever cast away desire, fear and passion, verily is liberated.

Having known Me, as the Enjoyer of sacrifice and of austerity, the mighty Ruler of all the worlds, and the Lover of all beings, he goeth to Peace.

SIXTH DISCOURSE

The Blessed Lord said:

He that performeth such action as is duty, independently

of the fruit of action, he is an ascetic, he is a Yogî, not he that is without fire and without rites.

That which is called renunciation know thou that as yoga, O Pândava; nor doth any one become a Yogî with the formative will unrenounced.

For a Sage who is seeking yoga, action is called the means, for the same Sage, when he is enthroned in yoga, serenity is called the means.

When a man feeleth no attachment either for the objects of sense or for actions, renouncing the formative will, then he is said to be enthroned in yoga.

Let him raise the self by the Self, and not let the self become depressed; for verily is the Self the friend of the self, and also the Self the self's enemy;

The Self is the friend of the self of him in whom the self by the Self is vanquished; but to the unsubdued self, the Self verily becometh hostile as an enemy.

The higher Self of him who is Self-controlled and peaceful is uniform in cold and heat, pleasure and pain, as well as in honour and dishonour.

The Yogî who is satisfied with wisdom and knowledge, unwavering, whose senses are subdued, to whom a lump of earth, a stone and gold are the same, is said to be harmonised.

He who regards impartially lovers, friends, and foes, strangers, neutrals, foreigners and relatives, also the righteous and unrighteousness, he excelleth.

Let the Yogî constantly engage himself in yoga, remaining in a secret place by himself, with thought and self subdued, free from hope and greed.

In a pure place, established on a fixed seat of his own, neither very much raised nor very low, made of a cloth, a black antelope skin, and kusha grass, one over the other,

There, having made the mind one-pointed, with thought and the functions of the sense subdued, steady on his seat, he should practise yoga for the purification of the self.

Holding the body, head and neck erect, immovably steady, looking fixedly at the point of the nose, with unseeing gaze,

The self serene, fearless, firm in the vow of the Brahmachârî, the mind controlled, thinking on Me, harmonised, let him sit aspiring after Me.

The Yogî, ever united thus with the Self, with the mind controlled, goeth to Peace, to the supreme Bliss that abideth in Me.

Verily yoga is not for him who eateth too much, nor who abstaineth to excess, nor who is too much addicted to sleep, nor even to wakefulness, O Arjuna.

Yoga killeth out all pain for him who is regulated in eating and amusement, regulated in performing actions, regulated in sleeping and waking.

When his subdued thought is fixed on the Self, free from longing after all desirable things, then it is said: "he is harmonised."

As a lamp in a windless place flickereth not, to such is likened the Yogî of subdued thought, absorbed in the yoga of the Self.

That in which the mind finds rest, quieted by the practice of yoga; that in which he, seeing the Self by the Self, in the Self is satisfied;

That in which he findeth the supreme delight which the Reason can grasp beyond the senses, wherein established, he moveth not from the Reality;

Which, having obtained, he thinketh there is no greater gain beyond it; wherein established, he is not shaken even by heavy sorrow;

That should be known by the name of yoga, this disconnection from the union with pain. This yoga must be clung to with a firm conviction and with undesponding mind.

Abandoning without reserve all desires born of the imagination, by the mind curbing in the aggregate of the senses on every side,

Little by little let him gain tranquillity by means of Reason controlled by steadiness; having made the mind abide in the Self, let him not think of anything.

As often as the wavering and unsteady mind goeth forth, so often reining it in, let him bring it under the control of the Self.

Supreme joy is for the Yogî whose mind is peaceful, whose passion-nature is calmed, who is sinless and of the nature of the Eternal.

The Yogî who thus, ever harmonising the self, hath put away sin, he easily enjoyeth the infinite bliss of contact with the Eternal.

The self, harmonised by yoga, seeth the Self abiding in all beings, all beings in the Self; everywhere he seeth the same.

He who seeth Me everywhere, and seeth everything in Me, of him will I never lose hold, and he shall never lose hold of Me.

He who, established in unity, worshippeth Me, abiding in

all beings, that Yogî liveth in Me, whatever his mode of living.

He who, through the likeness of the Self, O Arjuna, seeth equality in everything, whether pleasant or painful, he is considered a perfect Yogî.

Arjuna said:

This yoga which Thou hast declared to be by equanimity, O Madhusûdana, I see not a stable foundation for it, owing to restlessness;

For the mind is verily restless, O Krishna; it is impetuous, strong and difficult to bend; I deem it as hard to curb as the wind.

The Blessed Lord said:

Without doubt, O mighty-armed, the mind is hard to curb and restless; but it may be curbed by constant practice and by dispassion.

Yoga is hard to attain, methinks, by a self that is uncontrolled; but by the Self-controlled it is attainable by properly directed energy.

Arjuna said:

He who is unsubdued but who possesseth faith, with the mind wandering away from yoga, failing to attain perfection in yoga, what path doth he tread, O Krishna?

Fallen from both, is he destroyed like a rent cloud, unsteadfast, O mighty-armed, deluded in the path of the Eternal?

Deign, O Krishna, to completely dispel this doubt of mine; for there is none to be found save Thyself able to destroy this doubt.

The Blessed Lord said:

O son of Prithâ, neither in this world nor in the life to come is there destruction for him; never doth any who worketh righteousness, O beloved, tread the path of woe.

Having attained to the worlds of the pure-doing, and having dwelt there for immemorial years, he who fell from yoga is reborn in a pure and blessed house.

Or he may even be born into a family of wise Yogîs; but such a birth as that is most difficult to obtain in this world.

There he recovereth the characteristics belonging to his former body, and with these he again laboureth for perfection, O joy of the Kurus.

By that former practice he is irresistibly swept away. Only wishing to know yoga, even the seeker after yoga goeth beyond the Brâhmic word.

But the Yogî, labouring with assiduity, purified from sin, fully perfected through manifold births, he reacheth the supreme goal.

The Yogî is greater than the ascetics; he is thought to be greater than even the wise; the Yogî is greater than the men of action; therefore become thou a Yogî, O Arjuna.

And among all Yogîs, he who, full of faith, with the inner Self abiding in Me, adoreth Me, he is considered by Me to be the most completely harmonised.

SEVENTH DISCOURSE

The Blessed Lord said:

With the mind clinging to Me, O Pârtha, performing yoga, refuged in Me, how thou shalt without doubt know Me to the uttermost, that hear thou.

I will declare to thee this knowledge and wisdom in its completeness, which, having known, there is nothing more here needeth to be known.

Among thousands of men scarce one striveth for perfection; of the successful strivers scarce one knoweth Me in essence.

Earth, water, fire, air, ether, Mind and Reason also and Egoism—these are the eightfold division of My nature.

This is the inferior. Know My other nature, the higher, the life-element, O mighty-armed, by which the universe is upheld.

Know this to be the womb of all beings. I am the source of the forthgoing of the whole universe and likewise the place of its dissolving.

There is naught whatsoever higher than I, O Dhanañjaya. All this is threaded on Me, as rows of pearls on a string.

I the sapidity in waters, O son of Kuntî, I the radiance in moon and sun; the Word of Power in all the Vedas, sound in ether, and virility in men;

The pure fragrance of earth and the brilliance in fire am I: the life in all beings am I, and the austerity in ascetics.

Know Me, O Pârtha, as the eternal seed of all beings. I am the Reason of the Reason-endowed, the splendour of splendid things am I.

And I the strength of the strong, devoid of desire and passion. In beings, I am desire not contrary to duty, O Lord of the Bharatas.

The natures that are harmonious, active, slothful, these know as from Me; not I in them, but they in Me.

All this world, deluded by these natures made by the three qualities, knoweth not Me, above these, imperishable.

This divine illusion of Mine, caused by the qualities, is hard to pierce; they who come to Me, they cross over this illusion.

The evil-doing, the deluded, the vilest men, they come not to Me, they whose wisdom is destroyed by illusion, who have embraced the nature of demons.

Fourfold in division are the righteous ones who worship Me, O Arjuna: the suffering, the seeker for knowledge, the self-interested, and the wise, O Lord of the Bharatas.

Of these, the wise, constantly harmonised, worshipping the One, is the best; I am supremely dear to the wise, and he is dear to Me.

Noble are all these, but I hold the wise as verily Myself; he, Self-united, is fixed on Me, the highest path.

At the close of many births the man full of wisdom cometh unto Me: "Vâsudeva is all," saith he, the Mahâtmâ, very difficult to find.

They whose wisdom hath been rent away by desires go forth to other Shining Ones, resorting to various external observances, according to their own natures.

Any devotee who seeketh to worship with faith any such aspect, I verily bestow the unswerving faith of that man.

He, endowed with that faith, seeketh the worship of such a one, and from him he obtaineth his desires, I verily decreeing the benefits;

Finite indeed the fruit; that belongeth to those who are of small intelligence. To the Shining Ones go the worship-pers of the Shining Ones, but My devotees come unto Me.

Those devoid of Reason think of Me, the Unmanifest, as having manifestation, knowing not My supreme nature, imperishable, most excellent.

Nor am I of all discovered, enveloped in My creative

illusion. This deluded world knoweth Me not, the unborn, the imperishable.

I know the beings that are past, that are present, that are to come, O Arjuna, but no one knoweth Me.

By the delusion of the pairs of opposites, sprung from attraction and repulsion, O Bhârata, all beings walk this universe wholly deluded, O Parantapa.

But those men of pure deeds, in whom sin is come to an end, they, freed from the delusive pairs of opposites, worship Me, steadfast in vows.

They who refuged in Me strive for liberation from birth and death, they know the Eternal, the whole Self-knowledge and all Action.

They who know Me as the knowledge of the Elements, as that of the Shining Ones, and as that of the Sacrifice, they, harmonised in mind, know Me verily even in the time of forthgoing.

EIGHTH DISCOURSE

Arjuna said:

What is that Eternal, what Self-knowledge, what Action, O Purushottama? And what is declared to be the knowledge of the Elements, what is called the knowledge of the Shining Ones?

What is knowledge of Sacrifice in this body, and how, O Madhusûdana? And how at the time of forthgoing art Thou known by the Self-controlled?

The Blessed Lord said:

The indestructible, the supreme, is the Eternal; His essential nature is called Self-knowledge; the emanation that causes the birth of beings is named Action;

Knowledge of the Elements concerns My perishable nature, and knowledge of the Shining Ones concerns the life-giving energy; the knowledge of sacrifice tells of Me, as wearing the body, O best of living beings.

And he who, casting off the body, goeth forth thinking upon Me only at the time of the end, he entereth into My being; there is no doubt of that.

Whosoever at the end abandoneth the body, thinking upon any being, to that being only he goeth, O Kaunteya, ever to that conformed in nature.

Therefore at all times think upon Me only, and fight. With mind and Reason set on Me, without doubt thou shalt come to Me.

With the mind not wandering after aught else, harmonised by continual practice, constantly meditating, O Pârtha, one goeth to the Spirit, supreme, divine.

He who thinketh upon the Ancient, the Omniscient, the All-Ruler, minuter than the minute, the Supporter of all, of form unimaginable, refulgent as the sun beyond the darkness,

In the time of forthgoing, with unshaken mind, fixed in devotion, by the power of yoga drawing together his life-breath in the centre of the two eye-brows, he goeth to this Spirit, supreme, divine.

That which is declared indestructible by the Veda-knowers, that which the controlled and passion-free enter, that desiring which Brahmachârya is performed, that path I will declare to thee with brevity.

All the gates closed, the mind confined in the heart, the life-breath fixed in his own head, concentrated by yoga,

"Aum!" the one-syllabled Brahman, reciting, thinking upon Me, he who goeth forth, abandoning the body, he goeth on the highest path.

He who constantly thinketh upon Me, not thinking ever of another, of him I am easily reached, O Pârtha, of this ever harmonised Yogi.

Having come to Me, these Mahâtmâs come not again to birth, the place of pain, non-eternal; they have gone to the highest bliss.

The worlds, beginning with the world of Brahmâ, they come and go, O Arjuna; but he who cometh unto Me, O Kaunteya, he knoweth birth no more.

The people who know the day of Brahmâ, a thousand ages in duration, and the night, a thousand ages in ending, they know day and night.

From the unmanifested all the manifested stream forth at the coming of day; at the coming of night they dissolve, even in That called the unmanifested.

This multitude of beings going forth repeatedly, is dissolved at the coming of night; by ordination, O Pârtha, it streams forth at the coming of day.

Therefore verily there existeth, higher than that unmanifested, another unmanifested, eternal, which, in the destroying of all beings, is not destroyed.

That unmanifested, "the Indestructible," It is called; It is named the highest Path. They who reach It return not. That is My supreme abode.

He, the highest Spirit, O Pârtha, may be reached by unswerving devotion to Him alone, in whom all beings abide, by whom all This is pervaded.

That time wherein going forth, Yogîs return not, and also that wherein going forth they return, that time shall I declare to thee, O prince of the Bharatas.

Fire, light, day-time, the bright fortnight, the six months of the northern path—then, going forth, the men who know the Eternal go to the Eternal.

Smoke, night-time, the dark fortnight also, the six months of the southern path—then the Yogî, obtaining the moonlight, returneth.

Light and darkness, these are thought to be the world's everlasting paths; by the one he goeth who returneth not, by the other he who returneth again.

Knowing these paths, O Pârtha, the Yogî is nowise per-plexed. Therefore in all times be firm in yoga, O Arjuna.

The fruit of meritorious deeds, attached in the Vedas to sacrifices, to austerities, and also to almsgiving, the Yogî pas-seth all these by having known this, and goeth to the supreme and ancient Seat.

NINTH DISCOURSE

The Blessed Lord said:

To thee, the uncarping, verily shall I declare this pro-foundest Secret, wisdom with knowledge combined, which, having known, thou shalt be freed from evil.

Kingly Science, kingly Secret, supreme Purifier, this, intuitional, according to righteousness, very easy to perform, imperishable.

Men without faith in this knowledge, O Parantapa, not reaching Me, return to the paths of this world of death.

By Me all this world is pervaded in My unmanifested

aspect; all beings have root in Me, I am not rooted in them.

Nor have beings root in Me; behold My sovereign yoga! The support of beings, yet not rooted in beings, My Self their efficient cause.

As the mighty air everywhere moving is rooted in the Akâsha, so all beings rest rooted in Me—thus know thou.

All beings, O Kaunteya, enter My lower nature at the end of a world-age; at the beginning of a world-age again I emanate them.

Hidden in Nature, which is Mine own, I emanate forth again and again all this multitude of beings, helpless, by the force of Nature.

Nor do these works bind me, O Dhanañjaya, enthroned on high, unattached to actions.

Under Me, as supervisor, Nature sends forth the moving and unmoving; because of this, O Kaunteya, the universe revolves.

The foolish disregard Me, when clad in human semblance, ignorant of My supreme nature, the great Lord of beings;

Empty of hope, empty of deeds, empty of wisdom, senseless partaking of the deceitful, brutal, and demoniacal nature.

Verily the Mahâtmas, O Pârtha, partaking of My divine nature, worship with unwavering mind, having known Me, the imperishable source of beings.

Always magnifying Me, strenuous, firm in vows, prostrating themselves before Me, they worship Me with devotion, ever harmonised.

Others also sacrificing with the sacrifice of wisdom,

worship Me as the One and the Manifold everywhere present.

I the oblation; I the sacrifice; I the ancestral offering; I the fire-giving herb; the mantra I; I also the butter; I the fire; the burnt-offering I;

I the Father of this universe, the Mother, the Supporter, the Grandsire, the Holy One to be known, the Word of Power, and also the Rik, Sâma, and Yajur,

The Path, Husband, Lord, Witness, Abode, Shelter, Lover, Origin, Dissolution, Foundation, Treasure-house, Seed imperishable.

I give heat; I hold back and send forth the rain; immortality and also death, being and non-being am I, Arjuna.

The knowers of the three, the Soma-drinkers, the purified from sin, worshipping Me with sacrifice, pray of Me the way to heaven; they, ascending to the holy world of the Ruler of the Shining Ones, eat in heaven the divine feasts of the Shining Ones.

They, having enjoyed the spacious heaven-world, their holiness withered, come back to this world of death. Following the virtues enjoined by the three, desiring desires, they obtain the transitory.

To those men who worship Me alone, thinking of no other, to those, ever harmonious, I bring full security.

Even the devotees of other Shining Ones who worship full of faith, they also worship Me, O son of Kuntî, though contrary to the ancient rule.

I am indeed the enjoyer of all sacrifices, and also the Lord, but they know Me not in Essence, and hence they fall.

They who worship the Shining Ones go to the Shining Ones; to the ancestors go the ancestor-worshippers; to the

Elementals go those who sacrifice to Elementals; but My worshippers come unto Me.

He who offereth to Me with devotion a leaf, a flower, a fruit, water, that I accept from the striving self, offered as it is with devotion.

Whatsoever thou doest, whatsoever thou eatest, whatsoever thou offerest, whatsoever thou givest, whatsoever thou doest of austerity, O Kaunteya, do thou that as an offering unto Me.

Thus shalt thou be liberated from the bonds of action, yielding good and evil fruits; thyself harmonised by the yoga of renunciation, thou shalt come unto Me when set free.

The same am I to all beings; there is none hateful to Me nor dear. They verily who worship Me with devotion, they are in Me, and I also in them.

Even if the most sinful worship Me, with undivided heart, he too must be accounted righteous, for he hath rightly resolved;

Speedily he becometh dutiful and goeth to eternal peace. O Kaunteya, know thou for certain that My devotee perisheth never.

They who take refuge with Me, O Pârtha, though of the womb of sin, woman, Vaishyas, even Shûdras, they also tread the highest Path.

How much rather then holy Brâhmanas and devoted royal saints; having obtained this transient joyless world, worship thou Me.

On Me fix thy mind; be devoted to Me; sacrifice to Me; prostrate thyself before Me; harmonised thus in the Self, thou shalt come unto Me, having Me as thy supreme goal.

TENTH DISCOURSE

The Blessed Lord said:

Again, O mighty-armed, hear thou My supreme word, that, desiring thy welfare, I will declare to thee who art beloved.

The multitude of the Shining Ones, or the great Rishis, know not My forthcoming, for I am the beginning of all the Shining Ones and the great Rishis.

He who knoweth Me, unborn, beginningless, the great Lord of the world, he, among mortals without delusion, is liberated from all sin.

Reason, wisdom, non-illusion, forgiveness, truth, self-restraint, calmness, pleasure, pain, existence, non-existence, fear, and also courage,

Harmlessness, equanimity, content, austerity, alms-giving, fame and olboquy, are the various characteristics of being issuing from Me.

The seven great Rishis, the ancient Four, and also the Manus, were born of My nature and mind; of them this race was generated.

He who knows in essence that sovereignty and yoga of Mine, he is harmonised by unfaltering yoga; there is no doubt thereof.

I am the Generator of all; all evolves from Me; understanding thus, the wise adore Me in rapt emotion.

Mindful of Me, their life hidden in Me, illuminating each other, ever conversing about Me, they are content and joyful.

To these, ever harmonious, worshipping, in love, I give the yoga of discrimination by which they come unto Me.

Out of pure compassion for them, dwelling within their

Self, I destroy the ignorance-born darkness by the shining lamp of wisdom.

Arjuna said:

Thou art the supreme Eternal, the supreme Abode, the supreme Purity, eternal, divine Man, primeval Deity, unborn, the Lord!

All the Rishis have thus acclaimed Thee, as also the divine Rishi, Nârada; so Asita, Devala, and Vyâsa; and now Thou Thyself tellest it me.

All this I believe true that Thou sayest to me, O Keshava. Thy manifestation, O Blessed Lord, neither Shining Ones nor Dânavas comprehend.

Thyself indeed knowest Thyself by Thyself, O Purushottama! Source of beings, Lord of beings, Shining One of Shining Ones, Ruler of the world!

Deign to tell without reserve of Thine own divine glories, by which glories Thou remainest, pervading these worlds.

How may I know Thee, O Yogi, by constant meditation? In what, in what aspects art Thou to be thought of by me, O blessed Lord?

In detail tell me again of Thy yoga and glory, O Janârdana; for me there is never satiety in hearing Thy life-giving words.

The Blessed Lord said:

Blessed be thou! I will declare to thee My divine glory by its chief characteristics, O best of the Kurus; there is no end to details of Me.

I, O Gudâkesha, am the Self, seated in the heart of all beings; I am the beginning, the middle, and also the end of all beings.

Of the Âdityas I am Vishnu; of radiances the glorious Sun;

I am Marîchi of the Maruts, of the asterisms the Moon am I.

Of the Vedas I am the Sâma-Veda; I am Vâsava of the Shining Ones; and of the senses I am the mind; I am of living beings the intelligence.

And of the Rudras Shankara am I; Vittesha of the Yakshas and Râkshasas; and of the Vasus I am Pâvaka; Meru of high mountains am I.

And know Me, O Pârtha, of household priests the chief, Brihaspati; of generals I am Skanda; of lakes I am the ocean.

Of the great Rishis, Bhrigu; of speech I am the one syllable; of sacrifices I am the sacrifice of silent repetitions; of immovable things the Himâlaya.

Ashvattha of all trees; and of divine Rishis Nârada, of Gandharvas Chitraratha; of the perfected the Muni Kapila.

Uchchaishravâ of horses know Me, nectar-born; Airâvata of lordly elephants; and of men the monarch.

Of weapons I am the thunderbolt; of cows I am Kâmadhuk; I am Kandarpa of the progenitors; of serpents Vâsuki am I.

And I am Ananta of Nâgas; Varuna of sea-dwellers I; and of ancestors Aryamâ; Yama of governors am I.

And I am Prahlâda of Daityas; of calculators Time am I; and of wild beasts I the imperial beast; and Vainateya of birds.

Of purifiers I am the wind; Râma of warriors I; and I am Makara of fishes; of streams the Gangâ am I.

Of creations the beginning and the ending and also the middle am I, O Arjuna. Of sciences the science concerning the Self; the speech of orators I.

Of letters the letter A am I, and the dual of all the compounds; I also everlasting Time; I the Supporter, whose face turns everywhere.

And all-devouring Death am I, and the origin of all to come; and of feminine qualities, fame prosperity, speech, memory, intelligence, firmness, forgiveness.

Of hymns also Brihatsâman; Gâyatrî of metres am I; of months I am Mârgashîrsha; of seasons the flowery.

I am the gambling of the cheat, and the splendour of splendid things I; I am victory, I am determination, and the truth of the truthful I.

Of the Vrîshnis Vâsudeva am I; of the Pârdavas Dhanañjaya; of the Sages also I am Vyâsa; of poets Ushanâ the Bard.

Of rulers I am the sceptre; of those that seek victory I am statesmanship; and of secrets I am also silence; the knowledge of knowers am I.

And whatsoever is the seed of all beings, that am I, O Arjuna; nor is there aught, moving or unmoving, that may exist bereft of Me.

There is no end of My divine powers, O Parantapa, What has been declared is only illustrative of My infinite glory.

Whatsoever is glorious, good, beautiful, and mighty, understand thou that to go forth from a fragment of My splendour.

But what is the knowledge of all these details to thee, O Arjuna? Having pervaded this whole universe with one fragment of Myself, I remain.

ELEVENTH DISCOURSE
Arjuna said:

This word of the Supreme Secret concerning the Self,

Thou has spoken out of compassion; by this my delusion is taken away.

The production and destruction of beings have been heard by me in detail from Thee, O Lotus-eyed, and also Thy imperishable greatness.

O supreme Lord, even as Thou describest Thyself, O best of beings, I desire to see Thy Form omnipotent.

If thou thinkest that by me It can be seen, O Lord, Lord of Yoga, then show me Thine imperishable Self.

The Blessed Lord said:

Behold, O Pârtha, forms of Me, a hundredfold, a thousandfold, various in kind, divine, various in colours and shapes.

Behold the Âdityas, the Vasus, the Rudras, the two Ashvins and also the Maruts; behold many marvels never seen ere this, O Bhârata.

Here, today, behold the whole universe, movable and immovable, standing in one in My body, O Gudâkesha, with aught else thou desirest to see.

But verily thou art not able to behold Me with these thine eyes; the divine eye I give unto thee. Behold My sovereign Yoga.

Sanjaya said:

Having thus spoken, O King, the great Lord of Yoga, Hari, showed to Pârtha His supreme form as Lord.

With many mouths and eyes, with many visions of marvel, with many divine ornaments, with many upraised divine weapons;

Wearing divine necklaces and vestures, anointed with divine unguents, the God all-marvellous, boundless, with face turned everywhere.

If the splendour of a thousand suns were to blaze out together in the sky, that might resemble the glory of that Mahâtmâ.

There Pândava beheld the whole universe, divided into manifold parts, standing in one in the body of the God of Gods.

Then he, Dhananjaya, overwhelmed with astonishment, his hair upstanding, bowed down his head to the God, and with joined palms spake.

Arjuna said:

Within Thy form, O God, the Gods I see,
All grades of beings with distinctive marks;
Brahmâ, the Lord, upon His lotus throne,
The Rishis all and Serpents, the Divine.
With mouths, eyes, arms, breasts, multitudinous,
I see Thee everywhere, unbounded Form.
Beginning, middle, end, nor source of Thee,
Infinite Lord, infinite Form, I find;
Shining, a mass of splendour everywhere,
With discus, mace, tiara, I behold:
Blazing as fire, as sun, dazzling the gaze
From all sides in the sky, immeasurable.
Loftly beyond all thought, unperishing,
Thou treasure-house supreme; all-immanent,
Eternal Dharma's changeless Guardian, Thou;
As immemorial Man I think of Thee.
Nor source, nor midst, nor end; infinite force,
Unnumbered arms, the sun and moon Thine eyes!
I see Thy face, as sacrificial fire
Blazing, its splendour burneth up the worlds.

By thee alone are filled the earth, the heavens,
And all the regions that are stretched between;
The triple worlds sink down, O mighty One,
Before Thine awful manifested Form.
To Thee the troops of Suras enter in,
Some with joined palms in awe invoking Thee:
Banded Maharshis, Siddhas, "Svasti!" cry,
Chanting Thy praises with resounding songs.
Rudras, Vasus, Sâdhyas and Âdityas,
Vishvas, the Ashvins, Maruts, Ushmapas,
Gandharvas, Yakshas, Siddhas, Asuras,
In wondering multitudes beholding Thee.
Thy mighty Form, with many mouths and eyes,
Long-armed, with thighs and feet innumerate,
Vast-bosomed, set with many fearful teeth,
The worlds see terror-struck, as also I.
Radiant Thou touchest heaven; rainbow-hued,
With opened mouths and shining vast-orbed eyes.
My inmost self is quaking, having seen,
My strength is withered, Vishnu, and my peace.
Like Time's destroying flames I see Thy teeth,
Upstanding, spread within expanded jaws;
Nought know I anywhere, no shelter find,
Mercy, O God! refuge of all the worlds!
The sons of Dhritarâshtra, and with them
The multitude of all these kings of earth,
Bhîshma, and Drona, Sûta's royal son,
And all the noblest warriors of our hosts,
Into Thy gaping mouths they hurrying rush,
Tremendous-toothed and terrible to see;

Some caught within the gaps between Thy teeth
Are seen, their heads to powder crushed and ground.
As river-floods impetuously rush,
Hurling their waters into ocean's lap,
So fling themselves into Thy flaming mouths,
In haste, these mighty men, these lords of earth.
As moths with quickened speed will headlong fly
Into a flaming light, to fall destroyed,
So also these, in haste precipitate,
Enter within Thy mouths destroyed to fall.
On every side, all-swallowing, fiery-tongued,
Thou lickest up mankind, devouring all;
Thy glory filleth space: the universe
Is burning, Vishnu, with Thy blazing rays.
Reveal Thy Self; What awful Form art Thou?
I worship Thee! Have mercy, God supreme!
Thine inner being I am fain to know;
This Thy forthstreaming Life bewilders me.
The Blessed Lord said:
Time am I, laying desolate the world,
Made manifest on earth to slay mankind!
Not one of all these warriors ranged for strife
Escapeth death; thou shalt alone survive.
Therefore stand up! win for thyself renown,
Conquer thy foes, enjoy the spacious realm.
By Me they are already overcome,
Be thou the outward cause, left-handed one.
Drona and Bhîshma and Jayadratha,
Karna, and all the other warriors here
Are slain by me. Destroy then fearlessly

Fight! thou shalt crush thy rivals in the field.

Sanjaya said:

Having heard these words of Keshava, he who weareth
a diadem, with joined palms, quaking, and prostrating himself, spake again to Krishna, stammering with fear, casting
down his face.

Arjuna said:

Hrishîkesha! in Thy magnificence
Rightly the world rejoiceth, hymning Thee;
The Râkshasas to every quarter fly
In fear; the hosts of Siddhas prostrate fall.
How should they otherwise, O loftiest Self!
First Cause! Brahmâ Himself less great than Thou.
Infinite, God of Gods, home of all worlds,
Unperishing, Sat Asat, That supreme!
First of the Gods, most ancient Man Thou art,
Supreme receptacle of all that lives;
Knower and known, the dwelling-place on high;
In Thy vast Form the universe is spread.
Thou art Vâyu and Yama, Agni, moon,
Varuna, Father, Grandsire of all;
Hail, hail to Thee! a thousand times all hail!
Hail unto Thee! again, again, all hail!
Prostrate in front of Thee, prostrate behind,
Prostrate on every side to Thee, O All.
In power boundless, measureless in strength,
Thou holdest all; then Thou Thyself art All.
If, thinking Thee but friend, importunate,

O Krishna! or O Yâdava! O friend!
I cried, unknowing of Thy majesty,
And careless in the fondness of my love;
If jesting, I irreverence showed to Thee,
At play, reposing, sitting or at meals,
Alone, O sinless One, or with my friends,
Forgive my error, O Thou boundless One.
Father of worlds, of all that moves and stands,
Worthier of reverence than the Guru's self,
There is none like to Thee. Who passeth Thee?
Pre-eminent Thy power in all the worlds.
Therefore I fall before Thee; with my body
I worship as is fitting; bless Thou me.
As father with the son, as friend with friend,
With the beloved as lover, bear with me.
I have seen That which none hath seen before,
My heart is glad, yet faileth me for fear;
Show me, O God, Thine other Form again,
Mercy, O God of Gods, home of all worlds.
Diademed, mace and discus in Thy hand,
Again I fain would see Thee as before:
Put on again Thy four-armed shape, O Lord,
O thousand-armed, of forms innumerate.
The Blessed Lord said:
Arjuna, by My favour thou hast seen
This loftiest form by Yoga's self revealed!
Radiant, all-penetrating, endless, first,
That none except thyself hath ever seen.
Nor sacrifice nor Vedas, alms nor works,
Nor sharp austerity, nor study deep,

Can win the vision of this Form for man.

Foremost of Kurus, thou alone hast seen.

Be not bewildered, be thou not afraid,

Because thou hast beheld this awful Form;

Cast fear away, and let thy heart rejoice;

Behold again Mine own familiar shape.

Sanjaya said:

Vâsudeva, having thus spoken to Arjuna, again manifested His own Form, and consoled the terrified one, the
Mahâtma again assuming a gentle form.

Arjuna said:

Beholding again Thy gentle human Form, O Janârdana, I
am now collected, and am restored to my own nature.

The Blessed Lord said:

This Form of Mine beholden by thee is very hard to see.
Verily the Gods ever long to behold this Form.

Nor can I be seen as thou hast seen Me by the Vedas, nor
by austerities, nor by alms, nor by offerings.

But by devotion to Me alone I may thus be perceived,
Arjuna, and known and seen in essence, and entered, O
Parantapa.

He who doeth actions for Me, whose supreme good I am,
My devotee, freed from attachment, without hatred of any
being, he cometh unto Me, O Pândava.

TWELFTH DISCOURSE

Arjuna said:

Those devotees who ever harmonised worship Thee, and

those also who worship the Indestructible, the Unmanifested, whether of these is more learned in yoga?

The Blessed Lord said:

They who with mind fixed on Me, ever harmonised worship Me, with faith supreme endowed, these in My opinion, are best in yoga.

They who worship the Indestructible, the Ineffable, the Unmanifested, Omnipresent and Unthinkable, the Unchanging, Immutable, Eternal,

Restraining and subduing the senses, regarding everything equally, in the welfare of all rejoicing, these also come unto Me.

The difficulty of those whose minds are set on the Unmanifested is greater; for the path of the Unmanifested is hard for the embodied to reach.

Those verily who, renouncing all actions in Me and intent on Me, worship meditating on Me, with wholehearted yoga,

These I speedily lift up from the ocean of death and existence, O Pârtha, their minds being fixed on Me.

Place thy mind in Me, into Me let thy Reason enter; then without doubt thou shalt abide in Me hereafter.

But if thou art not able firmly to fix thy mind on Me, then by the yoga of practice seek to reach Me, O Dhananjaya.

If also thou art not equal to constant practice, be intent on My service; performing actions for My sake, thou shalt attain perfection.

If even to do this thou hast not strength, then taking refuge in union with Me, renounce all fruit of action, with the self controlled.

Better indeed is wisdom than constant practice; than wisdom meditation is better: than meditation renunciation of the fruit of action; on renunciation follows peace.

He who beareth no ill-will to any being, friendly and compassionate, without attachment and egoism, balanced in pleasure and pain, and forgiving,

Ever content, harmonious, with the self controlled, resolute, with mind and Reason dedicated to Me, he, My devotee, is dear to Me.

He from whom the world doth not shrink away, who doth not shrink away from the world, freed from the anxieties of joy, anger and fear, he is dear to Me.

He who wants nothing, is pure, expert, passionless, untroubled, renouncing every undertaking, he, My devotee, is dear to Me.

He who neither loveth nor hateth, nor grieveth, nor desireth, renouncing good and evil, full of devotion, he is dear to Me.

Alike to foe and friend, and also in fame and ignominy, alike in cold and heat, pleasures and pains, destitute of attachment,

Taking equally praise and reproach, silent, wholly content with what cometh, homeless, firm in mind, full of devotion, that man is dear to Me.

They verily who partake of this life-giving wisdom as taught herein, endued with faith, I their Supreme Object, devotees, they are surpassingly dear to Me.

THIRTEENTH DISCOURSE
Arjuna said:

Matter and Spirit, also the Field and the Knower of the

Field, Wisdom and that which ought to be known, these I fain would learn, O Keshava.

The Blessed Lord said:

This body, son of Kuntî, is called the Field; that which knoweth it is called Knower of the Field by the Sages.

Understand Me as the Knower of the Field in all Fields, O Bhârata. Wisdom as to the Field and the Knower of the Field, that in My opinion is the Wisdom.

What the Field is and of what nature, how modified, and whence it is, and what He is and what His powers, hear that now briefly from Me.

Rishis have sung in manifold ways, in many various chants, and in decisive Brahma-sûtra words, full of reasonings.

The great Elements, Individuality, Reason and also the Unmanifested, the ten senses, and the one, and the five pastures of the senses;

Desire, aversion, pleasure, pain, combination, intelligence, firmness, these, briefly described, constitute the Field and its modifications.

Humility, unpretentiousness, harmlessness, rectitude, service of the teacher, purity, steadfastness, self-control,

Indifference to the objects of the senses, and also absence of egoism, insight into the pain and evil of birth, death, old age and sickness,

Unattachment, absence of self-identification with son, wife or home, and constant balance of mind in wished-for and unwished-for events,

Unflinching devotion to Me by yoga, without other object, resort to sequestered places, absence of enjoyment in the company of men.

Constancy in the Wisdom of the Self, understanding of the object of essential wisdom; that is declared to be the Wisdom; all against it is ignorance.

I will declare that which ought to be known, that which being known immortality is enjoyed—the beginningless supreme Eternal, called neither being nor non-being.

Everywhere That hath hands and feet, everywhere eyes, heads, and mouths; all-hearing, He dwelleth in the world, enveloping all;

Shining with all sense-faculties without any senses; unattached supporting everything; and free from qualities enjoying qualities.

Without and within all beings, immovable and also movable; by reason of His subtlety imperceptible; at hand and far away is That.

Not divided amid beings, and yet seated distributively; That is to be known as the supporter of beings; He devours and He generates.

That, the Light of all lights, is said to be beyond darkness; Wisdom, the object of Wisdom, by Wisdom to be reached, seated in the hearts of all.

Thus the Field, Wisdom and the Object of Wisdom, have been briefly told. My devotee, thus knowing, enters into My Being.

Know thou that Matter and Spirit are both without beginning; and know thou also that modifications and qualities are all Matter-born.

Matter is called the cause of the generation of causes and effects; Spirit is called the cause of the enjoyment of pleasure and pain.

Spirit seated in Matter useth the qualities born of Matter; attachment to the qualities is the cause of his births in good and evil wombs.

Supervisor and permitter, supporter, enjoyer, great Lord and also the supreme Self: thus is styled in this body the supreme Spirit.

He who thus knoweth Spirit and Matter with its qualities, in whatsoever condition he may be, he shall not be born again.

Some by meditation behold the Self in the self by the Self; others by the Sâñkhya Yoga, and others by the Yoga of Action;

Others also, ignorant of this, having heard of it from others, worship; and these also cross beyond death, adhering to what they had heard.

Whatsoever creature is born, immobile or mobile, know thou, O best of the Bharatas, that it is from the union between the Field and the Knower of the Field.

Seated equally in all beings, the supreme Lord, unperishing within the perishing—he who thus seeth, he seeth.

Seeing indeed everywhere the same Lord equally dwelling, he doth not destroy the Self by the self, and thus treadeth the highest Path.

He who seeth that Prakriti verily performeth all actions, and that the Self is actionless, he seeth.

When he perceiveth the diversified existence of beings as rooted in One, and spreading forth from it, then he reacheth the Eternal.

Being beginningless and without qualities, the imperishable supreme Self, though seated in the body, O Kaunteya, worketh not nor is affected.

As the omnipresent ether is not affected, by reason of its subtlety, so seated everywhere in the body the Self is not affected.

As the one sun illumineth the whole earth, so the Lord of the Field illumineth the whole Field, O Bhârata.

They who by the eye of Wisdom perceive this difference between the Field and the Knower of the Field, and the liberation of beings from Matter, they go to the Supreme.

FOURTEENTH DISCOURSE

The Blessed Lord said:

I will again proclaim that supreme Wisdom, of all wisdom the best, which all the Sages having known have gone hence to the supreme Perfection.

Having taken refuge in this Wisdom and being assimilated to My own nature, they are not re-born even in the emanation of a universe, nor are disquieted in the dissolution.

My womb is the great Eternal; in that I place the germ; thence cometh the birth of all beings, O Bhârata.

In whatsoever wombs mortals are produced, O Kaunteya, the Eternal is their mighty womb, I their generating father.

Harmony, Mobility, Inertia, such are the qualities, Matter-born; they bind fast in the body, O great-armed one, the indestructible dweller in the body.

Of these Harmony, from its stainlessness, luminous and healthy, bindeth by the attachment to bliss and the attachment to wisdom, O sinless one.

Mobility, the passion-nature, know thou, is the source of

attachment and thirst for life, O Kaunteya, that bindeth the dweller in the body by the attachment to action.

But Inertia, know thou, born of unwisdom, is the deluder of all dwellers in the body; that bindeth by heedlessness, indolence and sloth, O Bhârata.

Harmony attacheth to bliss, Mobility to action, O Bhârata. Inertia, verily having shrouded wisdom, attacheth on the contrary to heedlessness.

Now Harmony prevaileth, having overpowered Mobility and Inertia, O Bhârata. Now Mobility, having overpowered Harmony and Inertia; and now Inertia, having overpowered Harmony and Mobility.

When the wisdom-light streameth forth from all the gates of the body, then it may be known that Harmony is increasing.

Greed, outgoing energy, undertaking of actions, restlessness, desire—these are born of the increase of Mobility, O best of the Bhâratas.

Darkness, stagnation and heedlessness and also delusion—these are born of the increase of Inertia, O joy of the Kurus.

If Harmony verily prevaileth when the embodied goeth to dissolution, then he goeth forth to the spotless worlds of the great Sages.

Having gone to dissolution in Mobility, he is born among those attached to action; if dissolved in Inertia, he is born in the wombs of the senseless.

It is said the fruit of a good action is harmonious and spotless; verily the fruit of Mobility is pain, and the fruit of Inertia unwisdom.

From Harmony wisdom is born, and also greed from Mobility; heedlessness and delusion are of Inertia, and also unwisdom.

They rise upwards who are settled in Harmony; the Active dwell in the midmost place; the Inert go downwards, enveloped in the vilest qualities.

When the Seer perceiveth no agent other than the qualities, and knoweth That which is higher than the qualities, he entereth into My nature.

When the dweller in the body hath crossed over these three qualities, whence all bodies have been produced, liberated from birth, death, old age and sorrow, he drinketh the nectar of immortality.

Arjuna said:

What are the marks of him who hath crossed over the three qualities, O Lord? How acteth he, and how doth he go beyond these three qualities?

The Blessed Lord said:

He, O Pândava, who hateth not radiance, nor outgoing energy, nor even delusion, when present, nor longeth after them, absent;

He who, seated as a neutral, is unshaken by the qualities; who saying; "The qualities revolve," standeth apart, immovable,

Balanced in pleasure and pain, self-reliant, to whom a lump of earth, a rock and gold are alike; the same to loved and unloved, firm, the same in censure and in praise,

The same in honour and ignominy, the same to friend and foe, abandoning all undertakings—he is said to have crossed over the qualities.

And he who serveth Me exclusively by the yoga of devotion, he, crossing beyond the qualities, he is fit to become the Eternal.

For I am the abode of the Eternal, and of the indestructible nectar of immortality, of immemorial righteousness, and of unending bliss.

FIFTEENTH DISCOURSE

The Blessed Lord said:

With roots above, branches below, the Ashvattha is said to be indestructible; the leaves of it are hymns; he who knoweth it is a Veda-knower.

Downwards and upwards spread the branches of it, nourished by the qualities; the objects of the senses its buds; and its roots grow downwards, the bonds of action in the world of men.

Nor here may be acquired knowledge of its form, nor its end, nor its origin, nor its rooting-place; this strongly-rooted Ashvattha having been cut down by the unswerving weapon of non-attachment,

That path beyond may be sought, treading which there is no return. I go indeed to that Primal Man whence the ancient energy forthstreamed.

Without pride and delusion, victorious over the vice of attachment, dwelling constantly in the Self, desire pacified, liberated from the pairs of opposites known as pleasure and pain, they tread, undeluded, that indestructible path.

Nor doth the sun lighten there, nor moon, nor fire; having gone thither they return not; that is My supreme abode.

A portion of Mind own Self, transformed in the world of life into an immortal Spirit, draweth round itself the senses of which the mind is the sixth, veiled in Matter.

When the Lord acquireth a body and when He abandoneth it, He seizeth these and goeth with them, as the wind takes fragrances from their retreats.

Enshrined in the ear, the eye, the touch, the taste and the smell, and in the mind also, He enjoyeth the objects of the senses.

The deluded do not perceive Him when He departeth or stayeth, or enjoyeth, swayed by the qualities; the wisdom-eyed perceive.

Yogîs also, struggling, perceive Him, established in the Self; but, though struggling, the unintelligent perceive Him not, their selves untrained.

That splendour issuing from the sun that enlighteneth the whole world, that which is in the moon and in fire, that splendour know as from Me.

Permeating the soil, I support beings by My vital energy, and having become the delicious Soma I nourish all plants.

I, having become the Fire of Life, take possession of the bodies of breathing things, and united with the life-breaths I digest the four kinds of food.

And I am seated in the hearts of all, and from Me memory and wisdom and their absence. And that which is to be known in all the Vedas am I; and I indeed the Veda-knower and the author of the Vedânta.

There are two energies in this world, the destructible and the indestructible; the destructible is all beings, the unchanging is called the indestructible.

The highest energy is verily Another, declared as the supreme Self, He, who pervading all, sustaineth the three worlds, the indestructible Lord.

Since I excel the destructible, and am more excellent also than the indestructible, in the world and in the Veda I am proclaimed the supreme Spirit.

He who undeluded knoweth Me thus as the Supreme spirit he, all-knowing, worshippeth Me with his whole being, O Bhârata.

Thus by Me this most secret teaching hath been told, O sinless one. This known, he hath become illuminated, and hath finished his work, O Bhârata.

SIXTEENTH DISCOURSE

Fearlessness, cleanness of life, steadfastness in the Yoga of wisdom, almsgiving, self-restraint and sacrifice and study of the Scripture, austerity and straightforwardness,

Harmlessness, truth, absence of wrath, renunciation, peacefulness, absence of crookedness, compassion to living beings, uncovetousness, mildness, modesty, absence of fickleness,

Vigour, forgiveness, fortitude, purity, absence of envy and pride—these are his who is born with the divine properties, O Bhârata.

Hypocrisy, arrogance and conceit, wrath and also harshness and unwisdom, are his who is born, O Pârtha, with demoniacal properties.

The divine properties are deemed to be for liberation, the demonical for bondage. Grieve not, thou art born with divine properties, O Pândava.

Twofold is the animal creation in this world, the divine

and the demoniacal; the divine hath been described at length; hear from Me, O Pârtha, the demoniacal.

Demoniacal men know neither right energy nor right abstinence; nor purity, nor even propriety, nor truth is in them.

"The universe is without truth, without (moral) basis," they say; "without a God, brought about by mutual union, and caused by lust and nothing else."

Holding this view, these ruined selves of small understanding, of fierce deeds, come forth as enemies for the destruction of the world.

Surrendering themselves to insatiable desires, possessed with vanity, conceit and arrogance, holding evil ideas through delusion, they engage in action with impure resolves.

Giving themselves over to unmeasured thought whose end is death, regarding the gratification of desires as the highest, feeling sure that this is all,

Held in bondage by a hundred ties of expectation, given over to lust and anger, they strive to obtain by unlawful means hoards of wealth for sensual enjoyments.

"This today by me hath been won, that purpose I shall gain; this wealth is mine already, and also this shall be mine in future.

"I have slain this enemy, and others also I shall slay. I am the Lord, I am the enjoyer, I am perfect, powerful, happy;

"I am wealthy, well-born; what other is there that is like unto me? I will sacrifice, I will give (alms), I will rejoice." Thus deluded by unwisdom,

Bewildered by numerous thoughts, enmeshed in the web of delusion, addicted to the gratifications of desire, they fall downwards into a foul hell.

Self-sufficing, obstinate, filled with the pride and intoxication of wealth, they perform lip-sacrifices for ostentation,
contrary to scriptural ordinance.

Given over to egoism, power, insolence, lust and wrath,
these malicious ones hate Me in the bodies of others and in
their own.

These haters, evil, pitiless, vilest among men in the
world, I ever throw down into demoniacal wombs.

Cast into a demoniacal womb, deluded birth after birth,
attaining not to Me, O Kaunteya, they sink into the lowest
depths.

Triple is the gate of this hell, destructive of the self—
lust, wrath and greed; therefore let man renounce these three.

A man liberated from these three gates of darkness, O son
of Kunti, accomplisheth his own welfare and thus reacheth
the highest goal.

He who having cast aside the ordinances of the
Scriptures, followeth the promptings of desire, attaineth not
to perfection, nor happiness, nor the highest goal.

Therefore let the Scriptures be thy authority, in deter-
mining what ought to be done, or what ought not to be
done. Knowing what hath been declared by the ordinances
of the Scriptures, thou oughtest to work in this world.

SEVENTEENTH DISCOURSE

Arjuna said:

Those that sacrifice full of faith, but casting aside the
ordinances of the Scriptures, what is verily their condition,
O Krishna? Is it one of Purity, Passion or Darkness?

The Blessed Lord said:

Threefold is by nature the inborn faith of the embodied—pure, passionate and dark. Hear thou of these.

The faith of each is shaped to his own nature, O Bhârata. The man consists of his faith; that which his faith is, he is even that.

Pure men worship the Gods; the passionate the gnomes and giants; the others, the dark folk, worship ghosts and troops of nature-spirits.

The men who perform severe austerities, unenjoined by the Scripture, wedded to vanity and egoism, impelled by the force of their desires and passions,

Unintelligent, tormenting the aggregated elements forming the body, and Me also, seated in the inner body, know these demoniacal in their resolves.

The food also which is dear to each is threefold, as also sacrifice, austerity and almsgiving. Hear thou the distinction of these.

The foods that augment vitality, energy, vigour, health, joy and cheerfulness, delicious, bland, substantial and agreeable, are dear to the pure.

The passionate desire foods that are bitter, sour, saline, over-hot, pungent, dry and burning, and which produce pain, grief and sickness.

That which is stale and flat, putrid and corrupt, leavings also and unclean, is the food dear to the dark.

The sacrifice which is offered by men without desire for fruit as enjoined by the ordinances, under the firm belief that sacrifice is a duty, that is pure.

The sacrifice offered with a view verily to fruit, and also

indeed for self-gratification, O best of the Bharatas; know thou that to be of passion.

The sacrifice contrary to the ordinances, without distributing food, devoid of words and power and without gifts, empty of faith, is said to be of darkness.

Worship given to the Gods, to the twice-born, to the teachers and to the wise, purity, straightforwardness, continence and harmlessness, are called the austerity of the body.

Speech causing no annoyance, truthful, and beneficial, the practice of the study of the Scriptures, are called the austerity of speech.

Mental happiness, equilibrium, silence, self-control, purity of nature—this is called the austerity of the mind.

This threefold austerity, performed by men with the utmost faith, without desire for fruit, harmonised, is said to be pure.

The austerity which is practised with the object of gaining respect, honour and worship, and for ostentation, is said to be of passion, unstable and fleeting.

That austerity done under a deluded understanding, with self-torture, or with the object of destroying another, that is declared of darkness.

That alms given to one who does nothing in return, believing that a gift ought to be made, in a fit place and time, to a worthy person, that alms is accounted pure.

That given with a view to receiving in return, or looking for fruit again, or grudgingly, that alm is accounted of passion.

That alms given at unfit place and time, and to unworthy persons, disrespectfully and contemptuously, that is declared of darkness.

"Aum Tat Sat," this has been considered to be the threefold designation of the Eternal. By that were ordained of old Brâhmanas, Vedas and sacrifices.

Therefore with the pronunciation of "Aum" the acts of sacrifice, gift and austerity, as laid down in the ordinances, are always commenced by the knowers of the Eternal.

With the pronunciation of "Tat" and without aiming at fruit are performed the various acts of sacrifice, austerity and gift, by those desiring liberation.

"Sat" is used in the sense of reality and goodness likewise, O Pârtha, the word "Sat" is used in the sense of a good work.

Steadfastness in sacrifice, austerity and gift is also named "Sat," and an action for the sake of the supreme is also called "Sat."

Whatsoever is wrought without faith, oblation, gift, austerity, or other deed, "Asat" it is called, O Pârtha; it is nought, here or hereafter.

EIGHTEENTH DISCOURSE
Arjuna said:

I desire, O mighty-armed, to know severally the essense of renunciation, O Hrishîkesha, and of relinquishment, O Keshinishûdana.

The Blessed Lord said:

Sages have known as renunciation the renouncing of works with desire; the relinquishing of the fruit of all actions is called relinquishment by the wise.

"Action should be relinquished as an evil," declare some thoughtful men; "acts of sacrifice, gift and austerity should not be relinquished," say others.

Hear my conclusions as to that relinquishment, O best of the Bharatas: since relinquishment, O tiger of men, has been explained as threefold.

Acts of sacrifice, gift and austerity should not be relinquished, but should be performed; sacrifice, gift and also austerity are the purifiers of the intelligent.

But even these actions should be done leaving aside attachment and fruit, O Pârtha; that is my certain and best belief.

Verily renunciation of actions that are prescribed is not proper; the relinquishment thereof from delusion is said to be of darkness.

He who relinquisheth an action from fear of physical suffering, saying "Painful," thus performing a passionate relinquishment, obtaineth not the fruit of relinquishment.

He who performeth a prescribed action, saying, "It ought to be done," O Arjuna, relinquishing attachment and also fruit, that relinquishment is regarded as pure.

The relinquisher pervaded by purity, intelligent and with doubts cut away, hateth not unpleasurable action nor is attached to pleasurable.

Nor indeed can embodied beings completely relinquish action; verily he who relinquisheth the fruit of action he is said to be a relinquisher.

Good, evil and mixed—threefold is the fruit of action hereafter for the non-relinquisher; but there is none ever for the renouncer.

These five causes, O mighty-armed, learn of Me as declared in the Sâñkhya system for the accomplishment of all actions:—

The body, the actor, the various organs, the divers kinds of energies, and the presiding deities also, the fifth.

Whatever action a man performeth by his body, speech

and mind, whether right or the reverse, these five are the cause thereof.

That being so, he verily who—owing to untrained Reason—looketh on his Self, which is isolated, as the action, he, of perverted intelligence, seeth not.

He who is free from the egoistic notion, whose Reason is not affected, though he slay these peoples, he slayeth not, nor is bound.

Knowledge, the knowable and the knower, the threefold impulse to action; the organ, the action, the actor, the threefold constituents of action.

Knowledge, action and actor in the category of qualities are also said to be severally threefold, from the difference of qualities; hear thou duly these also.

That by which one indestructible Being is seen in all beings, inseparate in the separated, know thou that knowledge as pure.

But that knowledge which regardeth the several manifold existences in all beings as separate, that knowledge know thou as of passion.

While that which clingeth to each one thing as if it were the whole, without reason, without grasping the reality, narrow, that is declared to be dark.

An action which is ordained, done by one undesirous of fruit, devoid of attachment, without love or hate, that is called pure.

But that action that is done by one longing for desires, or again with egoism, or with much effort, that is declared to be passionate.

The action undertaken from delusion, without regard to capacity and to consequences—loss and injury to others—

that is declared to be dark.

Liberated from attachment, not egoistic, endued with firmness and confidence, unchanged by success or failure, that actor is called pure.

Impassioned, desiring to obtain the fruit of actions, greedy, harmful, impure, moved by joy and sorrow, such an actor is pronounced passionate.

Discordant, vulgar, stubborn, cheating, malicious, indolent, despairful, procrastinating, that actor is called dark.

The division of Reason and of firmness also, threefold according to the qualities, hear thou related, unreservedly and severally, O Dhananjaya.

That which knoweth energy and abstinence, what ought to be done and what ought not to be done, fear and fearlessness, bondage and liberation, that Reason is pure, O Pârtha.

That by which one understandeth awry Right and Wrong, and also what ought to be done and what ought not to be done, that Reason, O Pârtha, is passionate.

That which, enwrapped in darkness, thinketh Wrong to be Right, and seeth all things subverted, that Reason O Pârtha, is of darkness.

The unwavering firmness by which, through yoga, one restraineth the activity of the mind, of the life-breaths and of the sense-organs, that firmness, O Pârtha, is pure.

But the firmness, O Arjuna, by which, from attachment desirous of fruit, one holdeth fast duty, desire and wealth, that firmness, O Pârtha, is passionate.

That by which one from stupidity doth not abandon sleep, fear, grief, despair, and also vanity, that firmness, O Pârtha, is dark.

And now the threefold kinds of pleasure hear thou from Me, O bull of the Bharatas. That in which one by practice rejoiceth, and which putteth an end to pain;

Which at first is as venom but in the end is as nectar; that pleasure is said to be pure, born of the blissful knowledge of the Self.

That which from the union of the senses with their objects at first is as nectar, but in the end is like venom, that pleasure is accounted passionate.

That pleasure which both at first and afterwards is delusive of the self, arising from sleep, indolence and heedlessness dark, that is declared tâmasic.

There is not an entity, either on the earth or again in heaven among the Shining Ones, that is liberated from these three qualities, born of matter.

Of Brâhmanas, Kshattriyas, Vaishyas and Shûdras, O Parantapa, the duties have been distributed, according to the qualities born of their own natures.

Serenity, self-restraint, austerity, purity, forgiveness and also uprightness, wisdom, knowledge, belief in God, are the Brâhmana duty, born of his own nature.

Prowess, splendour, firmness, dexterity, and also not flying from battle, generosity, the nature of a ruler, are the Kshattriya duty, born of his own nature.

Ploughing, protection of kine, and trade are the Vaishya duty, born of his own nature. Action of the nature of service is the Shûdra duty, born of his own nature.

Man reacheth perfection by each being intent on his own duty. Listen thou how perfection is won by him who is intent on his own duty.

He from whom is the emanation of beings, by Whom all This is pervaded, by worshipping Him in his own duty a man winneth perfection.

Better is one's own duty, though destitute of merits, than the well-executed duty of another. He who doeth the duty laid down by his own nature incurreth not sin.

Congenital duty, O son of Kuntî, though defective, ought not to be abandoned. All undertakings indeed are clouded by defects as fire by smoke.

He who Reason is everywhere unattached, the self subdued, dead to desires, he goeth by renunciation to the supreme perfection of freedom from obligation.

How he who hath attained perfection obtaineth the Eternal, that highest state of wisdom learn thou from Me only succinctly, O Kaunteya.

United to the Reason purified, controlling the self by firmness, having abandoned sound and the other objects of the senses, having laid aside passion and malice,

Dwelling in solitude, abstemious, speech, body and mind subdued, constantly fixed in meditation and yoga, taking refuge in dispassion,

Having cast aside egoism, violence, arrogance, desire, wrath, covetousness, selfless and peaceful—he is fit to become the Eternal.

Becoming Brahman, serene in the Self, he neither grieveth nor desireth; the same to all beings, he obtaineth supreme devotion unto Me.

By devotion he knoweth Me in essence, who and what I am; having thus known Me in essence he forthwith entereth into the Supreme.

Though ever performing all actions, taking refuge in Me, by My grace he obtaineth the eternal indestructible abode.

Renouncing mentally all works in Me, intent on Me, resorting to the yoga of discrimination have thy thought ever on Me.

Thinking on Me, thou shalt overcome all obstacles by My grace; but if from egoism thou wilt not listen, thou shalt be destroyed utterly.

Entrenched in egoism, thou thinkest, "I will not fight;" to no purpose thy determination; nature will constrain thee.

O son of Kuntî, bound by thine own duty, born of thin own nature, that which from delusion thou desirest not to do, even that helplessly thou shalt perform.

The Lord dwelleth in the hearts of all beings, O Arjuna, by His illusive power, causing all beings to revolve, as though mounted on a potter's wheel.

Flee unto Him for shelter with all thy being, O Bhârata; by His grace thou shalt obtain supreme peace, the everlasting dwelling place.

Thus hath wisdom, more secret than secrecy itself, been declared unto thee by Me; having reflected on it fully, then act thou as thou listest.

Listen thou again to My supreme word, most secret of all; beloved art thou of Me, and steadfast of heart, therefore will I speak for thy benefit.

Merge thy mind in Me, be My devotee, sacrifice to Me, prostrate thyself before Me, thou shalt come even to Me. I pledge thee My troth; thou art dear to Me.

Abandoning all duties, come unto Me alone for shelter; sorrow not, I will liberate thee from all sins.

Never is this to be spoken by thee to anyone who is without asceticism, nor without devotion nor to one who desireth not to listen, nor yet to him who speaketh evil of Me.

He who shall declare this supreme secret among My devotees, having shown the highest devotion for Me, without doubt he shall come to Me.

Nor is there any among men who performeth dearer service to Me than he, nor any other shall be more beloved by Me on earth than he.

And he who shall study this sacred dialogue of ours, by him I shall be worshipped with the sacrifice of wisdom. Such is My mind.

The man also who, full of faith, merely heareth it unreviling, even he, freed from evil, obtaineth the radiant worlds of the righteous.

Has this been heard, O son of Pritha, with one-pointed mind? Has thy delusion, caused by unwisdom, been destroyed, O Dhananjaya?

Arjuna said:

Destroyed is my delusion. I have gained knowledge through Thy grace, O Immutable One. I am firm, my doubts have fled away. I will do according to Thy word.

Sanjaya said:

I heard this marvellous dialogue of Vâsudeva and of the great-souled Pârtha, causing my hair to stand on end;

By the favour of Vyâsa I listened to this secret and supreme yoga from the Lord of Yoga, Krishna Himself speaking before mine eyes.

O King, remembering, remembering this marvellous and holy dialogue between Keshava and Arjuna, I rejoice again and again.

Remembering, remembering, also that most marvelous form of Hari, great is my wonder, O King. I rejoice, again and again.

Wherever is Krishna, Yoga's Lord, wherever is Pârtha, the archer, assured are there prosperity, victory and happiness. So I think.

To the Blessed Krishna be homage. May there be happiness.

Thus the Bhagavad-Gîtâ hath ending.

Peace be to all Worlds.

THE

Prologue by Sirdar Ikbal ali Shah {

QUR'AN

The Qur'an is nothing but the old books refined of human alloy, and contains transcendent truths embodied in all sacred scriptures with complete additions, necessary for the development of all human faculties. It repeats truths given in the Holy Vedas, in the Bible, in the words of the Gita, in the sayings of Buddha and all other prophets, and adds what was not in them, and gives new laws to meet the contingencies of the present time when the different members of God's family who lived apart from each other in the days of old revelations had come close one to the other.

INTRODUCTION

HUSTON SMITH

THE BLEND OF ADMIRATION, respect, and affection that the Muslim feels for Muhammad is an impressive fact of history. They see him as a man who experienced life in exceptional range. Not only was he a shepherd, merchant, hermit, exile, soldier, lawmaker, prophet-priest-king, and mystic; he was also an orphan, for many years the husband of one wife much older than himself, a many times bereaved father, a widower, and finally the husband of many wives, some much younger than himself. In all of these roles he was exemplary. All this is in the minds of Muslims as they add to the mention of his name the benediction, "Blessings and peace be upon him." Even so, they never mistake him for the earthly center of their faith. That place is reserved for the bible of Islam, the Koran.

Literally, the word *al-qur'an* in Arabic (and hence "koran,") means a recitation. Fulfilling that purpose, the Koran is perhaps the most recited (as well as read) book in the world. Certainly, it is the world's most memorized book, and possibly the one that exerts the most influence on those who read it. So great was Muhammad's regard for its contents that (as we have seen) he considered it the only major miracle God worked through him—God's "standing miracle," as he called it. That he himself, unschooled to the extent that he was unlettered (*ummi*) and could barely write his name, could have produced a book that provides the ground plan of all knowledge and at the same time is grammatically perfect and without poetic peer—this, Muhammad, and with him all Muslims, are convinced defies belief. He put the point in a rhetorical question: "Do you ask for a greater miracle than this, O unbelieving people, than to have your language chosen as the language of that incomparable Book, one piece of which puts all your golden poetry to shame?"

Four-fifths the length of the New Testament, the Koran is divided into 114 chapters or *surahs*, which (with the exception of the short first chapter that figures in the Muslim's daily prayers) are arranged in order of decreasing length. Thus Surah Two has 286 verses, Surah Three has 200, down to Surah One Hundred Fourteen, which has only six.

Muslims tend to read the Koran literally. They consider it the earthly facsimile of an Uncreated Koran in almost exactly the way that Christians consider Jesus to have been the human incarnation of God. The comparison that reads, "If Christ is God incarnate, the Koran is God inlibriate" (from *liber*, Latin for book) is inelegant but not inaccurate. The created Koran is the instantiation, in letters and sounds, of the Koran's limitless essence in its Uncreated Form. Not that there are two Korans, of course. Rather, the created Koran is the formal crystallization of the infinite reality of the Uncreated Koran. Two levels of reality are operative here. There is the Divine Reality of the Uncreated Koran, and there is the earthly reality of the created Koran. When the created Koran is said to be a miracle, the miracle referred to is the presence of the Uncreated Koran within the letters and sounds of its created (and therefore necessarily in certain ways circumscribed) manifestation.

The words of the Koran came to Muhammad in manageable segments over twenty-three years through voices that seemed at first to vary and sometimes sounded like "the reverberating of bells," but which gradually condensed into a single voice that identified itself as Gabriel's. Muhammad had no control over the flow of the revelation; it descended on him independent of his will. When it arrived he was changed into a special state that was externally discernible. Both his appearance and the sound of his voice would change. He reported that the words assaulted him as if they were solid and heavy: "For We shall charge thee with a word of weight" (73:5; all such references in this chapter are to *surah* and verse[s] in the Koran). Once they descended while he was riding a camel. The animal sought vainly to support the added weight by adjusting its legs. By the time the revelation ceased, its belly was pressed against the earth and its legs splayed out. The words that Muhammad exclaimed in these often trance-like states were memorized by his followers and recorded on bones, bark, leaves, and scraps of parchment, with God preserving their accuracy throughout.

The Koran continues the Old and New Testaments, God's earlier revelations, and presents itself as their culmination: "We made a covenant of old with the Children of Israel [and] you have nothing of guidance until you observe the Torah and the Gospel" (5:70, 68). This entitles Jews and Christians to be included with Muslims as "People of the Book." (Because the context of the koranic revelation is the Middle East, religions of other lands are not mentioned, but their existence is implied and in principle validated, as in the following verses: "To every people we have sent a messenger. . . . [Some] We have mentioned to you, and [some] we have not mentioned to you" [10:47, 4:164]). Nevertheless, Muslims regard the Old and New Testaments as sharing two defects from which the Koran is free. For circumstantial reasons they record only portions of Truth. Second, the Jewish and Christian Bibles were partially corrupted in transmission, a fact that explains the occasional discrepancies that occur between their accounts and parallel ones in the Koran. Exemption from these two limitations makes the Koran the final and infallible revelation of God's will. Its second chapter says explicitly: "This is the Scripture whereof there is no doubt."

From the outside things look otherwise, for from without the Koran is all but impenetrable. No one has ever curled up on a rainy weekend to read the Koran. Carlyle confessed that it was "as toilsome reading as I ever undertook; a wearisome, confused jumble, crude, incondite. Nothing but a sense of duty could carry any European through the Koran." Sir Edward Gibbon said much the same: "The European will peruse with impatience its endless incoherent rhapsody of fable and precept, and declamation, which seldom excites a sentiment or an idea, which sometimes crawls in the dust, and is sometimes lost in the clouds." How are we to understand the discrepancy of the Koran as read from within and from without?

The language in which it was proclaimed, Arabic, provides an initial clue. "No people in the world," writes Philip Hitti, "are so moved by the word, spoken or written, as the Arabs. Hardly any language seems capable of exercising over the minds of its users such irresistible influence as Arabic." Crowds in Cairo, Damascus, or Baghdad can be stirred to the highest emotional pitch by statements that, when translated, seem banal. The rhythm, melodic cadence, the rhyme produce a powerful hypnotic effect. Thus the power of the koranic revelation lies not only in the literal meaning of its words but also in the language in which this meaning incorporated, including its sound. The Koran was from the first a vocal phenomenon; we remember that we are to "recite" in the name of the Lord! Because content and container are here inseparably fused, translations cannot possibly convey the emotion, the fervor, and the mystery that the Koran holds in the original. This is why, in sharp contrast to Christians, who have translated their Bible into every known script, Muslims have preferred to teach others the language in which they believe God spoke finally with incomparable force and directness.

Language, however, is not the only barrier the Koran presents to outsiders, for in content too it is like no other religious text. Unlike the Upanishads, it is not explicitly metaphysical. It does not ground its theology in dramatic narratives as the Indian epics do, nor in historical ones as do the Hebrew scriptures; nor is God revealed in human form as in the Gospels and the *Bhagavad-Gita*. Confining ourselves to the Semitic scriptures, we can say that whereas the Old and New Testaments are directly historical and indirectly doctrinal, the Koran is directly doctrinal and indirectly historical. Because the overwhelming thrust of the Koran is to proclaim the unity, omnipotence, omniscience, and mercy of God—and correlatively the total dependence of human life upon him—historical facts are in its case merely reference points that have scarcely any interest in themselves. This explains why the prophets are cited without any chronological order; why historical occurrences are sometimes recounted so elliptically as to be unintelligible without commentaries; and why the biblical stories that the Koran refers to are presented in an unexpected, abbreviated, and dry manner. They are stripped of their epic character and inserted as didactic examples of the infinitely various things that declare God's praise. When the Lord-servant relationship is the essential point to get across, all else is but commentary and allusion.

Perhaps we shall be less inclined to fault the Koran for the strange face it presents to foreigners if we note that foreign scriptures present their own problems to Muslims. To speak only of the Old and New Testaments, Muslims express disappointment in finding that those texts do not take the form of Divine speech and merely report things that happened. In the Koran God speaks in the first person. Allah describes himself and makes known his laws. The Muslim is therefore inclined to consider each individual sentence of the Holy Book as a separate revelation and to experience the words themselves, even their sounds, as a means of grace. "The Qur'an does not document what is other than itself. It is not about the truth: it is the truth." By contrast the Jewish and Christian Bibles seem more distant from God for placing religious meaning in reports of events instead of God's direct pronouncements.

The Koran's direct delivery creates, for the reader, a final problem that in other scriptures is eased by greater use of narrative and myth. One discerning commentator on the Koran puts this point as follows: "The seeming incoherence of the text has its cause in the incommensurable disproportion between the Spirit [Uncreated Koran] and the limited resources of human language. It is as though the poverty-stricken coagulation which is the language of mortal man were under the formidable pressure of the Heavenly Word broken into a thousand fragments, or as if God in order to express a thousand truths, had but a dozen words at his command and so was compelled to make use of allusions heavy with meaning, of ellipses, abridgements and symbolical syntheses."

Putting comparisons behind us, it is impossible to over-emphasize the central position of the Koran in the elaboration of any Islamic doctrine. With large portions memorized in childhood, it regulates the interpretation and evaluation of every event. It is a memorandum for the faithful, a reminder for daily doings, and a repository of revealed truth. It is a manual of definitions and guarantees, and at the same time a road map for the will. Finally, it is a collection of maxims to meditate on in private, deepening endlessly one's sense of the divine glory. "Perfect is the Word of your Lord in truth and justice" (6:115).

THE QUR'AN

PREFACE

IN THE NAME of the most merciful GOD.

Praise be to GOD, the LORD of all creatures; the most merciful, the king of the day of judgment. Thee do we worship, and of thee do we beg assistance. Direct us in the right way, in the way of those to whom thou hast been gracious; not of those against whom thou art incensed, nor of those who go astray.

THE COW

There is no doubt in this book; *it is* a direction to the pious, who believe in the mysteries *of faith*, who observe the appointed times of prayer, and distribute *alms* out of what we have bestowed on them; and who believe in that *revelation*, which hath been sent down unto thee, and that which

hath been sent down *unto the prophets* before thee, and have
firm assurance in the life to come: these are directed by their
LORD, and they shall prosper. As for the unbelievers, it will
be equal to them whether thou admonish them, or
do not admonish them; they will not believe. GOD hath
sealed up their hearts and their hearing; a dimness covereth
their sight, and they shall suffer a grievous punishment.
There are some who say, We believe in GOD and the last
day, but are not *really* believers; they seek to deceive GOD,
and those who do believe, but they deceive themselves only,
and are not sensible thereof. There is an infirmity in their
hearts, and GOD hath increased that infirmity; and they
shall suffer a most painful punishment because they have disbelieved. When one saith unto them, Act not corruptly in
the earth, they reply, Verily, we are men of integrity. Are
not they themselves corrupt doers? but they are not sensible
thereof. And when one saith unto them, Believe ye as others
believe; they answer, Shall we believe as fools believe? Are
not they themselves fools? but they know it not. When they
meet those who believe, they say, We do believe: but when
they retire privately to their devils, they say, We really *hold*
with you, and only mock *at those people*: GOD shall mock at
them, and continue them in their impiety; they shall wander
in confusion. These are *the men* who have purchased error at
the price of *true* direction: but their traffic hath not been
gainful, neither have they been *rightly* directed. They are
like unto one who kindleth a fire, and when it hath enlightened all around him, GOD taketh away their light and
leaveth them in darkness, they shall not see; *they are* deaf,
dumb and blind, therefore will they not repent. Or like a

stormy cloud from heaven, fraught with darkness, thunder, and lightning, they put their fingers in their ears, because of the noise of the thunder, for fear of death; GOD encompasseth the infidels: the lightning wanteth but little of taking away their sight; so often as it enlighteneth them, they walk therein, but when darkness cometh on them, they stand still; and if GOD so pleased, He would certainly deprive them of their hearing and their sight, for GOD is almighty. O men *of Mecca*! serve your LORD who hath created you, and those who have been before you: peradventure ye will fear *him*; who hath spread the earth as a bed for you, and the heaven as a covering, and hath caused water to descend from heaven, and thereby produced fruits for your sustenance. Set not up therefore any equals unto GOD, against your own knowledge. If ye be in doubt concerning that *revelation* which we have sent down unto our servant, produce a chapter like unto it, and call upon your witnesses, besides GOD, if ye say truth. But if ye do *it* not, nor shall *ever be able to* do *it*, justly fear the fire whose fuel is men and stones, prepared for the unbelievers. But bear good tidings unto those who believe, and do good works, that they shall have gardens watered by rivers; so often as they eat of the fruit thereof for sustenance, they *shall* say, This is what we have formerly eaten of; and they shall be supplied with *several sorts of fruit* having a mutual resemblance to one another. There shall they enjoy wives subject to no impurity, and there shall they continue for ever. Moreover GOD will not be ashamed to propound in a parable a gnat, or even a more despicable thing: for they who believe will know it to be the truth from their LORD; but the unbelievers will say,

What meaneth GOD by this parable? he will thereby mislead many, and will direct many thereby: but he will not
mislead *any* thereby, except the transgressors, who make
void the covenant of GOD after the establishing thereof, and
cut in sunder that which GOD hath commanded to be
joined, and act corruptly in the earth; they shall perish.
How *is it that* ye believe not in GOD? Since ye were dead,
and he gave you life; he will hereafter cause you to die, and
will again restore you to life; then shall ye return unto him.
It is he who hath created for you whatsoever is on earth,
and then set his mind to *the creation* of heaven, and formed it
into seven heavens; he knoweth all things. When thy LORD
said unto the angels, I am going to place a substitute on
earth, they said, Wilt thou place there one who will do
evil therein, and shed blood? but we celebrate thy praise,
and sanctify thee. GOD answered Verily I know that which
ye know not; and he taught Adam the names of all things,
and then proposed them to the angels, and said, Declare
unto me the names of these things if ye say truth. They
answered, Praise be unto thee, we have no knowledge but
what thou teachest us, for thou art knowing and wise. GOD
said, O Adam, tell them their names. And when he had told
them their names, GOD said, Did I not tell you that I know
the secrets of heaven and earth, and know that which ye
discover, and that which ye conceal? And when we said
unto the angels, Worship Adam, they *all* worshipped *him*,
except Eblis, *who* refused, and was puffed up with pride,
and became of the *number of* unbelievers. And we said, O
Adam, dwell thou and thy wife in the garden, and eat *of the
fruit* thereof plentifully wherever ye will; but approach not

this tree, lest ye become of *the number of* the transgressors. But Satan caused them to forfeit *paradise*, and turned them out of *the state of happiness* wherein they had been; whereupon we said, Get ye down, the one of you and enemy unto the other; and there shall be a dwelling place for you on earth, and a provision for a season. And Adam learned words *of prayer* from his LORD, and GOD turned unto him, for he is easy to be reconciled and merciful. We said, Get ye all down from hence; hereafter shall there come unto you a direction from me, and whoever shall follow my direction, on them shall no fear come, neither shall they be grieved; but they who shall be unbelievers, and accuse our signs of falsehood, they shall be the companions of *hell* fire, therein shall they remain for ever. O children of Israel, remember my favour wherewith I have favoured you; and perform *your* covenant with me, and I will perform *my* covenant with you; and revere me: and believe in the *revelation* which I have sent down, confirming that which is with you, and be not the first who believe not therein, neither exchange my signs for a small price; and fear me. Clothe not the truth with vanity, neither conceal the truth against your own knowl- edge; observe the stated times of prayer, and pay your legal alms, and bow down yourselves with those who bow down. Will ye command men to do justice, and forget your own souls? yet ye read the book *of the law*: do ye not there- fore understand? Ask help with perseverance and prayer; this indeed is grievous, unless to the humble, who *seriously* think they shall meet their LORD, and that to him they shall return. O children of Israel, remember my favour where- with I have favoured you, and that I have preferred you above all nations: dread the day *wherein one* soul shall not make satisfaction for *another* soul, neither shall any intercession be accepted from them, nor shall any compensation be received, neither shall they be helped. *Remember* when we delivered you from the people of Pharaoh, who grievously oppressed you, they slew your male children, and let your females live: therein was a great trial from your LORD. And when we divided the sea for you and delivered you, and drowned Pharaoh's people while ye looked on. And when we treated with Moses forty nights; then ye took the calf *for your God*, and did evil; yet afterwards we forgave you, that peradventure ye might give thanks. And when we gave Moses the book *of the law*, and the distinction *between good and evil*, that peradventure ye might be directed. And when Moses said unto his people, O my people, verily ye have injured your own souls, by your taking the calf *for your God*; therefore be turned unto your Creator, and slay those among you *who have been guilty of that crime*; this will be better for you in the sight of your Creator: and *thereupon* he turned unto you, for he is easy to be reconciled, and merciful. And when ye said, O Moses, we will not believe thee, until we see GOD manifestly; therefore a punishment came upon you, while ye looked on; then we raised you to life after ye had been dead, that peradventure ye might give thanks. And we caused clouds to overshadow you, and manna and quails to descend upon you, *saying*, Eat of the good things which we have given you for food: and they injured not us, but injured their own souls. And when we said, Enter into this city, and eat *of the provisions* thereof plentifully as ye will; and enter the gate worshipping, and say, Forgiveness! we will pardon you your sins, and give increase unto the well-doers. But the ungodly changed the expression into another, different from what had been spoken unto them; and we sent down upon the ungodly indignation from heaven, because they had transgressed. And when Moses asked drink for his people, we said, Strike the rock with thy rod; and there gushed thereout twelve fountains *according to the number of the tribes*, and all men knew their *respective* drinking-place. Eat and drink of the bounty of GOD, and commit not evil in the earth, acting unjustly. And when ye said, O Moses, we will by no means be satisfied with one *kind of* food; pray unto thy LORD therefore for us, that he would produce for us of that which the earth bringeth forth, herbs, and cucumbers, and garlic, and lentils, and onions; Moses answered, Will ye exchange that which is better, for that which is worse? Get ye down into Egypt, for *there* shall ye find what ye desire: and they were smitten with vileness and misery, and drew on themselves indignation from GOD. This *they suffered*, because they believed not in the signs of GOD, and killed the prophets unjustly; this, because they rebelled and transgressed. Surely those who believe, and those who Judaize, and Christians, and Sabians, whoever believeth in GOD, and the last day, and doth that which is right, they shall have their reward with their LORD ; *there shall come* no fear on them, neither shall they be grieved. *Call to mind* also when we accepted your covenant, and lifted up the mountain *of Sinai* over you, *saying*, Receive *the law* which we have given you, with a resolution *to keep it*, and remember that which is contained therein, that ye may beware. After this ye again turned back, so that if it had not been for GOD's indulgence and mercy towards you, ye had certainly been destroyed. Moreover ye know *what befell* those of your nation who transgressed on the sabbath day; We said unto them, Be ye *changed into* apes, driven away *from the society of men*. And we made them an example unto those who were contemporary with them, and unto those who came after them, and a warning to the pious. And when Moses said unto his people, Verily GOD commandeth you to sacrifice a cow; they answered, Dost thou make a jest of us? Moses said, GOD forbid that I should be *one* of the foolish. They said, Pray for us unto thy LORD, that he would show us what *cow* it is. Moses answered, He saith, She is neither an old cow, nor a young heifer, but of a middle age between both: do ye therefore that which ye are commanded. They said, Pray for us unto thy LORD, that he would show us what colour she is of. Moses answered, He saith, She is a red cow, intensely red, her colour rejoiceth the beholders. They said, Pray for us unto thy LORD, that he would *further* show us what *cow* it is, for *several* cows with us are like one another, and we, if GOD please, will be directed. Moses answered, He saith, She is a cow not broken to plough the earth, or water the field, a sound one, there is no blemish in her. They said, Now hast thou brought the truth. Then they sacrificed her; yet they wanted little of leaving it undone. And when ye slew a man, and contended among yourselves concerning him, GOD brought forth *to light* that which ye concealed. For we said, Strike *the dead body* with part of *the sacrificed cow*: so GOD raiseth the dead to life, and showeth you his signs, that peradventure ye may understand. Then were your hearts hardened after this, even as stones, or exceeding *them* in hardness: for from some stones have rivers bursted forth, others have been rent in sunder, and water hath issued from them, and others have fallen down for fear of GOD. But GOD is not regardless of that which ye do. Do ye therefore desire that *the Jews* should believe you? yet a part of them heard the word of GOD, and then perverted it, after they had understood it, against their own conscience. And when they meet the true believers, they say, We believe: but when they are privately assembled together, they say, Will ye acquaint them with what GOD hath revealed unto you, that they may dispute with you concerning it in the presence of your LORD ? Do ye not therefore understand? Do not they know that GOD knoweth that which they conceal as well as that which they publish? But there are illiterate men among them, who know not the book *of the law*, but only lying stories, although they think otherwise. And woe unto them who transcribe *corruptly* the book *of the law* with their hands, and then say, This is from GOD: that they may sell it for a small price. Therefore woe unto them because of that which their hands have written; and woe unto them for that which they have gained. They say, The fire *of hell* shall not touch us but for a *certain* number of days. Answer, Have ye received any promise from GOD *to that purpose?* for GOD will not act contrary to his promise: or do ye speak concerning GOD that which ye know not? Verily whoso doth evil, and is encompassed by his iniquity, they *shall be* the companions of *hell* fire, they shall remain therein for ever: but they who believe and do good works, they shall be the companions of paradise, they shall continue therein for ever. *Remember* also, when we accepted the covenant of the children of Israel, *saying,* Ye shall not worship *any other* except GOD, and *ye shall show* kindness to *your* parents and kindred, and to orphans, and to the poor, and speak that which is good unto men, and be constant at prayer, and give alms. Afterwards ye turned back, except a few of you, and retired afar off. And when we accepted your covenant, *saying,* Ye shall not shed your *brother's* blood, nor dispossess one another of your habitations. Then ye confirmed *it,* and were witnesses *thereto.* Afterwards ye were they who slew one another, and turned several of your *brethren* out of their houses, mutually assisting each other against them with injustice and enmity; but if they come captives unto you, ye redeem them: yet it is *equally* unlawful for you to dispossess them. Do ye therefore believe in part of the book *of the law,* and reject other part thereof? But whoso among you doth this, shall have no other reward than shame in this life, and on the day of resurrection they shall be sent to a most grievous punishment; for GOD is not regardless of that which ye do. These are they who have purchased this present life, at the price of that which is to come; wherefore their punishment shall not be mitigated, neither shall they be helped. We formerly delivered the book *of the law* unto Moses, and caused apostles to succeed him, and gave evident miracles to Jesus the son of Mary, and strengthened him with the holy spirit. Do ye therefore, whenever an apostle cometh unto you with that which your souls desire not, proudly reject *him,* and accuse some of imposture, and slay others? *The Jews* say, Our hearts are uncircumcised: but GOD hath cursed them with their infidelity, therefore few shall believe. And when a book came unto them from GOD, confirming *the scrip-*

tures which were with them, although they had before prayed for assistance against those who believed not, *yet* when that came unto them which they knew *to be from God*, they would not believe therein: therefore the curse of GOD shall be on the infidels. For a vile *price* have they sold their souls, that they should not believe in that which GOD hath sent down; out of envy, because GOD sendeth down his favours to such of his servants as he pleaseth: therefore they brought on themselves indignation on indignation; and the unbelievers shall suffer an ignominious punishment. When one saith unto them, Believe in that which GOD hath sent down: they answer, We believe in that which hath been sent down unto us: and they reject what *hath been revealed* since, although it be the truth, confirming that which is with them. Say, Why therefore have ye slain the prophets of GOD in times past, if ye be true believers? Moses formerly came unto you with evident signs, but ye afterwards took the calf *for your god* and did wickedly. And when we accepted your covenant, and lifted the mountain of *Sinai* over you, *saying*, Receive *the law* which we have given you, with a resolution *to perform it*, and hear; they said, We have heard, and have rebelled: and they were made to drink down the calf into their hearts for their unbelief. Say, A grievous thing hath your faith commanded you, if ye be true believers. Say, If the future mansion with GOD be *prepared* peculiarly for you, exclusive of the rest of mankind, wish for death, if ye say truth: but they will never wish for it, because of that which their hands have sent before them; GOD knoweth the wicked doers; and thou shalt surely find them of all men the most covetous of life, even *more* than the idolaters: one of them would desire his life to be prolonged a thousand years, but none shall reprieve himself from punishment, that his life may be prolonged: GOD seeth that which they do. Say, Whoever is an enemy to Gabriel (for he hath caused *the Korân* to descend on thy heart, by permission of GOD, confirming that which was before *revealed*, a direction, and good tidings to the faithful); whosoever is an enemy to GOD, or his angels, or his apostles, or to Gabriel, or Michael, verily GOD is an enemy to the unbelievers. And now we have sent down unto thee evident signs, and none will disbelieve them but the evil-doers. Whenever they make a covenant, will some of them reject it? yea, the greater part of them do not believe. And when there came unto them an apostle from GOD, confirming that *scripture* which was with them, some of those to whom the scriptures were given, cast the book of GOD behind their backs, as if they knew it not: and they followed *the device* which the devils devised against the kingdom of Solomon; and Solomon was not an unbeliever; but the devils believed not, they taught men sorcery, and that which was sent down to the two angels at *Babel*, Harût and Marût: yet those two taught no man until they had said Verily we are a temptation, therefore be not an unbeliever. So men learned from those two *a charm* by which they might cause division between a man and his wife; but they hurt none thereby, unless by GOD's permission; and they learned that which would hurt them, and not profit them; and yet they knew that he who bought that *art* should have no part in the life to come, and woeful *is the price* for which they have sold their souls, if they knew it. But if they had believed and feared

God, verily the reward *they would have had* from GOD would have been better, if they had known it. O true believers, say not *to our apostle*, Raïna; but say, Ondhorna; and hearken: the infidels shall suffer a grievous punishment. It is not the desire of the unbelievers, either among those unto whom the scriptures have been given, or among the idolaters, that any good should be sent down unto you from your LORD : but GOD will appropriate his mercy unto whom he pleaseth; for GOD is exceeding beneficent. Whatever verse we shall abrogate, or cause *thee* to forget, we will bring a better than it, or one like unto it. Dost thou not know that GOD is almighty? Dost thou not know that unto GOD belongeth the kingdom of heaven and earth? neither have ye any protector or helper except GOD. Will ye require of your apostle according to that which was formerly required of Moses? but he hath exchanged faith for infidelity, hath already erred from the straight way. Many of those unto whom the scriptures have been given, desire to render you again unbe-lievers, after ye have believed; out of envy from their souls, even after the truth is become manifest unto them, but for-give *them*, and avoid *them*, till GOD shall send his command; for GOD is omnipotent. Be constant in prayer, and give alms; and what good ye have sent before for your souls, ye shall find it with GOD; surely GOD seeth that which ye do. They say, Verily none shall enter paradise, except they who are Jews or Christians: this is their wish. Say, Produce your proof *of this*, if ye speak truth. Nay, but he who resigneth himself to GOD, and doth that which is right, he shall have his reward with his LORD ; there shall *come* no fear on them, neither shall they be grieved. The Jews say, The Christians are *grounded* on nothing; and the Christians say, The Jews are *grounded* on nothing: yet they *both* read the scriptures. So likewise say they who know not the *scripture*, according to their saying. But GOD shall judge between them on the day of the resurrection, concerning that about which they *now* disagree. Who is more unjust than he who prohibiteth the temples of GOD, that his name should be remembered therein, and who hasteth to destroy them? Those men cannot enter therein, but with fear: they shall have shame in this world, and in the next a grievous punishment. To GOD *belongeth* the east and the west; therefore, withersoever ye turn yourselves to pray, there is the face of GOD; for GOD is omnipresent and omniscient. They say, GOD hath begotten children: GOD forbid! To him *belongeth* whatever is in heaven, and on earth; all is possessed by him, the Creator of heaven and earth; and when he decreeth a thing, he only saith unto it, Be, and it is. And they who know not *the scriptures* say, Unless GOD speak unto us, or thou show us a sign, *we will not believe.* So said those before them, according to their saying: their hearts resemble each other. We have already shown manifest signs unto people who firmly believe; we have sent thee in truth, a bearer of good tidings, and a preacher; and thou shalt not be questioned concerning the companions of hell. But the Jews will not be pleased with thee, neither the Christians, until thou follow their religion; say, The direction of GOD is the *true* direction. And verily if thou follow their desires, after the knowledge which hath been given thee, thou shalt find no patron or protector against GOD. They to whom we have given the book *of the* Korân, and who read it with its true reading, they believe therein; and whoever believeth not therein, they shall perish. O children of Israel, remember my favour wherewith I have favoured you, and that I have preferred you before all nations; and dread the day wherein *one* soul shall not make satisfaction for *another* soul neither shall any compensation be accepted from them, nor shall any intercession avail, neither shall they be helped. *Remember* when the LORD tried Abraham by *certain* words, which he fulfilled: *God* said, Verily I will constitute thee a model of religion unto mankind; he answered, And also of my posterity; *God* said, My covenant doth not comprehend the ungodly. And when we appointed the *holy* house *of Mecca* to be the place of resort for mankind, and a place of security; and *said*, Take the station of Abraham for a place of prayer; and we convenanted with Abraham and Ismael, that they should cleanse my house for those who should compass *it*, and those who should be devoutly assiduous *there*, and those who should bow down and worship. And when Abraham said, LORD, make this a territory of security, and bounteously bestow fruits on its inhabitants, such of them as believe in GOD and the last day; *God* answered, And whoever believeth not, I will bestow on him little, afterwards I will drive him to the punishment of *hell* fire; an ill journey shall it be! And when Abraham and Ismael raised the foundations of the house, *saying*, LORD, accept *it* from us, for thou art he who heareth and knoweth: LORD, make us also resigned unto thee, and of our posterity a people resigned unto thee, and show us our holy ceremonies, and be turned unto us, for thou art easy to be reconciled, and merciful: LORD, send them likewise an apostle from among them, who may declare thy signs unto them, and teach them the book *of the Korân* and wisdom, and may purify them; for thou art mighty and wise. Who will be averse to the religion of Abraham, but he whose mind is infatuated? Surely we have chosen him in this world, and in that which is to come he shall be one of the righteous. When his LORD said unto him, Resign thyself *unto me*; he answered, I have resigned myself unto the LORD of all creatures. And Abraham bequeathed this *religion* to his children, and Jacob *did the same, saying,* My children, verily GOD hath chosen this religion for you, therefore die not, unless ye also be resigned. Were ye present when Jacob was at the point of death? when he said to his sons, Whom will ye worship after me? They answered, We will worship thy GOD, and the GOD of thy fathers, Abraham, and Ismael, and Isaac, one GOD, and to him will we be resigned. That people are now passed away, they have what they have gained, and ye shall have what ye gain; and ye shall not be questioned concerning that which they have done. They say, Become Jews or Christians that ye may be directed. Say, Nay *we follow* the religion of Abraham the orthodox, who was no idolater. Say, We believe in GOD, and that which hath been sent down unto us, and that which hath been sent down unto Abraham, and Ismael, and Isaac, and Jacob, and the tribes, and that which was delivered unto Moses, and Jesus, and that which was delivered unto the prophets from their LORD : We make no distinction between any of them, and to *God* are we resigned. Now if they believe according to what ye believe, they are surely directed, but if they turn back, they are is schism. GOD shall support thee against them, for he is the hearer, the wise. The baptism of GOD *have we received*, and who is better than GOD to baptize? him do we worship. Say, Will ye dispute with us concerning GOD, who is our LORD, and your LORD ? we have our works, and ye have your works, and unto him we are sincerely devoted. Will ye say, Truly Abraham, and Ismael, and Isaac, and Jacob, and the tribes were Jews or Christians? Say, Are ye wiser, or GOD? And who is more unjust than he who hideth the testimony which he hath *received* from GOD? But GOD is not regardless of that which ye do. That people are passed away, they have what they have gained, and ye shall have what ye gain, nor shall ye be questioned concerning that which they have done.(II.) The foolish men will say, What hath turned them from their Keblah, towards which they formerly *prayed*? Say, Unto GOD *belongeth* the east and the west: he directeth whom he pleaseth into the right way. Thus have we placed you, *O Arabians*, an intermediate nation, that ye may be witnesses against *the rest of* mankind, and that the apostle may be witness against you. We appointed the Keblah towards which thou didst formerly *pray*, only that we might know him who followeth the apostle, from him who turneth back on his heels; though this *change* seem a great matter, unless unto those whom GOD hath directed. But GOD will not render your faith of none effect; for GOD is gracious and merciful unto man. We have seen thee turn about thy face towards heaven *with uncertainty*, but we will cause thee to turn thyself towards a Keblah that will please thee. Turn therefore thy face towards the holy temple *of Mecca*; and wherever ye be, turn your faces towards that *place*. They to whom the scripture hath been given, know this to be truth from their LORD . GOD is not regardless of that which ye do. Verily although thou shouldest show unto those to whom the scripture hath been given all kinds of signs, yet they will not follow thy Keblah, neither shalt thou follow their Keblah; nor will one part of them follow the Keblah of the other. And if thou follow their desires, after the knowledge which hath been given thee, verily thou wilt become *one* of the ungodly. They to whom we have given the scripture know *our apostle*, even as they know their own children; but some of them hide the truth, against their own knowledge. Truth is from thy LORD, therefore thou shalt not doubt. Every sect hath a certain tract *of heaven* to which they turn themselves *in prayer*; but do ye strive to run after good things: wherever ye be, GOD will bring you all back *at the resurrection*, for GOD is almighty. And from what place soever thou comest forth, turn thy face towards the holy temple; for this is truth from thy LORD ; neither is GOD regardless of that which ye do. From what place soever thou comest forth, turn thy face towards the holy temple; and wherever ye be, thitherward turn your faces, lest men have matter of dispute against you; but as for those among them who are unjust doers, fear them not, but fear me, that I may accomplish my grace upon you, and that ye may be directed. As we have sent unto you an apostle from among you, to rehearse our signs unto you, and to purify you, and to teach you the book *of the Korân* and wisdom, and to teach you that which ye knew not: therefore remember me, and I will remember you, and give thanks unto me, and be not unbelievers. O *true* believers, beg assistance with patience and prayer, for GOD is with the patient. And say not of those who are slain in fight for the religion of GOD, that *they are* dead; yea, *they are* living: but ye do not understand. We will surely prove you *by afflicting you* in some measure with fear, and hunger, and decrease of wealth, and *loss* of lives, and *scarcity* of fruits: but bear good tidings unto the patient, who when a misfortune befalleth them, say, We are GOD's, and unto him shall we surely return. Upon them shall be blessings from their LORD and mercy, and they are the rightly directed. Moreover Safa and Merwah are *two* of the monuments of GOD: whoever therefore goeth on pilgrimage to the temple *of Mecca* or visiteth *it*, it shall be no crime in him if he compass them both. And as for him who voluntarily performeth a good work; verily GOD is grateful and knowing. They who conceal any of the evident signs, or the direction which we have sent down, after what we have manifested unto men in the scripture, GOD shall curse them; and they who curse shall curse them. But as for those who repent and amend, and make known *what they concealed*, I will be turned unto them, for I am easy to be reconciled and merciful. Surely they who believe not, and die in their unbelief, upon them shall be the curse of GOD, and of the angels, and of all men; they shall remain under it for ever, their punishment shall not be alleviated, neither shall they be regarded. Your GOD is one GOD, there is no GOD but He, the most merciful. Now in the creation of heaven and earth, and the vicissitude of night and day, and in the ship which saileth in the sea, *loaden* with what is profitable for mankind, and in the *rain*-water which GOD sendeth from heaven, quickening thereby the dead earth, and replenishing the same with all sorts of cattle, and in the change of winds, and the clouds that are compelled to do service between heaven and earth, are signs to people of understanding: yet some men take idols beside GOD, and love them as with the love *due to* GOD; but the true believers are more fervent in love towards GOD. Oh that they who act unjustly did perceive, when they behold their punishment, that all power belongeth unto GOD, and that he is severe in punishing! When those who have been followed, shall separate themselves from their followers, and shall see the punishment, and the cords *of relation* between them shall be cut in sunder; the followers shall say, If we could return *to life*, we would separate ourselves from them, as they have *now* separated themselves from us. So GOD will show them their works; they shall sigh grievously, and shall not come forth from the fire *of hell*. O men, eat of that which is lawful and good on the earth; and tread not in the steps of the devil, for he is your open enemy. Verily he commandeth you evil and wickedness, and that ye should say that of GOD which ye know not. And when it is said unto them *who believe not*, Follow that which GOD hath sent down; they answer, Nay, but we will follow that which we found our fathers practise. What? though their fathers knew nothing, and were not *rightly* directed? The unbelievers are like unto one who crieth aloud to that which heareth not so much as *his* calling, or the sound of *his* voice. *They are* deaf, dumb, and blind, therefore they do not understand. O true believers, eat of the good things which we have bestowed on you for food, and return thanks unto GOD, if ye serve him. Verily he hath forbidden you *to eat* that which dieth of itself, and blood, and swine's flesh, and that on which any other name but GOD's hath been invoked. But he who is forced by necessity, not lusting, nor returning *to transgress,* it shall be no crime in him *if he eat of those things,* for GOD is gracious and merciful. Moreover they who conceal *any part* of the scripture which GOD hath sent down unto them, and sell it for a small price, they shall swallow into their bellies nothing but fire; GOD shall not speak unto them on the day of resurrection, neither shall he purify them, and they shall suffer a grievous punishment. These are they who have sold direction for error, and pardon for punishment: but how great will their suffering be in the fire! This *they shall endure,* because GOD sent down the book *of the Korân* with truth, and they who disagree concerning that book, are certainly in a wide mistake. It is not righteousness that ye turn your faces *in prayer* towards the east and the west, but righteousness is of him who believeth in GOD and the last day, and the angels and the scriptures, and the prophets; who giveth money for *God's* sake unto his kindred, and unto orphans, and the needy, and the stranger, and those who ask, and for redemption of captives; who is constant at prayer, and giveth alms; and of those who perform their covenant, when they have covenanted, and who behave themselves patiently in adversity, and hardships, and in time of violence: these are they who are true, and these are they who fear *God.* O true believers, the law of retaliation is ordained you for the slain: the free *shall die* for the free, and the servant for the servant, and a woman for a woman: but he whom his brother shall forgive, may be prosecuted, *and obliged to make satisfaction* according to what is just, and a fine shall be set on him with humanity. This is indulgence from your LORD, and mercy. And he who shall transgress after this, *by killing the murderer*, shall suffer a grievous punishment. And in this law of retaliation ye have life, O ye of understanding, that peradventure ye may fear. It is ordained you, when any of you is at the point of death, if he leave any goods, *that he bequeath* a legacy to his parents, and kindred, according to what shall be reasonable. This is a duty *incumbent* on those who fear GOD. But he who shall change *the legacy*, after he heath heard it *bequeathed by the dying person*, surely the sin thereof shall be on those who change it, for GOD is he who heareth and knoweth. Howbeit he who apprehendeth from the testator any mistake or injustice, and shall compose *the matter* between them, that shall be no crime in him, for GOD is gracious and merciful. O true believers, a fast is ordained you, as it was ordained unto those before you, that ye may fear *God*. A certain number of days *shall ye fast*: but he among you who shall be sick, or on a journey, *shall fast an equal* number of other days. And those who can *keep it, and do not*, must redeem *their neglect* by maintaining of a poor man. And he who voluntarily dealeth better *with the poor man than he is obliged*, this shall be better for him. But if ye fast it will be better for you, if ye knew it. The month of Ramadân *shall ye fast*, in which the Korân was sent down *from heaven*, a direction unto men, and declarations of direction, and the distinction *between good and evil*. Therefore let him among you who shall be present in this month, fast the same *month*; but he who shall be sick, or on a journey, *shall fast the like* number of other days. GOD would *make this* an ease unto you, and would not *make it* a difficulty unto you; that ye may fulfil the number *of days*, and glorify GOD, for that he hath

directed you, and that ye may give thanks. When my servants ask thee concerning me, Verily I am near; I will hear
the prayer of him that prayeth, when he prayeth unto me:
but let them hearken unto me, and believe in me, that they
may be rightly directed. It is lawful for you on the night of
the fast to go in unto your wives, they are a garment unto
you, and ye are a garment unto them. GOD knoweth that ye
defraud yourselves *therein*, wherefore he turneth unto you,
and forgiveth you. Now therefore go in unto them; and
earnestly desire that which GOD ordaineth you, and eat and
drink, until ye can plainly distinguish a white thread from
a black thread by the daybreak: then keep the fast until
night, and go not in unto them, but be constantly present in
the places of worship. These are the prescribed bounds of
GOD, therefore draw not near them *to transgress them*. Thus
GOD declareth his signs unto men, that ye may fear *him*.
Consume not your wealth among yourselves in vain; nor present it unto judges, that ye may devour part of men's substance unjustly, against your own consciences. They will ask
thee concerning the phases of the moon. Answer, They are
times appointed unto men, and to *show the season of* the pilgrimage to *Mecca*. It is not righteousness that ye enter *your*
houses by the back part thereof, but righteousness is of him
who feareth *God*. Therefore enter *your* houses by their doors;
and fear GOD, that ye may be happy. And fight for the religion of GOD against those who fight against you, but transgress not *by attacking them first*, for GOD loveth not the
transgressors. And kill them wherever ye find them, and
turn them out of that whereof they have dispossessed you;
for temptation *to idolatry* is more grievous than slaughter: yet

fight not against them in the holy temple, until they attack you therein; but if they attack you, slay them *there*. This shall be the reward of the infidels. But if they desist, GOD is gracious and merciful. Fight therefore against them, until there be no temptation *to idolatry*, and the religion be GOD's: but if they desist, then let there be no hostility, except against the ungodly. A sacred month for a sacred month, and the holy limits *of Mecca, if they attack you therein, do ye also attack them therein in* retaliation; and whoever transgresseth against you *by so doing*, do ye transgress against him in like manner as he hath transgressed against you, and fear GOD, and know that GOD is with those who fear *him*. Contribute *out of your substance* towards the defence of the religion of GOD, and throw not *yourselves* with your own hands into perdition; and do good, for GOD loveth those who do good. Perform the pilgrimage *of Mecca*, and the visitation of GOD; and if ye be besieged, *send* that offering which shall be the easiest; and shave not your heads, until your offering reacheth the place of sacrifice. But whoever among you is sick, or is trou-bled with any distemper of the head, must redeem *the shav-ing of his head* by fasting, or alms, or some offering. When ye are secure *from enemies,* he who tarrieth in the visitation *of the temple of Mecca* until the pilgrimage, shall *bring* that offering which shall be the easiest. But he who findeth not *anything to offer*, shall fast three days in the pilgrimage, and seven when ye are returned: they shall be ten *days* complete. This *is incumbent* on him whose family shall not be present at the holy temple. And fear GOD, and know that GOD is severe in punishing. The pilgrimage *must be performed in* the known months; whosoever therefore purposeth to go on pilgrimage therein, let him not know a woman, nor transgress, nor quarrel in the pilgrimage. The good which ye do, GOD knoweth it. Make provision *for your journey*; but the best provision is piety: and fear me, O ye of understanding. It shall be no crime in you, if ye seek an increase from your LORD, *by trading during the pilgrimage.* And when ye go in procession from Arafat, remember GOD near the holy monument; and remember him for that he hath directed you, although ye were before this of *the number of* those who go astray. Therefore go in procession from whence the people go in procession, and ask pardon of GOD, for GOD is gracious and merciful. And when ye have finished your holy ceremonies, remember GOD, according as ye remember your fathers, or with a more reverent commemoration. There are some men who say, O LORD, give us *our portion* in this world; but such shall have no portion in the next life: and there are others who say, O LORD, give us good in this world, and also good in the next world, and deliver us from the torment of *hell* fire. They shall have a portion of that which they have gained: GOD is swift in taking and account. Remember GOD the *appointed* number of days: but if any haste *to depart from the valley of Mina* in two days, it shall be no crime in him. And if any tarry longer, it shall be no crime in him, in him who feareth GOD. Therefore fear GOD, and know that unto him ye shall be gathered. There is a man who causeth thee to marvel by his speech concerning this present life, and calleth GOD to witness that which is in his heart, yet he is most intent in opposing thee; and when he turneth away *from thee,* he hasteth to act corruptly in the earth, and to destroy that which is sown, and springeth up but GOD loveth not corrupt doing. And if one say unto him, Fear GOD; pride seizeth him, together with wickedness; but hell shall be his reward, and an unhappy couch shall it be. There is also a man who selleth his soul for the sake of those things which are pleasing unto GOD; and GOD is gracious unto his servants. O true believers, enter into the true religion wholly, and follow not the steps of Satan, for he is your open enemy. If ye have slipped after the declarations of our will have come unto you, know that GOD is mighty and wise. Do the infidels expect less than that GOD should come down to them overshadowed with clouds, and the angels also? but the thing is decreed, and to GOD shall all things return. Ask the children of Israel how many evident signs we have showed them; and whoever shall change the grace of GOD, after it shall have come unto him, verily GOD will be severe in punishing him The present life was ordained for those who believe not, and they laugh the faithful to scorn; but they who fear GOD shall be above them, on the day of the resurrection: for GOD is bountiful unto whom he pleaseth without measure. Mankind was of one faith, and GOD sent prophets bearing good tidings, and denouncing threats, and sent down with them the scripture in truth, that it might judge between men of that concerning which they disagreed: and none disagreed concerning it, except those to whom the same scriptures were delivered, after the declarations of GOD's will had come unto them, out of envy among themselves. And GOD directed those who believed, to that truth concerning which they disagreed, by his will: for GOD directeth whom he pleaseth into the right way. Did ye think ye should enter paradise, when as yet no such thing had happened unto you, as *hath happened* unto those who have been before you? They suffered calamity and tribulation, and were afflicted; so that the apostle, and they who believed with him, said, When *will* the help of GOD *come?* Is not the help of GOD nigh? They will ask thee what they shall bestow *in alms:* Answer, The good which ye bestow, *let it be given* to parents, and kindred, and orphans, and the poor, and the stranger. Whatsoever good ye do, GOD knoweth it. War is enjoined you *against the Infidels;* but this is hateful unto you: yet perchance ye hate a thing which is better for you, and perchance ye love a thing which is worse for you: but GOD knoweth and ye know not. They will ask thee concerning the sacred month, *whether they may* war therein: Answer, To war therein is grievous; but to obstruct the way of GOD, and infidelity towards him, and *to keep men* from the holy temple, and to drive out his people from thence, is more grievous in the sight of GOD, and the temptation *to idolatry* is more grievous than to kill *in the sacred months.* They will not cease to war against you, until they turn you from your religion, if they be able: but whoever among you shall turn back from his religion, and die an infidel, their works shall be vain in this world and the next; they shall be the companions of *hell* fire, they shall remain therein for ever. But they who believe, and who fly for the sake of religion, and fight in GOD's cause, they shall hope for the mercy of GOD; for GOD is gracious and merciful. They will ask thee concerning wine and lots. Answer, In both there is great sin, and *also some* things of use unto men; but their sinfulness is greater than their use. They will ask thee also what they shall bestow *in alms:* Answer, What ye

have to spare. Thus GOD showeth *his* signs unto you, that
peradventure ye might seriously think of this present world,
and of the next. They will also ask thee concerning orphans:
Answer, To deal righteously with them is best; and if ye
intermeddle with *the management of what belongs to* them, *do them
no wrong*; they are your brethren: GOD knoweth the corrupt
dealer from the righteous; and if GOD please, he will surely
distress you, for GOD is mighty and wise. Marry not *women
who are* idolators, until they believe: verily a maid-servant
who believeth is better than an idolatress, although she
please you *more*. And give not *women who believe* in marrige to
the idolaters, until they believe; for verily a servant who is
a true believer, is better than an idolater, though he please
you *more*. They invite unto *hell* fire, but GOD inviteth paradise and pardon through his will, and declareth his signs
unto men, that they may remember. They will ask thee also
concerning the courses of women: Answer, They are a pol-
lution: therefore separate yourselves from women in their
courses, and go not near them until they be cleansed. But
when they are cleansed, go in unto them as GOD hath commanded you, for GOD loveth those who repent, and loveth
those who are clean. Your wives are your tillage; go in
therefore unto your tillage in what manner soever ye will:
and do first some act *that may be profitable* unto your souls; and
fear GOD, and know that ye must meet him; and bear good
tidings unto the faithful. Make not GOD the object of your
oaths, that ye will deal justly, and be devout, and make
peace among men; for GOD is he who heareth and knoweth.
GOD will not punish you for an inconsiderate word in your
oaths; but he will punish you for that which your hearts

have assented unto: GOD is merciful and gracious. They who vow *to abstain* from their wives, are *allowed* to wait four months: but if they go back *from their vow*, verily GOD is gracious and merciful; and if they resolve on a divorce, GOD is he who heareth and knoweth. The *women who are* divorced shall wait concerning themselves until they have their courses thrice, and it shall not be lawful for them to conceal that which GOD hath created in their wombs, if they believe in GOD and the last day; and their husbands will act more justly to bring them back at this *time*, if they desire a reconciliation. The women ought also *to behave towards their husbands* in like manner as *their husbands should behave* towards them, according to what is just: but the men ought to have a superiority over them. GOD is mighty and wise. Ye may divorce *your wives* twice; and then either retain *them* with humanity, or dismiss *them* with kindness. But it is not lawful for you to take away anything of what ye have given them, unless both fear that they cannot observe the ordinances of GOD. And if ye fear that they cannot observe the ordinances of GOD, it shall be no crime in either of them on account of that for which *the wife* shall redeem herself. These are the ordinances of GOD; therefore transgress them not; for whoever transgresseth the ordinances of GOD, they are unjust doers. But if *the husband* divorce her a *third time*, she shall not be lawful for him again, until she marry another husband. But if he *also* divorce her, it shall be no crime in them, if they return to each other, if they think they can observe the ordinances of GOD; and these are the ordinances of GOD, he declareth them to people of understanding. But when ye divorce women, and they have fulfilled their prescribed time, either retain them with humanity, or dismiss them with kindness; and retain them not by violence, so that ye transgress; for he who doth this, surely injureth his own soul. And make not the signs of GOD a jest: but remember GOD's favour towards you, and that he hath sent down unto you the book *of the Korân*, and wisdom, admonishing you thereby; and fear GOD, and know that GOD is omniscient. But when ye have divorced *your* wives, and they have fulfilled their prescribed time, hinder them not from marrying their husbands, when they have agreed among themselves according to what is honourable. This is given in admonition unto him among you who believeth in GOD, and the last day. This is most righteous for you, and most pure. GOD knoweth, but ye know not. Mothers *after they are divorced* shall give suck unto their children two full years, to him who desireth the time of giving suck to be completed; and the father shall be obliged to maintain them and clothe them *in the mean time*, according to that which shall be reasonable. No person shall be obliged beyond his ability. A mother shall not be compelled *to what is unreasonable* on account of her child, nor a father on acount of his child. And the heir *of the father* shall be obliged to do in like manner. But if they choose to wean *the child before the end of two years*, by common consent and on mutual consideration, it shall be no crime in them. And if ye have a mind to provide a nurse for your children, it shall be no crime in you, in case ye fully pay what ye offer *her*, according to that which is just. And fear GOD, and know that GOD seeth whatever ye do. Such of you as die, and leave wives *their wives* must wait concerning themselves four months and ten *days*, and when they shall have fulfilled their term, it shall be no crime in you, for that which they shall do with themselves, according to what is reasonable. GOD well knoweth that which ye do. And it shall be no crime in you, whether ye make public overtures of marriage unto *such* women, *within the said four months and ten days*, or whether ye conceal *such your designs* in your minds: GOD knoweth that ye will remember them. But make no promise unto them privately, unless ye speak honourable words; and resolve not on the knot of marriage, until the prescribed time be accomplished; and know that GOD knoweth that which is in your minds, therefore beware of him, and know that GOD is gracious and merciful. It shall be no crime in you, if ye divorce your wives, so long as ye have not touched them, nor settled any dowry on them. And provide for them (he who is at his ease must *provide* according to his circumstances, and he who is straitened according to his circumstances) necessaries, according to what shall be reasonable. *This is* a duty *incumbent* on the righteous. But if ye divorce them before ye have touched them, and have already settled a dowry on them, *ye shall give them* half of what ye have settled, unless they release *any part*, or he release *part* in whose hand the knot of marriage is; and if ye release *the whole*, it will approach nearer unto piety. And forget not liberality among you, for GOD seeth that which ye do. Carefully observe the *appointed* prayers, and the middle prayer, and be assiduous *therein*, with devotion towards GOD. But if ye fear *any danger, pray* on foot or on horseback; and when ye are safe, remember GOD, how he hath taught you what as yet ye knew not. And such of you as shall die and leave wives, ought to bequeath their wives a year's maintenance, without putting them out *of their houses*: but if they go out *voluntarily*, it shall be no crime in you, for that which they shall do with themselves, accorking to what shall be reasonable; GOD is mighty and wise. And unto those who are divorced, a reasonable provision *is also due; this is* a duty *incumbent* on those who fear God. Thus GOD declareth his signs unto you, that ye may understand. Hast thou not considered those who left their habitations (and they were thousands) for fear of death? And GOD said unto them, Die; then he restored them to life, for GOD is gracious towards mankind; but the greater part of men do not give thanks. Fight for the religion of GOD, and know that GOD is he who heareth and knoweth. Who is he that will lend unto GOD on good usury? verily he will double it unto him manifold; for GOD contracteth and extendeth *his hand* as he pleaseth, and to him shall ye return. Hast thou not considered the assembly of the children of Israel, after *the time of* Moses; when they said unto their prophet *Samuel*, Set a king over us, that we may fight for the religion of GOD? *The prophet* answered, If ye are enjoined to go to war, will ye be near refusing to fight? They answered, And what should ail us that we should not fight for the religion of GOD, seeing we are dispossessed of our habitations, and *deprived* of our children? But when they were enjoined to go to war, they turned back, except a few of them: and GOD knew the ungodly. And their prophet said unto them, Verily GOD hath set Talût king over you: they answered, How shall he reign over us, seeing we are more worthy of the kingdom than he, neither is he possessed of great riches? *Samuel* said, Verily GOD hath chosen him before you, and hath caused him to increase in knowledge and stature, for GOD giveth his kingdom unto whom he pleaseth; GOD is bounteous and wise. And their prophet said unto them, Verily the sign of hsi kingdom shall be, that the ark shall come unto you: therein shall be tranquillity from your LORD, and the relics which have been left by the family of Moses, and the family of Aaron; the angels shall bring it. Verily this shall be a sign unto you, if ye believe. And when Talût departed with his soldiers, he said, Verily GOD will prove you by the river: for he who drinketh threreof, shall not be on my side (but he who shall not taste thereof he shall be on my side) except he who drinketh a draught out of his hand. And they drank thereof, except a few of them. And when they had passed *the river*, he and those who believed with him, they said, We have no strength to-day against Jalut and his forces. But they who considered that they should meet GOD *at the resur-rection*, said, How often hath a small army discomfited a great army, by the will of GOD? and GOD is with those who patiently persevere. And when they went forth to battle against Jalut and his forces, they said, O LORD, pour on us patience, and confirm our feet, and help us against the unbelieving people. Therefore they discomfited them, by the will of GOD, and David slew Jalut. And GOD gave him the kingdom and wisdom, and taught him his will; and if GOD had not prevented men, the one by the other, verily the earth had been corrupted: but GOD is benificent towards *his* creatures. These are the signs of GOD: we rehearse them unto thee with truth, and thou art surely *one* of those who have been sent *by* GOD. (III.) These are the apostles; we have preferred some of them before others:

some of them hath GOD spoken unto, and hath exalted the degree of others of them. And we gave unto Jesus the son of Mary manifest signs, and strengthened him with the holy spirit. And if GOD had pleased, they who came after those *apostles* would not have contended among themselves, after manifest signs had been shown unto them. But they fell to variance; therefore some of them believed, and some of them believed not; and if GOD had so pleased, they would not have contended among themselves, but GOD doth what he will. O true believers, give *alms* of that which we have bestowed on you, before the day cometh wherein there shall be no merchandizing, nor friendship, nor intercession. The infidels are unjust doers. GOD! there is no GOD but he; the living, the self-subsisting: neither slumber nor sleep seizeth him; to him *belongeth* whatsoever is in heaven, and on earth. Who is he that can intercede with him, but through his good pleasure? He knoweth that which is past, and that which is to come unto them, and they shall not comprehend anything of his knowledge, but so far as he pleaseth. His throne is extended over heaven and earth, and the preserva- tion of both is no burden unto him. He is the high, the mighty. Let there be no violence in religion. Now is right direction manifestly distinguished from deceit: whoever therefore shall deny Tagut, and believe in GOD, he shall surely take hold on a strong handle, which shall not be broken; GOD is he who heareth and seeth. GOD is the patron of those who believe; he shall lead them out of dark- ness into light: but *as to* those who believe not, their patrons are Tagut; they shall lead them from the light into darkness; they shall be the companions of *hell* fire, they shall remain therein for ever. Hast thou not considered him who disputed with Abraham concerning his LORD, because GOD had given him the kingdom? When Abraham said, My LORD is he who giveth life, and killeth: he answered, I give life, and I kill. Abraham said, Verily GOD bringeth the sun from the east, now do thou bring it from the west. Whereupon the infidel was confounded; for GOD directeth not the ungodly people. Or *hast thou not considered* how he *behaved* who passed by a city which had been destroyed, even to her foundations? He said, How shall GOD quicken this *city*, after she hath been dead? And GOD caused him to die for an hundred years, and afterwards raised him to life. *And God* said, How long hast thou tarried *here?* He answered, A day, or part of a day. *God* said, Nay, thou hast tarried *here* an hundred years. Now look on thy food and the drink, they are not yet corrupted; and look on thine ass: and this *have we done* that we might make thee a sign unto men. And look on the bones *of thine ass*, how we raise them, and afterwards clothe them with flesh. And when *this* was shown unto him, he said, I know that GOD is able to do all things. And when Abraham said, O LORD, show me how thou wilt raise the dead; *God* said, Dost thou not yet believe? He answered, Yea; but *I ask this* that my heart may rest at ease. *God* said, take therefore four birds, and divide them; then lay a part of them on every mountain; then call them, and they shall come swiftly unto thee: and know that GOD is mighty and wise. The similitude of those who lay out their substance for advancing the religion of GOD, is as a grain *of corn* which produceth seven ears, and in every ear an hundred grains; for GOD giveth twofold unto whom he

pleaseth: GOD is bounteous and wise. They who lay out
their substance for the religion of GOD, and afterwards
follow not what they have *so* laid out by reproaches or mischief, they shall have their reward with their LORD ; upon
them shall no fear come, neither shall they be grieved. A fair
speech, and to forgive, is better than alms followed by mischief. GOD is rich and merciful. O true believers, make not
your alms of none effect by reproaching, or mischief, as he
who layeth out what he hath to appear unto men *to give alms*,
and believeth not in GOD and the last day. The likeness of
such a one is as a flint covered with earth, on which a violent rain falleth, and leaveth it hard. They cannot prosper in
anything which they have gained, for GOD directeth not
the unbelieving people. And the likeness of those who lay
out their substance from a desire to please GOD, and for an
establishment for their souls, is as a garden on a hill, on
which a violent rain falleth, and it bringeth forth its fruits
twofold; and if a violent rain falleth not on it, yet the dew
falleth thereon: and GOD seeth that which ye do. Doth any of
you desire to have a garden of palm-trees and vines, through
which rivers flow, wherein he may have all *kinds of* fruits,
and that he may attain to old age, and have a weak offspring? then a violent fiery wind shall strike it, so that it
shall be burned. Thus GOD declareth his signs unto you,
that ye may consider. O true believers, bestow *alms* of the
good things which ye have gained, and of that which
we have produced for you out of the earth, and choose not
the bad thereof, to give it *in alms* such as ye would not
accept yourselves, otherwise than by connivance: and know
that GOD is rich and worthy to be praised. The devil

threateneth you with poverty, and commandeth you filthy
covetousness; but GOD promiseth you pardon from himself
and abundance: GOD is bounteous and wise. He giveth
wisdom unto whom he pleaseth; and he unto whom wisdom
is given, hath received much good: but none will consider,
except the *wise* of heart. And whatever alms ye shall give, or
whatever vow ye shall vow, verily GOD knoweth it; but the
ungodly shall have none to help *them*. If ye make your alms
to appear, it is well; but if ye conceal them, and give them
unto the poor, this *will be* better for you, and will atone for
your sins: and GOD is well informed of that which ye do.
The direction of them belongeth not unto thee; but GOD
directeth whom he pleaseth. The good that ye shall give *in
alms shall redound* unto yourselves; and ye shall not give unless
out of desire of *seeing* the face of GOD. And what good thing
ye shall give *in alms*, it shall be repaid you, and ye shall not
be treated unjustly; unto the poor who are wholly
employed in fighting for the religion of GOD, and cannot go
to and fro in the earth; whom the ignorant man thinketh
rich, because of their modesty: thou shalt know them by
this mark, they ask not men with importunity; and what
good ye shall give *in alms*, verily GOD knoweth it. They
who distribute *alms of* their substance night and day, in private and in public, shall have their reward with the LORD
; on them shall no fear come, neither shall they be grieved.
They who devour usury shall not arise *from the dead*, but as he
ariseth whom Satan hath infected by a touch: this *shall
happen to them* because they say, Truly selling is but as usury:
and yet GOD hath permitted selling and forbidden usury.
He therefore who when there cometh unto him an admoni-

tion from his LORD, abstaineth *from usury for the future*, shall have what is past *forgiven him*, and his affair belongeth unto GOD. But whoever returneth *to usury*, they shall be the companions of *hell* fire, they shall continue therein for ever. GOD shall take his blessing from usury, and shall increase alms: for GOD loveth no infidel, or ungodly person. But they who believe and do that which is right, and observe the stated times of prayer, and pay their legal alms, they shall have their reward with their LORD: there shall come no fear on them, neither shall they be grieved. O true believers, fear GOD, and remit that which remaineth of usury, if ye *really* believe; but if ye do it not, hearken unto war, *which is declared against you* from GOD and his apostle: yet if ye repent, ye shall have the capital of your money. Deal not unjustly *with others*, and ye shall not be dealt with unjustly. If there be any *debtor* under a difficulty *of paying his debt*, let *his creditor* wait till it be easy *for him to do it*; but if ye remit it as alms, it will be better for you, if ye knew it. And fear the day wherein ye shall return unto GOD; then shall every soul be paid what it hath gained, and they shall not be treated unjustly. O true believers, when ye bind yourselves one to the other in a debt for a certain time, write it down; and let a writer write between you according to justice, and let not the writer refuse writing according to what GOD hath taught him; but let him write, and let him who oweth the debt dictate, and let him fear GOD his LORD, and not diminish ought thereof. But if he who oweth the debt be foolish, or weak, or be not able to dictate himself, let his agent dictate according to equity; and call to witness two witnesses of your *neighbouring* men; but if there be not two men, *let there be* a man and two women of those whom ye shall choose for witnesses: if one of those *women* should mistake, the other of them will cause her to recollect. And the witnesses shall not refuse, whensoever they shall be called. And disdain not to write it down, be it a large *debt*, or be it a small one, until its time *of payment*: this will be more just in the sight of GOD, and more right for bearing witness, and more easy, that ye may not doubt. But if it be a present bargain which ye transact between yourselves, it shall be no crime in you, if ye write it not down. And take witnesses when ye sell one to the other, and let no harm be done to the writer, nor to the witness; *which* if ye do, it will surely be injustice in you: and fear GOD, and GOD will instruct you, for GOD knoweth all things. And if ye be on a journey, and find no writer, *let* pledges *be* taken: but if one of you trust the other, let him who is trusted return what he is trusted with, and fear GOD his LORD. And conceal not the testimony, for he who concealeth it hath surely a wicked heart: GOD knoweth that which ye do. Whatever is in heaven and on earth is GOD's; and whether ye manifest that which is in your minds, or conceal it, GOD will call you to account for it, and will forgive whom he pleaseth, and will punish whom he pleaseth; for GOD is almighty. The apostle believeth in that which hath been sent down unto him from his LORD, and the faithful *also*. Every one *of them* believeth in GOD, and his angels, and his scriptures, and his apostles: we make no distinction at all between his apostles. And they say, We have heard, and do obey: *we implore* thy mercy, O LORD, for unto thee must we return. GOD will not force any soul beyond its capacity: it shall have *the good* which it gaineth, and it shall suffer *the evil* which it gaineth. O LORD, punish us not, if we forget, or act sinfully: O LORD, lay not on us a burden like that which thou hast laid on those who have been before us; neither make us, O LORD, to bear what we have not strength to *bear*, but be favourable unto us, and spare us, and be merciful unto us. Thou art our patron, help us therefore against the unbelieving nations.

THE FAMILY OF IMRAN

There is no GOD but GOD, the living, the self-subsisting: He hath sent down unto thee the book *of the Korân* with truth, confirming that which was *revealed* before it; for he had formerly sent down the law and the gospel, a direction unto men; and he had also sent down the distinction *between good and evil*. Verily those who believe not the signs of GOD, shall suffer a grievous punishment; for GOD is mighty, able to revenge. Surely nothing is hidden from GOD, *of that which is on earth*, or in heaven: it is he who formeth you in the wombs, as he pleaseth; there is no GOD but he, the mighty,. the wise. It is he who hath sent down unto thee the book wherein are some verses clear to be understood, they are the foundation of the book; and others are parabolical. But they whose hearts are perverse will that which is parabolical therein, out of love of schism, and a desire of the interpretation thereof; yet none knoweth the interpretation thereof, except GOD. But they who are well grounded in knowledge say, We believe therein, the whole is from our LORD ; and none will consider except the prudent. O LORD, cause not our hearts to swerve *from truth*, after thou hast directed us: and give us from thee mercy, for thou art he who giveth. O

LORD, thou shalt surely gather mankind together, unto a day *of resurrection*: there is no doubt of it, for GOD will not be contrary to the promise. As for the infidels, their wealth shall not profit them anything, nor their children, against GOD: they shall be the fuel of *hell* fire. According to the wont of the people of Pharaoh, and of those who went before them, they charged our signs with a lie; but GOD caught them in their wickedness, and GOD is severe in punishing. Say unto those who believe not, Ye shall be overcome, and thrown together into hell; and unhappy couch *shall it be*. Ye have already had a miracle *shown you* in two armies, which attacked each other: one army fought for GOD's true religion, but the other were infidels; they saw *the faithful* twice as many as themselves in *their* eyesight; for GOD strengtheneth with his help whom he pleaseth. Surely herein was an example unto men of understanding. The love and eager desire of wives, and children, and sums heaped up of gold and silver, and excellent horses, and cattle, and land, is prepared for men: this is the provision of the present life; but unto GOD shall be the most excellent return. Say, Shall I declare unto you better *things* than this? For those who are devout *are prepared* with their LORD, gardens through which rivers flow; therein shall they continue for ever: and *they shall enjoy* wives free from impurity, and the favour of GOD; for GOD regardeth *his* servants; who say, O LORD, we do sincerely believe; forgive us therefore our sins, and deliver us from the pain of *hell* fire: the patient, and the lovers of truth, and the devout, and the almsgivers, and those who ask pardon *early* in the morning. GOD hath borne witness that there is no GOD but he; and the angels, and *those who are* endowed with wisdom, *profess the same*; who executeth righteousness; there is no GOD but he; the mighty, the wise. Verily the *true* religion in the sight of GOD, is Islâm; and they who had received the scriptures dissented not *therefrom*, until after the knowledge *of God's unity* had come unto them, out of envy among themselves; but whosoever believeth not in the signs of GOD, verily GOD will be swift in *bringing him to* account. If they dispute with thee, say, I have resigned myself unto GOD, and he who followeth me *doth the same*: and say unto them who have received the scriptures, and to the ignorant, Do ye profess *the religion of* Islâm? Now if they embrace Islâm, they are surely directed; but if they turn their backs, verily unto thee *belongeth* preaching *only*; for GOD regardeth his servants. And unto those who believe not in the signs of GOD, and slay the prophets without a cause, and put those men to death who teach justice; denounce unto them a painful punishment. These are they whose works perish in this world, and in that which is to come; and they shall have none to help them. Hast thou not observed those unto whom part of the scripture was given? They were called unto the book of GOD, that it might judge between them; then some of them turned their backs, and retired afar off. This *they did* because they said, The fire *of hell* shall by no means touch us, but for a *certain* number of days: and that which they had falsely devised, hath deceived them in their religion. How then *will it be with them*, when we shall gather them together at the day *of judgment*, of which there is no doubt; and every soul shall be paid that which it hath gained, neither shall they be treated unjustly? Say, O GOD, who possessest the king dom; thou givest the kingdom unto whom thou wilt, and thou takest away the kingdom from whom thou wilt: thou exaltest whom thou wilt, and thou humblest whom thou wilt: in thy hand is good, for thou art almighty. Thou makest the night to succeed the day: thou bringest forth the living out of the dead, and thou bringest forth the dead out of the living; and providest food for whom thou wilt without measure. Let not the faithful take the infidels for their protectors, rather than the faithful: he who doth this shall not be *protected* of GOD at all; unless ye fear any danger from them: but GOD warneth you to beware of himself; for unto GOD must ye return. Say, Whether ye conceal that which is in your breasts, or whether ye declare it, GOD knoweth it: for he knoweth whatever is in heaven, and whatever is on earth: GOD is almighty. On the *last* day every soul shall find the good which it hath wrought, present; and the evil which it hath wrought, it shall wish that between itself and that were a wide distance: but GOD warneth you to beware of himself; for GOD is gracious unto his servants. Say, If ye love GOD, follow me: *then* GOD shall love you, and forgive you your sins; for GOD is gracious and merciful. Say, Obey GOD, and *his* apostle: but if ye go back, verily GOD loveth not the unbelievers. GOD hath surely chosen Adam, and Noah, and the family of Abraham, and the family of Imrân above the *rest of the* world; a race *descending* the one from the other: GOD is he who heareth and knoweth. *Remember* when the wife of Imrân said, LORD, verily I have vowed unto thee that which is in my womb, to be dedicated *to thy service*: accept *it* therefore of me; for thou art he who heareth and knoweth. And when she was delivered of it, she said, LORD, verily I have brought forth a female (and GOD well knew what she had brought forth), and a male is not as a female: I have called her Mary; and I commend her to thy protection, and *also* her issue, against Satan driven away with stones. Therefore the LORD accepted her with a gracious acceptance, and caused her to bear an excellent offspring. And Zacharias took care of *the child*; whenever Zacharias went into the chamber to her, he found provisions with her: *and* he said, O Mary, whence hadst thou this? she answered, This is from GOD: for GOD provideth for whom he pleaseth without measure. There Zacharias called on his LORD, *and* said, LORD give me from thee a good offspring, for thou art the hearer of prayer. And the angels called to him, while he stood praying in the chamber, *saying*, Verily GOD promiseth thee *a son named* John, who shall bear witness to the Word *which cometh* from GOD; an honourable person, chaste, and one of the righteous prophets. He answered, LORD, how shall I have a son, when old age hath overtaken me, and my wife is barren? *The angel* said, So GOD doth that which he pleaseth. *Zacharias* answered, LORD, give me a sign. *The angel* said, Thy sign shall be, that thou shalt speak unto no man for three days, otherwise than by gesture: remember thy LORD often, and praise *him* evening and morning. And when the angels said, O Mary, verily GOD hath chosen thee, and hath purified thee, and hath chosen thee above *all* the women of the world: O Mary, be devout towards thy LORD, and worship, and bow down with those who bow down. This is a secret history: we reveal it unto thee, although thou wast not present with them when they threw in their rods *to cast lots* which of them should have the education of Mary: neither wast thou with them, when they strove among themselves. When the angels said, O Mary, verily GOD sendeth thee good tidings, *that thou shalt bear* the Word, *proceeding* from himself; his name shall be CHRIST JESUS the son of Mary, honourable in this world and in the world to come, and *one* of those who approach near *to the presence of God*; and he shall speak unto men in the cradle, and when he is grown up; and he shall be *one* of the righteous: she answered, LORD, how shall I have a son, since a man hath not touched me? *the angel* said, So GOD createth that which he pleaseth: when he decreeth a thing, he only saith unto it, Be, and it is: *God* shall teach him the scripture, and wisdom, and the law, and the gospel; and *shall appoint him his* apostle to the children of Israel; *and he shall say*, Verily I come unto you with a sign from you LORD ; for I will make before you, of clay, as it were the figure of a bird; then I will breathe thereon, and it shall become a bird, by the permission of GOD: and I will heal him that hath been blind from his birth, and the leper: and I will raise the dead by the permission of GOD: and I will prophesy unto you what ye eat, and what ye lay up for store in your houses. Verily herein will be a sign unto you, if ye believe. And I *come* to confirm the Law which was *revealed* before me, and to allow unto you as lawful, part of that which hath been forbidden you: and I come unto you with a sign from your LORD ; therefore fear GOD, and obey me. Verily GOD is my LORD, and your LORD: therefore serve him. This is the right way. But when Jesus perceived their unbelief, he said, Who *will be* my helpers towards GOD? The apostles answered, We *will be* the helpers of GOD; we believe in

GOD, and do thou bear witness that we are true believers.
O LORD, we believe in that which thou has sent down, and
we have followed thy apostle; write us down therefore
with those who bear witness *of him*. And *the Jews* devised a
stratagem *against him*, but GOD devised a stratagem *against
them*; and GOD is the best deviser of stratagems. When
GOD said, O Jesus, verily I will cause thee to die, and I will
take thee up unto me, and I will deliver thee from the unbelievers; and I will place those who follow thee above the
unbelievers, until the day of resurrection: then unto me shall
ye return, and I will judge between you of that concerning
which ye disagree. Moreover, as for the infidels, I will
punish them with a grievous punishment in this world, and
in that which is to come; and there shall be none to help
them. But they who believe, and do that which is right, he
shall give them their reward; for GOD loveth not the
wicked doers. These signs and this prudent admonition do
we rehearse unto thee. Verily the likeness of Jesus in the
sight of GOD is as the likeness of Adam: he created him out
of the dust, and then said unto him, Be; and he was. *This is*
the truth from thy LORD ; be not therefore *one* of those who
doubt: and whoever shall dispute with thee concerning
him, after the knowledge which hath been given thee, say
unto them, Come, let us call together our sons, and your sons,
and our wives, and your wives, and our selves, and your
selves; then let us make imprecations and lay the curse of
GOD on those who lie. Verily this is a true history: and
there is no GOD but GOD; and GOD is most mighty, and
wise. If they turn back, GOD well knoweth the evil-doers.
Say, O ye who have received the scripture, come to a just

determination between us and you; that we worship not *any* except GOD, and associate no creature with him; and that the one of us take not the other for lords, beside GOD. But if they turn back, say, Bear witness that we are true believers. O ye to whom the scriptures have been given, why do ye dispute concerning Abraham, since the Law and the Gospel were not sent down until after him? Do ye not therefore understand? Behold ye are they who dispute concerning that which ye have some knowledge in; why therefore do ye dispute concerning that which ye have no knowledge of? GOD knoweth, but ye know not. Abraham was neither a Jew, nor a Christian; but he was of the true religion, one resigned *unto God*, and was not of the *number of the* idolators. Verily the men who are the nearest *of kin* unto Abraham, are they who follow him; and this prophet, and they who believe *on him*: GOD is the patron of the faithful. Some of those who have received the scriptures desire to seduce you; but they seduce themselves only, and they perceive *it* not. O ye who have received the scriptures, why do ye not believe in the signs of GOD, since ye are witnesses *of them*? O ye who have received the scriptures, why do ye clothe truth with vanity, and knowingly hide the truth? And some of those to whom the scriptures were given, say, Believe in that which hath been sent down unto those who believe, in the beginning of the day, and deny *it* in the end thereof; that they may go back *from their faith*: and believe him only who followeth your religion. Say, Verily the *true* direction is the direction of GOD, that there may be given unto some other *a revelation* like unto what hath been given unto you. Will they dispute with you before your LORD ?

Say, Surely excellence is in the hand of GOD, he giveth it unto whom he pleaseth; GOD is bounteous and wise: he will confer peculiar mercy on whom he pleaseth; for GOD is endued with great beneficence. There is of those who have received the scriptures, unto whom if thou trust a talent, he will restore it unto thee; and *there is also* of them, unto whom if thou trust a dinâr, he will not restore it unto thee, unless thou stand over him continually *with great urgency*. This *they do* because they say, We are not obliged to observe justice with the heathen: but they utter a lie against GOD, knowingly. Yea; whoso keepeth his covenant, and feareth GOD, GOD surely loveth those who fear *him*. But they who make merchandise of GOD's covenant, and of their oaths, for a small price, shall have no portion in the next life, neither shall GOD speak to them or regard them on the day of resurrection, nor shall he cleanse them; but they shall suffer a grievous punishment. And there are certainly some of them, who read the scriptures perversely, that ye may think *what they read* to be really in the scriptures, yet it is not in the scripture; and they say, This is from GOD; but it is not from GOD: and they speak that which is false concerning GOD, against their own knowledge. It is not *fit* for a man, that GOD should give him a book *of revelations*, and wisdom, and prophecy; and then he should say unto men, Be ye worshippers of me, besides GOD; but *he ought to say*, Be ye perfect in knowledge and in works, since ye know the scriptures, and exercise yourselves therein. *God* hath not commanded *you* to take the angels and the prophets for *your* Lords: Will he command *you* to become infidels, after ye have been true believers? And *remember* when GOD accepted the covenant of the prophets, *saying,* This verily *is* the scripture and the wisdom which I have given you: hereafter shall an apostle come unto you, confirming the truth of that *scripture* which is with you; ye shall surely believe on him, and ye shall assist him. *God* said, Are ye firmly resolved, and do ye accept my covenant on this *condition?* They answered, We are firmly resolved: *God* said, Be ye therefore witnesses; and I also bear witness with you: and whosoever turneth back after this, they are surely the transgressors. Do they therefore seek any other religion but GOD's? since to him is resigned whosoever is in heaven or on earth, voluntarily, or of force: and to him shall they return. Say, We believe in GOD, and that which hath been sent down unto us, and that which was sent down unto Abraham, and Ismael, and Isaac, and Jacob, and the tribes, and that which was delivered to Moses, and Jesus, and the prophets from their LORD; we make no distinction between any of them; and to him are we resigned. Whoever followeth any other religion than Islâm, it shall not be accepted of him: and in the next life he shall be of those who perish. How shall GOD direct men who have become infidels after they had believed, and borne witness that the apostle was true, and manifest declarations *of the divine will* had come unto them? for GOD directeth not the ungodly people. Their reward shall be, that on them *shall fall* the curse of GOD, and of angels, and of all mankind: they shall remain under the same for ever; their torment shall not be mitigated, neither shall they be regarded; except those who repent after this, and amend; for GOD is gracious and merciful. Moreover they who become infidels after they have believed, and yet increase in infidelity, their repentance shall in no wise be accepted, and they are those who go astray. Verily they who believe not, and die in their unbelief, the world full of gold shall in no wise be accepted from any of them, even though he should give it for his ransom; they shall suffer a grievous punishment, and they shall have none to help them. (IV.) Ye will never attain unto righteousness, until ye give in alms of that which ye love: and whatever ye give, GOD knoweth it. All food was permitted unto the children of Israel, except what Israel forbade unto himself before the Pentateuch was sent down. Say *unto the Jews*, Bring hither the Pentateuch and read it, if ye speak truth. Whoever therefore contriveth a lie against GOD after this, they will be evil-doers. Say, GOD is true: follow ye therefore the religion of Abraham the orthodox; for he was no idolater. Verily the first house appointed unto men *to worship in* was that which is in Becca; blessed, and a direction to all creatures. Therein are manifest signs: the place where Abraham stood; and whoever entereth therein, shall be safe. And *it is a duty* towards GOD, *incumbent* on those who are able to go thither, to visit this house; but whosoever disbelieveth, verily GOD needeth not *the service of* any creature. Say, O ye who have received the scriptures, why do you not believe in the signs of GOD? Say, O ye who have received the scriptures, why do ye keep back from the way of GOD him who believeth? Ye seek to make it crooked, and yet are witnesses *that it is the right*: but GOD will not be unmindful of what ye do. O true believers, if ye obey some of those who have received the scripture, they will render you infidels, after ye have believed: and how can ye be infidels, when the signs of GOD are read unto you, and his apostle is among you? But he who cleaveth firmly unto GOD, is already directed into the right way. O believers, fear GOD with his true fear; and die not unless ye also be true believers. And cleave all *of you* unto the covenant of GOD, and depart not *from it*, and remember the favour of GOD towards you: since ye were enemies, and he reconciled your hearts, and ye became companions and brethren by his favour: and ye were on the brink of a pit of fire, and he delivered you thence. Thus GOD declareth unto you his signs, that ye may be directed. Let there be people among you, who invite to the best *religion*; and command that which is just, and forbid that which is evil; and they shall be happy. And be not as they who are divided, and disagree *in matters of religion*, after manifest proofs have been brought unto them: they shall suffer a great torment. On the day *of resurrection some* faces shall become white, and *other* faces shall become black. And unto them whose faces shall become black, *God will say*, Have ye returned unto *your* unbelief, after ye had believed? therefore taste the punishment, for that ye have been unbelievers: but they whose faces shall become white *shall be* in the mercy of GOD, therein shall they remain for ever. These are the signs of GOD: we recite them unto thee with truth. GOD will not deal unjustly with *his* creatures. And to GOD *belongeth* whatever is in heaven and on earth; and to GOD shall *all* things return. Ye are the best nation that hath been raised up unto mankind: ye command that which is just, and ye forbid that which is unjust, and ye believe in GOD. And if they who have received the scriptures had believed, it had surely been the better for them: there are believers among them, but the greater part of them are transgressors. They shall not hurt you, unless with a *slight* hurt; and if they fight against you, they shall turn their backs to you, and they shall not be helped. They are smitten with vileness wheresoever they are found; unless *they obtain security* by *entering into* a treaty with GOD, and a treaty with men: and they draw on themselves indignation from GOD, and they are afflicted with poverty. This *they suffer*, because they disbelieved the signs of GOD, and slew the prophets unjustly; this, because they were rebellious, and transgressed. *Yet* they are not *all* alike: there are of those who have received the scriptures, upright people; they meditate on the signs of GOD in the night season, and worship; they believe in GOD and the last day; and command that which is just, and forbid that which is unjust, and zealously strive *to excel* in good works: these are of the righteous. And ye shall not be denied *the reward of* the good which ye do; for GOD knoweth the pious. As for the unbelievers, their wealth shall not profit them at all, neither their children, against GOD: they *shall be* the companions of *hell* fire; they shall continue therein for ever. The likeness of that which they lay out in this present life, is as a wind wherein there is a scorching cold: it falleth on the standing corn of those men who have injured their own souls, and destroyeth it. And GOD dealeth not unjustly with them; but they injure their own souls. O true believers, contract not an intimate friendship *with any* besides yourselves: they will not fail to corrupt you. They wish for that which may cause you to perish: their hatred hath already appeared from out of their mouths; but what their breasts conceal is yet more inveterate. We have already shown you signs *of their ill will towards you*, if ye understand. Behold, ye love them, and they do not love you: ye believe in all the scriptures, and when they meet you, they say, We believe; but when they assemble privately together, they bite their fingers' ends out of wrath against you. Say *unto them*, Die in your wrath: verily GOD knoweth the innermost part of *your* breasts. If good happen unto you, it grieveth them; and if evil befall you, they rejoice at it. But if ye be patient, and fear *God*, their subtlety shall not hurt you at all; for GOD comprehendeth whatever they do. *Call to mind* when thou wentest forth early from thy family, that thou mightest prepare the faithful a camp for war; and GOD heard and knew *it*; when two companies of you were anxiously thoughtful, so that ye became faint-hearted; but GOD was the supporter of them both; and in GOD let the faithful trust. And GOD had already given you the victory at Bedr, when ye were inferior *in number*; therefore fear GOD, that ye may be thankful. When thou saidst unto the faithful, Is it not enough for you, that your LORD should assist you with three thousand angels, sent down *from heaven?* Verily if ye persevere, and fear *God*, and *your enemies* come upon you suddenly, your LORD will assist you with five thousand angels, distinguished *by their horses and attire*. And this GOD designed only as good tidings for you that your hearts might rest secure: for victory is from GOD alone, the mighty, the wise. That he should cut off the uttermost part of the unbelievers, or cast them down, or that they should be overthrown and unsuccessful, *is nothing to thee*. It is no business of thine; whether *God* be turned unto them, or whether he punish them; they are surely unjust doers. To GOD belongeth whatsoever is in heaven and on earth: he spareth whom he pleaseth, and he punisheth whom he pleaseth; for GOD is merciful. O true believers, devour not usury, doubling it twofold; but fear GOD, that ye may prosper: and fear the fire which is prepared for the unbelievers; and obey GOD, and *his* apostle, that ye may obtain mercy. And run with emulation to *obtain* remission from your LORD, and paradise, whose breath *equalleth* the heavens and the earth, which is prepared for the godly; who give alms in prosperity and adversity; who bridle then anger and forgive men: for GOD loveth the beneficent. And who, after they have committed a crime, or dealt unjustly with their own souls, remember GOD, and ask pardon for their sins (for who forgiveth sins except GOD?) and perse-vere not in what they have done knowingly: their reward shall be pardon from their LORD, and gardens wherein rivers flow, they shall remain therein for ever: and how excellent is the reward of those who labour! There have already been before you examples of punishment *of infidels,* therefore go through the earth, and behold what hath been the end of those who accuse *God's apostles* of imposture. This *book* is a declaration unto men, and a direction, and an admo-nition to the pious. And be not dismayed, neither be ye grieved; for ye shall be superior *to the unbelievers* if ye believe. If a wound hath happened unto you *in war,* a like wound hath already happened unto the *unbelieving* people: and we cause these days *of different success* interchangeably to succeed each other among men; that GOD may know those who believe, and may have martyrs from among you (GOD loveth not the workers of iniquity); and that GOD might prove those who believe, and destroy the infidels. Did ye imagine

that ye should enter paradise, when as yet GOD knew not
those among you who fought strenuously *in his cause;* nor
knew those who persevered with patience? Moreover ye
did sometime wish for death before that ye met it; but ye
have now seen it, and ye looked on, *but retreated from it.*
Mohammed is no more than an apostle; the *other* apostles
have already deceased before him: if he did therefore, or be
slain, will ye turn back on your heels? but he who turneth
back on his heels, will not hurt GOD at all; and GOD will
surely reward the thankful. No soul can die unless by the
permission of GOD, according to *what is written in* the book
containing the determinations of things. And whoso
chooseth the reward of this world, we will give him
thereof: but whoso chooseth the reward of the world to
come, we will give him thereof; and we will surely reward
the thankful. How many prophets have encountered those
who had many myriads *of troops:* and yet they desponded not
in their mind for what had befallen them in fighting for the
religion of GOD, and were not weakened, neither behaved
themselves in an abject manner? GOD loveth those who persevere patiently. And their speech was no other than that
they said, Our LORD forgive us our offences, and our trans-
gressions in our business; and confirm our feet, and help us
against the unbelieving people. And GOD gave them the
reward of this world, and a glorious reward in the life to
come; for GOD loveth the well-doers. O ye who believe, if
ye obey the infidels, they will cause you to turn back on
your heels, and ye will be turned back and perish: but GOD
is your LORD; and he is the best helper. We will surely cast
a dread into the hearts of the unbelievers, because they have

associated with GOD that concerning which he sent them down no power: their dwelling shall be the fire *of hell*; and the receptacle of the wicked shall be miserable. GOD had already made good unto you his promise, when ye destroyed them by his permission, until ye became faint-hearted, and disputed concerning the command *of the apostle*, and were rebellious; after *God* had shown you what ye desired. Some of you chose this present world, and others of you chose the world to come. Then he turned you *to flight* from before them, that he might make trial of you (but he hath now pardoned you; for GOD is endued with beneficence toward the faithful); when ye went up *as ye fled*, and looked not back on any; while the apostle called you, in the uttermost part of you. Therefore *God* rewarded you with affliction on affliction, that ye be not grieved *hereafter* for the *spoils* which ye fail of, nor for that which befalleth you; for GOD is well acquainted with whatever ye do. Then he sent down upon you after affliction security; soft sleep which fell on some part of you; but *other* part were troubled by their own souls; falsely thinking of GOD a foolish imagination, saying, Will anything of the matter *happen* unto us? Say, Verily the matter *belongeth* wholly unto GOD. They concealed in their minds what they declared not unto thee; saying, If anything of the matter had happened unto us, we had not been slain here. Answer, If ye had been in your houses, verily they would have gone forth to fight, whose slaughter was decreed, to the places where they died, and *this came to pass* that GOD might try what was in your breasts, and might discern what was in your hearts; for GOD knoweth the innermost parts of the breasts *of men*. Verily they among you who turned their backs on the day whereon the two armies met each other *at Ohod*, Satan caused them to slip, for some *crime* which they had committed: but now hath GOD forgiven them; for GOD is gracious and merciful. O true believers, be not as they who believe not, and said of their brethren, when they had journeyed in the land or had been at war, If they had been with us, those had not died, nor had these been slain: *whereas what befell them was so ordained* that GOD might make it *matter of* sighing in their hearts. GOD giveth life, and causeth to die: and GOD seeth that which ye do. Moreover if ye be slain, or die in defence of the religion of GOD; verily pardon from GOD, and mercy, is better than what they heap together *of worldly riches*. And if ye die, or be slain, verily unto GOD shall ye be gathered. And as to the mercy *granted unto the disobedient* from GOD, thou, O *Mohammed*, hast been mild towards them; but if thou hadst been severe and hard-hearted, they had surely separated themselves from about thee. Therefore forgive them, and ask pardon for them: and consult them in the affair *of war*; and after thou hast deliber-ated, trust in GOD; for GOD loveth those who trust *in him*. If GOD help you, none shall conquer you; but if he desert you, who is it that will help you after him? Therefore in GOD let the faithful trust. It is not *the part* of a prophet to defraud, for he who defraudeth, shall bring with him what he hath defrauded *any one of*, on the day of the resurrection. Then shall every soul be paid what he hath gained; and they shall not be treated unjustly. Shall he therefore who fol-loweth that which is well pleasing unto GOD, be as he who bringeth on himself wrath from GOD, and whose receptacle is hell? an evil journey shall it be *thither*. There shall be

degrees *of rewards and punishments* with GOD, for GOD seeth
what they do. Now hath GOD been gracious unto the
believers when he raised up among them an apostle of their
own nation, who should recite his signs unto them, and
purify them, and teach them the book *of the Korân* and
wisdom; whereas they were before in manifest error. After
a misfortune hath befallen you *at Ohod* (ye had already
obtained two equal advantages), do ye say, Whence *cometh*
this? Answer, This is from yourselves: for GOD is almighty.
And what happened unto you, on the day whereon the two
armies met, was certainly by the permission of GOD; and
that he might know the faithful, and that he might know
the ungodly. It was said unto them, Come, fight for the religion of GOD, or drive back *the enemy*: they answered, If we
had known *ye went out* to fight, we had certainly followed
you. They were on that day nearer unto unbelief than they
were to faith; they spake with their mouths what was not
in their hearts: but GOD perfectly knew what they concealed; who said of their brethren, *while themselves* stayed *at
home*, if they had obeyed us, they had not been slain. Say,
Then keep back death from yourselves, if ye say truth. Thou
shalt in no wise reckon those who have been slain *at Ohod* in
the cause of GOD, dead; nay, they are sustained alive with
their LORD, rejoicing for what GOD of his favour hath
granted them; and being glad for those who, coming after
them, have not as yet overtaken them; because there shall no
fear come on them, neither shall they be grieved. They are
filled with joy for the favour *which they have received* from
GOD, and *his* bounty; and for that GOD suffereth not the
reward of the faithful to perish. They who hearkened unto

GOD and *his* apostle, after a wound had befallen them *at Ohod*, such of them as do good works, and fear GOD, shall have a great reward; unto whom *certain* men said, Verily the men *of Mecca* have already gathered *forces* against you, be ye therefore afraid of them: but *this* increaseth their faith, and they said, GOD is our support, and the most excellent patron. Wherefore they returned with favour from GOD, and advantage; no evil befell them: and they followed what was well pleasing unto GOD; for GOD is endowed with great liberality. Verily that devil would cause you to fear his friends: but be ye not afraid of them; but fear me, if ye be true believers. They shall not grieve thee, who emulously hasten unto infidelity; for they shall never hurt GOD at all. GOD will not give them a part in the next life, and they shall suffer a great punishment. Surely those who purchase infidelity with faith, shall by no means hurt GOD at all, but they shall suffer a grievous punishment. And let not the unbelievers think, because we grant them lives long and prosperous, that it is better for their souls: we grant them long and prosperous lives only that their iniquity may be increased; and they shall suffer an ignominious punishment. GOD is not *disposed* to leave the faithful in the condition which ye are now in, until he sever the wicked from the good; nor is GOD *disposed* to make you acquainted with what is a hidden secret, but GOD chooseth such of his apostles as he pleaseth, *to reveal his mind unto*: believe therefore in GOD, and his apostles; and if ye believe, and fear *God*, ye shall receive a great reward. And let not those who are covetous of what GOD of his bounty hath granted them, imagine that *their avarice* is better for them: nay, rather it is worse for them. That which they have covetously reserved shall be bound as a collar about their neck, on the day of the resurrection: unto GOD *belongeth* the inheritance of heaven and earth; and GOD is well acquainted with what ye do. GOD hath already heard the saying of those who said, Verily GOD is poor, and we are rich: we will surely write down what they have said, and the slaughter which they have made of the prophets without a cause; and we will say *unto them*, Taste ye the pain of burning. This *shall they suffer* for the *evil* which their hands have sent before them, and because GOD is not unjust towards mankind; who *also* say, Surely GOD hath commanded us, that we should not give credit to *any* apostle, until *one* should come unto us with a sacrifice, which should be consumed by fire. Say, Apostles have already come unto you before me, with plain proofs, and with the *miracle* which ye mention: why therefore have ye slain them, if ye speak truth? If they accuse thee of imposture, the apostles before thee have also been accounted impostors, who brought evident demonstrations, and the scriptures, and the book which enlightened *the understanding*. Every soul shall taste of death, and ye shall have your rewards on the day of resurrection; and he who shall be far removed from *hell* fire, and shall be admitted into paradise, shall be happy: but the present life is only a deceitful provision. Ye shall surely be proved in your possessions, and *in* your persons; and ye shall bear from those unto whom the scripture was delivered before you, and from the idolaters, much hurt: but if ye be patient, and fear *God*, this is a matter that is absolutely determined. And when GOD accepted the covenant of those to whom the book *of the law* was given, *saying*, Ye shall surely publish it unto mankind, ye shall not hide it; yet they threw it behind their backs, and sold it for a small price; but woeful *is the price* for which they have sold *it*. Think not that they who rejoice at what they have done, and expect to be praised for what they have not done; think not, O *prophet*, that they shall escape from punishment, for they shall suffer a painful punishment; and unto GOD *belongeth* the kingdom of heaven and earth; GOD is almighty. Now in the creation of heaven and earth, and the vicissitude of night and day, are signs unto those who are endued with understanding; who remember GOD standing, and sitting, and *lying* on their sides; and meditate on the creation of heaven and earth, *saying*, O LORD, thou has not created this in vain; far be it from thee: therefore deliver us from the torment of *hell* fire: O LORD, surely whom thou shalt throw into the fire, thou wilt also cover with shame; nor shall the ungodly have any to help them. O LORD, we have heard of a preacher inviting *us* to the faith, *and saying*, Believe in your LORD: and we believed. O LORD, forgive us therefore our sins, and expiate our evil deeds from us, and make us to die with the righteous. O LORD, give us also *the reward* which thou hast promised by thy apostles; and cover us not with shame on the day of resurrection; for thou art not contrary to the promise. Their LORD therefore answereth them, *saying*, I will not suffer the work of him among you who worketh to be lost, whether he be male or female: the one of you is from the other. They therefore who have left their country, and have been turned out of their houses, and have suffered for my sake, and have been slain in battle; verily I will expiate their evil deeds from them, and I will surely bring them into gardens watered by rivers; a reward from GOD: and with GOD is the most excellent reward. Let not the prosperous dealing of the unbelievers in the land deceive thee: *it is but* a slender provision; *and* then their receptacle shall be hell; an unhappy couch *shall it be.* But they who fear their LORD shall have gardens through which rivers flow, they shall continue therein for ever: this is the gift of GOD; for what is with GOD shall be better for the righteous *than short-lived worldly prosperity.* There are some of those who have received the scriptures, who believe in GOD, and that which hath been sent down unto you, and that which hath been sent down to them, submitting themselves unto GOD; they tell not the signs of GOD for a small price: these shall have their reward with their LORD; for GOD is swift in taking an account. O true believers, be patient, and strive to excel in patience, and be constant-minded, and fear GOD, that ye may be happy.

LIGHT

Thus Sura have we sent down *from heaven;* and have ratified the same: and we have revealed therein evident signs, that ye may be warned. The whore, and the whoremonger, shall ye scourge with an hundred stripes. And let not compassion towards them prevent you from *executing* the judgment of GOD; if ye believe in GOD and the last day: and let some of the true believers be witnesses of their punishment. The whoremonger shall not marry *any other* than a harlot, or an idolatress. And a harlot shall no *man* take in marriage, except a whoremonger, or an idolater. And this *kind of marriage* is forbidden the true believers. But *as to* those who accuse women of reputation *of whoredom*, and produce not four witnesses *of the fact*, scourge them with fourscore stripes, and receive not their testimony for ever; for such are infamous prevaricators: excepting those who shall afterwards repent, and amend; for *unto such will* GOD *be* gracious *and* merciful. They who shall accuse *their wives* of adultery, and shall have no witnesses *thereof* besides themselves; the testimony *which shall be required* of one of them *shall be*, that he swear four times by GOD that he speaketh the truth: and the fifth *time that he imprecate* the curse of GOD on him, if he be a liar. And it shall avert the punishment from *the wife*, if she swear four times by GOD that he is a liar; and if the fifth *time she imprecate* the wrath of GOD on her, if he speaketh the truth. If *it were* not *for* the indulgence of GOD towards you, and his mercy, and that GOD is easy to be reconciled, *and* wise; *he would immediately discover your crimes. As to* the party among you who have published the falsehood *concerning* Ayesha, think it not to be an evil unto you: on the contrary, it is better for you. Every man of them *shall be punished* according to the injustice of which he hath been guilty; and he among them who hath undertaken to aggravate the same, shall suffer a grievous punishment. Did not the faithful men, and the faithful women, when ye heard this, judge in their own minds for the best; and say, This is a manifest falsehood? Have they produced four witnesses thereof? wherefore since they have not produced the witnesses, they are surely liars in the sight of GOD. *Had it* not *been for* the indulgence of GOD towards you, and his mercy, in this world and in that which is to come, verily a grievous punishment had been inflicted on you, for the *calumny* which ye have spread:

when ye published that with your tongues, and spoke that with your mouths, of which ye had no knowledge; and esteemed it to be light, whereas it was a matter of importance in the sight of GOD. When ye heard it, did ye say, It belongeth not unto us, that we should talk of this *matter*: GOD forbid! this is a grievous calumny? GOD warneth you, that ye return not to the like *crime* for ever; if ye be true believers. And GOD declareth unto you *his* signs; for GOD *is* knowing *and* wise. Verily they who love that scandal be published of those who believe, shall receive a severe punishment *both* in this world, and in the next. GOD knoweth, but ye know not. *Had it not been for* the indulgence of GOD towards you, and his mercy, and that GOD *is* gracious *and* merciful, *ye had felt his vengeance*. O true believers, follow not the steps of the devil: for whosoever shall follow the steps of the devil, he will command him filthy crimes, and that which is unlawful. If *it were* not *for* the indulgence of GOD, and his mercy towards you, there had not been so much as one of you cleansed *from his guilt* for ever: but GOD cleanseth whom he pleaseth; for GOD *both* hereth *and* knoweth. Let not those among you who possess abundance *of wealth*, and *have* ability, swear that they will not give unto *their* kindred, and the poor, and those who have fled their country for the sake of GOD's true religion: but let them forgive, and act with benevolence *towards them*. Do ye not desire that GOD should pardon you? And GOD *is* gracious *and* merciful. Moreover they who falsely accuse modest women, who behave in a negligent manner, *and are* true believers, shall be cursed in this world, and *in* the world to come; and they shall suffer a severe punishment. One day their own tongues shall bear witness against them, and their hands, and their feet, concerning that which they have done. On that day shall GOD render unto them their just due: and they shall know that GOD is the evident truth. The wicked women *should be joined* to the wicked men, and the wicked men to the wicked women; but the good women *should be married* to the good men, and the good men to the good women. These shall be cleared from *the calumnies* which *slanderers* speak *of them*: they shall obtain pardon, and an honourable provision. O true believers, enter not any houses, besides your own houses, until ye have asked leave, and have saluted the family thereof: this *is* better for you; peradventure ye will be admonished. And if ye shall find no person in the *houses*, yet do not enter them, until leave be granted you: and if it be said unto you, Return back; do ye return back. This *will be* more decent for you; and GOD knoweth that which ye do. It shall be no crime in you, that ye enter uninhabited houses, wherein ye may meet with a convenience. GOD knoweth that which ye discover, and that which ye conceal. Speak unto the true believers, that they restrain their eyes, and keep themselves from immodest actions: this will be more pure for them; for GOD is well acquainted with that which they do. And speak unto the believing women, that they restrain their eyes, and preserve their modesty, and discover not their ornaments, except what *necessarily* appeareth thereof: and let them throw their veils over their bosoms, and not show their ornaments, unless to their husbands, or their fathers, or their husbands' fathers, or their sons, or their husbands' sons, or their brothers, or their brothers' sons, or their sisters' sons, or their women, or the *captives* which their right hands shall possess, or unto such men as attend *them*, and have no need *of women*, or unto children, who distinguish not the nakedness of women. And let them not make a noise with their feet, that their ornaments which they hide may *thereby* be discovered. And be ye all turned unto GOD, O true believers, that ye may be happy. Marry those who are single among you, and such as are honest of your men-servants, and your maid-servants: if they be poor, GOD will enrich them of his abundance; for GOD *is* bounteous *and* wise. And let those who find not a match, keep themselves *from fornication*, until GOD shall enrich them of his abundance. And unto such of your slaves as desire a written instrument *allowing them to redeem themselves on paying a certain sum*, write *one*, if ye know good in them; and give them of the riches of GOD, which he hath given you. And compel not your maid-servants to prostitute themselves, if they be willing to live chastely; that ye may seek the casual *advantage* of this present life: but whoever shall compel them *thereto*, verily GOD *will be* gracious *and* merciful *unto such women* after their compulsion. And now have we revealed unto you evident signs, and a *history* like unto some *of the histories* of those who have gone before you, and an admonition unto the pious. GOD *is* the light of heaven and earth: the similitude of his light is as a niche in a wall, wherein a lamp *is placed, and* the lamp *enclosed* in a *case of glass*; the glass *appears* as it were a shining star. It is lighted with *the oil of* a blessed tree, an olive neither of the east, nor of the west: it wanteth little but that the oil thereof would give light, although no fire touched it. *This is* light *added* unto light: GOD will direct unto his light whom he pleaseth. GOD propoundeth parables unto men; for GOD knoweth all things. In the houses which GOD hath permitted to be raised, and that his name be commemorated therein: men celebrate his praise in the same morning and evening, whom neither merchandiz‐ ing, nor selling diverteth from the remembering of GOD, and the observance of prayer, and the giving of alms; fearing the day whereon *men's* hearts and eyes shall be troubled; that GOD may recompense them according to the utmost merit of what they shall have wrought, and may add unto them of his abundance *a more excellent reward*; for GOD bestoweth on whom he pleaseth without measure. But *as to* the unbeliev‐ ers, their works are like the vapour in a plain, which the thirsty *traveller* thinketh to be water, until when he cometh thereto, he findeth it *to be* nothing; but he findeth GOD with him, and he will fully pay him his account; and GOD is swift in taking an account: or, as the darkness in a deep sea, covered by waves *riding* on waves, above which are clouds, being *additions of* darkness one over the other; when *one* stretcheth forth his hand, he is far from seeing it. And unto whomsoever GOD shall not grant *his* light, he shall enjoy no light at all. Dost thou not perceive that all *creatures* both in heaven and earth praise GOD; and the birds *also*, extending their wings? Every one knoweth his prayer, and his praise: and GOD knoweth that which they do. Unto GOD *belongeth* the kingdom of heaven and earth; and unto GOD *shall be* the return *at the last day*. Dost thou not see that GOD gently driveth forward the clouds, and gathereth them together, and then layeth them on heaps? Thou also seest the rain, which falleth from the midst thereof; and GOD sendeth down from heaven *as it were* mountains, wherein there is hail;

he striketh therewith whom he pleaseth, and turneth the same away from whom he pleaseth: the brightness of his lightning wanteth but little of taking away the sight. GOD shifteth the night, and the day: verily herein is an instruction unto those who have sight. And GOD hath created every animal of water; one of them goeth on his belly, and another of them walketh upon two feet, and another of them walketh upon four *feet*: GOD createth that which he pleaseth; for GOD is almighty. Now have we sent down evident signs: and GOD directeth whom he pleaseth into the right way. The *hypocrites* say, We believe in GOD, and on *his* apostle; and we obey *them*: yet a part of them turneth back, after this; but these are not *really* believers. And when they are summoned before GOD and his apostle, that he may judge between them; behold, a part of them retire: but if the right had been on their side, they would have come and submitted themselves unto him. Is there an infirmity in their hearts? Do they doubt? Or do they fear lest GOD and his apostle act unjustly towards them? But themselves are the unjust doers. The saying of the true believers, when they are summoned before GOD and his apostle, that he may judge between them, is no other than that they say, We have heard, and do obey: and these are they who shall prosper. Whoever shall obey GOD and his apostle, and shall fear GOD, and shall be devout towards him; these shall enjoy great felicity. They swear by GOD, with a most solemn oath, that if thou commandest them, they will go forth *from their houses and possessions*. Say, Swear not *to a falsehood*: obedience *is more* requisite: and GOD is well acquainted with that which ye do. Say, Obey GOD, and obey the apostle: but if ye turn back, verily it is expected of him that he perform his duty, and of you that ye perform your duty; and if ye obey him, ye shall be directed: but the duty of our apostle is only public preaching. GOD promiseth unto such of you as believe, and do good works, that he will cause them to succeed the unbelievers in the earth, as he caused those who were before you to succeed the infidels of their time; and that he will establish for them their religion which pleaseth them, and will change their fear into security. They shall worship me; and shall not associate any other with me. But whoever shall disbelieve after this; they will be the wicked doers. Observe prayer, and give alms, and obey the apostle: that ye may obtain mercy. Think not that the unbelievers shall frustrate the designs of GOD on earth: and their abode hereafter shall be hell fire; a miserable journey shall it be thither! O true believers, let your slaves and those among you who shall not have attained the age of puberty, ask leave of you, before they come into your presence, three times in the day; namely, before the morning prayer, and when ye lay aside your garments at noon, and after the evening prayer. These are the three times for you to be private: it shall be no crime in you, or in them, if they go in to you without asking permission after these times, while ye are in frequent attendance, the one of you on the other. Thus GOD declareth his signs unto you; for GOD is knowing and wise. And when your children attain the age of puberty, let them ask leave to come into your presence at all times, in the same manner as those who have attained that age before them, ask leave. Thus GOD declareth his signs unto you; and GOD is knowing and wise. As to such women as are past childbearing, who hope not to marry again, because of their advanced age; it shall be no crime in them, if they lay aside their outer garments, not showing *their* ornaments; but if they abstain *from this, it will be* better for them. GOD *both* heareth *and* knoweth. It shall be no crime in the blind, nor shall it be any crime in the lame, neither shall it be any crime in the sick, or in yourselves, that ye eat in your houses, or in the house of your fathers, or the houses of your mothers, or in the houses of your brothers, or the houses of your sisters, or the houses of your uncles on the father's side, or the houses of your aunts on the father's side, or the houses of your uncles on the mother's side, or the houses of your aunts on the mother's side, or *in those houses* the keys whereof ye have in your possession, or *in the house* of your friend. It shall not be any crime in you whether ye eat together, or separately. And when ye enter any houses, salute one another on the part of GOD, with a blessed and a welcome salutation. Thus GOD declareth his signs unto you, that ye may understand. Verily they only *are* true believers, who believe in GOD and his apostle, and when they are assembled with him on any affair, depart not, until they have obtained leave of him. Verily they who ask leave of thee, are those who believe in GOD and his apostle. When therefore they ask leave of thee *to depart*, on account of any business of their own, grant leave unto such of them as thou shalt think fit, and ask pardon for them of GOD; for GOD *is* gracious *and* merciful. Let not the calling of the apostle be esteemed among you, as your calling the one to the other. GOD knoweth such of you as privately withdraw themselves *from the assembly*, taking shelter behind one another. But let those who withstand his command, take heed; lest some calamity befall them *in the life to come. Doth* not whatever is in heaven and on earth *belong* unto GOD? He well knoweth what ye are about: and on a certain day they shall be assembled before him; and he shall declare unto them that which they have done; for GOD knoweth all things.

Y. S.

I *swear* by the instructive Korân, that thou art *one* of the messengers *of God, sent* to *show* the right way. *This is a* revelation of the most mighty, the merciful *God:* that thou mayest warn a people whose fathers were not warned, and who live in negligence. *Our* sentence hath justly been pronounced against the greater part of them; wherefore they shall not believe. We have put yokes on their necks, which *come* up to *their* chins; and they are forced to hold up their heads; and we have set a bar before them, and a bar behind them; and we have covered them with darkness; wherefore they shall not see. *It shall be* equal unto them whether thou preach unto them, or do not preach unto them; they shall not believe. But thou shalt preach *with effect* unto him only who followeth the admonition *of the Korân,* and feareth the Merciful in secret. Wherefore bear good tidings unto him, of mercy, and an honourable reward. Verily we will restore the dead to life, and will write down *their works* which they shall have sent before them, and their footsteps *which they shall have left behind them;* and everything do we set down in a plain register. Propound unto them as an example the inhabitants of the city *of Antioch,* when the apostles *of Jesus* came thereto; when we sent unto them two *of the said apostles,* but they charged them with imposture. Wherefore we strengthened *them* with a third. And they said, Verily we *are* sent unto you *by* God. *The inhabitants* answered, Ye are no other than men, as we *are;* neither hath the Merciful revealed anything *unto you*; ye only publish a lie. The *apostles* replied, Our LORD knoweth that we *are* really sent unto you; and our duty is only public preaching. *Those of Antioch* said, Verily we presage evil from you; if ye desist not *from preaching*, we will surely stone you, and a painful punishment shall be inflicted on you by us. The *apostles* answered, Your evil presage is with yourselves; although ye be warned, *will ye persist in your errors!* Verily ye *are* a people who transgress *exceedingly*. And a certain man came hastily from the farther parts of the city, *and* said, O my people, follow the messengers *of* GOD; follow him who demandeth not any reward of you; for these are *rightly* directed. What *reason* have I that I should not worship him who hath created me? For unto him shall ye return. Shall I take *other* gods besides him? If the merciful be pleased to afflict me, their intercession will not avail me at all, neither can they deliver *me*; then should I be in a manifest error. Verily I believe in your LORD ; wherefore hearken unto me. *But they stoned him; and as he died*, it was said *unto him*, Enter thou into paradise. *And* he said, O that my people knew how merciful GOD hath been unto me! For he hath highly honoured me. And we sent not down against his people, after *they had slain* him, an army from heaven, nor *the other instruments of destruction* which we sent down *on unbelievers in former days*: there was only one cry *of Gabriel from heaven*, and behold, they *became* utterly extinct. O the misery of men! No apostle cometh unto them, but they laugh him to scorn. Do they not consider how many genera-tions we have destroyed before them? Verily they shall not return unto them; but all of them in general *shall be* assembled before us. *One* sign *of the resurrection* unto them *is* the dead earth; we quicken the same *by the rain*, and produce thereout *various sorts of* grain, of which they eat. And we make therein gardens of palm-trees, and vines; and we cause springs to gush forth in the same: that they may eat of the fruits thereof, and of the labour of their hands. Will they not therefore give thanks? Praise be unto him who hath created all the different kinds, *both* of *vegetables*, which the earth bringeth forth, and of their own species, *by forming the two sexes*, and also *the various sorts* of things which they know not. The night also *is* a sign unto them: we withdraw the day from the same, and behold, they *are* covered with darkness: and the sun hasteneth to his place of rest. This *is* the dispo-sition of the mighty, the wise GOD. And for the moon have we appointed *certain* mansions, until she *change and* return *to be* like the old branch of a palm-tree. It is not expedient that the sun should overtake the moon *in her course;* neither doth the night outstrip the day: but each *of these luminaries* moveth in a *peculiar* orbit. It *is* a sign also unto them, that we carry their offspring in the ship filled *with merchandise;* and that we have made for them *other conveniences* like unto it, whereon they ride. If we please, we drown them, and *there is* none to help them; neither are they delivered, unless through our mercy, and that they may enjoy *life* for a season. When it is said unto them, Fear that which is before you, and that which is behind you, that ye may obtain mercy; *they withdraw from thee:* and thou dost not bring them one sign, of the signs of their LORD, but they turn aside from the same. And when it is said unto them, Give alms of that which GOD hath bestowed on you; the unbelievers say unto those who believe, *by way of mockery*, Shall we feed him whom GOD can feed, if he pleaseth? Verily ye *are* in no other than a manifest error. And they say, When will this promise *of the resurrection be fulfilled*, if ye speak truth? They only wait for one sounding *of the trumpet*, which shall overtake them while they are disputing together; and they shall not *have time to* make any disposition *of their effects*, neither shall they return to their family. And the trumpet shall be sounded *again*, and behold they shall come forth from *their* graves, and hasten unto their LORD . They shall say, Alas for us! Who hath awakened us from our bed? This is what the Merciful promised *us*; and *his* apostles spoke the truth. It shall be but one sound *of the trumpet*, and behold, they *shall be* all assembled before us. On this day no soul shall be unjustly treated in the least; neither shall ye be rewarded, but according to what ye shall have wrought. On this day the inhabitants of paradise shall be wholly taken up with joy: they and their wives *shall rest* in shady groves, leaning on magnificent couches. There shall they have fruit, and they shall obtain whatever they shall desire. Peace *shall be* the word spoken *unto the righteous*, by a merciful LORD: but *he shall say unto the wicked*, Be ye separated this day, O ye wicked, *from the righteous*. Did I not command you, O sons of Adam, that ye should no worship Satan; because he *was* an open enemy unto you? And *did I not say*, Worship me; this *is* the right way? But now hath he seduced a great multitude of you: did ye not therefore understand? This is hell, with which ye were threatened: be ye cast into the same this day, to be burned; for that ye have been unbelievers. On this day we will seal up their mouths, *that they shall not open them in their own defence*; and their hands shall speak unto us, and their feet shall bear witness of that which they have committed. If we pleased we could put out their eyes, and they might run with emulation in the way *they use to take;* and how should they see *their error?* And if we pleased we could transform them *into other shapes,* in their places *where they should be found;* and they should not be able to depart: neither should they repent. Unto whomsoever we grant a long life, him do we cause to bow down his body *through age.* Will they not therefore understand? We have not taught *Mohammed* the art of poetry; nor is it expedient for him *to be a poet.* This *book is* no other than an admonition *from God,* and a perspicuous Korân; that he may warn him who is living: and the sentence *of condemnation* will be justly executed on the unbelievers. Do they not consider that we have created for them, among the things which our hands have wrought, cattle *of several kinds,* of which they are possessors; and that we have put the same in subjection under them? Some of them *are* for their riding; and on some of them do they feed: and they receive *other* advantages therefrom; and *of their milk to they* drink. Will they not, therefore, be thankful? They have taken *other* gods, besides GOD, *in hopes* that they may be assisted *by them:* but they are not able to give them any assistance: yet *are* they a party of troops ready to *defend* them. Let not their speech, therefore, grieve thee: we know that which they privately conceal, and that which they publicly discover. Doth not man know that we have created him of seed? yet behold, he is an open disputer *against the resurrection:* and he propoundeth unto us a comparison, and forgetteth his creation. He saith, Who shall restore bones to life, when they are rotten? Answer, He shall restore them to life, who produced them the first time: for he is skilled in every *kind of* creation: who giveth you fire out of the green tree, and behold, ye kindle *your fuel* from thence. Is not he who hath created the heavens and the earth, able to create *new creatures* like unto them? Yea, certainly: for he *is* the wise Creator. His command, when he willeth a thing, *is* only that he saith unto it, Be and it is. Wherefore praise be unto him, in whose hand is the kingdom of all things, and unto whom ye shall return *at the last day.*

THE GENII

Say, It hath been revealed unto me that a company of genii attentively heard *me reading the Korân,* and said, Verily we have heard an admirable discourse; which directeth unto the right institution: wherefore we believe therein, and we will by no means associate any *other* with our LORD . He (may the majesty of our LORD be exalted!) hath taken no wife, nor *hath he begotten* any issue. Yet the foolish among us hath spoken that which is extremely false of GOD but we verily thought that neither man nor genius would by any mean have uttered a lie concerning GOD. And there are certain men who fly for refuge unto certain of the genii: but they increase their folly and transgression: and they also thought, as ye thought, that GOD would not raise any one to life. And we *formerly* attempted *to pry into what was transacting in* heaven; but we found the same filled with a strong guard *of angels,* and with flaming darts: and we sat on *some of the* seats thereof to hear *the discourse of the inhabitants;* but whoever listenth now findeth a flame laid in ambush for him, *to guard the celestial confines.* And we know not whether evil be *hereby* intended against those who *are* in the earth, or whether their LORD intendeth to direct them aright. *There are* some among us who are upright; and *there are* some among us who are otherwise: we are of different ways. And we verily thought that we could by no means frustrate GOD in the earth, neither could we escape him by flight: wherefore, when we had heard the direction *contained in the Korân*, we believed therein. And whoever believeth in his LORD, need not fear any diminution *of his reward*, nor any injustice. *There are some* Moslems among us; and *there are others* of us who swerve from righteousness. And whoso embraceth Islam, they earnestly seek true direction; but those who swerve from righteousness shall be fuel for hell. If they tread in the way *of truth*, we will surely water them with abundant rain; that we may prove them thereby; but whoso turneth aside from the admonition of his LORD, him will he send into a severe torment. Verily the places of worship *are set apart* unto GOD: wherefore invoke not any *other therein* together with GOD. When the servant of GOD stood up to invoke him, it wanted little but that *the genii* had pressed on him in crowds, *to hear him rehearse the Korân*. Say, Verily I call upon my LORD only, and I associate no *other god* with him. Say, Verily I am not able, *of myself*, to procure you either hurt or a right institution. Say, Verily none can protect me against GOD; neither shall I find any refuge besides him. *I can do no more* than publish *what hath been revealed unto me* from GOD, and his messages. And whosoever shall be disobedient unto GOD and his apostle, for him *is* the fire of hell *prepared;* they shall remain therein for ever. Until they see *the vengeance* with which they are threatened, *they will not cease their opposi-*tion: but then shall they know who *were* the weaker in a protector, and the fewer in number. Say, I know not whether *the punishment* with which ye are threatened *be* night, or whether my LORD will appoint for it a distant term. He knoweth the secrets of futurity; and he doth not communicate his secrets unto any, except an apostle in whom he is well pleased: and he causeth a guard *of angels* to march before him and beind him, that he may know that they have executed the commissions of their LORD: he comprehendeth whatever is with them, and counteth all things by number.

THE TERRITORY

I swear by this territory (and thou, O *prophet*, residest in this territory), and by the begetter, and that which he hath begotten; verily we have created man in misery. Doth he think that none shall prevail over him? He saith, I have wasted plenty of riches. Doth he think that none seeth him? Have we not made him two eyes, and a tongue, and two lips; and shown him the two highways *of good and evil*? Yet he attempteth not the cliff. What shall make thee to understand what the cliff *is*? *It is* to free the captive; or to feed, in the day of famine, the orphan who is of kin, or the poor man who lieth on the ground. *Whoso doth this*, and is *one* of those who believe, and recommend perseverance unto each other, and recommend mercy unto each other; these *shall be* the companions of the right hand. But they who shall disbelieve our signs, shall be the companions of the left hand: above them *shall be* arched fire.

THE WAR-HORSES

By the *war-horses* which run swiftly *to the battle*, with a panting noise; and by those which strike fire, by dashing *their hoofs against the stones;* and by those which make a sudden incursion *on the enemy* early in the morning, and therein raise the dust, and therein pass through the midst of the *adverse* troops, verily man *is* ungrateful unto his LORD ; and he *is* witness thereof: and he *is* immoderate in the love of *worldly* good. Doth he not know, therefore, when that which *is* in the graves shall be taken forth and that which *is* in *men's* breasts shall be brought to light, that their LORD *will,* on that day, *be* fully informed concerning them?

THE STRIKING

The striking! What *is* the striking? And what shall make thee to understand how *terrible* the striking *will be?* On that day men shall be like moths scattered abroad, and the mountains shall become like carded wool of various colours *driven by the wind.* Moreover he whose balance shall be heavy *with good works,* shall lead a pleasing life: but *as to* him whose balance shall be light, his dwelling *shall be* in the pit *of hell.* What shall make thee to understand how *frightful* the pit *of hell is? It is* a burning fire.

GOD'S UNITY

Say, *God* is one GOD; the eternal GOD: he begetteth not, neither is he begotten: and there is not any one like unto him.

MEN

Say, I fly for refuge unto the LORD of men, the king of men, the GOD of men, *that he may deliver me* from the mischief of the whisperer who slyly withdraweth, who whispereth evil suggestions into the breasts of men; from genii and men.

THE

TIBETAN BOOK

Prologue by the Dalai Lama {

OF THE DEAD

The Bardo Thodol, which has become known in the West as The Tibetan Book of the Dead, is one of the most important books our civilization has produced. We Tibetans have a reputation of being very spiritual, though we usually consider ourselves quite down-to-earth and practical. So we think of our systematic study and analysis of the human death process as a cautious and practical preparation for the inevitable. After all, there is not a single one of us who is not going to die, sooner or later. So how to prepare for death, how to undergo the death process with the least trauma, and what comes after death— these are matters of vital importance to every one of us. It would be impractical of us not to study these issues with the greatest of care and not to develop methods of dealing with death and the dying in a skillful, compassionate, and humane way. . . . Indeed, the reality of death has always been a major spur to virtuous and intelligent action in all Buddhist societies. It is not considered morbid to contemplate it, but rather liberating from fear, and even beneficial to the health of the living. . . . Naturally, most of us would like to die a peaceful death, but it is also clear that we cannot hope to die peacefully if our lives have been full of violence, or if our minds have mostly been agitated by emotions like anger, attachment, or fear. So if we wish to die well, we must lean how to live well: Hoping for a peaceful death, we must cultivate peace in our mind, and in our way of life.

INTRODUCTION

CARL JUNG

THE TIBETAN BOOK OF THE DEAD, or the *Bardo Thödol*, is a book of instructions for the dead and dying. Like the Egyptian Book of the Dead, it is meant to be a guide for the dead man during the period of his *Bardo* existence, symbolically described as an intermediate state of forty-nine days' duration between death and rebirth. The text falls into three parts. The first part, called *Chikhai Bardo*, describes the psychic happenings at the moment of death. The second part, or *Chönyid Bardo*, deals with the dream-state which supervenes immediately after death, and with what are called "karmic illusions." The third part, or *Sidpa Bardo*, concerns the onset of the birth-instinct and of prenatal events. . . . The purpose of the instruction is to fix the attention of the dead man, at each successive stage of delusion and entanglement, on the ever-present possibility of liberation, and to explain to him the nature of his visions. The text of the *Bardo Thödol* is recited by the lama in the presence of the corpse. . . .

The *Bardo Thödol*, fitly named by its editor, Dr. W. Y. Evans-Wentz, "The Tibetan Book of the Dead," caused a considerable stir in English-speaking countries at the time of its first appearance in 1927. It belongs to that class of writings which are not only of interest to specialists in Mahayana Buddhism, but which also, because of their deep humanity and their still deeper insight into the secrets of the human psyche, make an especial appeal to the layman who is seeking to broaden his knowledge of life. For years, ever since it was first published, the *Bardo Thödol* has been my constant companion, and to it I owe not only many stimulating ideas and discoveries, but also many fundamental insights. Unlike the Egyptian Book of the Dead, which always prompts one to say too much or too little, the *Bardo Thödol* offers one an intelligible philosophy addressed to human beings rather than to gods or primitive savages. Its philosophy contains the quintessence of Buddhist psychological criticism; and, as such, one can truly say that it is of an unexampled sublimity. Not only the "wrathful" but also the "peaceful" deities are conceived as samsaric projections of the human psyche, an idea that seems all too obvious to the enlightened European, because it reminds him of his own banal simplifications. But though the European can easily explain away these deities as projections, he would be quite incapable of positing them at the same time as real. The *Bardo Thödol* can do that, because, in certain of its most essential metaphysical premises, it has the enlightened as well as the unenlightened European at a disadvantage. The ever-present, unspoken assumption of the *Bardo Thödol* is the antinomian character of all metaphysical assertions, and also the idea of the qualitative difference of the various levels of consciousness and of the metaphysical realities conditioned by them. The background of this unusual book is not the niggardly European "either-or," but a magnificently affirmative "both-and." This statement may appear objectionable to the Western philosopher, for the West loves clarity and unambiguity; consequently, one philosopher clings to the position, "God is," while another clings equally fervently to the negation, "God is not." What would these hostile brethren make of an assertion like the following:

> Recognizing the voidness of thine own intellect to be Buddhahood and knowing it at the same time to be thine own consciousness, thou shalt abide in the state of the divine mind of the Buddha.

Such an assertion is, I fear, as unwelcome to our Western philosophy as it is to our theology. The *Bardo Thödol* is in the highest degree psychological in its outlook; but, with us, philosophy and theology are still in the medieval, pre-psychological stage where only the assertions are listened to, explained, defended, criticized and disputed, while the authority that makes them has, by general consent, been deposed as outside the scope of discussion.

Metaphysical assertions, however, are *statements of the psyche*, and are therefore psychological. To the Western mind, which compensates its well-known feelings of resentment by a slavish regard for "rational" explanations, this obvious truth seems all too obvious, or else it is seen as an inadmissible negation of metaphysical "truth." Whenever the Westerner hears the word "psychological," it always sounds to him like "*only* psychological." For him the "soul" is something pitifully small, unworthy, personal, subjective, and a lot more besides. He therefore prefers to use the word "mind" instead, though he likes to pretend at the same time that a statement which may in fact be very subjective indeed is made by the "mind," naturally by the "Universal Mind," or even—at a pinch—by the "Absolute" itself. This rather ridiculous presumption is probably a compensation for the regrettable smallness of the soul.

It is the psyche which, by the divine creative power inherent in it, makes the metaphysical assertion; it posits the distinctions between metaphysical entities. Not only is it the condition of all metaphysical reality, it *is* that reality.

With this great psychological truth the *Bardo Thödol* opens. The book is not a ceremonial of burial, but a set of instructions for the dead, a guide through the changing phenomena of the *Bardo* realm, that state of existence which continues for forty-nine days after death until the next incarnation. If we disregard for the moment the supratemporality of the soul—which the East accepts as a self-evident fact—we, as readers of the *Bardo Thödol*, shall be able to put ourselves without difficulty in the position of the dead man, and shall consider attentively the teaching set forth in the opening section. . . .

It is highly sensible of the *Bardo Thödol* to make clear to the dead man the primacy of the psyche, for that is the one thing which life does not make clear to us. We are so hemmed in by things which jostle and oppress that we never get a chance, in the midst of all these "given" things, to wonder by whom they are "given." It is from this world of "given" things that the dead man liberates himself; and the purpose of the instruction is to help him towards this liberation. We, if we put ourselves in his place, shall derive no lesser reward from it, since we learn from the very first paragraphs that the "giver" of all "given" things dwells within us. This is a truth which in the face of all evidence, in the greatest things as in the smallest, is never known, although it is often so very necessary, indeed vital, for us to know it. Such knowledge, to be sure, is suitable only for contemplatives who are minded to understand the purpose of existence, for those who are Gnostics by temperament and therefore believe in a saviour who, like the saviour of the Mandaeans, is called "knowledge of life" (Manda d'Hayye). Perhaps it is not granted to many of us to see the world as something "given." A great reversal of standpoint, calling for much sacrifice, is needed before we can see the world as "given" by the very nature of the psyche. It is so much more straightforward, more dramatic, impressive, and therefore more convincing, to see all the things that happen to me than to observe how I make them happen. Indeed, the animal nature of man makes him resist seeing himself as the maker of his circumstances. That is why attempts of this kind were always the object of secret initiations, culminating as a rule in a figurative death which symbolized the total character of this reversal. And, in point of fact, the instruction given in the *Bardo Thödol* serves to recall to the dead man the experiences of his initiation and the teachings of his guru, for the instruction is, at bottom, nothing less than an initiation of the dead into the *Bardo* life, just as the initiation of the living was a preparation for the Beyond. Such was the case, at least, with all the mystery cults in ancient civilizations from the time of the Egyptian and Eleusinian mysteries. In the initiation of the living, however, this "Beyond" is not a world beyond death, but a reversal of the mind's intentions and outlook, a psychological "Beyond" or, in Christian terms, a "redemption" from the trammels of the world and of sin. Redemption is a separation and deliverance from an earlier condition of darkness and unconsciousness, and leads to a condition of illumination and releasedness, to victory and transcendence over everything "given. . . ."

The book describes a way of initiation in reverse, which, unlike the eschatological expectations of Christianity, pre-pares the soul for a descent into physical being. The thor-oughly intellectualistic and rationalistic worldly-mindedness of the European makes it advisable for us to reverse the sequence of the *Bardo Thödol* and to regard it as an account of Eastern initiation experiences, though one is perfectly free, of one chooses, to substitute Christian symbols for the gods of the *Chönyid Bardo*.

The real purpose of this singular book is the attempt, which must seem very strange to the educated European of the twentieth century, to enlighten the dead on their journey through the regions of the *Bardo*. The Catholic Church is the only place in the world of the white man where any provi-sion is made for the souls of the departed. Inside the Protestant camp, with its world-affirming optimism, we only find a few mediumistic "rescue circles," whose main concern is to make the dead aware of the fact that they *are* dead. But, generally speaking, we have nothing in the West that is in any way comparable to the *Bardo Thödol*, except for certain secret writings which are inaccessible to the wider public and to the ordinary scientist. According to tradition, the *Bardo Thödol*, too, seems to have been included among the "hidden" books. . . . As such, it forms a special chapter in the magical "cure of the soul" which extends even beyond death. This cult of the dead is rationally based on the belief in the supra-temporality of the soul, but its irrational basis is to be found in the psychological need of the living to do something for the departed. This is an elementary need which forces itself upon even the most "enlightened" individuals when faced by the death of relatives and friends. That is why, enlightenment or no enlightenment, we still have all manner of ceremonies for the dead. If Lenin had to submit to being embalmed and put on show in a sumptuous mausoleum like an Egyptian pharaoh, we may be quite sure it was not because his followers believed in the resurrection of the body. Apart, however, from the Masses said for the soul in the Catholic Church, the provisions we make for the dead are rudimentary and on the lowest level, not because we cannot convince ourselves of the soul's immortality, but because we have rationalized the above-mentioned psychological need out of existence. We behave as if we did not have this need, and because we cannot believe in a life after death we prefer to do nothing about it. Simpler-minded people follow their own feelings, and, as in Italy, build themselves funeral monuments of gruesome beauty. The Catholic Masses for the soul are on a level considerably above this, because they are expressly intended for the psychic welfare of the deceased and are not a mere gratification of lachrymose sentiments. But the highest application of spiritual effort on behalf of the departed is surely to be found in the instructions of the *Bardo Thödol*. They are so detailed and thoroughly adapted to the apparent changes in the dead man's condition that every serious-minded reader must ask himself whether these wise old lamas might not, after all, have caught a glimpse of the fourth dimension and twitched the veil from the greatest of life's secrets.

Even if the truth should prove to be a disappointment, one almost feels tempted to concede at least some measure of reality to the vision of life in the *Bardo*. At any rate, it is unexpectedly original, if nothing else, to find the after-death state, of which our religious imagination has formed the most grandiose conceptions, painted in lurid colours as a terrifying dream-state of a progressively degenerative character. The supreme vision comes not at the end of the *Bardo*, but right at the beginning, at the moment of death; what happens afterward is an ever-deepening descent into illusion and obscuration, down to the ultimate degradation of new physical birth. The spiritual climax is reached at the moment when life ends. Human life, therefore, is the vehicle of the highest perfection it is possible to attain; it alone generates the karma that makes it possible for the dead man to abide in the perpetual light of the Voidness without clinging to any object, and thus to rest on the hub of the wheel of rebirth, freed from all illusion of genesis and decay. Life in the *Bardo* brings no eternal rewards or punishments, but merely a descent into a new life which shall bear the individual nearer to his final goal. But this eschatological goal is what he himself brings to birth as the last and highest fruit of the labours and aspirations of earthly existence. This view is not only lofty, it is manly and heroic. . . .

The *Bardo Thödol* began by being a "closed" book, and so it has remained, no matter what kind of commentaries may be written upon it. For it is a book that will only open itself to spiritual understanding, and this is a capacity which no man is born with, but which he can only acquire through special training and special experience. It is good that such to all intents and purposes "useless" books exist. They are meant for those "queer folk" who no longer set much store by the uses, aims, and meaning of present-day "civilization."

THE TIBETAN BOOK OF THE DEAD

HEY! NOBLE ONE, you named So-and-so! Now the time has come for you to seek the way. Just as your breath stops, the objective clear light of the first between will dawn . . . you are now proceeding. You have woken up with the worry, "What is happening to me?" Recognize that you are in the between! Now, since the life cycle is in suspension, all things dawn as lights and deities. All space dawns full of azure light. Now, from the central Buddha-land, All-pervading Drop, the Lord Vairochana appears before you, white bodied, sitting on a lion throne, holding in his hand an eight-spoked wheel, united with his consort Akasha Dhatvishvari. The natural purity of the consciousness aggregate, the blue light of the Reality Perfection wisdom, a clear and vivid color blue, frighteningly intense, shines piercingly from the heart center of this Vairochana couple, dazzling your eyes unbearably. Simultaneously the soft white light of the gods shines upon you and penetrates you in parallel with the bright blue light. At that time, influenced by negative evolution, you panic and are terrified of that bright blue light of Reality Perfection wisdom and you flee from it. And you feel a liking for the soft white light of the gods, and you approach it. But you must not panic at that blue light, the clear, piercing, brilliant, frightening supreme wisdom clear light! Do not fear it! It is the light ray of the Transcendent Lord, the Reality Perfection wisdom. Feel attracted to it with faith and reverence! Make it the answer to your prayer, thinking, "It is the light ray of the compassion of Lord Vairochana—I must take refuge in it!" It is the way Lord Vairochana comes to escort you through the straits of the between. It is the light ray of the compassion of Vairochana. Don't be enticed by the soft white light of the gods. Don't be attached to it! Don't long for it! If you cling to it, you will wander into the realm of the gods, and you will continue to cycle through the six realms of driven existence. It is an obstacle to cessation, the path of freedom. So don't look upon it, but be devoted to the brilliant penetrating blue light, aim your intense willpower toward Vairochana and repeat after me the following prayer:

When I roam the life cycle driven by strong delusion,
May the Lord Vairochana lead me on the path
Of the clear light of reality-perfection wisdom!
May his Consort Buddha Dhatvishvari back me on the way,
Deliver me from the dangerous straits of the between,

And carry me to perfect Buddhahood!

Thus praying with fierce devotion, you dissolve in rainbow light into the heart of the Vairochana couple, whence you will enter the central pure land Ghanavyuha, Dense Array, and become a Buddha by way of the Body of Perfect Beatitude!

Hey, noble one! Listen without wavering! On this second day, the white light that is the purity of the element water dawns before you. At this time, from the blue eastern pure land of Abhirati, Intense Delight, the blue Lord Vajrasattva Akshobhya arises before you seated on an elephant, carrying a five-pronged vajra scepter, in union with his consort Buddhalochana, attended by the male Bodhisattvas Kshitigarbha and Maitreya and the female Bodhisattvas Lasya and Pushpa—a group of six Archetype Deities. The white light of the Mirror wisdom, purity of the form aggregate, white and piercing, bright and clear, shines from the heart of the Vajrasattva couple before you, penetrating, unbearable to your eyes. At the same time the soft smoky light of the hells shines before you in parallel with the wisdom light. At that time, under the influence of hate you panic, terrified by that brilliant white light, and you flee from it. You feel a liking for that soft smoky light of the hells and you approach it. But now you must fearlessly recognize that brilliant white, piercing, dazzling clear light as wisdom. Be gladdened by it with faith and reverence! Pray and increase your love for it, thinking, "It is the light of the compassion of Lord Vajrasattva! I take refuge in it!" It is Lord Vajrasattva's shining upon you to escort you through the terrors of the between. It is the tractor-beam of the light of the compassion of Vajrasattva—have faith in it! Don't be enticed by that soft smoky light of hell! Hey! That is the path of destruction from the sins you have accumulated by your strong hatred! If you cling to it, you will fall into the hells; you will be stuck in the mire of unbearable ordeals of suffering, without any escape. It is an obstacle to the path of liberation. Don't look upon it, and abandon all hate! Don't cling to it! Don't long for it! Have faith in that dazzlingly bright white light! Aim your intense willpower toward Lord Vajrasattva and make the following prayer:

Alas! When I roam the life cycle driven by strong hate,
May the Lord Vajrasattva lead me on the path
Of the dear light of the mirror wisdom!
May his Consort Buddhalochana back me on the way,
Deliver me from the dangerous straits of the between,
And carry me to perfect Buddhahood!

By praying in this way with intense faith, you will dissolve into rainbow light in the heart of Lord Vajrasattva, and you will go to his eastern pure land Abhirati and attain Buddhahood in the Body of Perfect Beatitude.

Hey, noble one! Listen without wavering! On this third day, the yellow light that is the purity of the element earth dawns. At this time, from the yellow southern Buddha-land of Shrimat, the yellow Lord Ratnasambhava appears seated on a fine horse, carrying a precious wish-granting gem, in union with his consort Mamaki, attended by the male Bodhisattvas Akashagarbha and Samantabhadra and the female Bodhisattvas Mala and Dhupa—a group of six

Buddha deities in a background of rainbows, rays, and lights. The yellow light of the Equalizing wisdom, the purity of the sensation aggregate, yellow and piercing, dazzling and clear, adorned with glistening drops and droplets, shines from the heart of the Ratnasambhava couple before you, penetrating your heart center, unbearable to see with your eyes. At the same time, the soft blue light of the human realm shines before you, penetrating your heart in parallel with the wisdom light. At that time, under the influence of pride, you panic and are terrified by that brilliant, energetic yellow light, and you flee it. You feel a liking for that soft blue light of the human realms and you approach it. But at that time you must fearlessly recognize that brilliant yellow, piercing, dazzling clear light as wisdom. Upon it place your mind, relaxing your awareness in the experience of nothing more to do. Or again be gladdened by it with faith and reverence! If you can recognize it as the natural energy of your own awareness, without even having to feel faith or make prayers, you will dissolve indivisibly with all the images and light rays and you will become a Buddha. If you do not recognize it as the natural energy of your own awareness, then pray and increase your love for it, thinking, "It is the light ray of the compassion of Lord Ratnasambhava! I take refuge in it!" It is the tractor beam of the light rays of the compassion of Lord Ratnasambhava—have faith in it! Don't be enticed by that soft blue light of the human realms—for that is the path of destruction from the sins you have accumulated by your fierce pride! If you cling to it, you will fall into the human realms; you will experience the suffering of birth, sickness, old age, and death, and you will find no time for liberation from the life cycle. It is an obstacle blocking the path of lib-eration. Don't look upon it, and abandon all pride! Abandon its instinct! Don't cling to it! Don't long for it! Have faith in that dazzlingly bright yellow light! Aim your one-pointed willpower toward the Lord Ratnasambhava and make the following prayer:

Hey! When I roam the life cycle driven by strong pride,
May the Lord Ratnasambhava lead me on the path
Of the clear light of the equalizing wisdom!
May his Consort Buddha Mamaki back me on the way,
Deliver me from the dangerous straits of the between,
And carry me to perfect Buddhahood!

By praying in this way with intense faith, you will dis-solve into rainbow light in the heart of the Lord Ratnasambhava couple, and you will go to the southern pure land Shrimat and attain Buddhahood in the Body of Perfect Beatitude.

Hey, noble one! Listen without wavering! On this fourth day, the red light that is the purity of the element fire dawns. At this time, from the red western world of Sukhavati, the red Lord Amitabha appears before you seated on a peacock throne, carrying a lotus, in union with his con-sort Pandaravasini, attended by the male Bodhisattvas Avalokiteshvara and Manjushri and the female Bodhisattvas Gita and Aloka—a group of six Buddha deities in a back-ground of rainbows and lights. The red light of the Discriminating wisdom, purity of the conceptual aggregate, red and piercing, dazzling and clear, adorned with drops and

droplets, shines from the heart of the Amitabha couple, precisely penetrating your heart center, unbearable to see with
your eyes. Do not fear it! At the same time a soft yellow light
of the pretan realm shines before you, penetrating your heart
in parallel with the wisdom light. Do not indulge in it!
Abandon clinging and longing! At that time, under the influence of fierce passion, you panic and are terrified by that
brilliant, energetic red light, and you want to flee it. You
feel a liking for that soft yellow light of the pretan realms
and you approach it.

But at that time you must fearlessly recognize that brilliant red, piercing, dazzling clear light as wisdom. Upon it
place your mind, relaxing your awareness in the experience
of nothing more to do. Or again be gladdened by it with
faith and reverence! If you can recognize it as the natural
energy of your own awareness, without feeling faith, without making prayers, you will dissolve indivisibly with all
the images and light rays and you will become a Buddha. If
you do not recognize it as the natural energy of your own
awareness, then pray and hold your aspiration for it, thinking, "It is the light ray of the compassion of Lord Amitabha!
I take refuge in it!" It is the tractor beam of the light rays of
the compassion of Lord Amitabha—have faith in it! Don't
flee it! If you flee it, it still will not leave you! Don't fear it!
Don't be enticed by that soft yellow light of the pretan
realms! It is the path of the instincts of the sins you have
accumulated by your fierce attachment! If you cling to it, you
will fall into the pretan realms; you will experience the
intolerable suffering of hunger and thirst, and it will be an
obstacle blocking the path of liberation. Without clinging

to it, abandon your instinct for it! Don't long for it! Have faith in that dazzlingly bright red light! Aim your one-pointed will toward the Lord Amitabha couple and make the following prayer:

Hey! When I roam the life cycle driven by strong passion,
May the Lord Amitabha lead me on the path
Of the clear light of the discriminating wisdom!
May his Consort Buddha Pandaravasini back me on the way,
Deliver me from the dangerous straits of the between,
And carry me to perfect Buddhahood!

By praying in this way with intense faith, you will dissolve into rainbow light in the heart of the Lord Amitabha couple, and you will go to the western pure land Sukhavati and attain Buddhahood in the Body of Perfect Beatitude.

Hey, noble one! Listen without wavering! On this fifth day, the green light that is the purity of the element wind dawns. At this time, from the green northern Buddha-land of Prakuta, the green Lord Amoghasiddhi appears seated on an eagle throne, carrying a vajra cross, in union with his consort Samayatara, attended by the male Bodhisattvas Vajrapani and Sarvanivaranaviskambhin and the female Bodhisattvas Gandha and Nartya—a group of six Buddha deities in a background of rainbows and lights. The green light of the All-accomplishing wisdom, purity of the creation aggregate, green, piercing, dazzling and clear, adorned with glistening drops and droplets, shines from the heart of the Amoghasiddhi couple, precisely penetrating your heart center, unbearable to see with your eyes. Not fearing it, knowing it as the natural force of the wisdom of your own awareness, enter the experience of the great, unoccupied equanimity, free of attraction to the familiar and aversion to the alien! At the same time a soft, envy-made red light of the titan realm shines upon you together with the wisdom light-ray. Meditate upon it with attraction and aversion in balance. If you are of inferior mind, do not indulge in it! At that time, under the influence of fierce jealousy, you panic and are terrified by that brilliant, piercing green light, and you flee it in alarm. You enjoy and are attached to that soft red light of the titan realm and you approach it. But at that time you must fearlessly recognize that brilliant green, piercing, dazzling clear light as wisdom. Upon it relax your awareness in the experience of transcendence with nothing to do. Or again pray and increase your love for it, thinking "It is the light ray of the compassion of Lord Amoghasiddhi! I take refuge in it!" It is the All-accomplishing wisdom, the light ray of the tractor beam of the compassion of Lord Amoghasiddhi—have faith in it! Don't flee it! If you flee it, it still will not leave you! Don't fear it! Don't be enticed by that soft red light of the titan realms! It is the path of destruction from the negative evolutionary actions you have committed through your powerful jealousy! If you cling to it, you will fall into the titan realms; you will experience the intolerable suffering of interminable fighting, and it will be an obstacle blocking the path of liberation. Without clinging to it, abandon your instinct for it! Don't long for it! Have faith in that dazzling bright green light! Aim your one-pointed willpower toward the Lord Amoghasiddhi couple and make the following prayer:

Hey! When I roam the life cycle driven by strong envy,
May the Lord Amoghasiddhi lead me on the path
Of the clear light of the all-accomplishing wisdom!
May his Consort Buddha Samayatara back me on the way,
Deliver me from the dangerous straits of the between,
And carry me to perfect Buddhahood!

By praying in this way with intense faith, you will dissolve into rainbow light in the heart of the Lord Amoghasiddhi couple, and you will go to the northern pure land Prakuta and attain Buddhahood in the Body of Perfect Beatitude!

Hey, noble one! Listen without wavering! Up until yesterday, the visions of the five Buddha-clans appeared to you one by one. Though they were dearly described, under the influence of negative evolution you were panicked, and still up to now you are left behind here. If you had already recognized the natural shining of one of the wisdoms of the five clans as your own visions, it would have caused you to dissolve into rainbow light in the body of one of the five Buddha-clans and to attain Buddhahood in the Body of Beatitude. As it is, you did not recognize the light and you are still wandering here. Now behold without distraction! Now the vision of all the five clans and the vision of the joining of the four wisdoms have come to escort you in their direction. Recognize them!

Hey, noble child! The purity of the four elements is dawning as the four lights. In the center the Vairochana Buddha couple as described above appears from the pure land All-pervading Drop. In the east the Vajrasattva Buddha couple with retinue appears from the pure land Abhirati. In the south the Ratnasambhava Buddha couple with retinue as described above appears from the pure land Shrimat. In the west the Amitabha Buddha couple with retinue as described above appears from the lotus-heaped pure land Sukhavati. In the north the Amoghasiddhi Buddha couple with retinue as described above appears from the pure land Prakuta, in a rainbow light background.

Hey, noble child! Outside of those five Buddha-clan couples appear the fierce door guardians Vijaya, Yamantaka, Hayagriva, and Amertakundali; the fierce door guardian goddesses Ankusha, Pasha, Sphota, and Ghanta; and these six Lord Buddhas: Indra Shatakratu, the Buddha of the gods; Vemachitra, the Buddha of the titans; Shakyamuni, the Buddha of the humans; Simha, the Buddha of the animals; Jvalamukha, the Buddha of the pretans; and Dharmaraja, the Buddha of the hells. Also appearing is the All-around-goodness Samantabhadra Father-Mother, the general ancestor of all Buddhas. Altogether the host of the forty-two deities of the Beatific Body emerges from your own heart center and appears to you—recognize it as your own pure vision!

Hey, noble one! Those pure lands are not anywhere else—they abide in your own heart within its center and four directions. They now emerge from out of your heart and appear to you! Those images do not come from anywhere else! They are primordially created as the natural manifestation of your own awareness—so you should know how to recognize them!

Hey, noble one! Those deities, not great, not small, symmetrical, each with ornamentation, color, posture, throne, and gesture; those deities each pervaded by five mantras, each of the five circled by a five-colored rainbow aura; with male Bodhisattvas of each clan upholding the male part and female Bodhisattvas of each clan upholding the female part, with all the mandalas arising simultaneously whole—they are your Archetype Deities, so you should recognize them!

Hey, noble one! From the hearts of those five Buddha-clan couples four combined wisdom light rays dawn in your heart center, each extremely subtle and clear, like sun rays woven together in a rope.

Now first, from Vairochana's heart center, a cloth of the frighteningly brilliant white light rays of the reality-perfection wisdom dawns connecting to your heart center. Within that light-ray cloth, white drops glisten with their rays, like mirrors facing toward you, very clear, brilliant, and awesomely penetrating, with each drop itself naturally adorned with five other drops. Thus that light-ray cloth is adorned with drops and droplets without limit or center.

From the heart of Vajrasattva, the mirror wisdom, a cloth of blue light rays shines brilliantly upon you connecting to your heart center, on which shining blue drops like turquoise bowls facing down toward you, adorned by other drops and droplets, all shine upon you.

From the heart of Ratnasambhava, a cloth of the equalizing wisdom yellow light rays shines brilliantly upon you, on which golden drops like golden bowls adorned by other golden drops and droplets face down and dawn upon you.

From the heart center of Amitabha, the discriminating wisdom red light cloth shines brilliantly upon you, on which radiant red drops like coral bowls facing down to you, endowed with the deep luster of wisdom, very bright and penetrating, each adorned by five natural red drops—all these shine upon you adorned by drops and droplets without center or limit. These also shine upon you connecting to your heart center.

Hey, noble one! These all arise from the natural exercise of your own awareness. They do not come from anywhere else. So do not be attached to them! Do not be terrified of them! Relax in the experience of nonconceptualization. Within that experience all the deities and light rays will dissolve into you and you will become a Buddha!

Hey, noble one! Since the exercise of the wisdom of your awareness is not perfected, the all-accomplishing wisdom's green light does not shine.

Hey, noble one! These are called the vision of the four wisdoms in combination, the inner passageway of Vajrasattva. At that time, you should remember the orientation previously given by your spiritual teacher! If you remember that orientation, you will trust those visions, you will recognize reality like the child meeting the mother, or like the greeting of a long familiar person; and you will cease all reifying notions. Recognizing your visions as your own creations, you will trust your being held on the changeless path of pure reality, and you will achieve the samadhi of continuity. Your awareness will dissolve into the body of great effortlessness, and you will become a Buddha in the Beatific Body, never to be reversed.

Hey, noble one! Along with the wisdom lights, there also arise the impure, misleading visions of the six species; namely, the soft white light of the gods, the soft red light of the titans, the soft blue light of the humans, the soft green light of the animals, the soft yellow light of the pretans, and the soft smoky light of the hells. These six arise entwined in parallel with the pure wisdom lights. Therefore, don't seize or cling to any of those lights. Relax in the experience of nonperception! If you fear the wisdom lights and cling to the impure six-species life-cycle lights, you will assume a body of a being of the six species. You will not reach the time of liberation from the great ocean of suffering of the life cycle. You will experience only trouble.

Hey, noble one! If you lack the orientation given in the instruction of the spiritual teacher, and you fear and are terrified by the above images and pure wisdom lights, you will come to cling to the impure life-cycle lights. Do not do so! Have faith in those dazzling, piercing pure wisdom lights! Trust in them, thinking, "These light rays of the wisdom of the compassion of the Blissful Lords of the five clans have come to me to hold me with compassion—I must take refuge in them!" Not clinging, not longing for the misleading lights of the six species, aim your will one-pointedly toward the five Buddha-clan couples, and make the following prayer:

Hey! When I roam the life cycle driven by the five strong poisons,
May the Lord Victors of the five clans lead me on the path
Of the clear light of the four wisdoms in combination!
May the supreme five Consort Buddhas back me on the way,
And deliver me from the impure lights of the six realms!
Delivering me from the dangerous straits of the between,
May they carry me to the five supreme pure lands!

Hey, noble one! Listen without wavering! On the seventh day a five-colored rainbow-striped light will dawn to purify your instincts by immersion in reality. At that time, from the pure land of the angels, the Scientist Deity host will come to escort you. In the center of a mandala wreathed in rainbows and lights, the unexcelled Scientist of evolutionary development, Padmanarteshvara, will arise, his body lustrous with the five colors, his consort the Red Angel wound round his body, performing the dance of chopper and blood-filled skull bowl striking the gazing posture toward the sky.

From the east of that mandala the Stage-contemplating Scientist will arise, white, his expression smiling, his consort the White Angel wound round his body, performing the chopper and skull-bowl dance and the gesture of gazing into space. From the south of that mandala the Lifespan-master Scientist will arise, yellow with beautiful signs, his consort the Yellow Angel wound round his body, performing the chopper and skull-bowl dance and the gesture of gazing into space. From the west of that mandala the Great Seal Scientist will arise, red with a smiling expression, his consort the Red Angel wound round his body, performing the chopper and skull-bowl dance and the gesture of gazing into space. From the north of that mandala the Effortlessness Scientist will arise, green and smiling fiercely, his consort the Green Angel wound round his body, performing the chopper and skull-bowl dance and the gesture of gazing into space.

Ranged outside of those scientists, the infinite Angel host arises in order to escort the vow-holding devotee, and to punish the breakers of vows; they are the eight death-ground Angels, the four classes of Angels, the three holy place

Angels, the ten holy place Angels, the twenty-four holy land Angels, and the Heroes, the Heroines, and the warrior deities, along with all their defenders, the Dharma-protectors. All wear the six human bone ornaments, carry drums, thigh-bone trumpets, skull drums, human skin victory standards, human skin parasols and pennants, singed flesh incense, and play infinite different kinds of music. They fill the entire universe, rocking, dancing, and shaking, all their musical sounds vibrating as if to split your head open, and performing various dances.

Hey, noble one! Spontaneously purifying instincts in reality, the five-colored wisdom light striped like colored threads wound together dazzles, shimmers, and shines steadily, clear and brilliant, startlingly piercing; from the hearts of the five Scientist Lords it blinds your eyes and penetrates into your heart center. At the same time the soft green light of the animal realm dawns together with the wisdom light. At that time, under the influence of your instincts, you fear the five-colored light and flee from it, enticed by the soft green light of the animal realm. Therefore, don't be afraid of that energetic, piercing, five-colored light! Don't be terrified! Recognize it as wisdom! From within the light comes the thousand rolling thunders of the natural sound of teaching. The sound is fierce, reverberating, rumbling, stirring, like fierce mantras of intense sound. Don't fear it! Don't flee it! Don't be terrified of it! Recognize it as the exercise of your own awareness, your own perception. Do not be attached to that soft green light of the animal realms. Do not long for it! If you cling to it, you will fall into the delusion-dominated realm of the animals, and you will suffer infinite miseries of stupefaction, dumbness, and slavery, without any time of escape. So do not cling to it! Have faith in that penetrating bright, five-colored light! Aim your will one-pointedly toward the Lord Scientist Master Deity host! Aim your will with the thought:

This Scientist Deity host with its Heroes and Angels has come to escort me to the pure angelic heaven! O, you must know how beings such as me have accumulated no stores of merit and wisdom. We have not been taken up by the grip of the light rays of compassion of such a five-clan Deity host of the Blissful Buddhas of the three times. Alas! Such am I! Now, you the Scientist Deity host, from now on do not neglect me no matter what! Hold me with the tractor beam of your compassion! Right now draw me to the pure heaven of the Buddha Angels!

Then you should make the following prayer:

Hey! May the Scientist Deity host look upon me!
Please lead me on the path with your great love!
When I roam the life cycle driven by strong instincts,
May the Hero Scientists lead me on the path
Of the clear light of orgasmic wisdom!
May their consort Angel host back me on my way,
Deliver me from the dangerous straits of the between,
And carry me to perfect Buddhahood!

When you make this prayer with intense faith, you will dissolve into rainbow light at the heart center of the Scientist Deity host and without a doubt will be reborn in the perfect Angel heaven realm.

THE FIERCE DEITY REALITY BETWEEN

Hey, noble one! Listen without wavering! The peaceful between already dawned, but you did not recognize the light. So now you still must wander here. Now on this eighth day, the Heruka Fierce Deity host will arise. Do not waver! Recognize them! Hey, noble one! The great, glorious Buddha Heruka appears, wine maroon in color, with three faces, six arms, and four legs stretched out, his front face maroon, his right face white, his left face red, his entire body blazing with light rays. His eyes glare, fiercely terrifying, his eyebrows flash like lightning, his fangs gleam like new copper. He roars with laughter, "A la la," and "Ha ha ha," and he makes loud hissing noises like "shu-uu." His bright orange hair blazes upward, adorned with skull crown and sun and moon discs. His body is adorned with black snakes and a freshly severed head garland. His first right hand holds a wheel, the middle an ax, and the third a sword; his first left hand holds a bell, the middle a plowshare, and the third a skull bowl. His Consort Buddha Krodhishvari enfolds his body, her right arm embracing his neck, her left hand offering him sips of blood from her skull bowl. She clucks her tongue menacingly and roars just like thunder. Both are ablaze with wisdom flames, shooting out from their blazing vajra hairs. They stand in the warrior's posture on a throne supported by garudas. Thus they arise manifestly before you, having emerged from within your own brain! Do not fear them! Do not be terrified! Do not hate them! Recognize them as an image of your own awareness! He is your own Archetype Deity, so do not panic! In fact, they are really Lord Vairochana Father and Mother, so do not be afraid!

The very moment you recognize them, you will be liberated!

Hey, noble one! Listen without wavering! Now on the ninth day the Lord Vajra Heruka of the Vajra-clan will arise before you, emerging from within your brain. He is dark blue, with three faces, six arms, and four legs stretched out. His front face is dark blue, his right face white, his left face red. His first right hand holds a vajra, the middle a skull bowl, and the third an ax; his first left hand holds a bell, the middle a skull bowl, and the third a plowshare. His Consort Buddha Vajra Krodhishvari enfolds his body, her right arm embracing his neck, her left hand offering him sips of blood from her skull bowl. Thus they arise manifestly before you, having emerged from within your own brain! Do not fear them! Do not be terrified! Do not hate them! Recognize them as an image of your own awareness! They are your own Archetype Deity, so do not panic! In fact, they are really Lord Vajrasattva Father and Mother, so have faith in them! The very moment you recognize them, you will be liberated!

Hey, noble one! Listen without wavering! Now on the tenth day the Jewel-clan Heruka, Lord Ratna Heruka, will manifest to you, emerging from within your brain. He is dark yellow, with three faces, six arms, and four legs stretched out, his front face dark yellow, his right face white, his left face red. His first right hand holds a jewel, the middle a khatvanga staff, and the third a club; his first left hand holds a bell, the middle a skull bowl, and the third a trident. His Consort Buddha Ratna Krodhishvari enfolds his body, her right arm embracing his neck, her left hand offering him sips of blood from her skull bowl. Thus they arise manifestly before you, having emerged from within the southern part of

your own brain! Do not fear them! Do not be terrified!
Do not hate them! Recognize them as an image of your own
awareness! They are your own Archetype Deity, so do not
panic! In fact, they are really Lord Ratnasambhava Father
and Mother, so have faith in them! The very moment you recognize them, you will be liberated!

Hey, noble one! Listen without wavering! Now on the
eleventh day, the Lotus-clan Heruka, Lord Padma Heruka,
will manifest to you, emerging from within your brain. He is
dark red, with three faces, six arms, and four legs stretched
out, his front face dark red, his right face white, his left
face blue. His first right hand holds a lotus the middle a
khatvanga staff, and the third a rod; his first left hand
holds a bell, the middle a skull bowl filled with blood,
and the third a small drum. His Consort Buddha Padma
Krodhishvari enfolds his body, her right arm embracing his
neck, her left hand offering him sips of blood from her skull
bowl. Thus they arise manifestly before you, standing in
sexual union, having emerged from within your own brain!
Do not fear them! Do not be terrified! Do not hate them!
Feel delight! Recognize them as an image of your own
awareness! They are your own Archetype Deity, so do not
panic! In fact, they are really Lord Amitabha Father and
Mother, so have faith in them! The very moment you recognize them, you will be liberated!

Hey, noble one! Listen without wavering! Now on this
the twelfth day, the Lord Karma Heruka of the Karma-clan
will manifest before you, emerging from within your own
brain. He is dark green, with three faces, six arms, and four
legs stretched out, his front face dark green, his right face

white, his left face red. His first right hand holds a sword, the middle a khatvanga staff, and the third a rod; his first left hand holds a bell, the middle a skull bowl, and the third a plowshare. His Consort Buddha Karma Krodishvari enfolds his body, her right arm embracing his neck; her left hand offering him sips of blood from her skull bowl. Thus they arise manifestly before you, standing in sexual embrace, having emerged from the north of your own brain! Do not fear them! Do not be terrified! Do not hate them! Recognize them as an image of your own awareness! They are your own Archetype Deity, so do not panic! In fact, they are really Lord Amoghasiddhi Father and Mother, so have faith in them, feel deep reverence for them! The very moment you recognize them, you will be liberated!

Hey, noble one! Listen without wavering! The eight Gauri goddesses will emerge from within your brain and appear to you! Do not fear them! From the east of your brain appears to your east a white Gauri, her right hand holding a corpse as a club and her left hand holding a blood-filled skull bowl. Do not fear her! From the south, a yellow Chauri, aiming a bow and arrow; from the west, a red Pramoha, holding a crocodile victory standard; from the north, a black Vetali, holding a vajra and a blood-filled skull bowl; from the southeast, an orange Pukkasi, her right hand holding intestines, her left hand feeding them into her mouth; from the southwest, a dark green Ghasmari, her left hand holding a blood-filled skull bowl and her right hand holding a vajra, with which she stirs the blood and feeds it into her mouth; from the northwest, a pale yellow Chandali holding a body and head across her shoulders, her right hand holding a heart and her left hand feeding herself with the corpse; from the northeast, a dark blue Shmashani, feeding on a headless body; all these eight holy-ground Gauri goddesses emerge from within your brain and appear to you surrounding the five Herukas! Do not fear them!

Hey, noble one! Listen without wavering! After that, the eight Pishachi ghouls of the holy lands will appear to you! From the east, a dark maroon, lion-headed Simhasya, crossing her arms over her chest, holding a corpse in her mouth, and tossing her mane; from the south, a red, tiger-headed Vyaghrasya, crossing her arms downward staring hypnotically and gnashing her fangs; from the west, a black, jackal-headed Shrgalasya, with a razor in her right hand, holding and feeding on intestines in her left hand; from the north, a dark blue, wolf-headed Shvanasya, lifting a corpse up to her mouth with her two hands and staring hypnotically; from the southeast, a light yellow, vulture-headed Grdhrasya, carrying a corpse over her shoulder and holding a skeleton in her hand; from the southwest, a dark red, hawk-headed Kankhasya, carrying a corpse over her shoulder; from the northwest a black, crow-headed Kakasya, with a sword in her right hand, eating lungs and hearts; from the northeast, a dark blue, owl-headed Ulukasya, eating flesh and holding a vajra in her right hand and a sword in her left hand; all these holy-land Pishachi ghouls emerge from within your brain and appear to you surrounding the five Herukas! Do not fear them! Recognize whatever arises as the creativity of your own visionary awareness!

Hey, noble one! Listen without wavering! The four Door-guardian goddesses will emerge from your own brain and appear to you, so recognize them! From the east of your brain, a white, horse-headed Ankusha, with an iron hook in her right hand, and a blood-filled skull bowl in her left hand, will appear to your east. From the south, a yellow, pig-headed Pasha holding a noose; from the west, a red, lion-headed Shernkhala, holding an iron chain; from the north, a green, serpent-headed Ghanta holding a bell; these four Door-guardian goddesses will emerge from your brain and appear to you! Recognize them as being your own Archetype Deities!

Hey, noble one! Outside of these thirty fierce Heruka deities, the twenty-eight Ishvari goddesses with their various heads and their various implements will emerge from within your brain and appear to you. Do not fear them, but recognize them as the creativity of your own visionary awareness! At this time when you have arrived at the crucial moment of cessation, remember the instructions of your spiritual teacher!

Hey, noble one! From the east, the dark maroon, yak-headed Rakshasi holding a vajra; the orange, serpent-headed Brahmi holding a lotus; the dark green, leopard-headed Maheshvari holding a trident the blue, mongoose-headed Lobha holding a wheel; the red, mule-headed Kumari holding a javelin; the white, bear-headed Indrani holding an intestine-noose; these six eastern Yoginis emerge from your own brain and appear before you! Do not fear them!

Hey, noble one! From the south, the yellow, bat-headed Vajra holding a razor; the red, crocodile-headed Shanti holding a vase; the red, scorpion-headed Amerta holding a lotus; the white, hawk-headed Chandra holding a vajra; the dark green, box-headed Gada holding a club; the yellow-black, tiger-headed Rakshasi holding skull-bowl blood; these six southern Yoginis emerge from your own brain and appear before you! Do not fear them!

From the west, the dark green, vulture-headed Bhakshasi holding a club; the red, horse-headed Rati holding a human torso; the white, garuda-headed Mahabali holding a club; the red, dog-headed Rakshasi holding a vajra razor; the red, hoopoe-headed Kama aiming a bow and arrow; the red-green, deer-headed Vasuraksha holding a vase; these six western Yoginis emerge from within your brain and appear before you! Do not fear them!

Hey, noble one! From the north, the blue, wolf-headed Vayavi holding a banner; the red, ibex-headed Narini holding an impaling stake; the black, boar-headed Varahi holding a tusk-noose; the red, crow-headed Rati holding a child's skin; the green-black, elephant-headed Mahanasi holding a fresh corpse and drinking blood from a skull bowl; the blue, serpent-headed Varuni holding a serpent-noose; these six northern Yoginis will emerge from within your brain and appear before you! Do not fear them!

Hey, noble one! The four outer Door-guardian Yoginis will emerge from within your brain and appear before you! From the east, the white, cuckoo-headed Vajra holding an iron hook; from the south, the yellow, goat-headed Vajra holding a noose; from the west, the red, lion-headed Vajra holding an iron chain; from the north, the green-black, serpent-headed Vajra holding a bell; these four Door Yoginis will emerge from within your brain and appear before you! All these twenty-eight goddesses arise naturally from the creativity of the self-originating bodies of the fierce

Herukas—so you should recognize them as Buddha-wisdom!

Hey, noble one! The Truth Body arises from the voidness side as the peaceful deities! Recognize it! The Beatific Body arises from the clarity side as the fierce deities! Recognize it! At this time when the fifty-eight-deity Heruka host emerges from within your brain and appears before you, if you know that whatever arises is arisen from the natural energy of your own awareness, you will immediately become nondual with the Heruka Body and become a Buddha!

Hey, noble one! If you do not recognize that, you will cling to superficial reality, feel fear and hate, and flee these deities. You will go down again into excessive misery! If you do not recognize them you will perceive the whole Heruka Deity host as if they were Yamas, Lords of Death, and you will fear the Heruka deities. You will hate them! You will panic! You will faint! Your own visions having become devils, you will wander in the life cycle!

Hey, noble one! These mild and fierce deities at most will be as big as space, at medium will be as large as Sumeru, the planetary axis, at the least will be as large as eighteen times the height of your own body—so do not be afraid of them! All visible existence will arise as lights and deities! And all visions arising as lights and deities must be recognized as the natural energy of your own awareness. When your own energy dissolves nondually into these natural lights and deities, you will become a Buddha!

O my child! What you see and perceive, whatever terrifying visions occur, recognize them as your own visions! Recognize the clear light as the natural energy of your own awareness! If you so recognize, there is no doubt you will become a Buddha right away! The so-called "instantaneous perfect Buddhahood" will have come to pass! Remember this in your mind!

Hey, noble one! If now you do not recognize the light, and if you cling to terror, all the mild deities will arise as black Mahakala guardians! All the fierce deities will arise as Yama Dharmaraja deities! Your own visions having become devils, you will wander in the life cycle!

Hey, noble one! If you do not recognize your own visions, though you become expert in all scriptures of sutra and Tantra, though you practice the Dharma for an eon, you will not become a Buddha! If you recognize your own visions, with one key, one word, you will become a Buddha! If you do not recognize your own visions, then the moment you die, reality arises in the between in the image of Yama Dharmaraja the Lord of Death! The Yama Dharmaraja deities will arise at most filling all of space, at medium like huge mountains, filling the whole world. Their fanglike teeth protruding over their lips, their eyes like glass, their hair bound up on top of their heads, with protruding bellies, with thin necks, they carry punishment boards and shout, "Beat him!" and "Kill him!" They lick up your brains, they sever your head from your body, and they extract your heart and vital organs. Thus they arise, filling the world.

Hey, noble one! When it happens that such a vision arises, do not be afraid! Do not feel terror! You have a mental body made of instincts; even if it is killed or dismembered, it cannot die! Since in fact you are a natural form of voidness, anger at being injured is unnecessary! The Yama Lords of

Death are but arisen from the natural energy of your own awareness and really lack all substantiality. Voidness cannot injure voidness!

Except insofar as they arise from the natural creativity of your own awareness, you must firmly decide that all that you see—the mild and fierce deities, the Herukas, the animal-headed angels, the rainbow lights, and the Yama deities—none is substantially, objective existent! Once you understand that, then all the fears and terrors become liberated on the spot, you dissolve into nonduality and become a Buddha! If you so recognize them, you must feel intense faith, thinking "They are my Archetype Deities! They have come to escort me through the straits of the between! I take refuge in them!"

Be mindful of the Three Jewels! Remember whoever is your Archetype Deity! Call him or her by name! Pray to him or her, "I am wandering lost in the between—be my savior! Hold me with your compassion, O precious deity!" Call on your spiritual teacher by name, praying, "I am wandering lost in the between—be my savior! For compassion's sake, do not let me go!" Feel faith in the Heruka Deity host, and pray to them:

When I wander in the life cycle driven by powerful instincts,
May the host of mild and fierce Lords lead me on the path
Of the clear light that conquers terror-visions of hate and fear!
May the fierce Ishvari goddess hosts back me on the way,
Deliver me from the dangerous straits of the between,
And carry me to perfect Buddhahood!

Now that I wander alone, apart from my loved ones,
And all my visions are but empty images,
May the Buddhas exert the force of their compassion
And stop the fear- and hate-drawn terrors of the between!

When the five lights of brilliant wisdom dawn,
Fearless, bravely, may I know them as myself!
When the forms of the Lords mild and fierce arise,
Bold and fearless, may I recognize the between!
Now when I suffer by the power of negative evolution,
May the Archetype Deities dispel that suffering!
When reality crashes with a thousand thunders,
May they all become OM MANI PADME HUM!

When I'm pulled by evolution without recourse,
May the Compassionate Lord provide me refuge!
When I suffer due to evolutionary instincts,
May the clear light bliss samadhi dawn upon me!
May the five main elements not arise as enemies!
May I behold the pure lands of the five Buddha-clans!

Thus you should pray with intense reverence and faith! It is extremely important, since your fear and terror will thus disappear and you will surely become a Buddha in the Beatific Body! Do not waver!

ORIENTATION TO THE EXISTENCE BETWEEN

Hey, noble one! If you have not understood from the above, at this time, by power of evolution the vision will arise of your proceeding upward, on the level, or downward with head hanging. Now meditate on the Lord of Great Compassion! Remember him! Then, as already explained, you will have visions of hurricanes, blizzards, hailstorms, dense fogs, and being chased by many men, and you will seem to escape. Those without merit will seem to escape to a miserable place, but those with merit will seem to escape to a happy place. At that time, noble one, all the signs will arise showing the continent and place where you will be reborn. For this time there are many profound keys of instruction, so listen carefully! Even though you did not recognize freedom from the previous keys of orientation, here even those of the weakest practice can recognize freedom through the following keys, so listen!

Now, here, the method of blocking the womb door is very effective and important. There are two methods of blocking that door; blocking the entering person and blocking the womb door entered. First, the instruction for blocking the enterer.

Hey, noble one! You named So-and-so! Clearly visualize your Archetype Deity appearing like magic without intrinsic reality like the moon in water. If you are unsure about your Archetype Deity, then vividly envision Avalokiteshvara, thinking, "He is the Lord of Great Compassion!" Then dissolve the Archetype from the edges and contemplate the void clear light transparency of ultimate nonperception. That is the profound key. Using it, the Buddhas said, the womb will not be entered; so meditate in that way!

But if this still does not block the way and you are just about to enter a womb, there is the profound instruction to block the door of the womb about to be entered. So listen! Repeat after me the following from The Root Verses of the Six Betweens!

Hey! Now when the existence between dawns upon me,
I will hold my will with mind one-pointed,
And increase forcefully the impulse of positive evolution;
Blocking the womb door, I will remember to be revulsed.
Now courage and positive perception are essential;
I will give up envy, and contemplate all couples
As my Spiritual Mentor, Father and Mother.

Repeat this loud and clear and stir your memory. It is important to meditate on its meaning and put it into practice. As for its meaning, "Now when the existence between dawns upon me" means that you are now wandering within the existence between. A sign of that is that when you look in water you will not see your reflection. You have no shadow. You have no substantial flesh-and-blood body. These are signs that your mental body is wandering in the existence between. Now you must hold one-pointed in your mind the unwavering willpower. This one-pointed will is of chief importance. It is like reins to guide a horse. You can achieve whatever your will intends, so don't open your mind to negative evolution, but remember the teachings, instructions, initiations, authorizations, and inspirations you received in the human realm, such as this *Great Book of Natural Liberation Through Understanding in the Between*, and intensify the result of all good evolutionary actions. This is very important. Don't forget it! Don't be distracted! This is the exact time that determines whether you go up or you go down. Now is the time when indulgence in laziness definitely will bring on suffering. Now is the time when one-pointed positive willpower definitely brings on happiness. Hold one-pointed goodwill in your mind! Sustain forcefully the result of good action!

Now is the time to block the door of the womb! As the root verse says, blocking the womb door, remember to be revulsed! Now courage and positive perception are essential! That time is now. You should block the door of the womb. There are five methods to block the womb door; fix them well in your mind.

Hey, noble one! At this time you will have visions of couples making love. When you see them, don't enter between them, but stay mindful. Visualize the males and females as the Teacher, Father and Mother, prostrate to them, and make them visualized offerings! Feel intense reverence and devotion! Aim a strong will to request them to teach the Dharma, and the womb door will definitely be blocked.

If that does not block it, and you are about to enter the womb, then visualize them as Mentor Father-Mother, Archetype Deity Father and Mother, or Compassion Lord Father and Mother. Offer them visualized offerings! Form the powerful intention to receive spiritual attainments from them, and that will block the womb door.

If that does not block it, and you are again about to enter a womb, then third there is the instruction for reversing lust and hate. There are four modes of birth; egg birth, womb birth, magic birth, and warm-moisture birth. Egg birth and womb birth are alike. As before, you begin to see males and females engaged in love-making. If you enter the womb under the influence of lust and hate, whether you are reborn as horse, bird, dog, or human, if you are going to be male, you arise appearing to be male; you feel strong hate toward the father, and attraction and lust toward the mother. If you are going to be female, you appear as a female; you feel strong envy and jealousy toward the mother, you feel strong longing and lust for the father. Conditioned by that, you enter the path of the womb. You experience orgasmic bliss in the center of the union between white and red drops, and within the experience of that bliss you faint and lose consciousness. Your body develops through the embryonic stages of "custard," "gelatin," and so forth. Eventually you will be born outside the mother's womb. Once your eyes are open, you realize you have been born a puppy. Having been a human, now you are a dog. In the dog's kennel, you suffer. Or in the pig's sty, or in the anthill, or in the wormhole, or in the herds of cows or goats or sheep—born there you cannot return to the human state. Being extremely stupid, in the state of delusion you suffer various miseries. In this way you will cycle through the hells and the pretan realms, and will be tortured by limitless suffering. There is nothing more powerful, nothing more terrible than this. Alas! Alas! Those lacking the holy spiritual teacher's instruction fall down this deep abyss into the life cycle. They are tormented uninterruptedly by unbearable sufferings. So listen to what I say! Hold my personal instruction in your mind!

Now I will teach you an instruction to close the womb door by reversing lust and hate. Listen to it and remember it! As the verse says:

Blocking the door of the womb, I will remember to be
revulsed.
Now courage and positive perception are essential;
I will give up envy and contemplate all couples
As my Spiritual Mentor, Father and Mother.

As before, you will have strong feelings of envy; if reborn
as a male, you will lust for the mother and hate the father, if
reborn as a female you will lust for the father and hate the
mother. For that time, there is this profound instruction.

Hey, noble one! When such lust and hate arise, meditate
like this. "Alas! Such a creature of negative evolution as
myself will wander in the life cycle under the influence of
lust and hate. If I still persist in lust and hate, I will know
no end to my wanderings. I am in danger of being sunk forever in the ocean of miseries. Now I must give up lust and
hate entirely. Alas! I must hold intensely the one-pointed
will never to entertain lust and hate." The Tantras state that
this meditation itself will close the door of the womb.

Hey, noble one! Don't waver! Hold your will one pointed
in your mind! Even though you have done that, if the womb
door did not close and you are about to enter the womb, you
should block the womb door by the instruction of truthless
magical illusion. Meditate as follows: "Male and female,
father and mother, the thunderstorm, the hurricane, the thunder, terrifying visions, all phenomena are naturally like magical illusions. However they arise, they are truthless. All things
are untrue and false. Like mirages. Impermanent. Noneternal.
Why be attached to them? Why fear and hate them? It is to
see nothing as something. All of these are but visions of my

mind. The mind itself is as originally nonexistent as a magical illusion. So where—out there—do they come from? Since I never understood this in the past, I held the nonexistent to exist. I held the untrue to be true. I held illusion as truth. So for this long time I wandered in the life cycle. If I still now do not recognize the illusoriness of things, I will wander even longer in the life cycle, and I will be stuck in the quicksand of various miseries. So now I will recognize all these things as like a dream, a magical illusion, an echo, a fairy city, a mirage, a reflection, an optical illusion, the moon in water, lacking even a moment's truth-status, definitely untrue, and false."

Thus, holding these thoughts one-pointedly in mind, the truth-habit erodes, and, as the resulting freedom is impressed in your continuum, the deeper self-habit is reversed. As you thus deeply understand cosmic unreality, the womb door will definitely be blocked.

Yet even doing that, if the truth-habit does not erode, the womb door is not blocked, and you are about to enter the womb, again there is a profound instruction.

Hey, noble one! Even doing that, if the womb door is not blocked now, fifth, you should block the womb door by meditating on the dear light. This is how to contemplate. "Hey! All things are my own mind. That mind is voidness, free of creation and destruction." Thinking thus, do not artificially compose your mind. Like water being poured in water, let the mind flow into its own reality condition; release it into its own nature. Letting it relax easily and openly will decisively and definitely block the womb door for all four forms of rebirth. Thus meditate again and again until the womb door is blocked.

Hey, noble one! You, the deceased named So-and-so, listen to me! All the previous instructions for orientation have been given to you and still you do not understand. Now, since the womb door is not blocked, it is time to assume a body. You have many different authentic and profound instructions for the choosing of a womb. Hold them in your mind! Listen well with strong intent, and hold them in your mind!

Hey, noble one! Now signs and marks will arise about which continent you will be reborn in—recognize them! Now you should explore where to be reborn, you should choose a continent. If you are reborn in eastern Videha, you will see lakes and waters adorned with male and female geese. Think of renunciation and do not go there. If you are born there, your situation will be comfortable; but you should not go there as the Dharma is not available there. If you are going to be reborn in the southern Jambudvipa, you will see beautiful and comfortable houses. If you can go there do so. If you are to be reborn in western Godaniya, you will see lakes adorned with male and female horses. Turn back and do not go there. Although it is very enjoyable, the Dharma has not spread there, so do not go there. If you are going to be reborn in northern Kuru, you see lakes adorned with cattle or with evergreen trees. Recognize these as signs of being reborn there. Do not go there! Though you will have long life and much fortune there, the Dharma is not available there. Do not go there!

If you are to be reborn as a god, you will see delightful, divine, multistoried mansions made of various jewels. It is alright to dwell there, so you may enter there. If you are to be reborn as a titan, you will see a pleasant grove and spinning wheels of fire; remember renunciation, and by all means do not go there! If you are to be reborn among the animals you will see caves, ant holes, and grass huts, as if through a fog. Do not go there! If you are to be reborn as a pretan, you will see charred stumps, black spots, dark ravines, darkness, and shadows. If you go there, reborn as a pretan, you will experience various sufferings of hunger and thirst. So don't go there! Remember renunciation! Be fiercely courageous! If you are to be reborn in the hells, you will hear the songs of negative evolution, or you will feel a helpless need to go there, and you will have visions of an island of darkness, a black house or a red house, black pits, and black roads. If you go there, you will be stuck in the hells. You will experience unbearable pains of heat and cold. You will never escape. You must take every care not to get caught there! By any means, never enter there at all! "Block the womb door and remember renunciation!" Now is the time when that is essential.

Hey, noble one! Though you might wish not to go on, helplessly you are chased by the butchers of evolution. You find yourself powerless to stop, you must go on. Ahead of you are butchers and killers to drag you along. You will feel as if you are fleeing from overwhelming darkness, hurricanes, tempests, harsh noises, snow and rain, hailstorms, thunderstorms, and violent blizzards. Escaping in panic, you will seek a refuge, and you will feel safe in the previously mentioned beautiful houses, in rock caves, in earthen caverns, in forest thickets, within the round blossoms of lotuses and so forth. Hiding in such places, you will think, "I must not leave here now!" And feeling so anxious about losing your place, you will become very attached to it. Feeling so anxious about meeting the terrors of the between if you go out, hating those terrors, you hide within and assume no matter what kind of inferior body, and you will come to experience various sufferings. All that is the sign that demons and ogres are troubling you. There is a profound, crucial instruction for you at this time. Listen to it and hold it in your mind!

At that time when you are helplessly chased by butchers and are overwhelmed by terror, instantaneously visualize all at once the Lord Chemchok Heruka, or Hayagriva, or Vajrapani, and so forth, whoever is your Archetype Deity; gigantic in size, with bulging limbs, terrifying, furious, able to crush all demons to dust. By his blessing and compassion, you will free yourself from those butchers, and you will gain the power to choose a good womb. This is the authentic profound key of the instruction; so hold it in your mind!

Hey, noble one! Further, the deities of the contemplation realms are reborn by the power of their samadhi. The majority of the demonic types such as the pretans, by changing their self-images while in the between manifest various magical transformations in bodies of pretans, demons, and ogres, and then become mental bodies just like them. The pretans of the underworld, the pretans of the sky realms, and the eighty thousand types of demons adopt their bodies just by changing their self-concepts. At such a time, if you remember the import of voidness, the Great Seal, it is best. If you cannot, you should practice meditation on magical illusion. If you cannot do that, free of any kind of attachment to anything, you should meditate on the greatly compassionate Archetype Deity, and attain enlightenment in the Beatific Body in the between.

Hey, noble one! Thus, if it becomes necessary by the power of evolution to enter the womb, you should now rely on the instruction for choosing the womb. Listen! Do not go to just any womb door that presents itself. If, due to the demonic butchers, you lose the power not to go, then meditate on Hayagriva. Since now you have subtle clairvoyance, you will be able to understand the nature of all places, so choose your place of rebirth wisely. There are two instructions, one for transmitting your soul into the pure Buddhalands, and one for choosing a womb door in the impure life cycle. You should now practice the following.

If you are the most intelligent type of person, to perform the soul-transmission to the angel realms you should formulate the following controlling intention: "Alas! I am sad that I have stayed here in this swamp of the life cycle for so long, beginninglessly for boundless, countless eons! Alas! During all the lifetimes of so many Buddhas, I have still not been liberated! I am revulsed and nauseated by this interminable life cycle. I am terrified of it. I totally repudiate it. I must now remember the methods of escaping it. I must now take miraculous rebirth in the blossom of a lotus in the presence of the Buddha Amitabha in the western pure-land universe, Sukhavati the Blissful!" It is essential here to make great effort to aim all your willpower in this way toward the western pure universe of Sukhavati. Whichever pure universe you have faith in—whether it is Amitabha's Sukhavati; Abhirati, the delightful land of Akshobhya; Ghanavyuha, the pure land of Vairochana; Alakavati, the earthly paradise of Vaishravana; Potalaka, the earthly paradise of Avalokiteshvara, or the lotus light palace of Padma

Sambhava in Udyana, if you aim your concentrated willpower at any one of these pure lands and hold it one-pointedly without distraction, you will be reborn immediately in that pure land. Further, if you wish to be reborn in the presence of the Dharma Lord Maitreya in the Tushita heaven, just aim your will, thinking, "Now that I am in this between, it is time to visit the Dharma Lord Maitreya in his Tushita realm, I will go there!" You will be miraculously reborn in the heart of a lotus in the presence of Maitreya.

Again, if you cannot, or do not want to, proceed to any pure land, and must enter a womb, there is this instruction for choosing a womb in the impure life cycle. Listen to it! Choose your continent for rebirth as explained already. Using your clairvoyance, enter a womb in a place where the Dharma has spread. Caution is required, for even if you were to be reborn magically in a heap of dung, you would get the notion that the impure mass smelled delicious and you would be reborn in it by the force of your attraction. Therefore you should not adhere to whatever appearance occurs, and you must discount any signs that trigger attachment or aversion. Then choose a good womb. And here the willed intention is important; so you must create it as follows: "Hey! For the sake of all beings, I will be reborn as a world-ruling emperor, or of the priestly class, sheltering all beings like a great shade tree, or as the child of a holy man, an adept, or of a clan with an impeccable Dharma lineage, or in a family where the parents have great faith. I must succeed in this coming life, by adopting a body that has great merit, to enable me to accomplish the aims of all beings!" Aiming your will in this way you should enter the womb. At that time, the womb you have entered should appear to you as if magically trans-formed into a divine palace. You should pray to the Buddhas and the Bodhisattvas of the ten directions, the Archetype Deities, and especially to the Lord of Great Compassion. And you should visualize that they are all anointing you in consecration as you enter the womb.

In thus choosing the womb door, there is always danger of erring. Under the influence of evolution, you might see an excellent womb door as bad. You might see a bad womb door as excellent. So here the key instruction for choosing is important; do as follows: Even if a womb door appears to be excellent, do not become attached to it. Even if it appears bad, do not become averse to it. Enter it within the experi-ence of the universal loving equanimity, free of lust and hate and compulsive choosing between good and bad. This is the authentic profound key instruction.

Hey, noble one! If you cannot abandon lust and hate, and know how to choose a womb door, then, no matter what visions come to you, say the name of the Three Jewels, and go to them for refuge! Pray to the Lord of Great Compassion! Go forward with your head held high! Recognize that you are in the between! Abandon possessive love toward your dear ones left behind, your son, your daughter, your friends! They cannot help you now. Now go to the blue light of the human realm and the white light of the divine! Go to the beautiful jewel house and the pleasure garden!

CONTRIBUTORS

Karen Armstrong is widely respected for her studies
in comparative religions. She is the author of *The Gospel
According to Woman*, *Muhammad*, *In the Beginning* and, most
recently, the best-selling *A History of God*.

Marcus Borg was described by *The New York Times* as
"a leading figure among the new generation of Jesus scholars."
He is the author of ten books, including *Jesus: A New Vision*
and *Meeting Jesus Again for the First Time*.

Joseph Campbell's innovative studies in mythology
led him to translate the ancient Upanishads, the Arabian
Knights, and write a skeleton key to *Finnegan's Wake*. He is
author of the *The Hero with a Thousand Faces* and *The Masks of God*.

His Holiness the Dalai Lama is the spiritual head of
Tibet. Tenzin Gyatso was designated the 14th Dalai Lama
in 1937. After China's suppression of Tibet in 1959, he
was forced into permanent exile. In 1989, he was awarded
the Nobel Prize for Peace.

Sirdar Ikbal ali Shah, a modern descendant of the
prophet Muhammad, is the author of a definitive criticism
of the Qur'an, entitled *Islamic Sufism*.

Carl Jung, a Swiss psychoanalyst, was instrumental
in advancing the practice of psychology with his study
of "archetypes" of human experience. His collected works
encompass more than twenty volumes, and include
A Psychological Study of the Tibetan Book of the Dead.

Thomas Merton was a Trappist monk, peace activist, and prolific author. He became known at a young age for his classic autobiography, *The Seven Story Mountain*. Merton's true legacy is his introduction of Eastern religions to the West.

Barbara Stoler Miller was a leading translator of Sanskrit literature, including her respected version of *The Bhagavad-Gita*. She taught Asian Studies at Barnard College for 25 years.

Stephen Mitchell is widely known for his original studies and translations of spiritual writings and poetry. His books include *Tao te Ching*, *The Gospel According to Jesus*, and *The Enlightened Mind*.

Thomas Moore, writer and teacher, is the best-selling author of *Care of the Soul*, *Soul Mates* and *The Re-enchantment of Everyday Life*. He lived for twelve years as a Catholic Monk and holds a Ph.D. in religious studies.

Reynolds Price, the James B. Duke Professor of English at Duke University, is the author of more than two dozen books of fiction and non-fiction, including *The Promise of Rest*, *The Source of Light*, *The Three Gospels*, and *Letter to a Man in the Fire*.

Huston Smith is widely regarded as a foremost authority on the history of religions. Smith is currently Visiting Professor of Religious Studies at the University of California at Berkeley, and the author of the best-selling *The World's Religions*.

Jonathan Star is widely acclaimed for his writings on Eastern philosophy and his translations of Rumi and the Tao te Ching. His books include *Rumi, A Garden Beyond Paradise* and *Two Sons Rising*.

Henry David Thoreau was a writer, poet, and naturalist, best known for his journals that became *Walden, Or Life in the Woods*. His ruminations on Eastern religions are recorded in *A Week on the Concord and Merrimack Rivers*.

Herman Wouk is the author of the best-selling novels *The Caine Mutiny, The Winds of War*, and *War and Remembrance*. He has also written a book of non-fiction, *This is My God: The Jewish Way of Life*.

ACKNOWLEDGMENTS

Armstrong excerpt from *A History of God*. Copyright °1993 by Karen Armstrong. Used by permission of The Ballantine Publishing Group, a division of Random House, Inc.

Armstrong excerpt from *In the Beginning*. Copyright °1996 by Karen Armstrong. Used by permission of The Ballantine Publishing Group, a division of Random House, Inc.

Borg prologue °1999 by Marcus Borg. Used by permission of the author.

Campbell excerpt from *Myths to Live By* by Joseph Campbell. Copyright °1972 by Joseph Campbell. Reprinted by permission of Penguin Books Ltd.

Campbell excerpt from *Oriental Mythology* by Joseph Campbell. Copyright °1962 by Joseph Campbell, renewed in 1991 and reprinted by permission of Penguin Books USA Inc.

Cleary excerpt from *The Essential Koran*, by Thomas Cleary. Copyright °1994 by Thomas Cleary. Reprinted by permission of HarperCollins Publishers, Inc.

Jung excerpt from *Psyche and Symbol*, by C.G. Jung °1991 by Princeton University Press. Reprinted by permission of Princeton University Press.

Mitchell excerpt from *Tao Te Ching, an Illustrated Journey*, by Stephen Mitchell. Copyright °1999 by Frances Lincoln Limited. Reprinted by permission of HarperCollins Publishers Inc.

Merton excerpt from *Conjectures of a Guilty Bystander*, by Thomas Merton. Copywright °1966 by The Abby of Gethsemani. Used by permission of Doubleday, a division Random House, Inc.

Moore introduction °1999 by Thomas Moore. Used by permission of the author.

Price excerpt from *Three Gospels*, by Reynolds Price, °1996 Reynolds Price. Reprinted by permission of Touchstone, a division of Simon & Schuster.

Smith excerpt from *The World's Religions*, by Huston Smith. Copyright °1991 by Huston Smith. Reprinted by permission of HarperCollins Publishers Inc.

Star excerpt from *Rumi, In the Arms of the Beloved*, by Jonathan Star. Copyright °1997 by Jonathan Star. Used by permission of G.P. Putnam's Sons, a division of Penguin Putnam Inc.

Stoler excerpt from *The Bhagavad-Gita*, by Barbara Stoler Miller, Translation copyright °1986 by Barbara Stoler Miller. Used by permission of Bantam Books, a division of Random House, Inc.